Southern Historical Publications No. 19

THE LIFE

OF

ANDREW JACKSON

JOHN REID

AND

JOHN HENRY EATON

EDITED, WITH INTRODUCTION,
APPARATUS CRITICA, AND INDEX

BY FRANK LAWRENCE OWSLEY, JR.

PUBLISHED IN HONOR OF THE
AMERICAN REVOLUTION BICENTENNIAL, 1776–1976,
UNDER THE AUSPICES OF THE
ALABAMA BICENTENNIAL COMMISSION

THE UNIVERSITY OF ALABAMA PRESS
University, Alabama

CONTENTS

EDITOR'S ACKNOWLEDGMENTS

THE editor wishes to thank Auburn University for providing the financial assistance necessary to complete this project. He also wishes to express his appreciation to his wife, Mrs. Dorothy Owsley, to his mother, Mrs. Harriet C. Owsley, and to Miss Isabel Howell for their advice and clerical assistance. In addition he extends thanks to Mr. Bruce F. Nichols, Miss Kathleen Maehl, and Miss Madeleine Maehl for proofreading and to Mrs. Bettie Wegener and Mrs. Patricia Ponder for typing. He wishes to express his appreciation to Tennessee State Library and Archives for providing for reproduction a copy of the rare 1817 edition of this book. The editor is also greatly indebted to Mrs. Helen Reid Roberts for permitting him to use "Memoir of John Reid" which appears in this work as Appendix Y.

EDITOR'S INTRODUCTION

THE Life of Andrew Jackson, Major General In the Service of the United States: Comprising A History of the War in the South, From the Commencement of the Creek Campaign, to the Termination of Hostilities Before New Orleans, by John Reid and John Henry Eaton is the first biography of Andrew Jackson and covers his early life and activities during the War of 1812. This work was first published in 1817, only to be greatly revised in 1824 and again in 1828. These later revisions, some with different titles, had the effect of changing the book from a fairly accurate historical account into an utterly uncritical campaign biography of little merit.

The Reid-Eaton work is not only the earliest account of Jackson's exploits but can also be considered his official authorized biography. It was first proposed by Robert Y. Hayne, brother of Col. Arthur P. Hayne, of Jackson's staff, that an account of the General's military career be written by Dr. David Ramsay, the well-known South Carolina historian. Ramsay immediately agreed to undertake the project but unfortunately he was murdered before the work could proceed. He was shot by an insane person who apparently acted without reason. Several other possible authors were then suggested, including Thomas Cooper and Edward Livingston. Cooper was apparently not interested in the project, but Livingston conducted a fairly active correspondence with John Reid, Jackson's military secretary, concerning a biography of the General. Apparently Livingston dropped the project, since no Livingston manuscript has ever been located.[1]

Reid, having been used as a researcher by several interested authors, eventually decided to undertake the work himself. Many of his friends, including the General, encouraged him in this endeavor. When Reid presented Jackson with a prospectus of the book, the General gave it his full approval and wrote the following endorsement:

> Major Reid having made known to me his intention of publishing a history of the late campaign in the South, I think it very proper that the public should be made acquainted with the opportunities he has had of acquiring full and correct information on the subject which he proposed to write. He accompanied me as Aide-de-Camp during the Creek War and continued with me in that capacity after my appointment in the United States Army. He had and now has charge of my public papers and has ever possessed my unlimited confidence. The opportunities he has enjoyed, improved by the talents he possesses, will, I doubt not, enable him to satisfy the expectations of his friends.[2]

This decision to write about Jackson and his military career unquestionably pleased the General. John Reid was born in Bedford County, Virginia, in 1784 and received a classical education in that state prior to his move to Tennessee in 1807. He married Betsy, daughter of Abram Maury of Franklin, Tennessee, where he established himself in the practice of law. When Andrew Jackson raised a volunteer army in the Spring of 1813, for an expedition to Natchez, Mississippi, Reid was appointed aide to the General. This appointment was made on the recommendation of Colonel Thomas H. Benton. The young man became a devoted friend of Jackson and the conflict between Benton and Jackson which developed soon after his appointment does not seem to have affected the relationship between him and the General. During his service as Jackson's aide and secretary, Major Reid was the General's constant companion. So close was this association that Jackson frequently confided his private thoughts to the Major. In addition to being the General's confidant, Reid wrote many of Jackson's letters and proclamations, copying his style so nearly that it is not possible to tell which of the two men was actually the author.

Reid accompanied Jackson on the campaigns of the Creek War and was again his aide at the Battle of New Orleans. During the Fall of 1814 while the Pensacola campaign was in progress the young major left the service for a brief interval and made an unsuccessful attempt to win the Congressional seat vacated by Felix Grundy.[3] After his defeat, he rejoined Jackson at New Orleans. With the signing of the peace treaty, Reid remained there to defend Jackson at his trial by Judge Dominick Hall for contempt of court. He continued to serve Jackson as military aide after their return to Nashville.[4] In October 1815, Reid accompanied Andrew and Rachel Jackson to Washington ostensibly on military business. On the way as well as after their arrival in the city the little party were in the midst of a social whirl which was not lacking in political significance. They visited and were entertained by the President and other important people.[5] They left Washington on December 31, 1815, partly to escape the social life in which they had become involved and partly because of the General's health. Reid went for a visit with his family in Virginia and the Jacksons journeyed back to Tennessee, arriving in Nashville, February 1, 1816. One of the first letters received upon their arrival home was from Reid's family telling of John's sudden death in mid-January after an illness of only eighteen hours.

With Reid's death the book was left in an incomplete state with only the first four chapters finished. Jackson wrote Nathan Reid, Jr., February 8, 1816, "the book must be finished . . . if none of his friends or acquaintances in Virginia will undertake to finish the work, I will endeavour to get some person whose talents and integrity can be relied on to do justice to the work to compleat it for the benefit of his little family." [6]

After a short time John Henry Eaton was chosen to finish the work. Eaton was born in Halifax, North Carolina, on

June 18, 1790. He attended the University of North Carolina, and later studied law. After receiving an inheritance of 4800 acres of land in Williamson County, Tennessee, he moved, in 1808 or 1809, to Franklin, the county seat, where he earned a comfortable living managing his land and practicing law.

Reid and Eaton undoubtedly knew each other, since they both lived and practiced law in the small town of Franklin, Tennessee. Eaton was also aquainted with Jackson through his wife, Myra, who was a close friend of the Jackson family. Abram Maury, Reid's father-in-law, corresponded with Jackson about the choice of a person to complete the book which Reid had begun.[7] In a letter dated February 17, 1816, Maury wrote Jackson that judging from the contents of his letter of February 9, "I entertain the belief that it is your opinion as well as my own that the work begun by our friend can best be finished in the Western Country." [8] References were made to several other persons and it is not known exactly when Eaton was chosen but it could not have been very long after Reid's death for by March 20, 1817, he wrote Jackson from Philadelphia where he was attending to the publication of the volume.[9] Jackson's interest in the project continued and much of Eaton's writing was actually done at the Hermitage. It is almost certain that Jackson read and approved every line of the manuscript, probably as it was being written.[10] Clearly this close supervision by Jackson makes the work the nearest approach to an autobiography of the General. Since Jackson did not write his own memoirs, this fact alone gives the book considerable historical significance.

The Life of Andrew Jackson as first produced was written almost entirely from primary materials, and largely from manuscripts, since the authors had access both to Andrew Jackson's papers and the General himself. The papers were somewhat scattered after Jackson's death but the largest collection of them is located in the Library of Congress and the second largest group is in the Tennessee Historical Society. These collections still remain some of the best sources known to historians on the subject of the War of 1812 in the South. Although Reid and Eaton did not footnote their work, a careful examination of the Jackson Papers in these collections clearly indicates that they were the main sources in this book.[11] The authors also used *Niles' Register,* and other contemporary newspapers, which published many of the British records of the war. These materials, when added to Jackson's own information, provide the work with a balanced account of the war.

In addition to using the written accounts, Reid and Eaton interviewed many of the General's subordinates and friends.[12] These materials lend accuracy to the work, but Reid's own participation in the war makes the first four chapters of the work an eyewitness account, extremely valuable to the historian. The biography was written from the General's point of view, usually presenting him at his best. But while Jackson's virtues are praised, his faults are not entirely ignored. Because it was one of the first accounts, in print, of the War of 1812 in the South (only Latour's was earlier), it has avoided some of the errors found in later works. For example, the Reid-Eaton work numbered the persons killed at Fort Mims at around 300, instead of the exaggerated figure of 500 to 600 used by some recent scholars. Reid also correctly determined that the Spanish at Pensacola furnished the Creek Indians with ammunition only, not large quantities of arms as suggested in later works. Eaton attributes the victory at New Orleans to the excellent musketry and artillery fire of the Americans, rather than to rifle fire, which was credited in later accounts as being the decisive factor in that battle. While these are not major errors, the fact that the author's account is more nearly in agreement with the original records is a good indication of its accuracy.

After the publication of the first edition in 1817, there were many editions of *The Life of Andrew Jackson* but, unfortunately, the later printings were influenced by politics. In the elections of 1824 and 1828 when Jackson became a major candidate for the Presidency of the United States. John Eaton was a principal member and writer for the Nashville Junto, a small group composed of men who managed both of Jackson's campaigns, and it was in this capacity that he published numerous newspaper articles and revised the book for use as a campaign biography.

Although the 1824 edition mentions Reid's contribution in the preface, Eaton is listed on the title page as the only author. In appearance the 1824 reprint is similar to the first edition, but since it was intended to be campaign literature, it was printed on cheaper paper without the expensive maps found in the first edition. There are actually numerous revisions including minor word changes on nearly every page of the new printing. Most of these alterations are unimportant but there are some that are significant and change the book adversely. In converting the work from a history into a campaign biography, Eaton felt it was desirable to eliminate or explain away all material which was in any way critical of Jackson. A list of the General's faults such as his hot temper and stubborn disposition, which are mentioned in the first edition, are so explained away in this revision as to make them seem to be virtues, especially for a man who was to be President. This is a substantial change which dilutes the historical value of the book.

Another pattern of revision which is found in the 1824 edition is the tendency to discount the dissension between Jackson and some of his subordinate officers. Some of these controversies are almost entirely ignored, others are made to seem insignificant, and in almost all cases the names of the persons concerned are removed from the 1824 edition. Eaton undoubtedly hoped that many of these men, who were largely Tennessee militia officers, would support Jackson for the Presidency.

Still another method employed to transform the work into a political instrument was an attempt to increase the stature of Jackson. This was accomplished by inserting at strategic points a number of discourses praising the General. These exhortations not only severely damaged the work as a history but also made it very tedious reading in places. Eaton's revisions call the reader's attention to praiseworthy deeds of Jackson to a far greater degree than was done in the first edition. In the earlier work a successful action was often credited to Jackson and his subordinates, with the names of the other officers mentioned. In the revised work Eaton frequently transferred the entire credit to Jackson.

Apparently the 1824 edition was printed in large numbers and circulated over as much of the country as possible. Because of this widespread distribution, copies of this printing are far more numerous than the earlier edition. In fact, this first edition is so rare that outside of copies in the Nashville, Tennessee libraries and an imperfect copy in the Library of Congress, few of these books still exist. The 1824 edition, because it looks like the first edition and is readily available, has been much more widely used by scholars than the far superior earlier imprint. It is certain that this 1824 campaign biography, which was reprinted in facsimile in 1971, by Arno Press, is responsible for much of the unfavorable criticism which some scholars have leveled at the work.[13] Such a conclusion is especially justified since few historians seem to realize the degree to which later versions were revised and assume they are simply dealing with an unrevised reprint.[14]

Andrew Jackson, despite his plurality, was not elected President in 1824. Eaton, however, believed that his biography of the General had helped to stimulate this popularity. Accordingly when he managed Jackson's 1828 campaign he again revised the work and apparently tried to flood the market with the new edition. Two other versions, with varying titles, were prepared for distribution, disguised by additional material and the use of *nom-de-plumes*.

One of the 1828 editions included a brief account of the invasion of Florida in 1818 and the Seminole War, but most of the revisions simply enlarged on the 1824 changes. Eaton gave Jackson still more credit and in general further debased the book as good history. Few new discourses praising Jackson were added to the regular 1828 *Life of Andrew Jackson*, but instead, material not dealing with the General and anything offensive which might lose votes was omitted.

One of these 1828 editions showed a change in title, *Memoirs of Andrew Jackson, Late Major-General and Commander in Chief of the Southern Division of the Army of the United States*, listed its author as "a citizen of Massachusetts," and was published in Boston by Charles Ewer. This work was written by Eaton but much of the material was rearranged in an apparent effort to disguise it. There is the possibility that this was a pirated editon, but considering the intended use of the book in 1828, it seems almost certain that Eaton was responsible for printing and revision.

Still another life of Jackson which is attributed to Eaton was *Some Account of General Jackson, drawn up from the Hon. Mr. Eaton's very Circumstantial Narrative, and Other Well-Established Information Respecting Him*. This work lists its author as "a gentleman of the Baltimore bar," and was published in Baltimore by H. Vicary Matchett in 1828. Clearly intended as a campaign tract, this volume was printed in bold type on cheap paper and is only a summary of the earlier editions of Jackson's life. All of these works, including the regular 1828 Eaton edition, are part of the campaign literature and are almost entirely uncritical of Jackson.

Several more editions of the work appeared after 1828, but all of these seem to be reprints of the Charles Ewer 1828 book and either the author is not listed or they were signed by a citizen of Massachusetts. Most of the later printers even used the same plates as the Ewer edition, although the 1878 edition which was printed by Claxton, Remsen, Haffelfinger of Philadelphia, included a very brief account of Jackson as President of the United States. Since this volume was published long after Eaton's death in 1856 it is extremely unlikely that Eaton wrote this portion of the later book.[15]

Eaton apparently received considerable recognition for his book about Jackson. This personal recognition plus his friendship with the General may have been responsible for his appointment to fill the unexpired term of George W. Campbell in the United States Senate in 1818. He served as Senator from 1818 until 1829 when he resigned to become Secretary of War in Jackson's Cabinet. He held this post until 1831.

Eaton's second marriage to Peggy O'Neale gave him much notoriety and was the cause of a great deal of controversy precipitating the dismissal of Jackson's Cabinet. After Eaton's unsuccessful effort to return to the Senate from Tennessee, Jackson appointed him Governor of Florida, in which capacity he served for the years 1834-1836. Later he was appointed minister to Spain, serving from 1836 to 1840. Eaton's opposition to the nomination of Van Buren to the vice-presidency and to the presidency brought about an estrangement between him and Jackson and ended his political career. His remaining years were spent in Washington, where he died on November 17, 1856.[16]

It is the purpose of this printing to make the extremely rare first edition of the Reid-Eaton volume available once again to scholars and general readers. Since the 1817 edition is by far the superior historical account, it was chosen for reprinting, but in order that the reader may be made aware of the changes that have been made in the other editions of this book, major revisions from later printings have been added in an appendix and alterations which change the meaning of the work have been identified and noted. It was not considered desirable to indicate minor word changes which did not alter the meaning of the work. As there were usually several such amendments on each page, it would have created a useless distraction for the editor to note all of them. In addition to annotations concerning differences in the various editions, the editor has also provided notes where more recent scholarship has indicated the work to be in error or where the facts appear to need clarification. An index and an editor's bibliography have also been provided to aid scholars and general readers alike. Because the bulk of the work was written from the Jackson papers, personal accounts, and unidentified newspapers, it is not possible to create a formal bibliography of sources used by the authors. The editor believes that the time and effort spent in locating and annotating this extremely rare 1817 edition has been worthwhile because of its greater historical merit as compared with the more widely known later revisions.

NOTES

[1] Manuscript Division, Reference Department Library of Congress, *Index to the Andrew Jackson Papers, Library of Congress. President's Papers Index Series.* (Washington, 1967), v-vii.

[2] S. G. Heiskell, *Andrew Jackson and Early Tennessee History* (three volumes, Nashville, 1918-1921), II, 77.

[3] *Ibid.,* 64-75; *Index to the Andrew Jackson Papers,* v-vii; for a more detailed sketch of Reid's life and relationship with Jackson, see Helen Reid Roberts, "Memoir of John Reid," our Appendix Y.

[4] See below page 385-392.

[5] John Reid to John Coffee, November 21, 1815, Dyas Collection, Tennessee Historical Society, Tennessee State Library and Archives, Nashville, Tennessee.

[6] *Index to the Andrew Jackson Papers,* vii; Andrew Jackson to Nathan Reid, February 8, 1816, Andrew Jackson Papers, Library of Congress, Washington, D. C. (Microfilm copy in Tennessee State Library and Archives, Nashville, Tennessee.)

[7] Thomas P. Abernethy, "John Henry Eaton," Allen Johnson and Dumas Malone, ed. *Dictionary of American Biography* (New York, 1959) III, 609; Marquis James, *Andrew Jackson The Border Captain* (New York, 1933), 297-298, 321.

[8] Abram Maury to Andrew Jackson, February 17, 1816, Jackson Papers, Library of Congress.

[9] John H. Eaton to Jackson, March 20, 1817. Jackson Papers, Library of Congress.

[10] *Index to Andrew Jackson Papers,* ix.

[11] John Spencer Bassett, *The Life of Andrew Jackson* (New York, 1931) v-xi; Jackson Papers, Library of Congress; Jackson Papers, Tennessee Historical Society, Tennessee State Library and Archives; Roberts, "Memoir of John Reid," our Appendix Y.

[12] Reid to John Overton, July 2, 1815, Murdock Collection, Tennessee Historical Society, Eaton to Coffee, May 1, 1816, Dyas Collection.

[13] John H. Eaton, *The Life of Andrew Jackson* (New York, 1971. Facsimile reprint of 1824 edition).

[14] Abernethy, "John Henry Eaton," *DAB,* III, 609-610.

[15] See appendix for a full list of the editions of Reid and Eaton's *Life of Andrew Jackson.* Another work which is often credited to Eaton is *Memoirs of the Illustrious Citizen and Patriot, Andrew Jackson, late Major General in the Army of the United States: and Commander-in-*

Chief of the Division of the South by a citizen of Hagers-town, Maryland, Chambersburg, Pennsylvania; 1828. This book which has a similar
title to the Charles Ewer edition "by a citizen of Massachusetts" is often
mistaken for the latter publication. A cursory examination of the "Citizen of Hagers-town" edition will tend to strengthen the conclusion that
the two works are the same since their print, binding, general appearance
and to some extent their organization and chapter headings are very
similar. A close comparison of texts shows, however, that the "Citizen of
Hagers-town" book is a later printing of S. Putnam Waldo's *Memoirs
of Andrew Jackson Major-general in the Army of the United States; and
Commander in Chief the Division of the South,* Hartford, Connecticut:
S. Andrus, 1819. Waldo used the Reid and Eaton as a major source and
probably followed it entirely too closely. Nevertheless, the Waldo work
contains some material not found in the Reid and Eaton publication
and is phrased differently.

[16] Abernethy, "John Henry Eaton," *DAB*, III, 609-610.

Wheeler Pinx.ᵗ   Edwin sc.·

GENERAL JACKSON.

THE LIFE

OF

ANDREW JACKSON,

MAJOR GENERAL

IN THE SERVICE OF THE UNITED STATES

COMPRISING

A HISTORY OF THE WAR IN THE SOUTH,

FROM THE COMMENCEMENT OF THE

CREEK CAMPAIGN,

TO THE TERMINATION OF HOSTILITIES BEFORE

NEW ORLEANS.

COMMENCED

BY JOHN REID,

BREVET MAJOR, UNITED STATES' ARMY.

COMPLETED

BY JOHN HENRY EATON.

PHILADELPHIA:

PUBLISHED BY M. CAREY AND SON.

FOR THE BENEFIT OF THE CHILDREN OF JOHN REID.

LYDIA R. BAILEY, PRINTER.

1817.

PREFACE.

THE public have been for some time in expectation of this work: to the decision of the candid, who will make allowance for, and duly appreciate, the difficulties of the undertaking, it is now submitted. Who ventures on a detail of events, recent in the recollection of the world, hazards much, and can scarcely expect to escape censure. The numerous actors in, and spectators of, the scenes portrayed, entertaining different opinions of the facts as they transpired, and ascribing them to entirely different causes, become each a critic in his turn, accordingly as the narrative corresponds with, or is variant from his own opinion. The historian who traces events, at a period remote from their occurrence, stands on more favourable ground, and has fewer difficulties to encounter: he then proceeds in his undertaking without being acted upon by prejudice, or influenced by partiality. His readers, too, are similarly situated. But he who draws them at a moment when recollection treasures them, is oftentimes insensibly placed under the influence of both;—diverted from the course pointed out by truth;—ascribes events to motives that never induced them;—bestows censure where it is not due, and commendation where it is not merited.

To avoid errors so common, and to present things truly as they occur, has been the wish of the author, and he believes he has succeeded. He believes so, because he had no inducement to do otherwise, and because, having all the original papers in his possession, there was no avenue to error. unless from intention, and this he disclaims. He can therefore venture upon this assurance, that what is detailed may be taken as correct.

As regards the execution of the work, he has not much to offer to the consideration of the reader. It is his first effort, and he is willing to trust it to the world, without preface or apology ;—without supplicating its charity or indulgence in his favour; from no belief that ample room is not afforded, for both to be exercised in his behalf, but from a conviction that they are seldom or never extended, and that none has a right to ask for them, unless under peculiar circumstances. Whether he be competent to the task, is the duty of every man to inquire, before he undertakes to become an author; no sooner does he appear before the public in that character, than they have a right to infer, that he has entire confidence in his own qualifications, and may therefore with propriety judge him " according to his works."

2   It was not, however, a belief of this kind, that influenced on the present occasion : peculiar circumstances, and not choice, were the inducement. It is more, therefore, with a view of correctly stating the reasons, why he is placed before the public as an author, than to supplicate any indulgence for the defects which the work may be found to contain, that any thing is ventured to be said. His greatest regret, if he has any on the subject, is, that the events have not been portrayed by some masterly hand, that they might have been exhibited in a manner, worthy of him who gave them their existence.

It is some time, since major Reid submitted proposals for publishing to the world, "The Life of General Jackson." By those who knew him, it was a circumstance, hailed with pleasure, because they entertained a confidence, that the narrative would be faithful, and that he was well qualified to bestow every embellishment, necessary to render it interesting. His mind had been generously endowed by nature, and was richly stored with polite and elegant literature. The means of education had been liberally spread before him, nor had they been neglected. But before he could effect his object, he died. This event, deeply deplored, produced the necessity of either abandoning what had been already begun, or of prevailing on some person, to complete it. Through the entreaty of his relations and friends, the present author was led to the undertaking; not from a conviction that he would be able to present it, in a garb calculated to satisfy public expectation; but from a desire, that the infant children of one, who had rendered important services to his country, might not be so far injured by his death, as to lose the benefit, of what was supposed and hoped, might afford a sufficient fund for the purposes of their education.

This consideration, sufficiently weighty in itself, was the more cheerfully subscribed to, from a belief, that, perhaps, the greater part of the work was already digested, and only needed to be transcribed, and properly prepared for the press; for as yet the papers were in Virginia. Unforeseen difficulties, however, arose, when, on their arrival at Nashville, it was found, that scarcely one third of it had been prepared;* while the residue remained to be sought for, through an immense quantity of papers, without any arrangement or order. Many as were the difficulties presented, and troublesome as the research promised to be, yet the arrangement being already announced, it was too late to retract.

The brilliant achievements which had marked the course of general Jackson, and given to himself and his country a

* End of Chapter IV.

distinguished standing, had been already brought to public view; but garbled facts, and contradictory statements, had been so extensively circulated, that none knew things truly as they should be; and all, with impatience, looked for the appearance of a work, which should dispel doubt, and bring forth facts, substantially as they were. This anxiety in the public mind, added to a desire to have it published in time, to render the most essential service possible, to the children of the deceased, has caused its appearance earlier than was prompted by other considerations.

3   He, then, who shall read what is written, with a determination not to be pleased, because it is not so perfect as he himself could have made it, is desired to remember, that there is every imaginable difference between him, who has been accustomed to such pursuits, and, from habit, is enabled to give a happy arrangement to thought, and correctness to expression; and one who carries with him no such aid. But those who desire a correct view of those masterly exertions, which constantly hurried their actor to the most brilliant and uninterrupted successes;—who can be pleased with benevolence and generosity; and strength, and nerve, and decision of character, concentered in the same breast; —with a career, which, at every step, evinced an unshaken determination, to move forward for the benefit and exaltation of his country, at all hazards, and at every risk, will find much to admire. They will see the man, of whom they have already heard much, fearlessly encountering danger, and erecting himself in opposition to every design, that came in collision with the duty he owed to the station he occupied; and who, in moments of extreme difficulty, did not shrink from responsibility; but, bringing to his aid the slender resources within his reach, protected and saved an all-important and valuable portion of his country, at a time, when

her warmest votaries regarded the cause, in that quarter, as hopeless.

Whether the work shall be flatteringly received, or shall "drop still-born from the press," although of some concern to the author, is an event on which his peace and tranquillity of mind does not depend. A recollection, that the good opinion of the world is dependent on a thousand accidental circumstances,—is often "obtained without merit, and lost without crime," affords considerations, that neither hope nor fear can disturb. But that it shall be so far charitably received and patronized, as to afford advantages to the infant children of a friend, is desired. Their father is no more! but, as his representatives, they have claims of no common kind, on the liberality of the public. A character unstained by dishonour, and without reproach; a firmness unshaken, and a devotion to his country, are the inheritance he has left them. He was no inactive spectator of the trying scenes that are past. When danger threatened, he was foremost to meet it. Throughout the prosecution of the southern war, in the capacity of aid to the commanding general, he was active and valiant. Nor can any stronger evidence be furnished of his capacity, unquestioned merit, and distinguished services rendered, than that during the whole period, he carried with him the entire confidence and friendship of his general.

Of the proposals that were issued for its publication, few have been returned: an apprehension that the work would die with the author, occasioned them to be neglected and lost: it has therefore been put to press without the aid of that patronage, which had at first been extended, resting for future success on the considerations suggested, and the merit it may be found to contain.

4   It was desirable to avoid in the narrative, all those circumstances in which general Jackson was not directly concerned; but as the design of the original author was to give a complete history of the southern war, that plan has been pursued, and some events adverted to, in which the general had no immediate agency.

JOHN H. EATON.

Nashville, January, 1817.

NOTE.—Page 336, line 3, from the bottom, for " more than eight," read "fifteen."

THE LIFE

OF

ANDREW JACKSON.

CHAPTER I.

His birth, parentage, family, and education.—Engages in the American revolution, and is shortly after, with his brother, made a prisoner.—Their treatment and sufferings.—Commences the study of law.—His removal to the western country.—Becomes a member of the Tennessee convention, and afterwards a senator in the United States' congress.—Retires, and is appointed a judge of the state courts.—Declaration of war.—Tenders the services of 2500 volunteers to the president.—Ordered to the lower country.—His descent and return.

THE parents of Andrew Jackson were Irish. His father, (Andrew) the youngest son of his family, emigrated to America about the year 1765, bringing with him two sons, Hugh and Robert, both very young. Landing at Charleston, in South Carolina, he shortly afterwards purchased a tract of land, in what was then called the Waxsaw settlement, about forty-five miles above Camden; at which place the subject of this history was born, on the 15th of March, 1767. Shortly after his birth, his father died, leaving three sons to be

5

B

provided for by their mother. She appears to have been an exemplary woman, and to have executed the arduous duties which had devolved on her, with great faithfulness and success. To the lessons she inculcated on the youthful minds of her sons, was, no doubt, owing, in a great measure, that fixed opposition to British tyranny and oppression, which afterwards so much distinguished them. Often would she spend the winter's night, in recounting to them the sufferings of their grandfather, at the siege of Carrickfergus, and the oppressions exercised by the nobility of Ireland, over the labouring poor; impressing it upon them, as their first duty, to expend their lives, if it should become necessary, in defending and supporting the natural rights of man.

Inheriting but a small patrimony from their father, it was impossible that all the sons could receive an expensive education. The two eldest were therefore only taught the rudiments of their mother tongue, at a common country school. But Andrew, being intended by his mother for the ministry, was sent to a flourishing academy in the Waxsaw meeting house, superintended by Mr. Humphries. Here he was placed on the study of the dead languages, and continued until the revolutionary war, extending its ravages into that section of South Carolina, where he then was, rendered it necessary that every one should betake himself to the American standard, seek protection with the enemy, or flee his country. It was not an alternative that admitted of much deliberation. The natural ardor of his temper, deriving encouragement from the recommendations of his mother, whose feelings were

not less alive on the occasion than his own, quickly
determined him in the course to be pursued; and at
the tender age of fourteen, with his brother Robert, he
hastened to the American camp, and engaged in the
service of his country. His oldest brother, who had
previously joined the army, had lost his life at the battle of Stono, by the excessive heat of the weather, and
the fatigues of the day.

Both Andrew and Robert, were, at this period,
pretty well acquainted with the manual exercise, and
had some idea of the different evolutions of the field,
having been indulged by their mother in attending the
drill, and general musters.

The Americans being unequal, as well by the inferiority of their numbers, as their discipline, to engage
the British army in battle, retired before it, into the
interior of North Carolina; but when they learned,
that lord Cornwallis had crossed the Yadkin, they returned in small detachments to their native state. On
their arrival, they found lord Rawdon in possession of
Camden, and the whole country around in a state of
desolation. The British commander being advised of
the return of the settlers of Waxsaw; major Coffin was
immediately despatched thither, with a corps of light
dragoons, a company of infantry, and a considerable
number of tories, for their capture and destruction.
Hearing of their approach, the settlers, without delay,
appointed the Waxsaw meeting house as a place of rendezvous, that they might the better collect their scattered strength, and concert some system of operations.
About forty of them had accordingly assembled at this
point, when the enemy approached, keeping the tories,

CHAP.
I.

who were dressed in the common garb of the country, in front, whereby this little band of patriots was completely deceived, taking them for captain Nisbet's company, in expectation of which they had been waiting. Eleven of them were taken prisoners; the rest with difficulty fled, scattering and betaking themselves to the woods for concealment. Of those who thus escaped, though closely pursued, were Andrew Jackson and his brother, who, entering a secret bend in a creek, that was close at hand, obtained a momentary respite from danger, and avoided, for the night, the pursuit of the enemy. The next day, however, having gone to a neighbouring house, for the purpose of procuring something to eat, they were broken in upon, and made prisoners, by Coffin's dragoons, and a party of tories who accompanied them. They had approached the house by a route through the woods, and thereby eluded the vigilance of a sentinel who had been posted on the road. Being placed under guard, Andrew was ordered, in a very imperious tone, by a British officer, to clean his boots, which had become muddied in crossing a creek. This order he positively and peremptorily refused to obey; alleging that he looked for such treatment as a prisoner of war had a right to expect. Incensed at his refusal, the officer aimed a blow at his head with a drawn sword, which would, very probably, have terminated his existence, had he not parried its effects by throwing up his left hand, on which he received a severe wound. His brother, at the same time, for a similar offence, received a deep cut on the head, which afterwards occasioned his death. They were both now taken to gaol, where, separated and

8　Is made a prisoner by the British.

confined, they were treated with marked severity, un-
in consequence of a partial exchange, effected by the intercessions and exertions of their mother, and captain Walker, of the militia, they were both released. Captain Walker had, in a charge on the rear of the British army, succeeded in making thirteen prisoners, whom he gave in exchange for seven Americans, of which number were these two young men. Robert, during his confinement in prison, had suffered greatly; the wound on his head, all this time, having never been dressed, was followed by an inflammation of the brain, which, in a few days after his liberation, brought him to the grave. To add to the afflictions of Andrew, his mother, worn down by grief, and her incessant exertions to provide clothing and other comforts for the suffering prisoners, who had been taken from her neighbourhood, expired, in a few weeks after her son, near the lines of the enemy, in the vicinity of Charleston. Andrew, the last and only surviving child, confined to a bed of sickness, occasioned by the sufferings he had been compelled to undergo, whilst a prisoner, and by getting wet, on his return from captivity, was thus left in the wide world, without a human being with whom he could claim a near relationship. The small pox beginning, about the same time, to make its appearance upon him, had well nigh terminated his sorrows and his existence.

Having at length recovered from his complicated afflictions, he entered upon the enjoyment of his estate, which, although small, would have been sufficient, under prudent management, to have completed his

CHAP. education, on the liberal scale which his mother had
   I. designed.   Unfortunately, however, he, like too many
young men, sacrificing future prospects to present
gratification, expended it with rather too profuse a
hand.   Coming, at length, to foresee that he should
be finally obliged to rely on his own exertions, for
support and success in life, he again betook himself to
his studies, with increased industry.   He re-commenced under Mr. M'Culloch, in what was then called
the New Acquisition, near Hill's iron works.   Here
he revised the languages, devoting a portion of his
time to a desultory course of studies.

His education being now completed, so far as his
wasted patrimony, and the opportunities then afforded
in that section of the country, would permit; at the
age of eighteen, he turned his attention to acquiring a
profession, and preparing himself to enter on the busy
scenes of life.   The pulpit, for which he had been
designed by his mother, was now abandoned for the
bar; and, in the winter of 1784, he repaired to Salisbury, in North Carolina, and commenced the study of
law, under Spruce M'Cay, Esq. (afterwards one of
the judges of that state,) and continued it under colonel
John Stokes.   Having remained at Salisbury until the
winter of 1786, he obtained a license from the judges
to practice, and continued in the state until the spring
of 1788.

The observations he was enabled, during this time,
to make, satisfied him that this state presented few inducements to a young attorney; and recollecting that
he stood a solitary individual in life, without relations
to aid him in the onset, when innumerable difficulties

arise and retard success, he determined to seek a new CHAP.
country. But for this, he might have again returned I.
to his native state; but the death of every relation he
had, had wiped away all those recollections and circumstances which warp the mind to the place of its
nativity. The western parts of the state of Tennessee
were, about this time, often spoken of, as presenting
flattering prospects to adventurers. He immediately
determined to accompany judge M'Nairy thither, who
was appointed and going out to hold the first supreme
court that had ever sat in the state. Having reached
the Holston, they ascertained it would be impossible
to arrive at the time appointed for the session of the
court; and therefore determined to remain in that
country until fall. They re-commenced their journey
in October, and, passing through the wilderness, reached Nashville in the same month. It had not been
Jackson's intention, certainly, to make Tennessee the
place of his future residence; his visit was merely ex-
perimental, and his stay remained to be determined,
by the advantages that might be disclosed; but finding, soon after his arrival, that a considerable opening 9
was offered for the success of a young attorney, he determined to remain. His industry and attention soon
brought him forward, and introduced him to a profitable practice. Shortly afterwards, he was appointed attorney general for the district, in which capacity he
continued to act for several years.

Indian depredations being then frequent on the
Cumberland, every man became a soldier. Unassisted
by the government, the settlers were forced to rely for
security on their own bravery and exertions. Although

CHAP. young, no person was more distinguished than Andrew
   I.   Jackson, in defending the country against these preda-
tory incursions of the savages, who continually harassed the frontiers, and not unfrequently approached
the heart of the settlements, which were thin, but not
widely extended. He aided alike in garrisoning the
forts, and in pursuing and chastising the enemy.

In the year 1796, having, by his patriotism, firmness, and talents, secured to himself a distinguished
standing with all classes, he was chosen one of the
members of the convention, for establishing a constitution for the state. His good conduct and zeal for
the public interest, on this occasion, brought him more
conspicuously to view; and, without proposing or soliciting, he was, in the same year, elected a member of
the house of representatives, in congress, for the state
of Tennessee. The following year, his reputation
continuing to increase, and every bosom feeling a wish
10 to raise him to still higher honours, he was chosen a
member of the United States' senate.

The state of Tennessee, on its admission into the
Union, comprising but one military division, and general Conway, who commanded it, as major general,
dying about this time, Jackson, without being consulted on the subject, and without the least intimation
of what was in agitation, was chosen, by the field officers, to succeed him; which appointment he continued
to hold, until May, 1814, when he was constituted a
major general in the United States' service.

Growing tired of political life, for the intrigues of
which he found himself unqualified, and having for
two years voted in the minority in congress, he re-

signed his seat in the senate, in 1799. To this measure he was strongly urged, by a wish to make way
for general Smith, who, he conjectured, would, in that
capacity, be able to render more important services to
the government than himself. His country, unwilling
that his talents should remain inactive and unemployed,
again demanded his services. Immediately after his
resignation, he was appointed one of the judges of the
supreme court of the state. Sensibly alive to the difficult duties of this station, and impressed with the
great injury he might do to suitors, by erroneous
decisions, he advanced to the office with reluctance,
and in a short time resigned it; leaving it open for
those, who, he believed, were better qualified than
himself, to discharge its intricate and important duties.
Determined now to spend his life in tranquillity and   11
retirement, he settled himself on an elegant farm, ten
miles from Nashville, on the Cumberland river; where,
for several years, he enjoyed all the comforts of domestic and social intercourse. Abstracted from the
busy scenes of public life, surrounded by friends whom
he loved, and who entertained for him the highest veneration and respect, and blessed with an amiable and
affectionate consort, nothing seemed wanting to the
completion of that happiness he so anxiously desired
whilst in office. But a period approached, when all these
endearments were again to be abandoned, for the duties
of more active life. Great Britain, by multiplied outrages on our rights, as an independent and neutral nation, had provoked from our government a declaration
of war against her. This measure, though founded in
abundant cause, had been long forborne, and every at-

CHAP. tempt at conciliation made, without effect: when, at
  I.   length, it was resorted to, as the only alternative that
       could preserve the honour and dignity of the nation.
       General Jackson, ever devoted to the interest of his
       country, from that moment, knew no wish so strong as
       that of entering into her service, against a power, which,
       independent of public considerations, he had many
       private reasons for disliking. In her, he could trace
       the efficient cause, why, in early life, he had been left
       forlorn and wretched, without a single relation in the
       world. His proud and inflexible mind, however, could
       not venture to solicit an appointment in the army, now
       about be raised. He remained wholly unknown, until,
       at the head of the militia, employed against the Creek
       Indians, his constant vigilance, and the splendour of
       his victories, apprised the general government of those
       great military talents which he so eminently possessed,
       and conspicuously displayed, when opportunities for
       exerting them were afforded.
          The acts of congress, of the 6th of February, and
       July, 1812, afforded the means of bringing into view
       a display of those powers, which, unfortunately, being
       unknown, had too long slumbered in inaction. Under
       these acts, authorizing the president to accept the ser-
       vices of fifty thousand volunteers, he addressed the
       citizens of his division, and twenty-five hundred flock-
Tender of ed to his standard. A tender of them having been
services   made, in November he received orders to descend the
to govern-
ment.   Mississippi, for the defence of the lower country, which
       was then thought to be in danger. Accordingly, on
       the 10th of December, those troops rendezvoused at
       Nashville, prepared to advance to the place of their

destination; and, although the weather was then ex- CHAP.
cessively severe, and the ground covered with snow, I.
none could have displayed greater firmness. The
general was every where with them, inspiring them
with the ardour that animated his own bosom. The
cheerful spirit with which they submitted to hardships,
and bore privations, on the very onset of their military
career, as well as the order and subordination they so
readily observed, were happy presages of what might
be expected, when they should be directed to face an
enemy.

Having procured supplies, and made the necessary 1813.
arrangements for an active campaign, they proceeded,
the 7th of January, on their journey; and, descend- descends
ing the Ohio and Mississippi, through cold and ice, the Mis-
arrived and halted at Natchez. Here Jackson was in- sissippi,
structed to remain, until he should receive further orders. Having chosen a healthy site for the encampment of his troops, about two miles from Washington,
he devoted his time, with the utmost industry, to
training and preparing them for active service. The
clouds of war, however, in that quarter, having blown
over, he received an order from the secretary of war,
dated the 5th of January, directing him, on the receipt thereof, to dismiss those under his command,
from service, and to take measures for delivering over
every article of public property, in his possession, to
major general Wilkinson. When this order reached 12
his camp, there were one hundred and fifty on the
sick report, fifty-six of whom were unable to raise
their heads, and almost the whole of them destitute of
the means of defraying the expenses of their return:

the consequence, therefore, of a strict compliance
with the secretary's order, must have been, that many of the sick would have perished, whilst most of
the rest would, from necessity, have been compelled
to enlist in the regular army, under general Wilkinson.
Such alternatives were neither congenial with their
general's wishes, nor such as they had expected, on
adventuring with him; he had carried them from home,
and, the fate of war and disease apart, it was his duty,
he believed, to bring them back. Whether an expectation, that, by this plan, many of them would be
compelled into the regular ranks, had formed any part
of the motive that occasioned the order for their discharge, at so great a distance from home, cannot be
known; and it would be uncharitable to insinuate so serious and foul an accusation, without the strongest evidence to support it. Be this as it may, general Jackson
could not think of sacrificing or injuring an army that
had shown such devotedness to their country; and he
determined to disregard the order, and march them
back to their homes, where they had been embodied;
rather than discharge them where they would be exposed to the greatest hardships and dangers. To this
measure he was prompted, not only by the reasons
already mentioned, but by the consideration, that
many of the troops under his command were young
men, the children of his neighbours and acquaintances,
who had delivered them into his hands, as to a guardian, who, with parental solicitude, would watch over
and protect their welfare. To have abandoned them,
therefore, at such a time, and under such circumstances, would have drawn on him the merited censure

of the most deserving part of his fellow-citizens. Add
to this, those young men themselves, who were confined by sickness, learning the nature of the order he
had received, implored him, with tears in their eyes,
not to abandon them in so great an extremity, remind-
ing him, at the same time, of his assurances that he
would be to them as a father, and of the implicit confidence they had placed in his word. This was an
appeal, which it would have been difficult for the feelings of Jackson to have resisted, had it been without
the support of other weighty considerations; but, influenced by them all, he had no hesitation in coming
to a determination.

Having made known his resolution to the field officers, it met, apparently, their approbation; but those
officers, amongst whom were colonels Martin, Allcorn,   13
and Bradley, and those attached to the platoons, after
retiring from his presence, assembled late at night, in
secret caucus, and recommended to him an abandonment of his purpose, and an immediate discharge of
his troops. Great as was the astonishment, which this
measure excited in the general, it produced a still higher sentiment of indignation. In reply, he urged the
duplicity of their conduct, and reminded them, that although to those who possessed funds and health, such
a course could produce no inconvenience, yet to the
unfortunate soldier, who was destitute of both, no measure could be more calamitous. He concluded by
telling them, that his resolution not having been hastily formed, nor bottomed on light considerations, was
unalterably fixed; and that immediate preparations
must be made for carrying it into execution.

CHAP.
I.

He lost no time in making known to the secretary of war, the resolution he had adopted; to disregard the order he had given, and return his army to the place where he had received it. He painted in strong terms the evils it was calculated to produce, and expressed the astonishment he felt, that it should have originated with the famous author of the "Newburg Letters," the then redoubted advocate for soldiers' rights.

General Wilkinson, to whom the public property was directed to be delivered, learning that the determination had been taken, to march the troops back, and to take with them, so much of that property as should be necessary to their return, admonished Jackson, in a letter of solemn and mysterious import, of the awful and dangerous responsibility he was taking on himself, by that measure. General Jackson replied, that his conduct, and the consequences to which it might lead, had been deliberately weighed, and that he was prepared to abide the result. Wilkinson had previously given orders to his officers, to recruit from Jackson's army; they were advised, however, on their first appearance, that those troops were already in the service of the United States, and that thus situated, they should not be enlisted.

14

The quarter master, having been ordered to furnish the necessary transportation, for the conveyance of the sick and baggage to Tennessee, immediately set about the performance of the task; but, as the event proved, with no intention of executing it. Still, he continued to keep up the semblance of exertion; and the better to deceive, the very day before that, which had been appointed for breaking up the encampment,

and commencing the return march, eleven wagons arrived there by his order. The next morning, however,
when every thing was about to be packed up, the
quarter master entered the encampment, and discharg- 15
ed the whole. He was grossly mistaken in the man
he had to deal with, and had now played his own
tricks too far, to accomplish the object, which 'he
had, no doubt, been instructed to effect. Disregarding their dismissal, so evidently designed to prevent
his marching back his men, general Jackson seized
upon these wagons, yet within his lines, and used them
for the transportation of his sick. It deserves to be
recollected, that this quarter master, so soon as he had
received directions for furnishing transportation, despatched an express to general Wilkinson: and there
can be but little doubt, that the course of duplicity he
afterwards pursued, was a concerted plan between him
and that general, to defeat the design of Jackson; compel him to abandon the course he had adopted; and, in
this way, draw to the regular army many of the soldiers, who, from necessity, would be driven to enlist.
In this attempt, they were fortunately disappointed.
Adhering to his original purpose, he marched back
the whole of his division, to the section of country
whence they had been drawn, and dismissed them
from service, as he had been instructed.

To set an example, that might buoy up the sinking
spirits of his troops, in the long and arduous march
before them, he yielded up his horses to the sick, and
encountered all the hardships that were met by the soldiers. It was at a time of year when the roads were
extremely bad, and the swamps, lying in their passage,

CHAP. deep and full; yet, under these circumstances, he pla-
I. ced before his troops an example of patience, and hardship, that lulled to silence all complaints, and won to
him, still stronger than before, the esteem and respect
of every one. On arriving at Nashville, he communicated to the president of the United States, the course
he had pursued, and the reasons that had induced it.
If it had become necessary, he had sufficient grounds
on which he could have justified his conduct. Had he
suffered general Wilkinson to have accomplished what
was clearly his intention, it was an event which might,
at the moment, have benefited the service, by adding
an increased strength to the army; yet the example
would have been of so serious a character, that injury
would have been the final result. Whether the intention of thus forcing these men to enlist into the regular ranks, had its existence under the direction of the
government, or not, such would have been the universal belief; and all would have felt a deep abhorrence,
at beholding the patriots of the country sent off, under
pretence of danger, whilst the concealed design was,
by increasing their necessities, at a distance from home,
to compel them to an act which they would have ab-
stained from, under different circumstances. His conduct was approved of, and the expenses incurred directed to be paid.

CHAPTER II.

Indian preparation for hostilities.—Tecumseh arrives amongst
the southern tribes; his intrigues.—Civil wars of the Creeks.
—Destruction of Fort Mimms.—Expedition against the Indians.—Jackson joins the army, and enters the enemy's
country.—Scarcity of supplies in his camp.—Learns the
savages are embodied.—His address to his troops.—Seeks   16
to form a junction with the East Tennessee division, under
general Cocke.—Detaches general Coffee across the Coosa.
—Battle of Tallushatchee.

———

THE volunteers, who had descended the river, be-   CHAP.
ing discharged, early in May, there was little expectation   II.
that they would be again called for. Tennessee was
too remotely situated in the interior of the country, to
expect their services would be required at home, and
hitherto the British had discovered no serious intention
of waging operations against any part of Louisiana.
Their repose, however, was not of long duration.
The Creek Indians, inhabiting the country lying between the Chatahochee and Tombigbee, and extending   17
from the Tennessee river to the Florida line, had lately
manifested strong symptoms of hostility towards the
United States, from which they had received yearly
pensions, and every assistance which the most liberal
policy could bestow. This disposition was greatly
strengthened, by the means used by the northern Indians, who were then making preparations for a war
against the United States, and who wished to engage

D

CHAP. the southern tribes in the same enterprise. This they
II. believed to be of much importance; as, by assailing
the whole line of our frontiers at the same time, they
would be able, at once, to gratify their vengeance, and
enrich themselves with plunder.

An artful impostor had, about this time, sprung up
amongst the Shawnees, who, by passing for a prophet,
commissioned by "the Great Spirit," to communicate
his mandates and assurances to his red children, had
acquired, among his own and the neighbouring tribes,
the most astonishing influence. Clothed, as they believed him to be, with such high powers, they listened
to his most extravagant doctrines, and in them fully
confided. In a little time, he succeeded in kindling a
18   phrenzy and rage against the Anglo-Americans, which
soon after burst forth in acts of destructive violence.
Tecumseh His brother, Tecumseh, who became so famous during
arrives in the war, was despatched to the southern tribes, to ex-
the Creek
nation. cite the same temper. To the Creeks, as by far the
most numerous and powerful, as well as the most liable, from their situation and habits, to be influenced
by his suggestions, he directed his principal attention.
Having entered their nation, some time in the spring
19   of 1812, he repaired to Tookaubatcha, where he had
several conferences with the chiefs; but not meeting
with the encouragement he expected, he returned to
the Alabama, which he had previously visited, and
commenced his operations.

Finding here several leaders of great influence, who
readily entered into his views, he was enabled to carry
on his schemes with great success. Deriving his powers from his brother, *the Prophet*, whose extraordinary

commission and endowments were, before this, well understood by all the neighbouring tribes in the south; his authority was regarded with the highest veneration. He strongly interdicted all intercourse with the whites, and prevailed on the greater part of the Alabamians to throw aside the implements and clothing which that intercourse had furnished, and return again to their savage state, from which he represented them as highly culpable for having suffered themselves to be estranged. In a word, no means were left untried to excite them to the most deadly animosity and cruel war. To give additional weight to his councils, this designing missionary gave assurances of aid and support from Great Britain; whose power and riches he represented as almost without limits, and quite sufficient for the subjugation of the United States. So great an influence did his intrigues and discourses obtain over the minds of many, that it was with difficulty the most turbulent of them could be restrained from running immediately to arms, and committing depredations on the exposed frontiers. This hasty measure, however, he represented as calculated to defeat the great plan of operations which he was labouring to concert; and enjoined the utmost secrecy and quietness, until the moment should arrive, when, all their preparations being ready, they might be able to strike a general and decisive blow; in the mean time, they were to be industriously employed in collecting arms and ammunition, and other necessary implements of war.

Having ordained a chief prophet, whose word was to be regarded as infallible, and whose directions were

CHAP.
II.
to be implicitly followed; and established a regular gradation of inferior dependents, to scatter his doctrines through the different parts of the nation, Tecumseh set out to his own tribe, accompanied by several of the natives.

From this time, a regular communication was kept up, between the Creeks and the northern tribes, in relation to the great enterprise, which they were concerting together; whilst the parties, carrying it on, committed frequent depredations on the frontier settlers. By one of these, in the summer of 1812, several families had been murdered, in a shocking manner, near the mouth of the Ohio; and shortly afterwards, another party, entering the limits of Tennessee, butchered, with still greater barbarity, two families of women and children, on Duck river. Similar outrages were committed on the frontiers of Georgia, and were continued, at intervals, on the inhabitants of Tennessee, along her southern boundary.

22

These multiplied outrages at length attracted the attention of the general government; and, application was made, through their agent, (colonel Hawkins,) to the principal chiefs of the nation, who resolved to punish the murderers with death; and immediately appointed a party of warriors to carry their determination into execution. No sooner was this done, than the spirit of the greater part of the nation, which, from policy, had been kept, in a considerable degree, dormant, suddenly burst into a flame, and kindled a civil war.

It was not difficult for the friends of those murderers, who had been put to death, to prevail on others,

who secretly applauded the acts for which they suffer- CHAP.
ed, to enter warmly into their resentments against II.
those who had been concerned in bringing them to
punishment. An occasion was at hand, as they believed, fully authorizing them to throw aside all those
injunctions of secrecy, with regard to their hostile intentions, which had been imposed on them by Tecumseh and their prophets. This restraint, which, hitherto,
they had regarded with much difficulty, they now resolved to lay aside, and to execute their insatiate and
long-projected vengeance, not only on the white people,
but on those of their own nation, who, by this last act,
had unequivocally shown a disposition to preserve their
friendship with the former. The cloak of concealment
being now thrown aside, the war clubs* were immediately seen in every section of the nation; but more
particularly among the numerous hordes residing near
the Alabama. Brandishing these in their hands, they
rushed, in the first instance, on those of their own
countrymen, who had shown a disposition to preserve 1813.
their relations with the United States, and obliged them 23
to retire towards the white settlements, and place themselves in forts, to escape the first ebullition of their
rage. Encouraged by this success, and their numbers,
which hourly increased; and infatuated in the highest

---

* Instruments used by the Indian tribes, on commencing hos- 24
tilities; and which, when painted red, they consider a declaration of war. They are formed of a stick, about eighteen inches
in length, with a strong piece of sharp iron affixed at the end;
and in appearance resemble a hatchet. They use them principally in pursuit, and after they have been able to introduce
confusion into the ranks of an enemy.

CHAP. degree, by the predictions of their prophets, who as-
   II.   sured them, that " the Great Spirit" was on their side,
         and would enable them to triumph over all their ene-
         mies ; they began to make immediate preparations for
         extending their ravages to the white settlements. Fort
         Mimms, situated in the Tensaw settlement, in the Mis-
         sissippi territory, was the first point destined to satiate
         their cruelty and vengeance. It contained, at that time,
         about one hundred and fifty men, under the command
         of major Beasley, besides a considerable number of
         women and children, who had betaken themselves to it
   25   for security. Having collected a supply of ammunition,
         from the Spaniards, at Pensacola, and assembled their
   26   warriors, to the number of six or seven hundred, the
         war party, on the 30th of August, commenced their
Destruc- assault on the fort ; and having succeeded in carrying
tion of
fort   it, put to death nearly three hundred persons, including
Mimms.   women and children, with the most savage barbarity.
         The slaughter was indiscriminate ; mercy was extend-
   27   ed to none ; and the tomahawk often cleft the mother
         and the child, at the same stroke. But seventeen of
         the whole number, in the fort, escaped, to bring intel-
         ligence of the dreadful catastrophe. This monstrous
         and unprovoked outrage no sooner reached Tennessee,
         than the whole state was thrown into a ferment, and
         nothing was thought or spoken of, but retaliatory ven-
         geance. Considerable excitement had already been
         produced, by brutalities of earlier date, and mea-
         sures had been adopted by the governor, in conformity
         with instructions from the secretary of war, for com-
         mencing a campaign against them ; but the massacre
         at Fort Mimms, which threatened to be followed by the

entire destruction of the Mobile and Tombigbee set- CHAP.
tlements, inspired a deep and universal sentiment of II.
solicitude, and an earnest wish for speedy and effectual operations.   The anxiety felt on the occasion, was
greatly increased, from an apprehension, that general
Jackson would not be able to command.   He was the
only man, known in the state, who was believed qualified to discharge the arduous duties of the station, and
who could carry with him, the complete confidence of
his soldiers.   He was at this time confined to his room,
with a fractured arm, and a wound in his body, by a   28
pistol ball, received in a private rencounter, some time
before : although this apprehension was seriously indulged, measures were industriously taken, to prepare
the expedition with the utmost despatch.

A numerous collection of respectable citizens, who
convened at Nashville, on the 18th of September, for
the purpose of devising the most effectual ways and
means of affording protection to their brethren in distress, after conferring with the governor and general
Jackson, who was still confined to his room, strongly
advised the propriety of marching a sufficient army into the heart of the Creek nation ; and accordingly recommended this measure, with great earnestness, to
the legislature, which, in a few days afterwards, commenced its session.   That body, penetrated with the
same sentiments which animated the whole country,
immediately enacted a law, authorizing the executive
to call into the field thirty-five hundred of the militia,
to be marched against the Indians ; and, lest the general government should omit to adopt them into their
service, 300,000 dollars were voted for their support.

CHAP.   Additional reasons were at hand, why active opera-
II.   tions should be commenced with the least possible delay.
The settlers were fleeing to the interior, and every day
brought intelligence, that the Creeks, collected in large
force, were bending their course towards the frontiers
Creek war. of Tennessee.   The governor now issued an order to
general Jackson, requiring him to call out, and rendezvous at Fayetteville, in the shortest possible time, two
thousand of the militia and volunteers of his division,
to repel any invasion that might be contemplated.
Colonel Coffee, in addition to five hundred cavalry,
already raised, and under his command, was authorized
and instructed to organize and receive into his regiment, any mounted riflemen, that might make a tender
of their services.

Having received these orders, Jackson directed colonel Coffee, with the force then under his command,
and such additional mounted riflemen as could be attached at a short notice, to hasten forward to the neighbourhood of Huntsville, and occupy some eligible position, for the defence of the frontier, until the infantry
could arrive ; when it was contemplated to push him
on, by the nearest route, to fort St. Stephens.   The
infantry, consisting, in part, of the late detachment of
volunteers, who descended the Mississippi, were directed to appear at the place appointed, on the 4th of
October, well equipped for active service.   He stated
to them the imperious necessity, which demanded
their services, and required them to be punctual; that
their frontiers were threatened with invasion by a savage
foe.   " Already are large bodies of the hostile Creeks
marching to your borders, with their scalping knives

unsheathed, to butcher your women and children :
time is not to be lost. We must hasten to the frontier,
or we shall find it drenched in the blood of our citizens! The health of your general is restored—he will
command in person."

Every exertion was now made, to hasten the preparations for a vigorous campaign. Orders were given to
the quarter master, to furnish the necessary munitions,
with the proper transportation; and to the contractors,
to provide ample supplies of provisions. The day of October 4.
their rendezvous being arrived, and the general not
being sufficiently recovered of his wound, to attend
in person, he sent, by his aid-de-camp, major Reid,
an address, to be read to the troops, accompanied by
an order for the establishment of the police of the
camp. In this address, he pointed to the unprovoked
injuries that had been so long inflicted by this horde of
merciless and cruel savages; and intreated his soldiers
to evince that zeal in the defence of their country,
which the importance of the moment so much required. "We are about to furnish these savages a Address
lesson of admonition;—we are about to teach them, to his
that our long forbearance has not proceeded from an troops.
insensibility to wrongs, or inability to redress them.
They stand in need of such warning. In proportion
as we have borne with their insults, and submitted to
their outrages, have they multiplied in number, and
increased in atrocity. But the measure of their offences
is at length filled. The blood of our women and children, recently spilled at Fort Mimms, calls for our vengeance; it must not call in vain. Our borders must
no longer be disturbed by the war whoop of these

CHAP.
II.
savages, or the cries of suffering victims. The torch that has been lighted up, must be made to blaze in the heart of their own country. It is time they should be made to feel the weight of a power, which, because it was merciful, they believed to be impotent. But how shall a war so long forborne, and so loudly called for by retributive justice, be waged? Shall we imitate the example of our enemies, in the disorder of their movements, and the savageness of their dispositions? Is it worthy the character of American soldiers, who take up arms to redress the wrongs of an injured country, to assume no better model than that furnished them by barbarians? No, fellow soldiers; great as are the grievances that have called us from our homes, we must not permit disorderly passions to tarnish the reputation we shall carry along with us;—we must and will be victorious; but we must conquer as men who owe nothing to chance, and who, in the midst of victory, can still be mindful of what is due to humanity!

" We will commence the campaign by an inviolable attention to discipline and subordination. Without a strict observance of these, victory must ever be uncertain, and ought hardly to be exulted in, even when gained. To what but the entire disregard of order and subordination, are we to ascribe the disasters which have attended our arms in the north, during the present war? How glorious will it be to remove the blots, which have tarnished the fair character bequeathed us by the fathers of our revolution! The bosom of your general is full of hope. He knows the ardour which animates you, and already exults in the triumph, which your strict observance of discipline and good order will render certain."

For the police of his camp, he announced the fol- CHAP.
lowing order: II.

" The chain of sentinels will be marked, and the
sentries posted, precisely at ten o'clock to day.

" No sutler will be suffered to sell spiritous liquors
to any soldier, without permission, in writing, from a
commissioned officer, under the penalties prescribed
by the rules and articles of war.

" No citizen will be permitted to pass the chain of
sentinels, after retreat beat in the evening, until reveille
in the morning. Drunkenness, the bane of all orderly
encampments, is positively forbidden, both in officers
and privates : officers, under the penalty of immediate
arrest ; and privates, of being placed under guard, there
to remain, until liberated by a court martial.

" At reveille beat, all officers and soldiers are to appear on parade, with their arms and accoutrements in
proper order.

" On parade, silence, the duty of a soldier, is positively commanded.

" No officer or soldier is to sleep out of camp, but
by permission obtained."

These rules, to those who had scarcely yet passed
the line that separates the citizen from the soldier, and
who had not yet laid aside the notions of self sovereignty, had the appearance of too much rigour ; but
the general well knew, that the expedition in which
they were embarked involved much hazard ; and
that, although such lively feelings were manifested
now, yet when hardships pressed, these might cease.
He considered it much safer, therefore, to lay before
them, at once, the rules of conduct to which they

CHAP.
II.
must conform; believing it might be more difficult to drive licentiousness from his camp, than to prevent its entrance.

Impatient to join his division, although his health was far from being restored, his arm only beginning to heal, the general, in a few days afterwards, set out for the encampment, and reached it on the 7th. Finding, on his arrival, that the requisition was not complete, either in the number of men, or the necessary equipments, measures were instantly taken to remedy the deficiency. Orders were directed to the several brigadiers in his division, to hasten immediately their respective quotas, fully equipped for active operations.

Circumstances did not permit him to remain at this place long enough to have the delinquencies complained of remedied, and the ranks of his army filled. Colonel Coffee had proceeded with his mounted volunteers, to cover Huntsville, and give security to the frontiers. On the night of the 8th, a letter was received from him, dated two days before, advising, that two Indians, belonging to the peace party, had just arrived at the Tennessee river, from Chinnaby's fort, on the Coosa, with information that the war party had despatched eight hundred or a thousand of their warriors, to attack the frontiers of Georgia; and, with the remainder of their forces, were marching against Huntsville, or Fort Hampton. In consequence of this intelligence, exertions were made to hasten a movement. Late on the following night, another express arrived, confirming the former statement, and representing the enemy, in great force, to be rapidly approaching the Tennessee. Orders were now given for preparing the line of march,

30

October.

and by nine o'clock the next day, the whole division CHAP.
was in motion. They had not proceeded many miles, II.
when they were met with intelligence that colonel
Gibson, who had been sent out by Coffee, to reconnoitre the movements of the enemy, had been killed
by their advance. A strong desire had been manifested to be led forward; that desire was now strengthened, by the information just received; and it was with
difficulty their emotions could be restrained. They
mended their pace, and before eight o'clock at night,
arrived at Huntsville, a distance of thirty-two miles.
Learning here, that the information was erroneous,
which had occasioned so hasty a movement, the general encamped his troops; having intended to march
them that night to the Tennessee, had it been confirmed. The next day, the line of march was resumed.
The influence of the late excitement was now visible
in the lassitude which followed its removal. Proceeding slowly, they crossed the Tennessee, at Ditto's
landing, and united in the evening with colonel Coffee's
regiment, which had previously occupied a commanding bluff, on the south bank of the river. From this
place, in a few days afterwards, Jackson detached colonel Coffee, with seven hundred men, to scour the
Black Warrior, a stream running from the north-east,
and emptying into the Tombigbee; on which were
supposed to be settled several populous villages of the
enemy. He himself remained at this encampment a
week, using the utmost pains, in training his troops for
service, and labouring incessantly to procure the necessary supplies for a campaign, which he had determined to carry directly into the heart of the enemy's

CHAP. country. Towards the latter object, his attention had
II. been invariably directed, and his industry employed,
from the time the expedition was projected.

31   With major general Cocke, who commanded the
division of East Tennessee militia, an arrangement had
been made, the preceding month, in which he had engaged to furnish large quantities of bread stuff, at Ditto's landing. The facility of procuring it in that quarter, and the convenient transportation afforded by the
river, left no doubt on the mind of Jackson, but that
the engagement would be punctually complied with.
To provide, however, against the bare possibility of a
failure, and to be guarded against all contingencies that
might happen, he had addressed his applications to various other sources. He had, on the same subject, written
in the most pressing manner, to the governor of Georgia, with whose forces it was proposed to act in concert; to colonel Meigs, agent to the Cherokee nation
of Indians; and to general White, who commanded
the advance of the East Tennessee troops. Previously to his arrival at Huntsville, he had received assurances from the two latter, that a considerable supply of
flour, for the use of his army, had been procured, and
was then at Hiwassee, where boats were ready to transport it. From general Cocke himself, about the same
time, a letter was received, stating that a hundred and
fifty barrels of flour were then on the way to his encampment, and expressing a belief, that he should be
able to procure, and forward on immediately, a thousand barrels more. With pressing importunity, he had
addressed himself to the contractors, and they had giv-
en him assurances, that on his crossing the Tennessee,

they would be prepared with twenty days' rations, for his whole command; but finding, on his arrival at Ditto's, that their preparations were not in such forwardness as he had been led to expect, he was compelled, for a time, to suspend any general operations. Calculating, however, with great confidence, on exertions, which, he had been promised, should be unremitting; and on the speedy arrival of those supplies, descending the river, which had been already unaccountably delayed; he hoped, in a few days, to be placed in a situation to act efficiently. Whilst he was encouraged by these expectations, Shelocta, the son of Chinnaby, a principal chief among the friendly Creeks, arrived at his camp, to solicit his speedy movement, for the relief of his father's fort, which was then threatened by a considerable body of the war party, who had advanced to the neighbourhood of the Ten Islands, on the Coosa. Influenced by his representations, Jackson, on the 18th, gave orders for taking up the line of march on the following day, and notified the contractors of this arrangement, that they might be prepared to issue, immediately, such supplies as they had on hand; but, to his great astonishment, he then, for the first time, was apprised of their entire inability to supply him, whilst on his march. Having drawn what they had in their power to furnish, amounting to only a few days' rations, they were deposed, and others appointed, on whose industry and performance, he believed, he might more safely rely. The scarcity of his provisions, however, at a moment like the present, when there was every appearance that the enemy might be met, and a blow stricken to advantage, was

CHAP.
II.

not sufficient to wave his determination, already taken. The route he would have to make, to gain the fort, lay, for a considerable distance, up the river : might not the boats, long expected from Hiwassee, and which he felt strongly assured must be near at hand, be met with on the way ? He determined to proceed ; and, having passed his army and baggage wagons over several mountains of stupendous size, and such as were thought almost impassable by foot passengers, he arrived, on the 22d of October, at Thompson's creek, which empties into the Tennessee, twenty-four miles above Ditto's. Here he proposed the establishment of a permanent depot, for the reception of supplies, to be sent either up or down the river. Disappointed in the hopes with which he had adventured on his march, he remained here several days, in expectation of the boats that were coming to his relief. Thus harassed at the first onset, by difficulties wholly unexpected ; and fearing that the same disregard of duty might induce a continuance, he lost no time in opening every avenue to expedient, that the chances of future failure might be diminished. To general Flournoy, who commanded at Mobile, he applied, urging him to procure bread stuff, and have it forwarded up the Alabama, by the time he should arrive on that river. The agent of the Choctaws, colonel M'Kee, who was then on the Tombigbee, was addressed in the same style of intreaty. Expresses were despatched to general Cocke and general White, who, with the advance of the East Tennessee division, had arrived at the Look Out mountain, in the Cherokee nation, urging them to hasten on supplies. The assistance of the governor of

32

Tennessee, was also earnestly besought. To facilitate CHAP.
the exertions of the contractors, and to assure success, II.
every thing within his reach was attempted: several
persons of wealth and patriotism, in Madison county,
were solicited to afford them all the aid in their power; and, to induce them more readily to extend it, their
deep interest, immediately at stake, was pointed to,
and their deplorable and dangerous situation, should
necessity compel him to withdraw his army, and leave
them exposed to the mercy of the savages.

Whilst these measures were taking, two runners,
from Turkey town, despatched by Path-killer, a chief   33
of the Cherokees, arrived at the camp. They brought
information, that the enemy, from nine of the hostile
towns, were assembling in great force near the Ten
Islands; and solicited, that immediate assistance should
be afforded the friendly Creeks and Cherokees, in their
neighbourhood, who were exposed to such imminent
danger. His want of provisions was not yet remedied;
but, distributing the partial supply that was on hand,
he resolved to proceed, in expectation that the relief
he had so earnestly looked for, would, in a little while,
arrive, and be forwarded on. To prepare his troops
for an engagement, which he foresaw was soon to take
place, he thus addressed them:

" You have, fellow soldiers, at length penetrated the Address.
country of your enemies. It is not to be believed,
that they will abandon the soil that embosoms the bones
of their forefathers, without furnishing you an opportunity of signalizing your valour. Wise men do not
expect; brave men will not desire it. It was not to
travel unmolested, through a barren wilderness, that

CHAP.
II.
you quitted your families and homes, and submitted to so many privations; it was to avenge the cruelties, committed upon our defenceless frontiers, by the inhuman Creeks, instigated by their no less inhuman allies; you shall not be disappointed. If the enemy flee before us, we will overtake, and chastise him; we will teach him, how dreadful, when once aroused, is the resentment of freemen. But it is not by boasting, that punishment is to be inflicted, or victory obtained. The same resolution, that prompted us to take up arms, must inspire us in battle. Men thus animated, and thus resolved, barbarians can never conquer; and it is an enemy, barbarous in the extreme, that we have now to face. Their reliance will be, on the damage they can do you, whilst you are asleep, and unprepared for action: their hopes shall fail them, in the hour of experiment. Soldiers, who know their duty, and are ambitious to perform it, are not to be taken by surprise. Our sentinels will never sleep, nor our soldiers be unprepared for action: yet, whilst it is enjoined upon the sentinels, vigilantly to watch the approach of the foe, they are, at the same time, commanded not to fire at shadows. Imaginary danger must not deprive them of entire self possession. Our soldiers will lie with their arms in their hands: and the moment an alarm is given, they will move to their respective positions, without noise, and without confusion; they will be thus enabled to hear the orders of their officers, and to obey them with promptitude.

" Great reliance will be placed, by the enemy, on the consternation they may be able to spread through our ranks, by the hideous yells with which they commence their battles; but brave men will laugh at such efforts to alarm them.   It is not by bellowings and screams, that the wounds of death are inflicted.   You will teach these noisy assailants, how weak are their weapons of warfare, by opposing them with the bayonet; what Indian ever withstood its charge? what army, of any nation, ever withstood it long?

"Yes, soldiers, the order for a charge, will be the signal for victory.   In that moment, your enemy will be seen, fleeing in every direction before you.   But in the moment of action, coolness and deliberation must be regarded; your fires made with precision and aim; and when ordered to charge with the bayonet, you must proceed to the assault with a quick and firm step; without trepidation or alarm.   Then shall you behold the completion of your hopes in the discomfiture of your enemy.   Your general, whose duty, as well as inclination, is to watch over your safety, will not, to gratify any wishes of his own, rush you unnecessarily into danger.   He knows, however, that it is not in assailing an enemy, that men are destroyed; it is when retreating, and in confusion. Aware of this, he will be prompted as much by a regard for your lives, as your honour.   He laments that he has been compelled, even incidentally, to hint at a retreat when speaking to freemen, and to soldiers.   Never, until you forget all that is due to yourselves and your country, will you have any practical understanding of that word.   Shall an enemy, wholly unacquainted with military evolution, and who rely more for victory on their grim visages, and hideous yells, than upon their bravery, or their weapons; shall such an enemy, ever drive before them, the well-trained youths of our country, whose bosoms pant for glory, and a desire to avenge the wrongs they have received? Your general will not live to behold such a spectacle; rather would he rush into the thickest of the enemy, and submit himself to their scalping knives; but he has no fears of such a result. He knows the valour of the men he commands, and how certainly that valour, regulated as it will be, will lead to victory. With his soldiers he will face all dangers, and with them participate in the glory of conquest."

Having thus prepared the minds of his men, and brought to their view the kind of foe, with whom they were shortly to contend; and having also, by his expresses, instructed general White, to form a junction with him, and to hasten on all the supplies, in his power to command; with about six days' rations of meat, and less than two of meal, he again put his army in motion, to meet the enemy. Although there was some hazard, in advancing into a country where relief was not to be expected, with such limited preparation, yet believing that his contractors, lately installed, would exert themselves to the utmost, to forward supplies; and well aware that his delaying longer might be productive of many disadvantages, his determination was taken, to set out in quest of the enemy. He replied to the Path-killer, by his runners, that he should proceed immediately for the Coosa, and solicited him to be diligent in making discoveries of the situation and collected forces of the savages, and to give him the result of his inquiries.

" The hostile Creeks," he remarked to him, "will CHAP. not attack you, until they have had a brush with me; II. and that, I think, will put them out of the notion of fighting, for some time."

He requested that if he had, or could any how procure, provisions for his army, he would send them, or advise where they might be had: "You shall be well paid, and have my thanks into the bargain. I shall stand most in need of corn meal, but shall be thankful for any kind of meat; and indeed for whatever will support life."

The army had advanced but a short distance, when unexpected embarrassments were again presented. Information was received, by which it was clearly ascertained, that the present contractors, who had been so much and so certainly relied on, could not, with all their exertions, procure the necessary supplies. Major Rose, in the quarter master's department, who had been sent back to Madison, to aid them in their endeavours, having satisfied himself, as well from their own admissions, as from evidence derived from other sources, that their want of funds, and consequent want of credit, rendered them a very unsafe dependence, returned, and disclosed the facts to the general. He stated, that there were there persons of fortune and industry, who would be willing to contract for the army, if it were necessary. Jackson lost no time in embracing this plan, and gave the contract to Mr. Pope, upon whose means and exertions, he hoped, every reliance might be safely reposed. To the other contractors he wrote, informing them of the change that had been made, and the reasons that had induced it.

"I am advised," said he, "that you have candidly acknowledged, that you have it not in your power to execute the contract in which you have engaged. Do not think I mean to cast any reflection—very far from it. I am exceedingly pleased with the exertions you have made, and feel myself under many obligations of gratitude for them. The critical situation of affairs, when you entered into the contract, being considered, you have done all that individuals, in your circumstances, could have performed. But you must be well convinced, that any approbation which may be felt by the commander of an army, for past services, ought not to become the occasion of that army's destruction. From the admissions you have been candid enough to make, the scarcity which already begins to appear in camp, and the difficulties you are likely to encounter, in effecting your engagements, I am apprehensive I should be doing injustice to the army I command, were I to rely for support on your exertions—great as I know them to be. Whatever concerns myself, I may manage with any generosity or indulgence I please; but in acting for an army, I have no such discretion. I have therefore felt myself compelled to give the contract in which you are concerned, to another, who is abundantly able to execute it; on condition he indemnify you for the trouble you have been at."

This arrangement being made, the army continued its march, and having arrived within a few miles of the Ten Islands, was met by old Chinnaby, a leading chief of the Creek nation, and sternly opposed to the war party. He brought with him, and surrendered up, two of the hostile Creeks, who had been lately made

prisoners by his party. At this place, it was represent- CHAP.
ed, that they were within sixteen miles of the enemy, II.
who were collected, to the number of a thousand, to
oppose their passage. This information was little relied on, and afterwards proved untrue. Jackson continued his route, and in a few days reached the islands
of the Coosa; having been detained a day on the way,
for the purpose of obtaining small supplies of corn from
the neighbouring Indians. This acquisition to the
scanty stock on hand, whilst it afforded subsistence for
the present, encouraged his hopes for the future, as a
mean of temporary resort, should his other resources
fail.

In a letter to governor Blount, from this place, speaking of the difficulties with which he was assailed, he
observes:—" Indeed, sir, we have been very wretch-
edly supplied—scarcely two rations in succession have
been regularly drawn; yet we are not despondent.
Whilst we can procure an ear of corn a-piece, or any
thing that will answer as a substitute for it, we shall
continue our exertions, to accomplish the object for
which we were sent. The cheerfulness with which my
men submit to privations, and are ready to encounter
danger, does honour to the government whose rights
they are defending.

" Every mean within my power, for procuring the
requisite supplies for my army, I have taken, and am
continuing to take. East, west, north, and south have
been applied to, with the most pressing solicitation.
The governor of Georgia, in a letter received from him
this evening, informs me, that a sufficiency can be had
in his state; but does not signify that he is about to

CHAP. take any measures to procure it. My former contract-
II.   or has been superseded: no exertions were spared by
      him, to fulfil his engagements; yet the inconveniences
36   under which he laboured, were such as to render his
      best exertions unavailing. The contract has been of-
      fered to one who will be able to execute it: if he ac-
      cept it, my apprehensions will be greatly diminished."

37   On the 28th of October, colonel Dyer, who, on the
      march to the Ten Islands, had been detached from the
      main body, with two hundred cavalry, to attack Littafut-
      chee town, on the head of Canoe creek, which empties
      into the Coosa from the west, returned, bringing with
      him twenty-nine prisoners, men, women, and children;
      having destroyed the village.

          The sanguine expectations indulged, on leaving
      Thompson's creek,—that the advance of the East Ten-
      nessee militia would hasten to unite with him, was not
      yet realized. The express heretofore directed to general
      White, had not returned. Jackson, on the 31st, des-
      patched another, urging him to effect a speedy junction,
      and to bring with him all the bread stuff it should be
      in his power to procure; pointing out to him, at the
      same time, the great inconvenience and hazard to which
      he had been already exposed, for the want of punctu-
38   ality in himself and general Cocke. Owing to that
      cause, and the late failures of his contractors, he repre-
      sented his army as placed, at present, in a very preca-
      rious situation, and as dependent, in a great measure,
      for its support, on the exertions which he and general
      Cocke might be pleased to make; but assured him, at
      the same time, that, let circumstances transpire as they
      might, he would still endeavour to effect his purpose;

and, at all events, was resolved to hasten, with every CHAP.
practicable despatch, to the accomplishment of the ob- II.
ject for which he had set out. Believing the co-operation
of the East Tennessee troops essential to this end,
they were again instructed to join him without delay ;
for he could not conceive it to be correct policy, that
troops from the same state, pursuing the same object,
should constitute separate and distinct armies, and act
without concert, and independently of each other. He
entertained no doubt but that his order would be
promptly obeyed.

The next evening, a detachment, which had been
sent out the day before, returned to camp, bringing
with them, besides some corn and beeves, several negroes and prisoners of the war party.

Learning now, that a considerable body of the enemy
had posted themselves at Tallushatchee, on the south
side of the Coosa, about thirteen miles distant; general
Coffee was detached, with nine hundred men, (the
mounted troops having been previously organized into
a brigade, and placed under his command) to attack
and disperse them. With this force, he was enabled,
through the direction of an Indian pilot, to ford the
Coosa, at the Fish-dams, about four miles above the
Islands ; and having encamped beyond it, very early
the next morning proceeded to the execution of his
order. Having arrived within a mile and a half, he
formed his detachment into two divisions, and directed them to march so as to encircle the town, by
uniting their fronts beyond it. The enemy, hearing of
his approach, began to prepare for action, which was
announced by the beating of drums, mingled with yells

c

and war whoops. An hour after sun-rise, the action was commenced by captain Hammon's and lieutenant Patterson's companies of spies, who had gone within the circle of alignement, for the purpose of drawing the Indians from their buildings. No sooner had these

Battle of Tallus-hatchee.

companies exhibited their front in view of the town, and given a few scattering shot, than the enemy formed, . and made a violent charge. Being compelled to give way, they were pursued, until they reached the main body of the army, which immediately opened a general fire, and charged in their turn. The Indians retreated, firing, until they got around, and in their buildings, where an obstinate conflict ensued, and where those who maintained their ground persisted in fighting, as long as they could stand or sit, without manifesting fear, or soliciting quarter. Their loss was an hundred and eighty-six killed; among whom were, unfortunately, and through accident, a few women and children. Eighty-four women and children were taken prisoners, towards whom the utmost humanity was shown. Of the Americans, five were killed, and forty-one wounded. Two were killed with arrows, which, on this occasion, formed a principal part of the arms of the Indians ; each one having a bow and quiver, which he used after the first fire of his gun, until an opportunity occurred for re-loading.

Having buried his dead, and provided for his wounded, general Coffee, late on the evening of the same day, united with the main army, bringing with him about forty prisoners. Of the residue, a part were too badly wounded to be removed, and were therefore left, with a sufficient number to take care of

them.   Those which he brought in, received every
comfort and assistance their situation demanded, and,
for safety, were immediately sent into the settlements.

From the manner in which the enemy fought, the
killing and wounding others than their warriors was
not to be avoided.   On their retreat to their village,
after the commencement of the battle, they resorted to
their block houses, and strong log dwellings, whence
they kept up resistance, and resolutely maintained the
fight.   Thus mingled with their women and children,
it was impossible they should not be exposed to the
general danger; and thus many were injured, notwithstanding every possible precaution was taken to pre-
vent it.   39

CHAPTER III.

Endeavours to unite with the East Tennessee troops.—Establishment of Fort Strother.—Learns the enemy are embodied.—Marches to meet them.—Battle of Talladega.—Is compelled to return to his encampment, for want of supplies. —Discontents of his army.—Militia and volunteers mutiny. —Address to the officers.—Is compelled to abandon Fort Strother.—Hillabee clans sue for peace.—Letter from the Rev. Mr. Blackburn.—Answer.—The volunteers claim to be discharged.—Mutiny.—Address to them.—General Cocke arrives with part of his division.—General Coffee's brigade petitions for a discharge.—General Jackson's answer.—They abandon the service, and go home.

CHAP.   MEASURES were now taken, to establish a per-
III.   manent depot, on the north bank of the river, at the
        Ten Islands, to be protected by strong picketting and
1813.   block houses; after which, it was the intention of
        Jackson to proceed down the Coosa, to its junction
        with the Tallapoosa, near which it was expected, the
December main force of the enemy was collected. Well know-
        ing that it would take away much of the strength of
        his army, to occupy, in his advance, the different points
        necessary to the safety of his rear, it was desirable to
        unite, as soon as possible, with the troops from the
        east of Tennessee: to effect this, he again, on the 4th,
        despatched an express to general White, who had pre-
        viously, with his command, arrived at Turkey town, a
        Cherokee village, about twenty-five miles above, on

the same river, urging him to unite with him as soon CHAP.
as possible, and again intreating him on the subject of III.
provisions;—to bring with him such as he had on hand,
or could procure; and, if possible, to form some certain arrangement, that might insure a supply in future.

Anxious to proceed, and have his army serviceably   40
employed, which he believed practicable, as soon as a
junction could be effected; he again, on the morning
of the 7th, renewed his application to general White,
who still remained at Turkey town.

As yet, no certain intelligence was received, of any
collection of the enemy. The army was busily engaged
in fortifying and strengthening the site fixed on for a
depot, to which the name of Fort Strother had been
given. Late, however, on the evening of the 7th, a
runner arrived from Talladega, a fort of the friendly
Indians, distant about thirty miles below, with information, that the enemy had, that morning, encamped
before it in great numbers, and would certainly destroy
it, unless immediate assistance could be afforded.
Jackson, confiding in the statement, determined to lose
no time, in extending the relief which was solicited.
Understanding that general White was on his way to
join him, he despatched a messenger to meet him, directing him to reach his encampment in the course of
the ensuing night, and protect it in his absence. He
now gave orders for taking up the line of march, with
twelve hundred infantry, and eight hundred cavalry
and mounted gun men; leaving behind, the sick, the
wounded, and all his baggage, with a force which was
deemed sufficient for their protection, until the reinforcement from Turkey town should arrive. The   41

Indians, who had taken refuge in this besieged fort, had involved themselves in their present perilous situation, from a disposition to preserve their friendly relations with the United States. To suffer them to fall a sacrifice, from any tardiness of movement, would have been unpardonable; and unless relief were immediately extended, it might arrive too late. Acting under these impressions, the general concluded to move instantly forward to their assistance. By twelve o'clock at night, every thing was in readiness; and, in an hour afterwards, the army commenced crossing the river, about a mile above the camp,—each of the mounted men carrying one of the infantry behind him. The river, at this place, was six hundred yards wide, and it being necessary to send back the horses, for the remainder of the infantry, several hours were consumed, before a passage of all the troops could be effected. Nevertheless, though thus deprived of sleep, they continued the march with animation, and by evening had arrived within six miles of the enemy. In this march, Jackson used the utmost circumspection to prevent surprise; marching his army, as was his constant custom, in three columns, so that, by a speedy manœuvre, they might be thrown into such a situation, as to be capable of resisting an attack from any quarter. Having judiciously encamped his men on an eligible piece of ground, he sent forward two of the friendly Indians, and a white man, who had, for many years, been detained a captive in the nation, and was now acting as interpreter, to reconnoitre the position of the enemy. About eleven o'clock at night, they returned, with information, that the savages were posted within a quar-

ter of a mile of the fort, and appeared to be in great CHAP.
force; but that they had not been able to approach III.
near enough to ascertain either their numbers, or precise situation. Within an hour after this, a runner
arrived from Turkey town, with a letter from general
White, stating, that after having taken up the line of
march, to unite at Fort Strother, he had received orders from general Cocke, to change his course, and 42
proceed to the mouth of Chatuga creek. This unexpected and disagreeable intelligence filled Jackson with
astonishment and apprehensions; and dreading, lest the
enemy, by taking a different route, should attack his
encampment in his absence, he determined to lose no
time, in bringing him to battle. Orders were accordingly given to the adjutant general to prepare the line,
and by four o'clock in the morning, the army was
again in motion. The infantry proceeded in three columns; the cavalry in the same order, in the rear, with
flankers on each wing. The advance, consisting of a
company of artillerists, with muskets, two companies
of riflemen, and one of spies, marched about four hundred yards in front, under the command of colonel
Carroll, the inspector general; with orders, after commencing the action, to fall back on the centre, so as to
draw the enemy after them. At seven o'clock, having
arrived within a mile of the position they occupied, the
columns were displayed in order of battle. Two hundred and fifty of the cavalry, under lieutenant colonel
Dyer, were placed in the rear of the centre, as a corps
de reserve. The remainder of the mounted troops
were directed to advance, on the right and left, and,
after encircling the enemy, by uniting the fronts of their

CHAP.
III.
columns, and keeping their rear rested on the infantry, to face and press towards the centre, so as to leave them no possibility of escape. The remaining part of the army was ordered to move up, by heads of companies; general Hall's brigade occupying the right, and general Roberts's the left.

About eight o'clock, the advance having arrived within eighty yards of the enemy, who were concealed in a thick shrubbery, that covered the margin of a small rivulet, received a heavy fire, which they instantly returned with much spirit. Agreeably to their instructions, they fell back towards the centre, but not before they had dislodged the enemy from his position. The

Battle of Talladega.
Indians now screaming and yelling hideously, rushed forward in the direction of general Roberts's brigade; a few companies of which, alarmed by their numbers and yells, fled at the first fire. Jackson, to fill the chasm which was thus created, directed the regiment commanded by colonel Bradley, to be moved up, which,

43
from some unaccountable cause, had failed to advance, in a line with the others, and now occupied a position in rear of the centre: Bradley, however, to whom this order was given by one of the staff, could not be prevailed on to execute it in time, alleging, he was determined to remain on the eminence which he then possessed, until the enemy should approach and attack him. Owing to this failure, in the volunteer regiment, it became necessary to dismount the reserve, which, with great firmness, met the approach of the enemy, who were rapidly moving in this direction. The retreating militia, seeing their places supplied, rallied, and, recovering their former position in the line, aided

in checking the advance of the savages.   The action
now became general along the line, and in fifteen minutes the Indians were seen flying in every direction.
On the left, they were met and repulsed by the mounted riflemen; but on the right, owing to the halt of
Bradley's regiment, which was intended to occupy the
extreme right,—and to the circumstance of colonel Allcorn, who commanded one of the wings of the cavalry, having taken too large a circuit, a considerable
space was left between the infantry and the cavalry,   44
through which numbers escaped. The fight was maintained with great spirit and effect on both sides, as well
before, as after the retreat commenced; nor did the
savages escape the pursuit and slaughter, until they
reached the mountains, at the distance of three miles.

Jackson, in his report of this action, bestows high
commendation on the officers and soldiers. "Too
much praise," he observes, in the close of it, "cannot
be bestowed on the advance, led by colonel Carroll, for
the spirited manner in which they commenced and
sustained the attack; nor upon the reserve, commanded by lieutenant colonel Dyer, for the gallantry with
which they met, and repulsed the enemy.   In a word,
officers of every grade, as well as privates, realized the
high expectations I had formed of them, and merit the
gratitude of their country."

In this battle, the force of the enemy was one thousand and eighty, of whom two hundred and ninety-nine
were left dead on the ground; and it is believed that
many were killed in the flight, who were not found
when the estimate was made.   Probably few escaped
unhurt.   Their loss on this occasion, as stated since

CHAP. by themselves, was not less than six hundred: that
III.   of the Americans was fifteen killed, and eighty wounded, several of whom afterwards died. Jackson, after
collecting his dead and wounded, advanced his army
beyond the fort, and encamped for the night. The
Indians, who had been for several days shut up
by the besiegers, thus fortunately liberated from the
most dreadful apprehensions, and severest privations,
having for some time been entirely without water,
received the army with all the demonstrations of gratitude, that savages could give. Their manifestations
of joy for their deliverance, presented an interesting
and affecting spectacle. Their fears had been already
greatly excited, for it was the very day when they were
to have been assaulted, and when every soul within the
fort must have perished. All the provisions they could
spare, from their scanty stock, they sold to the general,
who, purchasing with his own money, distributed them
amongst the soldiers, who were almost destitute.

It was with great regret, that Jackson now found he
was without the means of availing himself fully of the
advantages of his victory; but the condition of his
posts in the rear, and the want of provisions, (having
left his encampment at Fort Strother with little more
than one day's rations,) compelled him to hasten back;
thus giving the enemy time to recover from their consternation, and to re-assemble their forces.

The cause which prevented general White from act-
45 ing in obedience to his order, and arriving at the Ten
Islands at a moment when it was so important, and so
confidently expected, was as yet unknown; the only
certainty upon the subject was, that for the pre-

sent it wholly thwarted his views, and laid him under CHAP. the necessity of returning. This mystery, hitherto III. inexplicable, was soon after explained, by a view of the order of general Cocke, under which White, being a brigadier in his division, chose to act, rather than under Jackson's. General Cocke stated to him, he had understood, Jackson had crossed the Coosa, and had an engagement with the Indians. " I have formed a council of officers here, and proposed these questions;—shall we follow him, or cross the river, and proceed to the Creek settlements on the Tallapoosa?—Both were decided unanimously : that he should not be followed, but that we should proceed in the way proposed." He remarked, that the decision had met his entire approbation; and directed White forthwith to unite with him at his encampment, where he should wait, fortifying it strongly for a depot, until he should arrive. " If," said he, " we follow general Jackson and his army, we must suffer for supplies; nor can we expect to gain a victory. Let us then take a direction, in which we can share some of the dangers and glories of the field. You will employ pilots, and advise me which side of the river you will move up." In this, as in every other measure, it seemed to be the studied aim of Cocke, to thwart the views, and arrest the successes of Jackson; and perhaps jealousy, in no inconsiderable degree, was the moving spring to his conduct. Both were major generals, from the state of Tennessee; sent on the same important errand,—to check an insolent foe, who had practised the most cruel and unprovoked outrages. Which of them should share the " dangers and glories of the field," was, perhaps, not so important to the country, as that they should, by acting in concert and harmony, endeavour to accomplish the grand object intended. National, and not individual advancement, was the inducement to carry an army into the field : and the best and most effectual mean of securing this, every officer, acting on liberal principles, should have constantly held in view.

Having buried his dead with all due honour, and provided litters for the wounded, he reluctantly commenced his return march, on the morning succeeding the battle. He confidently hoped, from the previous assurances of the contractors, that by the time of his return to Fort Strother, sufficient supplies would have arrived there ; but, to his inexpressible uneasiness, he found, that not a particle had been forwarded since his departure, and that what had been left was already consumed. Even his private stores, brought on at his own expense, and upon which he and his staff had hitherto wholly subsisted, had been, in his absence, distributed amongst the sick by the hospital surgeon, who had been previously instructed to do so, in the event their wants should require it. A few dozen biscuit, which remained on his return, were given to hungry applicants, without being tasted by himself or family, who were probably not less hungry than those who were thus relieved. A scanty supply of beef, taken from the enemy, or purchased of the Cherokees, was now the only support afforded. Thus left destitute, Jackson, with the utmost cheerfulness of temper, repaired to the bullock pen, and of the offal there thrown away, provided for himself and staff, what he was pleased to call, and seemed

Scarcity of provisions.

really to think, a very comfortable repast. Tripes, CHAP.
however, hastily provided in a camp, without bread or III.
seasoning, can only be palatable to an appetite very 47
highly whetted; yet this constituted, for several days,
the only diet at head quarters, during which time the
general seemed entirely satisfied with his fare. Neither this, nor the liberal donations by which he dis-
furnished himself, to relieve the suffering soldier, should
be ascribed to ostentation or design: the one flowed
from benevolence, the other from necessity, and a desire to place before his men an example of patience
and suffering, which he felt might be necessary, and
hoped might be serviceable. Of these two imputa-
tions, no human being, invested with rank and power,
was ever more deservedly free. Charity in him is
a warm and active propensity of the heart, urging him,
by an instantaneous impulse, to relieve the wants of
the distressed, without regarding, or even thinking
of the consequences. Many of those to whom it
was extended, had no conception of the source that
supplied them, and believed the comforts they received
were drawn from stores provided for the hospital department. 48

But while general Jackson remained wholly unmoved by his own privations, he was filled with solicitude and concern for his army. His utmost exertions,
unceasingly applied, were insufficient to remove the
sufferings to which he saw them exposed; and although
they were by no means so great as they themselves
represented, yet were undoubtedly such as to be se- 49
verely felt. Discontents, and a desire to return home,

arose, and presently spread through the camp; and these were still further embittered and augmented, by the arts of a few designing officers, who, believing that the campaign would now break up, hoped to make themselves popular, on the return, by encouraging and taking part in the complaints of the soldiery. It is a singular fact, that those officers who pretended, on this occasion, to feel the most sensibly for the wants of the army, and contrived the most effectually to instigate it to revolt, had never themselves been without provisions; and were, at that very moment, enjoying in abundance what would have relieved the distresses of many, had it been as generously and freely distributed as were their words of advice and condolence.

During this period of scarcity and discontent, small quantities of supplies were occasionally forwarded by the contractors; but not sufficient for present wants, and still less to remove the apprehensions that were indulged for the future. At length, revolt began to show itself openly. The officers and soldiers of the militia, collecting in their tents, and talking over their grievances, determined to abandon the camp. To this measure, there were good evidences for believing, that several of the officers of the old volunteer corps exerted themselves clandestinely, and with great industry, to instigate them; looking upon themselves somewhat in the light of veterans, from the discipline they had acquired in the expedition to the lower country, they were unwilling to be seen foremost, in setting an example of mutiny, and wished to make the defection of others a pretext for their own.

Jackson, apprized of their determination to abandon CHAP. III. him, resolved to oppose it, and, at all hazard, to prevent a departure. In the morning, when they were to carry their intentions into execution, he drew up the volunteers in front of them, with positive commands to prevent their progress, and compel them to return to their former position in the camp. The militia, seeing this, and fearing the consequences of persisting in their purpose, at once abandoned it, and returned to their quarters, without further murmuring; extolling, in the highest terms, the unalterable firmness of the general.

Mutiny of the militia

The next day, however, presented a singular scene. The volunteers, who, the day before, had been the instruments for compelling the militia to return to their duty, seeing the destruction of those hopes on which they had lately built, in turn began to mutiny themselves. Their opposition to the departure of the militia was but a mere pretence to escape suspicion; for they silently wished them success. They now determined to move off in a body, believing, from the known disaffection in the camp, that the general could find no means to prevent it. What was their surprise, however, when, on attempting to effectuate their resolves, they found the same men whom they had so lately opposed, occupying the very position which they had done the day previous, for a similar purpose, and manifesting a fixed determination to obey the orders of their general! All they ventured to do, was to take the example through, and, like them, move back in peace and quietness to their quarters. This was a curious change of circumstances, when we consider in how short a time it happened; but the conduct of the militia.

Mutiny of the volunteers.

on this occasion, must, in some measure, be ascribed to the gratification they felt, in being able to defeat the views of those, who had so lately thwarted their own. To this may be also added, the consciousness all must have entertained, that the privations of which they complained, were far less grievous than they had represented them; by no means sufficient to justify revolt, and not greater than a patriot might be expected to bear without a murmur. But, anxious to return to their families and kindred, and recount the late brilliant exploits of their first battle, they seized with eagerness every pretext for exoneration, and listened with too much docility to the representations of those, who were influenced by less honest feelings. Having many domestic considerations to attend to—the first ebullition of resentment being cooled, and the first impulse of curiosity gratified; there were no motives to retain them in the field, but a remaining sense of honour, and a fear of disgrace and punishment, should they abandon their post without a cause. But although these motives were sufficient for the present, those who were governed by them did not cease to wish, that a more plausible apology might offer for dispensing with their operation. The militia continued to show a much more obedient and patriotic disposition than the volunteers, who, having adopted a course which they discovered must finally involve them in dishonour, if it should fail, were exceedingly anxious for its success, and that it might have the appearance of being founded on justice. On this subject, the pretensions of the cavalry were certainly much better established; as they were entirely without forage, and without the prospect of obtaining any very soon. They petitioned therefore to be permitted to return into the settled parts of the country, pledging themselves, by their platoon and field officers, that if sufficient time were allowed them, to recruit the exhausted state of their horses, and to procure their winter clothing, they would return whenever called on. The general, unable, from many causes, to prosecute the campaign, granted the prayer of their petition, and they immediately set out on their return.

About this time, general Jackson's prospect of being able to maintain the conquests he had made, began to be cheered, by letters just received from the contractors, and principal wagon-master, stating, that sufficient supplies for the army were then on the road, and would shortly arrive at his camp. These letters he hastened to lay before the division, and at the same time invited the field and platoon officers to his quarters that evening, to consult on the measures proper to be pursued. Having assembled them, and well knowing that the flame of discontent, which had so lately shewn itself, was only for the present smothered, and might yet burst forth in serious injury, he addressed them in an animated speech, in which he extolled their patriotism and achievements; lamented the privations to which they had been exposed; and endeavoured to re-animate them by the prospect of speedy relief, which he expected with confidence on the following day. He spoke of the immense importance of the conquests they had already made, and of the dreadful consequences that must result, if they were now abandoned. " What," continued he, " is the present situation of our camp?

ɪ

a number of our fellow soldiers are wounded, and unable to help themselves. Shall it be said that we are
so lost to humanity, as to leave them in this condition?
Can any one, under these circumstances, and under
these prospects, consent to an abandonment of the
camp; of all that we have acquired in the midst of so
many difficulties, privations, and dangers; of what it
will cost us so much to regain; of what we never can
regain,—our brave wounded companions, who will be
murdered by our unthinking, unfeeling inhumanity?
Surely there can be none such! No, we will take with
us, when we go, our wounded and sick. They must
not,—shall not perish by our cold-blooded indifference.
But why should you despond? I do not, and yet your
wants are not greater than mine. To be sure, we do
not live sumptuously: but no one has died of hunger,
or is likely to die; and then how animating are our
prospects! Large supplies are at Deposit, and already
are officers despatched to hasten them on. Wagons
are on the way: a large number of beeves are in the
neighbourhood; and detachments are out to bring them
in.—All these resources surely cannot fail. I have no
wish to starve you—none to deceive you. Stay contentedly; and if supplies do not arrive in two days, we
will all march back together, and throw the blame of
our failure where it should properly lie; until then, we
certainly have the means of subsisting; and if we are
compelled to bear privations, let us remember that they
are borne for our country, and are not greater than many—perhaps most armies have been compelled to endure. I have called you together to tell you my feelings and my wishes; this evening, think on them seriously; and let me know yours in the morning."

On retiring to their tents, and deliberating on the measures most proper to be adopted in this emergency, the officers of the volunteer brigade came to this conclusion; that "nothing short of marching the army immediately back to the settlements, could prevent that disgrace, which must attend a forcible desertion of the camp by the soldiers." The officers of the militia determined differently, and reported a willingness to maintain the post a few days longer, that it might be ascertained whether or not a sufficiency of provisions could really be had. "If it can, let us proceed with the campaign;—if not, let us be marched back to where it can be procured." The general, who greatly preferred the latter opinion, was, nevertheless, disposed to gratify those, who appeared unwilling to submit to further hardships; and with this view ordered general Hall to march his brigade to Fort Deposit, and after satisfying their wants, to return, and act as an escort to the provisions. The second regiment, however, unwilling to be outdone by the militia, consented to remain; and the first proceeded alone. On this occasion, he could not forbear to remark, that men for whom he had ever cherished so warm an affection, and for whom he would at all times have made any sacrifice, desiring to abandon him at a moment when their presence was so particularly necessary, filled him with emotions which the strongest language was too feeble to express. "I was prepared," he continued, "to endure every evil but disgrace; and this, as I never can submit to myself, I can give no encouragement to in others."

Two days had elapsed since the departure of the volunteers, and no supplies had arrived. The militia, with great earnestness, now demanded a performance of the pledge that had been given,—that they should be marched back to the settlements. Jackson, on giving them an assurance that they should return, if relief did not reach them in two days, had indulged a confidence that it would certainly arrive by that time; and now felt more than ever certain, that it could not be far distant. Having, however, pledged himself, he could use no arguments or entreaties to detain them any longer, and immediately took measures for complying with their wishes. This was, to him, a moment of the deepest dejection. He foresaw how difficult it would be, ever to accomplish the object upon which his heart was so devotedly fixed, should he lose the men who were now with him; or even to regain the conquests he had made, if his present posts should fall into the hands of the enemy. While thus pondering on the gloomy prospect, he lifted up his hands and exclaimed, with a look and manner which showed how much he felt—"If only two men will remain with me, I will never abandon this post." Captain Gordon, of the spies, facetiously replied, "you have one, general, let us look if we can't find another," and immediately, with a zeal suited to the occasion, undertook, with some of the general staff, to raise volunteers; and in a little while succeeded in procuring one hundred and nine, who declared a determination to remain and protect the post. The general greatly rejoiced that he would not be compelled to an entire abandonment of his position, now set out towards Deposit, with the re-

mainder of the army, who were made distinctly to un- CHAP.
derstand, that on meeting supplies they were to return III.
and prosecute the campaign. This was an event,
which, as it had been expected and foretold, soon took
place: they had not proceeded more than ten or twelve
miles, when they met a hundred and fifty beeves; but
a sight which gave to Jackson so much satisfaction, was
to them the most disagreeable and unwelcome. Their
faces being now turned towards home, no spectacle
could be more hateful, than one which was to change
their destination. They were halted, and having satisfied their hungry appetites, the troops, with the exception of such as were necessary to proceed with the
sick and wounded, were ordered to return to the encampment,—he himself intending to see the contractors, and establish more effectual arrangements for the
future. So great was their aversion to returning, that
they preferred a violation of their duty, and their pledged honour. Low murmurings ran along the lines, and
presently broke out into open mutiny. In spite of the
order they had received, they began to revolt, and one
company was already moving off, in a direction towards home. They had proceeded some distance, before information of their departure was had by Jackson.
Irritated at their conduct, in attempting to violate the
promises they had given, and knowing that the success
of future operations depended on the result; the general pursued, until he came near a part of his staff,
and a few soldiers, who, with general Coffee, had halted about a quarter of a mile ahead. He ordered them
to form immediately across the road, and to fire on the
mutineers, if they attempted to proceed. Snatching

CHAP.
III.
up their arms, these faithful adherents presented a front which threw the deserters into affright, and caused them to retreat precipitately to the main body. Here, it was hoped, the matter would end, and that no further opposition would be made to returning. This expectation was not realized; a mutinous temper began presently to display itself throughout the whole brigade. Jackson having left his aid-de-camp, major Reid, engaged in making up some despatches, had gone out alone amongst his troops, who were at some little distance; on his arrival, he found a much more extensive mutiny, than that which had just been quell-

Mutiny.
ed. Almost the whole brigade had put itself into an attitude for moving forcibly off. A crisis had arrived; and feeling its importance, he determined to take no middle ground, but to triumph or perish. He was still without the use of his left arm; but, seizing a musket, and resting it on the neck of his horse, he threw himself in front of the column, and threatened to shoot the first man who should attempt to advance. In this situation he was found by major Reid and general Coffee, who, fearing from the length of his absence, that some disturbance had arisen, hastened where he was, and placing themselves by his side, awaited the result in anxious expectation. For many minutes the column preserved a sullen, yet hesitating attitude, fearing to proceed in their purpose, and disliking to abandon it. In the mean time, those who remained faithful to their duty, amounting to about two companies, were collected and formed at a short distance in advance of the troops, and in rear of the general, with positive directions to imitate his example

in firing, if they attempted to proceed. At length,
finding no one bold enough to advance, and overtaken by those fears that in the hour of peril always beset persons engaged in what they know to be a bad cause, they abandoned their purpose, and turning quietly round, agreed to return to their posts. It is very certain, that, but for the firmness of the general, at this critical moment, the campaign would for the present have been broken up, and would probably never have been re-commenced.

Shortly after the battle of Talladega, the Hillabee tribes, who had been the principal sufferers on that occasion, applied to general Jackson for peace; declaring their willingness to receive it on such terms as he might be pleased to dictate. His decision had been already returned, stating to them that his government had taken up arms, to bring to a proper sense of duty, a people, to whom she had ever shown the utmost kindness, and who, nevertheless, had committed against her citizens the most unprovoked depredations; and that she would lay them down only when certain that this object was attained.* "Upon those," continued he, "who are

Hillabee tribes sue for peace.

51

* This communication did not arrive in time:—general White, who had been detached for that purpose, having, on the morning on which it was written, attacked and destroyed their town, killed sixty, and made two hundred and fifty-six prisoners. The event was unfortunate; and in it may perhaps be found the reason why these savages, in their after battles, fought with the desperation they did, obstinately refusing to ask for quarter. They believed themselves attacked by Jackson's army; they knew they had asked peace upon his own terms. When, therefore, under these circumstances,

CHAP. disposed to become friendly, I neither wish nor intend
III. to make war; but they must afford evidences of the
sincerity of their professions; the prisoners and property they have taken from us, and the friendly Creeks,
must be restored; the instigators of the war, and the
murderers of our citizens, must be surrendered; the
latter must and will be made to feel the force of our
resentment.   Long shall they remember Fort Mimms
in bitterness and tears."

Having stated to general Cocke, whose division was
acting in this section of the nation, the propositions
that had been made by the Hillabee clans, with the answer he had returned; and urged him to detach to Fort
Strother six hundred of his men, to aid in the defence
of that place, during his absence, and in the operations
he intended to resume on his return; he proceeded to
Deposit and Ditto's landing, where the most effectual
means in his power were taken with the contractors,
for obtaining regular supplies in future.   They were
required to furnish, immediately, thirty days' rations
at Fort Strother, forty at Talladega, and as many at the
junction of the Coosa and Tallapoosa; two hundred
pack horses, and forty wagons, were put in requisition, to facilitate their transportation.   Understanding,
now, that the whole detachment, from Tennessee, had,
by the president, been received into the service of the

they saw themselves thus assailed, they no longer considered
that any pacific disposition they might manifest would afford
them protection from danger; and looked upon it as a war of
extermination.   In their battles, afterwards, there is no instance of their asking for quarter, or even manifesting a disposition to receive it.

United States, he persuaded himself that the difficulties CHAP. he had heretofore encountered, would not recur, and III. that the want of supplies would not again be a cause of impeding his operations. He now looked forward with sanguine expectations, to the speedy accomplishment of the objects of the expedition.

The volunteers, who were at Deposit, began to manifest the same unwillingness to return to their duty, that the militia had done, and were about to break out into the same spirit of mutiny and revolt; but were restrained by an animated address of the general, who, having assembled them together, painted, in the most glowing colours, all the consequences that were to be apprehended, if, from any defalcation of theirs, the campaign should be abandoned, or ineffectually prosecuted. By this mean, he succeeded, once more, in restoring quietness to his troops.

He now set out on his return to Fort Strother, and was delighted to find, by the progress of the works, the industry that had been used in his absence. But the satisfaction he felt, and the hopes he began to cherish, were of short continuance. Although he had succeeded in stilling the tumult of the volunteers, and in prevailing on them to return to their posts, it was soon discovered, he had not eradicated their deep-rooted aversion to a further prosecution of the war. Nothing is more difficult than to re-animate men who have once lost their spirits, or inspire with new ardour, those in whom it has lately become extinct. Even where the evils, which produced the change, are removed, apologies will be sought, and pretexts seized, for justifying and preserving the present tone of mind. The volun-

K

CHAP. teers, who had so lately clamoured about bread, now,
III. when they were no longer hungry, began to clamour,
with equal earnestness, about their term of service.
Having lately made an effort to forsake the drudgery
of the field, and failed, they were disposed to avail
themselves of any pretexts, seemingly plausible, to
obtain success. They insisted that the period, for
Volun- which they had undertaken to act, would end on the
teers claim
to be dis- 10th of December, that being the termination of a year
charged. from the day they had first entered into service; and
that although they had been a greater part of the time
disengaged, and unemployed, that recess was nevertheless to be taken in the computation. Jackson replied, that the law of congress, under which they had
been tendered and accepted, requiring one year's service out of two, could contemplate nothing less than an
actual service of three hundred and sixty-five days;
and, until that were performed, he could not, unless
specially authorized, undertake to discharge them.
But as this was a question not likely to be settled by
argument, and as the consequences were easily to be
foreseen, if they should persist in their demands, the
general began to think of providing other means for a
continuance of the campaign, that, even in the worst
extreme, he might not be unprepared to act. Ordering
general Roberts to return, and fill up the deficiencies in
Decem. 4. his brigade, he now despatched colonel Carroll and major Searcy, one of his aids-de-camp, into Tennessee, to
raise volunteers, for six months, or during the campaign; writing, at the same time, to many respectable
characters, he exhorted them to contribute all their
assistance to the accomplishment of this object. To a

letter, just received from the reverend Gideon Black- CHAP.
burn, assuring him that volunteers from Tennessee   III.
would eagerly hasten to his relief, if they knew their
services were wanted, he replied, " Reverend Sir,—
Your letter has been just received : I thank you for it;
I thank you most sincerely.   It arrived at a moment
when my spirits needed such a support.

" I left Tennessee with an army, brave, I believe,
as any general ever commanded.   I have seen them in
battle, and my opinion of their bravery is not changed.
But their fortitude—on this too I relied—has been too
severely tested.   Perhaps I was wrong, in believing
that nothing but death could conquer the spirits of
brave men.   I am sure I was ; for my men, I know,
are brave ; yet privations have rendered them discontented :—that is enough.   The expedition must nevertheless be prosecuted to a successful termination.
New volunteers must be raised, to conclude what has
been so auspiciously begun by the old ones.   Gladly
would I save these men from themselves, and insure
them a harvest which they have sown ; but if they will
abandon it to others, it must be so.

" You are good enough to say, if I need your assistance, it will be cheerfully afforded : I do need it greatly.   The influence you possess over the minds of men
is great and well-founded, and can never be better applied, than in summoning volunteers to the defence of
their country, their liberty, and their religion.   While
we fight the savage, who makes war only because he
delights in blood, and who has gotten his booty, when
he has scalped his victim, we are, through him, contending against an enemy of more inveterate character,

and deeper design—who would demolish a fabric cemented by the blood of our fathers, and endeared to us
by all the happiness we enjoy. So far as my exertions
can contribute, the purposes, both of the savage and
his instigator, shall be defeated ; and so far as yours
can, I hope—I know, they will be employed. I have
said enough.—I want men, and want them immediately."

Anxious to prosecute the campaign as soon as possible, that by employing his troops actively, he might
dispel from their minds those discontents so frequently
manifested, he wrote to general Cocke, desiring him
to unite with him, immediately, at the Ten Islands,
with fifteen hundred men. He assured him that the
mounted men, who had returned to the settlements for
subsistence, and to recruit their horses, would arrive
by the 12th of the month. He wished to commence
his operations directly, " knowing they would be prepared for it, and well knowing they would require it."
" I am astonished," he continued, " to hear that your
supplies continue deficient. In the name of God,
what is M'Gee doing, and what has he been about?
Every letter I receive from governor Blount, assures
me I am to receive plentiful supplies from him, and
seems to take for granted, notwithstanding all I have said
to the contrary, that they have been hitherto regularly
furnished. Considering the generous loan he obtained
for this purpose, and the facility of procuring bread
stuffs in East Tennessee, and transporting them by
water to Fort Deposit, it is to me wholly unaccountable that not a pound has ever arrived at that place.
This evil must continue no longer—it must be reme-

Decem. 6.

52

died. I expect, therefore, and through you must re- CHAP.
quire, that M'Gee, in twenty days, furnish at Deposit III.
every necessary supply."*

Whilst these measures were taking, the volunteers,
through several of their officers, were pressing on the Discontents and
consideration of the general, the subject of their term demands
of the
of service, and claiming to be discharged on the 10th troops.
instant. From colonel Martin, who commanded the
second regiment, he received a letter, dated the 4th, in
which was attempted to be detailed their whole ground
of complaint. He began by stating, that, much as it
pained him, he felt himself bound to disclose a very
unpleasant truth; that, on the 10th, the service would
be deprived of the regiment he commanded. He
seemed to deplore, with great sensibility, the scene
that would be exhibited on that day, should opposition

* Independent of an advantageous contract made with the government, the state of Tennessee had extended to this contract-
or a liberal loan, that immediate supplies might be forwarded.
Unfortunately, however, and it is a misfortune that will always
continue, so long as the present mode is persisted in, the contract was disregarded; nor did complaints on the subject cease,
even to the close of the war. Great as was the evil, no adequate remedy was at hand : nor was it confined to any particular section ; but in all directions, where our armies moved,
were complaints heard, and their operations frustrated, through
the misconduct of contractors. An advancing army, already
having within its reach decided advantages, is made to halt,
and to retrograde, or starve. The remedy is to sue the contractor; and, after twelve or eighteen months of law, a jury
decides how far he has or has not broken his covenant, In the
mean time, the government has lost the most decided advantages—advantages which, had they been secured, might have
saved millions of treasure, and thousands of lives.

be made to their departure; and still more sensibly, the consequences that would result from a disorderly abandonment of the camp. He stated, they had all thought themselves finally discharged, on the 20th of April last, and never knew to the contrary, until they saw the order of the 24th of September, requiring them to rendezvous at Fayetteville, on the 4th of October; for the first time, they then learned, that they owed further services, their discharge to the contrary notwithstanding. "Thus situated, there was considerable opposition to the order; on which the officers generally, as I am advised, and I know myself in particular, gave it as an unequivocal opinion, that their term of service would terminate on the 10th of December.

"They therefore look to their general, who holds their confidence, for an honourable discharge on that day; and that, in every respect, he will see that justice be done them. They regret that their peculiar situations and circumstances require them to leave their general, at a time when their services are important to the common cause.

"It would be desirable," he continued, "that those men, who have served with honour, should be honourably discharged, and that they should return to their families and friends, without even the semblance of disgrace; with their general they leave it to place them in that situation. They have received him as an affectionate father, whilst they have honoured, revered, and obeyed him; but, having devoted a considerable portion of their time to the service of their country, by which their domestic concerns are greatly deranged, they wish to return, and attend to their own affairs."

Although this communication announced the deter- CHAP.
mination of only a part of the volunteer brigade, he III.
had already abundant evidence that the defection was
general. The difficulties which the general had heretofore been compelled to encounter, from the discontents
of his troops, might well induce him to regret, that a
spirit of insubordination should again threaten to appear
in his camp. That he might, if possible, prevent it, he
hastened to lay before them the error and impropriety
of their views, and the consequences involved, should
they persist in their purpose.

"I know not," he observed, "what scenes will be
exhibited on the 10th instant, nor what consequences reply.
are to flow from them here or elsewhere; but as I shall
have the consciousness that they are not imputable
to any misconduct of mine, I trust I shall have the
firmness not to shrink from a discharge of my duty.

"It will be well, however, for those who intend to
become actors in those scenes, and who are about to
hazard so much on the correctness of their opinions,
to examine beforehand, with great caution and deliberation, the grounds on which their pretensions rest.
Are they founded on any false assurances of mine, or
upon any deception that has been practised towards
them? Was not the act of congress, under which they
are engaged, directed, by my general order, to be read
and expounded to them, before they enrolled themselves? That order will testify, and so will the recollection of every general officer of my division. It is
not pretended, that those who now claim to be discharged, were not legally and fairly enrolled, under the
act of congress, of the 6th of February, 1812. Have

they performed the service required of them by that act, and which they then solemnly undertook to perform? That required one year's service out of two, to be computed from the day of rendezvous, unless they should be sooner discharged. Has one year's service been performed? This cannot be seriously pretended. Have they then been discharged? It is said they have, and by me. To account for so extraordinary a belief, it may be necessary to take a review of past circumstances.

" More than twelve months have elapsed, since we were called upon to avenge the injured rights of our country. We obeyed the call! In the midst of hardships which none but those, to whom liberty is dear, could have borne without a murmur, we descended the Mississippi. It was believed our services were wanted, in the prosecution of the just war in which our country was engaged, and we were prepared to render them. But, though we were disappointed in our expectations, we established for Tennessee a name which will long do her honour. At length, we received a letter from the secretary of war, directing our dismission. You well recollect the circumstances of wretchedness in which this order was calculated to place us. By it, we were deprived of every article of public property ; no provision was made for the payment of our troops, or their subsistence on their return march ; whilst many of our sick, unable to help themselves, must have perished. Against the opinion of many, I marched them back to their homes, before I dismissed them. Your regiment, at its own request, was dismissed at Columbia. This was accompanied

with a certificate to each man, expressing the acts under which he had been enrolled, and the length of the
tour he had performed.   This it is which is now attempted to be construed " a final discharge;" but
surely it cannot be forgotten by any officer or soldier,
how sacredly they pledged themselves, before they
were dismissed, or received that certificate, cheerfully
to obey the voice of their country, if it should re-sum-
mon them into service: neither can it be forgotten, I
dare hope, for what purpose that certificate was given;
it was to secure, if possible, to those brave men, who
had shown such readiness to serve their country, certain extra emoluments, specified in the seventh section
of the act under which they had engaged, in the event
they were not recalled into service for the residue of
their term.

    " Is it true, then, that my solicitude for the interest
of the volunteers, is to be made by them a pretext for
disgracing a name which they have rendered illustrious? Is a certificate, designed solely for their benefit,
to become the rallying word for mutiny?—strange per-
version of feeling and of reasoning! Have I really any
power to discharge men, whose term of service has not
expired?   If I were weak or wicked enough to attempt the exercise of such a power, does any one believe, the soldier would be thereby exonerated from the
obligation he has voluntarily taken upon himself to his
government? I should become a traitor to the important concern which has been entrusted to my management, while the soldier, who had been deceived by a
false hope of liberation, would be still liable to redeem.

L

his pledge ;—I should disgrace myself, without bene-fiting you.

"I can only deplore the situation of those officers, who have undertaken to persuade their men, that their term of service will expire on the 10th. In giving their opinions to this effect, they have acted indiscreetly, and without sufficient authority. It would be the most pleasing act of my life, to restore them with honour to their families. Nothing would pain me more than that any other sentiments should be felt towards them, than those of gratitude and esteem. On all occasions, it has been my highest happiness to promote their interest, and even to gratify their wishes, where, with propriety, it could be done. When in the lower country, believing that, in the order for their dismissal, they had been improperly treated, I even solicited the government to discharge them, finally, from the obligations into which they had entered. You know the answer of the secretary of war ;—that neither he nor the president, as he believed, had the power to discharge them. How, then, can it be required of me to do so ?

"The moment it is signified to me, by any competent authority, even by the governor of Tennessee, to whom I have written on the subject, or by general Pinckney, who is now appointed to the command, that the volunteers may be exonerated from further service, that moment I will pronounce it, with the greatest satisfaction. I have only the power of pronouncing a discharge,—not of giving it, in any case ;—a distinction which I would wish should be borne in mind. Already have I sent to raise volunteers, on my own responsibility, to complete a campaign which has been

so happily begun, and thus far, so fortunately prose- CHAP.
cuted.   The moment they arrive, and I am assured, III.
that, fired by our exploits, they will hasten in crowds,
on the first intimation that we need their services, they
will be substituted in the place of those who are discontented here; the latter will then be permitted to return to their homes, with all the honour, which, under
such circumstances, they can carry along with them.
But I still cherish the hope, that their dissatisfaction
and complaints have been greatly exaggerated. I cannot, must not believe, that the "Volunteers of Tennessee," a name ever dear to fame, will disgrace themselves, and a country which they have honoured, by
abandoning her standard, as mutineers and deserters;
but should I be disappointed, and compelled to resign
this pleasing hope, one thing I will not resign—my
duty.   Mutiny and sedition, so long as I possess the
power of quelling them, shall be put down; and even
when left destitute of this, I will still be found, in the
last extremity, endeavouring to discharge the duty I
owe my country and myself."

To the platoon officers, who addressed him on the
same subject, he replied in nearly the same manner;
but discontent had taken too deep a hold, and had, by
designing men, been too artfully fomented, to be removed by any thing like argument or intreaty. At Mutiny.
ength, on the evening of the 9th, general Hall hastened
to the tent of Jackson, with information that his whole
brigade was in a state of mutiny, and making preparations for moving forcibly off. This was a measure
which every consideration of policy, duty, and honour,
required Jackson to oppose; and to this purpose, he

CHAP. instantly applied all the means he possessed. He im-
III. mediately issued the following general order:

" The commanding general being informed that an actual mutiny exists in his camp, all officers and soldiers are commanded to put it down.

" The officers and soldiers of the first brigade will, without delay, parade on the west side of the fort, and await further orders." The artillery company, with two small field pieces, being posted in the front and rear; and the militia, under the command of colonel Wynne, on the eminences, in advance, were ordered to prevent any forcible departure of the volunteers.

The general rode along the line, which had been formed agreeably to his orders, and addressed them by companies, in a strain of impassioned eloquence. He feelingly expatiated on their former good conduct, and the esteem and applause it had secured them; and pointed to the disgrace which they must heap upon themselves, their families, and country, by persisting, even if they could succeed, in their present mutiny. But he told them they should not succeed, but by passing over his body; that even in opposing their mutinous spirit, he should perish honourably,—by perishing at his post, and in the discharge of his duty. " Reinforcements," he continued, " are preparing to hasten to my assistance: it cannot be long before they will arrive. I am, too, in daily expectation of receiving information, whether you may be discharged, or not— until then, you must not, and shall not retire. I have done with intreaty,—it has been used long enough.—I will attempt it no more. You must now determine whether you will go, or peaceably remain: if you still persist

in your determination to move forcibly off, the point
between us shall soon be decided." At first they hesitated ;—he demanded an explicit and positive answer.
They still hesitated, and he commanded the artillerist
to prepare the match; he himself remaining in front of
the volunteers, and within the line of fire, which he intended soon to order. Alarmed at his apparent determination, and dreading the consequences involved in
such a contest; "Let us return," was presently lisped
along the line, and was soon after determined upon.
The officers now came forward, and pledged themselves for their men, who either nodded assent, or
openly expressed a willingness to retire to their quarters, and remain without further tumult, until information were had, or the expected aid should arrive. Thus
passed away a moment of the greatest peril,—pregnant
with the most important consequences.

54

Although the immediate execution of their purpose
was thus prevented, it was soon discovered that it was
not wholly abandoned, and that nothing could be expected from their future services. Jackson, therefore,
determined to rid himself, as soon as possible, of men,
whose presence answered no other end, than to keep
alive discontents in his camp. He accordingly prepared an order to general Hall, to march them to Nashville, and do with them as he should be directed by the
governor of Tennessee. Previous to promulgating
this, he resolved to make one further effort to retain
them, and to make a last appeal to their honour and
patriotism. For this purpose, having assembled them
before the fort, on the 13th, he directed his aid-de-camp
to read to them the following address :

"On the 10th of December, 1812, you assembled, at the call of your country. Your professions of patriotism, and ability to endure fatigue, were at once tested by the inclemency of the weather. Breaking your way through sheets of ice, you descended the Mississippi, and reached the point at which you were ordered to be halted and dismissed. All this you bore without murmuring. Finding that your services were not needed, the means for marching you back were procured; every difficulty was surmounted, and, as soon as the point from which you embarked was regained, the order for your dismissal was carried into effect. The promptness with which you assembled, the regularity of your conduct, your attention to your duties, the determination manifested, on every occasion, to carry into effect the wishes and will of your government, placed you on elevated ground. You not only distinguished yourselves, but gave to your state a distinguished rank with her sisters; and led your government to believe, that the honour of the nation would never be tarnished, when entrusted to the holy keeping of the "Volunteers of Tennessee."

"In the progress of a war, which the implacable and eternal enemy of our independence induced to be waged, we found that, without cause on our part, a portion of the Creek nation was added to the number of our foes. To put it down, the first glance of the administration fell on you; and you were again summoned to the field of honour. In full possession of your former feelings, that summons was cheerfully obeyed. Before your enemy thought you in motion, you were at Tallushatchee and Talladega. The thunder of your arms was

a signal to them, that the slaughter of your country- CHAP.
men was about to be avenged. You fought, you con- III.
quered! barely enough of the foe escaped, to recount
to their savage associates, your deeds of valour. You
returned to this place, loaded with laurels, and the ap-
plauses of your country.

" Can it be, that these brave men are about to become the tarnishers of their own reputation!—the de-
stroyers of a name, which does them so much honour?
Yes, it is a truth too well disclosed, that cheerfulness
has been exchanged for complaints:—murmurings
and discontents alone prevail. Men who a little while
since were offering up prayers, for permission to chastise the merciless savage,—who burned with impatience to teach them how much they had hitherto been
indebted to our forbearance; are now, when they could
so easily attain their wishes, seeking to be discharged.
The heart of your general has been pierced. The first
object of his military affections, and the first glory of
his life, were the volunteers of Tennessee! The very
name recalls to him a thousand endearing recollections.
But these men,—these volunteers, have become mutineers. The feelings he would have indulged, your
general has been compelled to suppress,—he has been
compelled by a regard to that subordination, so necessary to the support of every army, and which he is
bound to have observed, to check the disorder which
would have destroyed you. He has interposed his authority for your safety;—to prevent you from disgracing yourselves and your country. Tranquillity has
been restored in our camp,—contentment shall also be
restored; this can be done only by permitting those to

CHAP.
III.

retire, whose dissatisfaction proceeds from causes that cannot be controlled. This permission will now be given. Your country will dispense with your services, if you have no longer a regard for that fame, which you have so nobly earned for yourselves and her. Yes, soldiers, you who were once so brave, and to whom honour was so dear, shall be permitted to return to your homes, if you still desire it. But in what language, when you arrive, will you address your families and friends? Will you tell them that you abandoned your general, and your late associates in arms, within fifty miles of a savage enemy; who equally delights in shedding the blood of the innocent female and her sleeping babe, as that of the warrior contending in battle? Lamentable, disgraceful tale! If your dispositions are really changed; if you fear an enemy you so lately conquered; this day will prove it. I now put it to yourselves;—determine upon the part you will act, influenced only by the suggestions of your own hearts, and your own understandings. All who prefer an inglorious retirement, shall be ordered to Nashville, to be discharged, as the president or the governor may direct. Who choose to remain, and unite with their general, in the further prosecution of the campaign, can do so, and will thereby furnish a proof, that they have been greatly traduced; and that although disaffection and cowardice has reached the hearts of some, it has not reached theirs. To such my assurance is given, that former irregularities will not be attributed to them. They shall be immediately organized into a separate corps, under officers of their own choice; and in a little while, it is confidently believed,

an opportunity will be afforded of adding to the laurels CHAP.
you have already won."   III.

This appeal failed of the desired effect. Captain
Williamson alone agreed to remain. Finding that
their determination to abandon the service could not
be changed, and that every principle of patriotism
was forgotten, the general communicated his order
to general Hall, directing him to march his brigade
to Nashville, and await such instructions as he might
receive from the president, or the governor of Tennessee.   55

General Cocke had arrived on the 12th, with fifteen
hundred men; but it was found from his report, that Arrival of
no part of his troops were brought into the field under Cocke.
the requisition of the president of the United States;
and that the term of service of a greater part of them
would expire in a few days; and of the whole in a few
weeks. In consequence of this, he was ordered into
his district, to comply with that requisition, and to carry with him and discharge near their homes, those of
his troops, the period of whose service was within a
short time of being ended. The reason of this was explained in an address to the brigade, in which they
were entreated, when they should have obtained the
necessaries which a winter's campaign would require,
to return into the field, and aid in completing what had
been so successfully begun. Colonel Lilliard's regiment, which consisted of about eight hundred, and
whose term of service would not expire in less than
four weeks, was retained, to assist in defending the
present post, and in keeping open the communication

M

CHAP.
III.
with Deposit, until the expected reinforcements should
arrive.

Meantime the cavalry and mounted riflemen, who, under an express stipulation to return and complete the campaign, had been permitted to retire into the settlements, to recruit their horses and procure winter clothing, had, at the time appointed, re-assembled in the neighbourhood of Huntsville. But, catching the infection of discontent from the infantry, on their return march, they began now to clamour with equal earnestness for a discharge. The cavalry insisted that they were as well entitled to it as the infantry; and the riflemen, that they could not be held in service after the 24th, that being three months from the time they had been mustered: and that as that day was so near at hand, it was wholly useless to advance any farther.

Disaffection of general Coffee's brigade, which demands to be discharged.
General Coffee, who was confined at Huntsville by severe indisposition, employed all the means which his debilitated strength would allow him, to remove the dangerous impressions they had so readily imbibed, and to reclaim them to a sense of honour and of duty; but all his efforts proved unavailing. He immediately ordered his brigade to head quarters: they had proceeded as far as Ditto's ferry, when the greater part of them refusing to cross the river, returned in a tumultuous manner, committing on the route innumerable irregularities, which there was no force sufficient to restrain. Not more than seven hundred of the brigade could be gotten over; who, having marched to Deposit, were directed to be halted, until further orders could be obtained from general Jackson. At this place they committed the wildest extravagancies; profusely wast-

ing the public grain, which, with much difficulty and labour, had been collected there, for the purpose of the campaign; and indulging in every species of excess. Whilst thus rioting, they continued to clamour, vociferously, for their discharge. General Coffee finding his utmost efforts ineffectual, to restrain or to quiet them, wrote to Jackson, acquainting him with their conduct and demands, and enclosing a petition that had been addressed to him by the rifle regiment. In his letter he says, " I am of opinion, the sooner they can be gotten clear of the better; they are consuming the forage that will be necessary for others, and I am satisfied they will do no more good. I have told them, their petition would be submitted to you, who would decide upon it in the shortest possible time." This was truly disagreeable news to the general. Already sufficiently harassed by the discontents and opposition of his troops; now that they had retired, he looked anxiously forward, in hopes that the tranquillity of his camp would be no more assailed. On the brigade of Coffee, he had placed great reliance, and, from the pledges it had given him, entertained no fears but that it would return and act with him, as soon as he should be ready to proceed. He replied to general Coffee, and taking a view of the grounds and causes of their complaints, endeavoured to reconcile their objections, and persuade them to a discharge of the duties they had undertaken, and covenanted to perform.

The signers of that address, observes the general, commence by saying, " that jealousy is prevailing in our camp, with respect to the understanding between themselves and the government, relative to the service required of them; and believing it to be its policy to act fairly, are of opinion that a full explanation of their case will have a good effect, in promoting the cause in which they are engaged."

Jackson's reply to the demands of Coffee's brigade.
" What can have given rise to this jealousy, I am at a loss to conjecture; for surely no unfair practices were ever used by their government, to get them into the service, nor to keep them in it, longer than they had engaged to remain. How long that was, can be easily determined by the law, under which they were accepted. This was open to all, and must be presumed to have been understood by all. But for a complete answer, I send you and refer you to the written pledges, of both the field and platoon officers, before they returned to recruit their horses, and obtain their winter clothing. As they seem completely to have forgotten, remind them of all they contain,— of their assurances given, that, if what they asked were granted, they would return, at the shortest possible notice, prepared and willing to go through the winter service, or to the end of the campaign. Sensible of their necessities, and confiding fully in the promises they made, and signed with their own names, I permitted them, on the 22d ultimo, to return into the settlements, for the purpose of procuring fresh horses, and additional clothing; and required them, to which they readily agreed, to rendezvous in Madison, on the 8th instant. They have returned, and now, when every calculation is made upon their services, agreeably to the pledges that have been given, they send, (instead of coming,) this address. Under these circumstances, what " explanation of their case" do they

want? What explanation do they expect their general CHAP.
to give them? Barely to remind them of their written III.
pledges, without attempting any exposition of the law,
under which they have engaged, is surely a sufficient
answer.   An exposition of it will not be attempted by
me; not only because it is considered unnecessary, but
because my opinion on it has been already frequently
given.   56

" They, however, further remark, that " they are
returning like deserters, souring the minds of the people against the government and the officers, which will
prevent others from entering into the service of their
country, and paralyze the spirit of every citizen of
Tennessee."   That they are returning home, not only
" like deserters," but in the real genuine character of
such, is indeed a lamentable truth.   That they are also
endeavouring to sour the minds of the people against
the government and the officers, and that this attempt
will most probably be successful, and prevent many
from entering the service, is, I am fearful, too true.
But in the name of God, to whom is this to be ascribed
—to the government, or to their general? or rather is
it not more justly chargeable to themselves, who, having entered the camp from patriotic motives, as they
say,—having engaged with their government, and
pledged themselves to their general, to prosecute the
campaign, and avenge the injured rights of their country, forget both that engagement, and that pledge, and
all their boasted patriotism, at a moment when their
services are the most confidently expected, and the
most eminently needed.

" I cannot conceive how the idea has arisen, that they are attempted to be detained, without their consent. To say nothing of the length of service really required by the law under which they were accepted; have not the field officers given their written consent to remain, during the winter, or until the campaign be completed? Have they not also given a pledge for their men, and their officers commanding companies and platoons; and have not those company and platoon officers, too, given a similar assurance for themselves and their men? Let them look to these pledges, and blush at their conduct.

" They also remark, " If any tender of services, for a longer time than a tour of duty, (three months) has been made to the general government, we beg leave to say, it was without our consent or knowledge; and we are convinced that, in all contracts that are binding, both parties must fully understand and consent thereto. We wish to be permitted to return home, and to return under such circumstances, as will entitle us to be praised, instead of blamed, by those who so gallantly led us to battle."

" To this I answer, that no tender, for any specified term of service, was ever made to the general government, by me, or by any other, within my knowledge. As regards their *law remark*, that men, to be bound by a contract, must understand and consent to it, it will be a sufficient answer, that those who volunteer their services, under a public law, are presumed to understand fully all its provisions; or, at any rate, that those who sign an instrument drawn up by themselves, cannot reasonably be supposed ignorant of its contents, or unwilling to abide by its terms.   But they must be luke-warm patriots indeed, who, in the moment of danger and necessity, can halt in the discharge of their duty, to argue and quibble on the construction of laws and statutes.

" As to their wish " to be praised instead of censured," I am at a loss to conceive how such a sentiment should hold a place in the breasts of men, who are about to abandon the cause of their country, at such a moment as this, and under such engagements.   Even if it be possible for such men to desire praise ; from their present conduct they cannot expect it, nor believe themselves entitled to receive it.   Before they can have determined to enter upon such a course, they must undoubtedly have prepared their minds to meet all the contumely and contempt, that an indignant country can heap upon such wind-blown patriots ; who, when at home, clamoured so vociferously about her injured rights, and having taken up arms to defend them, abandon them, at a moment when they are most in danger.   A grosser aliment than praise must be the proper nutriment for such minds.   If it were possible that any doubt could exist, under the law by which their services were engaged, has not the utmost certainty been produced, by their own written undertakings, subsequently made ?   But on the question, whether their country, at this time, needs their services in the field, there can be no doubt.   And is patriotism to be measured by months, and weeks, and days ?   Is it by such a computation, that the volunteer, embarked in his country's defence, hopes to entitle himself to the thanks of that country, when her rights are assailed,

CHAP. and his efforts can protect them?—Be it so; let it be
III. even granted, that these men's engagements have expired under the law;—has their sacred pledge, in writing, and has their love of country expired? If these
cannot bind them to a faithful performance of their
duty, I know of nothing by which I can hope to hold
them."

57   To have addressed them in a less pointed and independent strain, and endeavoured to soothe their discontents by intreaty, might, at some other time, and under
different circumstances, have been better resorted to for
success; but the ineffectual attempts that had been
made with his infantry, who had forsaken the camp, in
spite of every thing that persuasion, threats, or honour
could suggest, left but a narrow basis, on which to
erect a hope of his being able to detain them. There
was but a single course left; to point them to the pledge
they had given, and appeal directly to their honour,
believing that if this were unsuccessful, there was
" nothing by which he could hope to hold them."

Jackson had just received a letter from the governor
of Tennessee, in answer to his frequent and pressing
inquiries, as to the disposition which should be made
Orders of of the volunteers. It recommended what had already,
governor
Blount, from necessity, been done; to dismiss—not discharge
respecting them, because the latter was not in the power of either
the volun-
teers. of them :—nor was their dismission to be given, because founded in right; but because, under existing circumstances, their presence could not prove beneficial,
but highly injurious. To induce them contentedly to
remain, the governor had suggested but one argument,
which had not already been unsuccessfully attempted;

"that it was very doubtful if the government would
pay them for the services they had already rendered,
if abandoned without her authority." It is true, that
avarice sometimes alters a determination, when other
considerations have failed of success; whether this appeal might not result beneficially with the cavalry,
whose presence was greatly desired, was at least worth
the trial. It was important, however, to bring it before them in a way to awaken inquiry, and guard
against offence. The letter was therefore enclosed for
their inspection, accompanied with these remarks :—
" I have just received a letter from governor Blount,
which I hasten to transmit to you, that you may avail
yourselves of whatever benefits and privileges it holds
out. You will perceive, that he does not consider he
has any power to discharge you,—neither have I :—
but you have my permission to retire from the service,
if you are still desirous of doing so, and are prepared
to risk the consequences."

These letters, so far from answering the desired end,
had a directly contrary effect. The governor's was no
sooner read, than they eagerly laid hold of it to support the resolution they had already formed; and without further ceremony or delay, abandoned the campaign, with their colonel, Allcorn, at their head, who,
so far from having endeavoured to reconcile them, is
believed, by secret artifices, to have fomented their
discontents.

So general was the dissatisfaction of this brigade,
and with such longing anxiety did they indulge the
hope of a speedy return to their homes, that their impatience did not permit them to wait the return of the

N

messenger from head quarters. Before an answer could reach general Coffee, they had broken up their encampment at Deposit, re-crossed the river, and proceeded four miles beyond Huntsville. On receiving it, Coffee had the brigade drawn up in solid column, and the letters, together with the pledge they had given, read to them; after which, the reverend Mr. Blackburn endeavoured, in an eloquent speech, in which he pointed out the ruinous consequences that were to be apprehended, if they persisted in their present purpose, to recall them to a sense of duty, and of honour; but they had formed their resolution too steadfastly, and had gone too extravagant lengths, to be influenced by the letter, the pledge, or the speech. As to the pledge, a few said they had not authorized it to be made; others, that as the general had not returned an immediate acceptance, they did not consider themselves bound by it; but the greater part candidly acknowledged, that they stood committed, and were without any justification for their present conduct. Nevertheless, except a few officers, and three or four privates, the whole persisted in the determination to abandon the service. Thus, in a tumultuous manner, they broke up, and, committing innumerable extravagancies, regardless alike of law and decency, continued their route to their respective homes.

CHAPTER IV.

—————

WHILST these unfortunate events were transpir-ing in the rear, matters were far from wearing a very encouraging aspect at head quarters. General Roberts' brigade of West Tennessee militia, at no time full, and at present consisting, in consequence of numerous desertions, of only about six hundred ; imitating the evil examples lately set before it, began, as the day on which they imagined themselves entitled to a discharge was approaching, to turn their attention towards home. Believing that three months constituted the tour of duty contemplated in the act, under which their services were engaged, they insisted that it would terminate on the 4th of the ensuing month. This, however, was a construction, that Jackson was by no means disposed to admit. It is true, the act

CHAP IV.

1813.

had not defined the term of their engagements; but it had specified the object of calling them out, viz. to subdue the Indians; and as that object was not yet attained, it was believed, that at present they were not entitled to a discharge. In addition to this, these troops, although raised by the state authority, had been, by the particular recommendation of their own legislature, received into the service of the general government, under the act of congress, authorizing the president to call out a hundred thousand militia, to serve for six months; unless by his own order they should be previously dismissed. So that, whether the act of congress, or the legislature of Tennessee, were taken as the rule of government in this case, it was believed there was no authority competent to extend to them a discharge, at the time they threatened to demand it. The militia of East Tennessee, having been specially mustered into service for three months, would, of course, be entitled to be dismissed, at the expiration of that period; hence colonel Lilliard's regiment, which constituted more than one half the present force at head quarters, would be lost to the service on the 14th of the next month.

With the failure of general Cocke, to bring into the field, the number and description of troops, which he had been ordered to raise, under the requisition of the president; as well as with the temper and demands of those who were in service, he kept the governor of Tennessee correctly advised; and omitted no opportunity of entreating him, in the most pressing manner, to take the earliest measures for supplying, by draft, or voluntary enlistment, the present deficiency, as well

as that which was so soon to be expected. To these
solicitations, he had now received the governor's answer, who stated, that, having ordered general Cocke
to bring into the field fifteen hundred of the detached
militia, as was required by the secretary of war, and a
thousand volunteers, under the act of the legislature of
Tennessee, of the 24th September, he did not feel
himself authorized to grant a new order, although the
first had not been complied with; that he viewed the
further prosecution of the campaign, attended as it was
with so many embarrassments, as a fruitless endeavour; and concluded by recommending, as advisable,
to withdraw the troops into the settlements, and suspend all active operations, until the general government should provide more effectual means, for conducting it to a favourable issue. Jackson, far from
having any intention to yield to this advice, was determined to oppose it. Still, however, he was greatly
concerned at the view the chief magistrate of his state
seemed to take of a question so important; and immediately proceeded to unfold himself fully, and to suggest the course, which, he believed, on the present occasion, it behoved them both to pursue; pointing out
the ruinous consequences, that might be expected to
result, from the adoption of the measure he had undertaken to recommend;—he continues:

" Had your wish, that I should discharge a part of
my force, and retire, with the residue, into the settlements, assumed the form of a positive order, it might
have furnished me some apology for pursuing such a
course; but by no means a full justification. As you
would have no power to give such an order, I could

CHAP.
IV.

1813.

not be inculpable in obeying, with my eyes open to the fatal consequences that would attend it. But a bare recommendation, founded, as I am satisfied it must be, on the artful suggestions of those fire-side patriots, who seek, in a failure of the expedition, an excuse for their own supineness; and upon the misrepresentations of the discontented from the army, who wish it to be believed, that the difficulties which overcame their patriotism are wholly insurmountable, would afford me but a feeble shield, against the reproaches of my country, or my conscience. Believe me, my respected friend, the remarks I make proceed from the purest personal regard. If you would preserve your reputation, or that of the state over which you preside, you must take a straight-forward, determined course; regardless of the applause or censure of the populace, and of the forebodings of that dastardly and designing crew, who, at a time like this, may be expected to clamour continually in your ears. The very wretches who now beset you with evil counsel, will be the first, should the measures which they recommend eventuate in disaster, to call down imprecations on your head, and load you with reproaches. Your country is in danger:—apply its resources to its defence! Can any course be more plain? Do you, my friend, at such a moment as the present, sit with your arms folded, and your heart at ease, waiting a solution of your doubts, and a definition of your powers? Do you wait for special instructions from the secretary at war, which it is impossible for you to receive in time for the danger that threatens? How did the venerable Shelby act, under similar circumstances; or rather, under circum-

stances by no means so critical? Did he wait for orders, to do what every man of sense knew—what every patriot felt—to be right? He did not; and yet how
highly and justly did the government extol his manly
and energetic conduct! and how dear has his name become to all the friends of their country!

" You say, that, having given an order to general
Cocke, to bring his quota of men into the field, your
power ceases; and that, although you are made sensible that he has wholly neglected that order, you can
take no measure to remedy the omission. Widely
different, indeed, is my opinion. I consider it your
imperious duty, when the men, called for by your order, founded upon that of the government, are known
not to be in the field, to see that they be brought there;
and to take immediate measures with the officer, who,
charged with the execution of your order, omits or ne-
glects to do it. As the executive of the state, it is
your duty to see that the full quota of troops be constantly kept in the field, for the time they have been
required. You are responsible to the government;
your officer to you. Of what avail is it, to give an
order, if it be never executed, and may be disobeyed
with impunity? Is it by empty orders, that we can
hope to conquer our enemies, and save our defenceless
frontiers from butchery and devastation? Believe me,
my valued friend, there are times, when it is highly
criminal to shrink from responsibility, or scruple about
the exercise of our powers. There are times, when
we must disregard punctilious etiquette, and think
only of serving our country. What is really our present situation? The enemy we have been sent to

CHAP. subdue, may be said, if we stop at this, to be only ex-
IV. asperated.   The commander in chief, general Pinck-
1813. ney, who supposes me, by this time, prepared for renewed operations, has ordered me to advance, and form
a junction with the Georgia army ; and, upon the expectation that I will do so, are all his arrangements
formed, for the prosecution of the campaign.   Will it
do, to defeat his plans, and jeopardize the safety of the
Georgia army ? The general government, too, believe,
and have a right to believe, that we have now not less
than five thousand men in the heart of the enemy's
country ; and on this opinion are all their calculations
bottomed; and must they all be frustrated, and I become
the instrument by which it is done ? God forbid !

" You advise me, too, to discharge, or dismiss from
service, until the will of the president can be known,
such portion of the militia, as have rendered three
months' service. This advice astonishes me, even more
than the former.   I have no such discretionary power ;
and it would be impolitic and ruinous to exercise it,
if I had. I believed, the militia who were not specially
received for a shorter period, were engaged for six
months, unless the objects of the expedition should be
sooner attained ; and in this opinion I was greatly
strengthened, by your letter of the 15th, in which you
say, when answering my inquiry upon this subject,
" the militia are detached for six months' service ;"
nor did I know, or suppose, you had a different
61 opinion, until the arrival of your last letter. This
opinion must, I suppose, agreeably to your request, be
made known to general Roberts' brigade, and then
the consequences are not difficult to be foreseen.

Every man belonging to it will abandon me on the
4th of next month; nor shall I have the means of
preventing it, but by the application of force, which,
under such circumstances, I shall not be at liberty to
use. I have laboured hard, to reconcile these men, to
a continuance in service, until they could be honourably discharged, and had hoped I had, in a great measure, succeeded; but your opinion, operating with
their own prejudices, will give a sanction to their conduct, and render useless any further attempts. They
will go; but I can neither discharge nor dismiss them.
Shall I be told, that, as they will go, it may as well be
peaceably permitted; can that be any good reason why
I should do an unauthorized act? Is it a good reason
why I should violate the order of my superior officer,
and evince a willingness to defeat the purposes of my
government? And wherein does the " sound policy"
of the measures that have been recommended consist?
or in what way are they " likely to promote the public
good?" Is it sound policy to abandon a conquest thus
far made, and deliver up to havoc, or add to the number of our enemies, those friendly Creeks and Cherokees, who, relying on our protection, have espoused
our cause, and aided us with their arms? Is it good
policy to turn loose upon our defenceless frontiers,
five thousand exasperated savages, to reek their hands
once more in the blood of our citizens? What! retrograde under such circumstances! I will perish first.
No, I will do my duty: I will hold the posts I have
established, until ordered to abandon them by the
commanding general, or die in the struggle;—long

o

since have I determined, not to seek the preservation of life, at the sacrifice of reputation.

"But our frontiers, it seems, are to be defended, and by whom? By the very force that is now recommended to be dismissed; for I am first told to retire into the settlements, and protect the frontiers; next, to discharge my troops; and then, that no measures can be taken for raising others. No, my friend, if troops be given me, it is not by loitering on the frontiers that I will seek to give protection;—they are to be defended, if defended at all, in a very different manner;—by carrying the war into the heart of the enemy's country. All other hopes of defence are more visionary than dreams. What then is to be done? I'll tell you what. You have only to act with the energy and decision the crisis demands, and all will be well. Send me a force engaged for six months, and I will answer for the result,—but withhold it, and all is lost,—the reputation of the state, and your's, and mine along with it."

This letter had considerable effect with the governor. On receiving it, he immediately ordered from the second division, twenty-five hundred of the militia, for a tour of three months, to rendezvous at Fayetteville, on the 28th of January. The command was given to brigadier general Johnston, with orders to proceed without delay, by detachments, or otherwise, to Fort Strother. He instructed general Cocke to execute the order he had received from Jackson, for raising from his division, his required quota of troops, and to bring them to the field as early as possible.

These measures were taken by the governor in opposition to his first views of their impropriety;—without any special directions from the government. If any
doubts, however, remained of the correctness of the
course adopted, they were soon after dispelled, by a
letter from the secretary of war, stating, that he was
" authorized to supply, by militia drafts or volunteers,
any deficiency that might arise, and without referring
on that head to the war department."

General Roberts, who had been ordered back to
supply the deficiencies in his brigade, returned on the
27th, with one hundred and ninety-one men, mustered
for three months.   Having halted them a few miles in
rear of the camp, he proceeded thither himself, to learn
of the commanding general, whether the troops he had
brought on would be received for the term they had
stipulated; as they were unwilling to advance further,
until this point were settled.   Jackson answered, that
although he greatly preferred they should be engaged for six months, or during the campaign, yet he
had no wish to alter any engagement they had made
with general Roberts, and would gladly receive them
for the period they had been mustered; at the expiration of which time he would discharge them.   Notwithstanding this assurance, with which he was instructed to make them acquainted, they yet determined,
for some unknown cause, to abandon their engagements, and return home, without gaining even a sight
of the camp.   To the misconduct and improper conversation of their general, was it justly to be attributed.
By halting them in the neighbourhood, until he could
go to head quarters, and " make terms" for their ac-

ceptance, he impressed them with the belief, that their obligations as yet extended only to himself; from which he promised to absolve them, if the terms he should be able to make, should be less favourable than they expected. And even after general Jackson had assented to all that was or could be asked in their behalf, and that assent had been reduced to writing, Roberts, either from not understanding what was done, or from a desire to injure the service, hastened back to his men,—informed them that he had been unable to effect an accomplishment of their object—seriously lamented having induced them from their homes, and concluded by gravely remarking, that he freely exonerated them from all the obligations they were under to him. They, just as gravely, concluded they would go no further; and, turning about, commenced their return home. The affair, however, was soon presented very differently to his mind. The careless indifference with which he had first treated it had subsided; and his fears took the alarm, on receiving from general Jackson, an order to parade immediately before the fort, the men he had reported to have brought into the field. He came forward, now, to excuse what had happened, and to solicit permission to go in pursuit of the refugees, whom he thought he should be able to bring back. Overtaking them, at the distance of twenty miles, he endeavoured, in a very gentle manner, to soothe their discontents, and prevail on them to return; but having been discharged, and absolved fully from the engagements they had at first entered into, they laughed at the folly of his errand. Unable to effect his object, he remained with them during the night; and, having

passed it with great jollity, set out in the morning for
camp, and his new recruits for home.   On arriving at
head quarters, he ascribed his failure to the practices
of certain officers, whom he named, and who, he said,
had stirred up a spirit of mutiny and desertion among
the men, to such a degree, that all his efforts to reclaim
them had proved unavailing. Jackson, who could not
view this incident with the same indifference that
Roberts had done, immediately issued an order, directing him to proceed, forthwith, in pursuit of the deserters, and have them apprehended, and brought back.
In the execution of this order, he was commanded to
call to his aid any troops in the United States' service,
within the county of Madison, or in the state of Tennessee, and to exert all his power and authority, as a military officer, within his own brigade; and in the event he
should not be able to collect a sufficient force to march
them safely to head quarters, to confine them in gaols,
and make report thereof, without delay.   This order
was accompanied with an assurance, that all who should
return willingly to their duty, except those officers
who had been reported as the instigators, would be
pardoned.   Many of the men, and several of the officers, who had been charged as encouraging the revolt,
learning the nature of the proceedings that were about
to be enforced against them, returned, of their own accord, to camp; and concurred in ascribing their late
misconduct entirely to their general.   He was afterwards arrested, and upon this and other charges exhibited against him, sentenced, by a court martial, to be
cashiered.

CHAP.   The day had arrived, when that portion of Roberts'
IV.   brigade, which had continued in service, claimed to
1814. be discharged; and insisted, that whether this were
given to them or not, they would abandon the cam-
63   paign, and return home. Jackson believed them not
entitled to it, and hence, that he had no right to give it;
but as governor Blount had said differently, and his
opinion, as he had required, had been promulgated,
he felt it was improper that he should attempt the exercise of force to detain them. Nevertheless, believing
it to be his duty to keep them, he issued a general order, commanding all persons, in the service of the
United States, under his command, not to leave the
encampment, without his written permission, under
the penalties annexed, by the rules and articles of war,
to the crime of desertion. This was accompanied by
an address, in which they were exhorted, by all those
motives which he supposed would be most likely to
have any influence, to remain at their posts, until they
could be legally discharged. Neither the order nor
the address availed any thing. On the morning of the
64   4th of January, the officer of the day, major Bradley,
reported, that, on visiting his guard, half after ten
o'clock, he found neither the officer, lieutenant Kearley, nor any of the sentinels at their posts. Upon this
Lieute- information, general Jackson ordered the arrest of
nant Kear- Kearley, who refused to surrender his sword, alleging
ley. it should protect him to Tennessee; that he was a
freeman, and not subject to the orders of general Jackson, or any body else. This being made known to
the general, he issued, immediately, this order to the
adjutant general: "You will forthwith cause the guards

to parade, with captain Gordon's company of spies,
and arrest lieutenant Kearley; and, in case you shall be
opposed, in the execution of this order, you are commanded to oppose force to force, and arrest him, at all
hazards.   Spare the effusion of blood, if possible; but
mutiny must, and shall be put down." Colonel Sitler,
with the guards and Gordon's company, immediately
proceeded in search, and found him at the head of his
company, on the lines, which were all formed, and
about to march off. He was ordered to halt, but refused. The adjutant general, finding it necessary, directed the guards to stop him; and again demanded
his sword, which he again refused to deliver. The
guards were commanded to fire on him, if he did not
immediately deliver it, and had already cocked their
guns. At this order, the lieutenant cocked his, and
his men followed his example. General Jackson, informed of what was passing, had hastened to the scene,
and arriving at this moment, personally demanded of
Kearley his sword, which he still obstinately refused to
deliver.   Incensed at the outrage, and viewing the
example as too dangerous to pass, he snatched a pistol
from his holster, and was already levelling it at the
breast of Kearley, when colonel Sitler, interposing between them, urged him to surrender his sword. At this
moment, Dr. Taylor, the friend of the lieutenant, drew
it from the scabbard, and handed it to the adjutant general, who refused to receive it. It was then returned to
Kearley, who now delivered it, and was placed under
guard. During this crisis, both parties remained with
their arms ready, and prepared for firing; and a scene
of bloodshed was narrowly escaped.

Kearley being confined, and placed under guard, soon became exceedingly penitent, and earnestly supplicated the general for a pardon. He stated, that the absence of the guards and sentinels from their post, was owing to the recommendation and advice of the brigade major, Myers; that his not delivering his sword, when it was first demanded, was owing to the influence and arguments of others, who persuaded him it was not his duty; that he had afterwards come to the determination to surrender himself, but was dissuaded by captains Metcalf and Dooley, who assured him it would be a sacrifice of character, and that they would protect him, in the hour of danger; why he still resisted, in the presence of the general, was, that being then at the head of his company, and having undertaken to carry them home, he was restrained, at the moment, by a false idea of honour. This application was aided by the certificate of several of the most respectable officers, then in camp, attesting his uniformly good behaviour heretofore, and expressing a belief that his late misconduct was wholly to be attributed to the interference of others. Influenced by these reasons, but particularly by the seductions which he believed had been practised upon him, by older and more experienced officers in his regiment, the general thought proper to order his liberation from arrest, and his sword to be restored to him. Never was a man more sensible of the favour he had received, or more devoted to his benefactor, than he afterwards became.

While these proceedings were taking place, the rest of the brigade, except captain Willis's company, and twenty-nine of his men, continued their march towards

home, leaving behind, for the further prosecution of
the campaign, and the defence of Fort Strother. colonel Lilliard's regiment of militia, whose term of service was within a few weeks of expiring; two small
companies of spies, and one of artillery. As Lilliard's
regiment had often professed a desire to be led against
the enemy, before they quitted the service, Jackson
flattered himself with the hope, that they would, for
this purpose, willingly remain in the field, a few days
beyond the period of their engagements. On the next
day, therefore, he caused the following address to be
read to that regiment.

"Major general Cocke having reported that your term
of service will expire on the 14th, I assume no claim
on you beyond that period. But, although I cannot
demand as a right, the continuance of your services, I
do not despair of being able to obtain them through
your patriotism. For what purpose was it that you
quitted your homes, and penetrated the heart of the
enemy's country? Was it to avenge the blood of your
fellow citizens, inhumanly slain by that enemy;—to
give security in future to our extended and unprotected frontier, and to signalize the valour by which you
were animated? Will any of these objects be attained
if you abandon the campaign at the time you contemplate? Not one! Yet an opportunity shall be afforded you, if you desire it. If you have been really
actuated by the feelings, and governed by the motives,
which, your commanding general supposes, influenced
you to take up arms, and enter the field in defence of
your rights, none of you will resist the appeal he now

Address
to the
East Ten- 65
nessee
troops.

P

CHAP.
IV.

1814.

makes, or hesitate to embrace with eagerness, the opportunity he is about to afford you.

"The enemy, more than half conquered, but deriving encouragement and hope from the tardiness of our operations, and the distractions which have unhappily prevailed in our camp, are again assembling below us. Another lesson of admonition must be furnished them. They must again be made to feel the weight of that power, which they have, without cause, provoked to war; and to know, that although we have been slow to take up arms, we will never again lay them from our hands, until we have secured the objects that impelled us to the resort. In less than eight days I shall leave this encampment, to meet and fight them. Will any of you accompany me? Are there any amongst you, who, at a moment like this, will not think it an outrage upon honour, for her feelings to be tested by a computation of time? What if the period for which you tendered your services to your country has expired,—is that a consideration with the valiant, the patriotic, and the brave, who have appeared to redress the injured rights of that country, and to acquire for themselves a name of glory? Is it a consideration with them, when those objects are still unattained, and an opportunity of acquiring them is so near at hand? Did such men enter the field like hirelings,—to serve for pay alone? Does all regard for their country, their families, and themselves, expire with the time, for which their services were engaged? Will it be a sufficient gratification to their feelings, that they served out three months, without seeing the enemy, and then abandoned the campaign, when the enemy was in the neighbourhood, and could be seen and conquered in ten days? Any retrospect they can make, of the sacrifices they have encountered, and the privations they have endured, can afford but little satisfaction under such circumstances;—the very mention of the Creek war, must cover them with the blushes of shame, and self-abasement. Having engaged for only three months, and that period having expired, you are not bound to serve any longer:—but are you bound by nothing else? Surely, as honourable and high-minded men, you must, at such a moment as the present, feel other obligations than the law imposes. A fear of the punishment of the law, did not bring you into camp;—that its demands are satisfied, will not take you from it. You had higher objects in view,—some greater good to attain. This, your general believes,—nor can he believe otherwise, without doing you great injustice.

" Your services are not asked for longer than twenty days; and who will hesitate making such a sacrifice, when the good of his country, and his own fame are at stake? Who, under the present aspect of affairs, will even reckon it a sacrifice? When we set out to meet the enemy, this post must be retained and defended; if any of you will remain, and render this service, it will be no less important, than if you had marched to the battle; nor will your general less thankfully acknowledge it. Tuesday next, the line of march will be taken up: and in a few days thereafter, the objects of the excursion will be effected. As patriotic men, then, I ask you for your services; and, thus long, I have no doubt you will cheerfully render them. I am well aware, that you are all anxious to return to your families and homes, and that you are entitled to do so; yet stay a little longer,—go with me, and meet the enemy, and you can then return, not only with the consciousness of having performed your duty, but with the glorious exultation, of having done even more than duty required."

What was hoped for, from this address, did not result. Difficulties were constantly pressing; and whilst one moment gave birth to expectation, the next served but to destroy it. Jackson had been already advised, that adequate numbers would shortly come to his relief; and until this could be accomplished, it was desirable to retain those already with him, to give to his posts greater protection. Whilst measures were adopting in Tennessee, to effect this fully, about a thousand volunteers were moving out, to preserve an appearance of opposition, and keep secure what had been already gained. With this force, added to what he already had, if in his power to keep them, he believed he would be able to advance on the enemy, make a diversion in favour of the Georgia army, and obtain other important advantages. With this view, he had addressed this regiment, and brought before them such considerations, as might be supposed calculated to excite a soldier's ardour. But, in answer to his address, colonel Lilliard replied, that having called upon the several captains in his regiment, to make a statement of those in their respective companies, who were willing to remain beyond the period of their engagement, it appeared that none would consent to do so, except captain Hamilton and three of his men.

As nothing but an unnecessary consumption of supplies was now to be expected from detaining them the
few days that yet remained of their term, orders were
given colonel Lilliard, to make the proper arrangements for taking up the line of march to Fort Armstrong, on the 10th; whence he was directed to proceed to Knoxville, and receive the orders of general
Cocke for their discharge.   Particular instructions
were given, to have the strictest police observed in his
camp, and the utmost order preserved on his march,
that no depredations might be committed on the persons or property of the Indians, through whose country
he was to pass; or on the citizens of Tennessee.

Meantime, the volunteers, lately raised, had arrived at Huntsville, where they were directed to remain, until sufficient supplies could be had at head
quarters.   Could they have proceeded directly on,
they would have reached the general sufficiently early
to have enabled him to proceed against the enemy,
before the period at which Lilliard's regiment would
have been entitled to a discharge. His exertions, to have
in readiness, the arrangements necessary to the accomplishment of this end, had been indefatigable.   General Cocke had been directed to give instructions to his
quarter master, to forward to Fort Strother the provisions that should arrive at Fort Armstrong; to proceed
thence to Ross', and make proper arrangements for the
speedy transportation, from that place to Deposit, of
all the bread stuff, which the contractor had been required to lay in at that depot; and to have procured
and sent from East Tennessee, a competent supply of
that article, as well for the troops then in the field, as

for those he had been ordered to raise. The more certainly to effect this object, he had, on the 20th of December, despatched his own quarter master, and adjutant general, to Deposit and Huntsville, to push on what should be collected, and on hand, at these places; and had, at the same time, despatched one of the sub-contractors from camp, with directions to examine the situation of the different depots; and, if found insufficient to meet the requisition he had made, to proceed immediately to the settlements in Tennessee, and lay in the necessary supplies. To the contractors themselves, he had addressed orders and exhortations almost without number; and, indeed, from every source, and through every channel that the hope of relief could be discerned, had he directed his exertions to obtain it.

Having thus strained every nerve, and unceasingly directed all his efforts towards the accomplishment of this object, he had, for a while, flattered himself with the hope that these multiplied endeavours would enable him to bring on his new troops in time for that combined movement with the East Tennessee militia, which he so much desired. So important did he consider this measure, that he was willing to subject himself to considerable hazard, rather than not effect it. To colonel Carroll he wrote, on learning that he was on his way, with the newly raised troops, "I am happy to hear of your success, in procuring volunteers. I shall receive, with open arms, those who, in this hour of need, so gallantly come forth, to uphold the sinking reputation of their state. I am more anxious than ever to re-commence operations, and indeed they have become more necessary than ever; yet I cannot move

without supplies. As this will meet you near where
the contractors are, you will be better able to ascertain
than I can inform you, when that happy moment will
arrive : and I pray you, use your best exertions to
have it brought about, with the least possible delay.
Until supplies, and the means of transportation can be
furnished, to justify another movement from this place,
it will be better that you remain where your horses can
be fed. I say this, upon the supposition that this will
shortly be done ; but were it certain that the same
causes of delay, which have so long retarded our operations, were still to continue, I would, at every risk,
and under every responsibility, take up the march, so
soon as the troops, now with you, could arrive. For
such a measure, I should seek my justification in the
imperiousness of the circumstances by which I am
surrounded ; and rely for success upon heaven, and the
enterprise of my followers.

" Partial supplies have arrived, for my use, at Fort
Armstrong, which will be ordered on to-morrow.
This, with the scanty stock on hand, will at least keep
us from starving a few weeks, until we can quarter
upon the enemy, or gain assistance from the country
below. General Claiborne, who is encamped eighty-
five miles above Fort Stoddart, writes me, that arrangements are made, to send supplies up the Alabama, to the junction of the Coosa and Tallapoosa.
Upon such resources will I depend, sooner than wait
until my army wastes away, or becomes, through inaction, unfit for service."

The hopes, however, which had been cherished, of
combined operations, with all the forces at that time

CHAP.
IV.
1814.
under his control, he was compelled, by the late events in his camp, to relinquish; but although these were highly discouraging, they were far from inducing him to despond. He was strongly persuaded of the necessity of proceeding; and determined, that as soon as it were possible, he would prosecute the campaign, with the feeble force he had at his command, deferring the period for more active operations, until the expected reinforcements, collecting in Tennessee, could be brought into the field.*

69

* These troops were calculated but for a single adventure, and no more. Colonel Carroll was unable to procure volunteers for six months, or during the campaign, as had been required by the order under which he acted. He had considered it so essential to have troops of some description engaged, that, rather than not obtain them at all, he had accepted them for sixty days, and taken them as mounted men, instead of infantry, which were not to be procured. This latter circumstance requiring a large quantity of supplies, occasioned them to be kept back much longer than would have been necessary, had they been troops of a different description. As there was no law, either of the state or general government, for a period so limited, which seemed too short to promise any very beneficial effects, the general was in doubt, whether or not to receive them; but, believing he might make a partial excursion, and thereby produce a diversion, favourable to the Georgia troops, who, relying on his co-operation, might be perhaps greatly endangered; and considering that their rejection might tend to the injury of the campaign, he finally concluded to accept them. Previously to doing so, he stated his objections, and the difficulties he felt; and endeavoured to prevail on them to enlarge their term of service: to this they would not agree; when, rather than lose them entirely, he consented to receive them.

On the second of January, colonel Carroll and Mr. CHAP.
Blackburn, having proceeded from Huntsville, arrived V.
at head quarters, to receive instructions, as to the man- 1814.
ner in which the volunteers should be organized; and
to learn the time when they would be required to be
brought up. Having reported their strength to be
eight hundred and fifty, they were directed to have Addition-
them formed, as had been desired, into two regiments, al troops
under officers of their own choice; and an order was arrive.
put into their hands, for general Coffee, who was then
at Huntsville, requiring him to march them to Fort
Strother, by the 10th instant. That officer, whose 70
feelings had been sufficiently harrowed by the late conduct and defection of his brigade, learning that those
troops were unwilling he should have the command of
them, had expressed a wish to general Jackson, that it
might not be assigned him; in consequence of which,
and their own request, the latter had determined, after
their arrival at his camp, that there should be no intermediate commander over them, between their colonels and himself. With this proposed arrangement,
and the nature and extent of the order borne to general Coffee, colonel Carroll and Mr. Blackburn were
instructed to make the troops acquainted; and were
particularly requested to use their best endeavours, to
remove any erroneous impressions that might have
been made upon their minds, by those who had so lately abandoned their duty, and who had laboured to instil
in others their own prejudices and passions. They
were charged, too, with the communication of a flattering address from the general, who considered it of
the utmost importance, to guard, by all the means in

his power, against the contamination of a corps, upon which his only hopes at present rested.

General Coffee, having received the instructions which general Jackson had sent him, immediately gave orders to colonels Perkins and Higgins, who had been chosen to the command of the two regiments, to march them directly for head quarters; explaining, in his order, the reasons that had induced him to issue it. To his entire astonishment, both these officers refused to obey it; alleging, in a written statement they made, that general Coffee had no command over them, and that they would disregard any he might attempt to exercise. Colonel Perkins, on its being shown him, by the brigade inspector, even went so far as to refuse to return it, or permit his taking a copy; thereby placing it out of his power, to make it known to the rest of the brigade.

Unwilling as Coffee was, to create any additional perplexities to the commanding general, or occasion new disturbances, at such a crisis; nevertheless, influenced by a regard for his own reputation, which he believed to be wantonly and wickedly assailed, by this contumacious refusal to obey an order which the occasion and his instructions required him to issue, he felt himself constrained to demand the arrest of those officers.

This application, with charges and specifications of so serious a nature, against his officers highest in command, placed Jackson in a very delicate situation. To commence the exercise of authority over troops wholly unacquainted with service, by the arrest of those in whom they had reposed such distinguished confidence,

might be attended with consequences fatal to his views, and the success of the contemplated expedi-
tion. On the other hand, he was fully sensible of the injury that had been done the feelings of an officer, acting under the authority of his instructions, and how much justice required them to be repaired : nor was he less sensible of the feeble reliance that could be reposed on men, who seemed to make a merit of dis-obedience and insubordination, especially if, from in-dulgence, they should derive encouragement to licen-tiousness. But however his mind might oscillate be-tween the evil consequences of either alternative, he knew that the course pointed out by duty was a plain one, should Coffee persist in his demand.

Notwithstanding the strong injunctions and weighty considerations that had been urged, to produce an expeditious movement, it was not until the 13th, that Perkins and Higgins reached head quarters, with their regiments. Finding, on their arrival, that they were likely to be noticed, on charges which their better-informed friends advised them would not only deprive them of command, but involve them in dis-grace, Higgins immediately came forward, and made an honourable and satisfactory concession. Colonel Perkins remained rather more obstinate; but after ba-lancing, for several days, between pride and prudence, he at length yielded, though with a bad grace, and of-fered general Coffee an apology, in which he pleaded ignorance of military duty, as an excuse for his mis-conduct. That the service, at a crisis so important, might not be injured by any private feuds, the charges were withdrawn.

Every preparation was now made, to hasten an accomplishment of the objects in view. The whole effective force consisted, at this time, by the reports, of little more than nine hundred men, and was, in reality, below that number.

Being addressed by the general, on the occasion; on the 15th, the mounted troops commenced their march, and moved to Wehogee creek, three miles from the fort. Jackson, with his staff, and the artillery company, joined them next morning, at that place, and continued the line of march to Talladega, where about 71 two hundred friendly Indians, Cherokees and Creeks, badly armed, and much discouraged at the weakness of his force, were added to his numbers, without increasing much his strength. Seldom, perhaps, has there been an expedition undertaken, fraught with 72 greater peril than this. A thousand men, entirely unacquainted with the duties of the field, were to be marched into the heart of an enemy's country, without a single hope of escape, but from victory, and that victory not to be expected, but from the wisest precaution, and most determined bravery. Although so pregnant with danger, to march was the only alternative that could be prudently adopted. No other could afford a diversion favourable to general Floyd, who was advancing with the army from Georgia, or give favourable results to the campaign, without which it must soon have been abandoned, for want of men to prosecute it. Another reason rendered such a movement proper, and indispensable. The officer commanding at Fort Armstrong had received intelligence, on which was placed the utmost reliance, that the war-

riors, from fourteen or fifteen towns on the Tallapoosa, CHAP.
were about to unite their forces, and attack that place ; IV.
which, for the want of a sufficient garrison, was in a
weak and defenceless situation. Of this, general Jack- 1814.
son had been advised. The present movement, above
all others, was best calculated to prevent the execution
of such a purpose, if it were in truth intended. On Expedi-
reaching Talladega, he received a letter from the tion
commandant at Fort Armstrong, confirmatory of the the In-
first information that had been obtained, and which left dians.
it no longer a matter of doubt, but an attack would
be waged against that depot. One also from general
Pinckney, by express, arrived, advising him that Floyd,
on the 10th instant, would move from Coweta, and in
ten days thereafter, establish a position at Tuckabat-
chee ; and recommended, if his force would allow him
to do no more, that he should advance against such of
the enemy's towns, as might be within convenient distance ; that, by having his troops employed, he might
keep disaffection from his ranks, and be, at the same
time, serviceably engaged in harassing the enemy. If,
therefore, he could have hesitated before, there was now
no longer any room to do so. By an expeditious
movement, he might save Fort Armstrong, and render
an essential service to general Floyd, by detaching a
part of the clans destined to proceed against him. The
force which might act against either, was understood
to be then collected in a bend of the Tallapoosa, near
the mouth of a creek called Emuckfaw, and thither he
determined, by the nearest route, to direct his course.

As he progressed on the march, a want of the necessary knowledge in his pilots, of subordination in his

troops, and skill in the officers who commanded them, became more and more apparent; but still their ardour to meet the enemy was not abated. Troops unacquainted with service are oftentimes more sanguine than veterans. The imagination too frequently portraying battles in the light of a frolic, keeps danger concealed, until, suddenly springing into view, it seems a monster too hideous to be withstood.

On the evening of the 21st, sensible, from the trails he had fallen in upon, fresh, and converging to a point, that he was in the neighbourhood of the enemy, Jackson encamped his little army in a hollow square, on an eligible site, upon the eminences of Emuckfaw, sent out his spies, posted his piquets, doubled his sentinels, and made the necessary arrangements to guard against attack. About midnight, the spies came in, and reported they had discovered a large encampment of Indians, at about three miles distance, who, from their whooping and dancing, were no doubt apprized of his arrival. Every thing was ready for their reception, if they meditated an attack, or to pursue in the morning, if they did not. At the dawn of day, the alarm guns of our sentinels, succeeded by shrieks and savage yells, announced their presence. They com-

Battle of
Emuckfaw
Jan. 22.

menced a furious assault on the left flank, commanded by colonel Higgins, which was met and opposed with great firmness. General Coffee, and colonels Carroll and Sitler, instantly repaired to the point of attack, and, by example and exhortation, encouraged the men to a performance of their duty. The action raged for half an hour; the brunt of which being against the left wing, it had become considerably weakened. It being now sufficiently light to ascertain, correctly, the position of the enemy, and captain Ferril's company having come up, and reinforced the left wing, the whole charged, under general Coffee, and a rout immediately ensued. The friendly Indians joining in the pursuit, they were chased about two miles, with considerable loss. We had five killed, and twenty wounded. Until it became light enough to discern objects, our troops derived considerable advantage from their camp fires ; these being placed at some distance without the encampment, afforded a decided superiority in a night attack, by enabling those within to fire, with great accuracy, on an approaching enemy, whilst they themselves remained invisible, in the dark.

The pursuit being over, Jackson detached general Coffee, with the Indians, and four hundred men, to destroy the enemy's encampment, unless he should find it too strongly fortified ; in which event, he was to give information immediately, and wait the arrival of the artillery. Coffee, having reconnoitred this position, and found it too strong to be assailed with the force he commanded, returned to camp. The wisdom of this determination was soon perceived. He had not returned more than half an hour, when a severe fire was made upon the piquets, posted on the right, accompanied with prodigious yelling. General Coffee, having obtained permission, proceeded to turn the left flank of the assailants. This detachment being taken from different corps, he placed himself at their head, and moved briskly forward. Those in the rear, availing themselves of this circumstance, continued to drop off, one by one, without his knowledge, until the whole number left with him, did not exceed fifty. It was fortunate, that the force of the enemy he had first to attack, was not greater. He found them occupying a ridge of open pine timber, covered with low underwood, which afforded them many opportunities for concealment. To deprive them of this advantage, which they are very dexterous in taking, Coffee ordered his men to dismount and charge them. This order was promptly obeyed, and some loss sustained in its execution; the general himself was wounded through the body, and his aid, major Donelson, killed by a ball through the head;—three of his men also fell. The enemy, driven back by the charge, took refuge on the margin of a creek, covered with reeds, where they lay concealed.

73

The savages having intended the attack on the right as a feint, now, with their main force, which had been concealed, made a violent onset on our left line, which they hoped to find weakened, and in disorder. General Jackson, however, who had apprehended their design, was prepared to meet it: this line had been ordered to remain firm in its position; and when the first gun was heard in that quarter, he had repaired thither in person, and strengthened it by additional forces. The first advance of the enemy, though sudden and violent, was sustained with firmness, and opposed with great gallantry. The battle was now maintained by the assailants, by quick and irregular firing, from behind logs, trees, shrubbery, and whatever could afford concealment: behind these, prostrating themselves after firing, and, re-loading, they would rise and again discharge their guns. After sustaining their fire

Second
battle of
Emuck-
faw.
Jan. 22.

in this way for some time, a charge, to dislodge them

from their position, was ordered: and the whole line under colonel Carroll, by a most brilliant and steady movement, broke in upon them, threw them into confusion, and they fled precipitately away. The pursuit commenced, and they were overtaken and destroyed in considerable numbers: their loss was great, but not certainly known.

In the mean time, general Coffee had been endeavouring, as far as prudence would permit him to make the attempt, to drive the savages on the right from the fastnesses into which they had retired; but finding that this could not be done, without much hazard, and considerable loss, he began to retire, towards the place where he had first dismounted. This expedient, designed for stratagem, produced the desired end. The enemy, presuming it a retreat, and to have been adopted in consequence of the severe firing they had heard on the left wing, now forsook their hiding places, and rapidly advanced upon him. That officer immediately availed himself of the opportunity thus afforded, of contending with them again on equal terms: and a severe conflict commenced, and continued about an hour, in which the loss on both sides was nearly equal. At this critical juncture, when several of the detachment had been killed, many wounded, and the whole greatly exhausted with fatigue; the dispersion of the enemy being effected on the left, a reinforcement was despatched by general Jackson, which, making its appearance on the enemy's left flank, put an end to the contest. General Coffee, although severely wounded, still continued the fight, and availing himself

CHAP. of the arrival of this additional strength, instantly or-
IV.   dered a charge; when the enemy, foreseeing their
       doom, fled in consternation, and were pursued with
1814. dreadful slaughter. It is believed that at this place
none escaped. Thus drew to a close, a day of almost
continual fighting.*

Having brought in and buried the dead, and dressed the wounded, preparations were made, to guard
against an attack by night, should one be attempted,
by ordering a breast-work of timber around the encampment; a measure the more necessary, as the spirits of our troops, most of whom had never before seen
an enemy, were observed visibly to flag, towards the
evening. Indeed, during the night, it was with the
utmost difficulty the sentinels could be kept at their
posts, who, expecting, every minute, the appearance
of the enemy, would, at the least noise, fire and run
in. The enemy, however, whose spies were around
our encampment all night, did not think proper to attack us in this position. The next day, general Jackson, having effected, as he believed, so far as he could,
the main objects of the expedition, a diversion in fa-

* The Indians had designed their plan of operations well,
though the execution did not succeed. It was intended to
bring on the attack at three different points, at the same time;
but a party of the Chealegrans, one of the tribes which compose
the Creek confederacy, who had been ordered to assail the
right extremity of our front line, instead of doing so, thought
it more prudent to proceed to their villages, happy to have
passed, undiscovered, the point they had been ordered to attack. But for this, the contest might have terminated less
advantageously.

vour of general Floyd, who was, at this juncture, supposed to be carrying on his operations, lower down on
the Tallapoosa, and the relief of Fort Armstrong, began to think of returning to the Ten Islands. Many
reasons concurred to render such a measure proper,
and indeed indispensable. Not having set out prepared to make a permanent establishment, his provisions were growing extremely scarce; and the country
itself afforded no means of subsistence, either for his
men or their horses. His wounded, many of whom
were exceedingly dangerous, required to be speedily
taken care of; whilst the present temper of his soldiery
precluded all hope that he should be able to effect any
thing further, of great consequence. Besides, if the
object were still further to cripple the enemy, this
would be more certainly attained, by commencing a
return, which, having the appearance of retreat, would
probably induce a pursuit, than by attacking them in
their strong holds; in which event, too, the diversion
contemplated would be the more complete, by drawing
them in a different direction. Determined by these
considerations, Jackson ordered litters to be formed, for
the transportation of the sick and wounded, and the
other preparations to be made, for a return march.
Every thing being ready, it was commenced at ten
o'clock next morning, and continued without interruption, until nearly night; when the army was encamped
a quarter of a mile on the south side of Enotichopco
creek, in the direction to the ford, at which it had been
passed, in proceeding out.

As it was pretty evident that the enemy had been in
pursuit during the day, a breast-work was thrown up,

with the utmost expedition, and every arrangement made to repel their attempts, should they meditate an attack, during the course of the night, or on the succeeding morning. The night having been permitted to wear away without any disturbance, and without any appearance of an enemy, the general was led to conjecture that an ambuscade had been prepared, and that an attack would be made on him, whilst crossing the creek in his front; which, being deep, and the banks rugged, and thickly covered with reeds, afforded many advantages for such a design. Near the crossing place, was a deep ravine, formed by the projection of two hills, overgrown with thick shrubbery and brown sedge, which afforded every convenience for concealment, whilst it entirely prevented pursuit. Along this route, the army, in going out, had passed; through it, as might have been expected, it would again return; and here, it was believed, an ambuscade would be formed, if any were intended. Acting under these impressions, and to guard against them, Jackson determined to take a different route. He secretly despatched, early next morning, a few pioneers, to ascertain and designate another crossing place below. A suitable one was soon discovered, at about six hundred yards distance from the old one; and thither the general now led his army; having formed his columns, and the front and rear guards, previously to commencing the march.

A handsome slope of open woodland led down to the new ford, where, except immediately on the margin of the creek, which was covered with a few reeds, there was nothing to obstruct the view. The front

guards, and part of the columns, had passed;—the CHAP.
wounded were also over, and the artillery just entering IV.
the creek, when an alarm gun was heard in the rear.
The Indians, finding the route had been changed, 1814.
quitted the defile where they expected to commence
the assault, and advanced upon a company, under the Battle of
command of captain Russell, which marched in the Enoti-
rear. Though assailed by greatly superior numbers, Jan. 23.
it returned the fire, and gradually retired, until it reached the rear guard, who, according to express instructions given, were, in the event of an attack, to face
about, and act as the advance; whilst the right and left
columns should be turned on their pivots, so as completely to loop the enemy, and render his destruction
sure. The right column of the rear guard was commanded by colonel Perkins, the left by lieutenant colonel Stump, and the centre column by colonel Carroll.
Jackson was just passing the stream, when the firing
and yelling commenced. Having instructed his aid
to form a line for the protection of the wounded, who
were but a short distance in advance, and afterwards to
turn the left column, he himself proceeded to the right,
for a similar purpose. What was his astonishment,
when, calculating on certain victory, he beheld the
right and left columns of the rear guard, after a feeble
resistance, precipitately give way, bringing with them
confusion and dismay, and obstructing the passage,
over which the principal strength of the army was to
be re-crossed! This shameful flight was well nigh being attended with the most fatal consequences; which
were alone prevented by the determined bravery of a
few. Nearly the whole of the centre column had fol-

lowed the example of the other two, and precipitated themselves into the creek: not more than twenty had remained, to oppose the violence of the first assault. The artillery company, commanded by lieutenant Armstrong, and composed of young men of the first families, who had volunteered their services, at the commencement of the campaign, formed with their muskets, before the piece of ordnance they had, and hastily dragged it from the creek to an eminence, from which they could play to advantage. Here an obstinate conflict ensued; the enemy endeavouring to charge and take it, whilst this company formed with their muskets, and resolutely defended it. These young men, the few who remained with colonel Carroll, and the gallant captain Quarles, who soon fell at their head, with Russell's spies, not exceeding one hundred in the whole, maintained, with the utmost firmness, a contest, for many minutes, against a force five times greater than their own, and checked the advance of a foe, already greatly inspirited, from the consternation his first shock had produced. Every man who there fought, seemed to prefer death to flight. The brave lieutenant Armstrong fell, at the side of his piece, by a wound in the groin, and exclaimed, as he lay, "Some of you must perish; but don't lose the gun." By his side, fell, mortally wounded, his associate and friend, Bird Evans, and the gallant captain Hamilton; who, having been abandoned by his men, at Fort Strother, with his two brothers and his aged father, had attached himself to the artillery company, as a private, and, in that capacity, showed how deserving he was to command, by the fidelity with which he

obeyed. In the mean time, general Jackson and his
staff had been enabled, by great exertions, to restore
something like order, out of confusion. The columns
were again formed, and put in motion ; and small detachments had been sent across the creek, to support
the little band, that there maintained their ground.
The enemy, perceiving a strong force advancing,
and being warmly assailed on their left flank, by captain Gordon, at the head of his company of spies, who
had advanced from the front, and re-crossed the creek,
in turn, were stricken with alarm, and fled away, leaving
behind their blankets, and whatever was likely to retard
their flight. Detachments were ordered on the pursuit,
who, in a chase of two miles, destroyed many, and
wholly dispersed them.

In despite of the active exertions made by general
Jackson, to restore order, they were, for some time,
unavailing, and the confusion continued. In addition
to the assistance received from his staff, who were
every where encouraging, and seeking to arrest the
flight of the columns, he derived much from the aid of
general Coffee. That officer, in consequence of the
wound he had received at Emuckfaw, had, the day
before, been carried in a litter. From the apprehensions indulged, that an attack would probably be made
upon them that morning, he had proceeded from the
encampment on horseback, and aided, during the action, with his usual calm and deliberate firmness. Indeed, all the officers of his brigade, who, having been
abandoned by their men, had formed themselves into
a corps, and followed the army without a command,
rendered manifest, now, the value of experience. This

was not a moment for rules of fancied etiquette. The very men who, a little time before, would have disdained advice, and spurned an order from any but their own commanders, did not scruple now to be regulated by those, who seemed to be so much better qualified, for extricating them from their present danger. The hospital surgeon, Dr. Shelby, appeared in the fight, and rendered important military services. The adjutant general, Sitler, than whom none displayed greater firmness, hastened across the creek, in the early part of the action, to the artillery company, for which he felt all the *esprit de corps*, having been once attached to it; and there remained, supporting them in their duties, and participating in their dangers. Captain Gordon, too, contributed greatly to dispel the peril of the moment, by his active sally on the left flank of the savages. Of the general himself, it is scarcely necessary to remark, that but for him, every thing must have gone to ruin. On him, all hopes were rested. In that moment of confusion, he was the rallying point, even for the spirits of the brave. Firm and energetic, and at the same time perfectly self-possessed, his example and his authority alike contributed to arrest the flying, and give confidence to those who maintained their ground. Cowards forgot their panic, and fronted danger, when they heard his voice, and beheld his manner; and the brave would have formed round his body a rampart with their own. In the midst of showers of balls, of which he seemed unmindful, he was seen performing the duties of subordinate officers, rallying the alarmed, halting them in their flight, forming his columns, and inspiriting them by his example. An army, suddenly dismayed, was thus

rescued from the destruction that lately appeared inevitable. Our total loss, in the several engagements,
on the 22d, and to-day, was only twenty killed, and
seventy-five wounded, some of whom, however, afterwards died. That of the enemy cannot be accurately
stated. The bodies of one hundred and eighty-nine
of their warriors were found; this, however, may be
considered as greatly below the real number; nor can
their wounded be even° conjectured. As had been
generally the case, the greatest slaughter was in the
pursuit. Scattered through the heights and hollows,
many of the wounded escaped, and many of the killed
were not ascertained. It is certain, however, as was
afterwards disclosed by prisoners, that considerably
more than two hundred of those who went out to battle, never returned; but those who got back, unwilling
it should be known they were killed, endeavoured to
have it believed, and so represented it, that they had
proceeded on some distant expedition, and would be
for some time absent.

After this battle, in which had been anticipated certain success, the enemy no more thought of harassing
our march. Having continued it, without interruption,
over high, broken, and, for the most part, barren land,
we encamped, on the night of the 26th, within three
miles of Fort Strother. Thus terminated an expedition
replete with peril, but attended with effects highly beneficial. Fort Armstrong was relieved; general Floyd
enabled to gain a victory at Autossee, where, but for
this movement, which had diverted much of the enemy's strength, he would most probably have met defeat; a considerable portion of the enemy's best forces

had been destroyed; and an end put to the hopes they had founded on our previous delays. Discontent had been kept from our ranks; the troops had been beneficially employed; and inactivity, the bane of every army, had been avoided. But perhaps the greatest good that resulted from the expedition was the effect produced on the minds of the people at home, from whom was to be collected a force sufficient to terminate the war. Experience has often proved the facility with which numbers are brought to a victorious standard; whilst the ranks of a defeated army are ever with difficulty filled. Any result, therefore, that was calculated to bring an efficient force into the field, was highly important and beneficial.

CHAPTER V.

The troops having reached, in safety, the post whence CHAP.
they had set out, and their term of service being with- V.
in a short time of expiring, the general determined to
discharge them. The information from Tennessee, 1814.
was, that there would soon be in the field a considerable force, enlisted for a period sufficient to effect a
termination of the Indian war. He was desirous of
having every thing in readiness, by the time of their
arrival, that they might be moved, without delay, into
active service. Detaining his late volunteers, therefore, a short time, to complete boats, for the transportation of his camp equipage and provisions down the Volun-
Coosa, he ordered them to be marched home, and to teers are
be honourably dismissed. The further service of his ed.
artillery company was also dispensed with. His parting interview with them was interesting and affecting; 76

they had rendered important services, and adhered to him, with great devotedness, in every vicissitude, and through every difficulty he had encountered, from the first commencement of the campaign. Although, from the high sense entertained of their bravery and fidelity, he would have gladly retained them, yet he was too well convinced of the many sacrifices these young men had made, of the bravery they had displayed, and the patience with which they had submitted to those moments of scarcity, that had raised up discontents and mutiny in his camp, not to feel a desire to gratify their wishes, and permit them, honourably, to retire from a service, which they had already so materially benefited.

A letter from Jackson to governor Blount, heretofore noticed, added to his own sense of the importance of the crisis, had induced him to issue an order, on the 3d, directing twenty-five hundred of the militia of the second division, to be detached, organized, and equipped, in conformity to an act of congress, of the 6th of April, 1812. These were to perform a tour of three months, to be computed from the time of rendezvous, which was appointed to be on the 28th instant. He had also required general Cocke to bring into the field, under the requisition of the secretary at war, the quota he had been instructed to raise, at the opening of the campaign. This officer, who had hitherto created so many obstacles, still appeared to desire nothing more ardently than a failure of the campaign. Although many difficulties were feigned, in the execution of the order, he was enabled to muster into service about two thousand, from his division.

February.

The militia are called out for three months.

77

These, however, as well as those called out from West
Tennessee, were but indifferently armed.

The thirty-ninth regiment, under colonel Williams,
also received orders to proceed to Jackson's head quarters, and act under his command, in the prosecution
of the war.   It arrived on the 5th or 6th of the month,
about six hundred strong.   Most of the men were
badly armed: but this evil was shortly afterwards remedied.

The quarter masters and contractors were already
actively engaged, and endeavouring to procure provisions, and the necessary transportations, for the army.
The failures, in regard to former enterprises, are to
be ascribed to these two departments; to the constant endeavour of the contractors, to procure provisions at a reduced price, in order to enhance their
profits, and to the fears which they entertained, lest,
if they should lay in a large store, it might spoil on
their hands.   Evils of this kind, growing out of the
very nature of the establishment, ought, long since,
to have convinced the government of the propriety of resorting to some other and better mode, for
supplying its armies, in times of war.   The inconveniences in the quarter master's department were,
indeed, less chargeable to them, than to causes they
could not control; for, to the extreme ruggedness of the
way, over which wagons had to pass, was to be added the real difficulty, in obtaining a sufficient number
on the frontiers.   That evils so severely felt, might,
for the future, be avoided, every facility was afforded these two departments, that the requisition, now
made upon them, might be promptly complied with.

To give, however, sufficient time, and to prevent any unnecessary press, the troops, advancing from East and West Tennessee, were directed to be halted in the rear of the depots, until ample stores, in advance, to justify immediate operations, should be laid in, and the requisite transportation provided.

About the middle of the month, in expectation that all things were in a state of readiness, from the strong assurances he had received, Jackson ordered the troops to advance, and form an union at head quarters, then at Fort Strother. Greatly to his surprise and mortification, he soon after learned, that the contractor from East Tennessee, had again failed in complying with his engagement, notwithstanding the ample means he possessed, and the full time that had been allowed him for that purpose. The troops, however, agreeably to the order, proceeded on their march. Those from the second division, under brigadier general Johnston, arrived on the 14th; which, added to the force under general Doherty, from East Tennessee, constituted about five thousand effectives. Composed, as this army was, of troops entirely raw, it was not to be expected, that any thing short of the greatest firmness in its officers could restrain that course of conduct and disorder, which had hitherto so unhappily prevailed.

The execution of a private, John Woods, who had been sentenced by a court martial, on a charge of mutiny, produced, at this time, the most salutary effects. That mutinous spirit, which had so frequently broken into the camp, and for a while suspended all active operations, remained to be checked. A fit occasion was now presented to evince, that although militia,

Execution
of John
Woods.

78

when at their fire-sides, at home, might boast an exemption from control, yet, in the field, those high notions were to be abandoned, and subordination observed. Painful as it was to the feelings of the general, he
viewed it as a sacrifice, essential to the preservation of
good order, and left the sentence of the court to be inflicted. The execution was productive of the happiest
effects; order was produced, and that opinion, so long
indulged, that a militia-man was for no offence to suffer
death, was, from that moment, abandoned, and a strict
obedience afterwards characterized the army.

Nothing was wanting, now, to put the troops in
motion, and actively to prosecute the war, but necessary supplies. Remonstrance, entreaty, and threats,
had long since been used, and exhausted. Every mean had been resorted to, to impress on the
minds of the contractors the necessity of urging forward, in faithful discharge of their duty; but the same
indifference and neglect were still persisted in. To
ward off the effects of such great evils,—evils which
he foresaw would again eventuate in discontent and
revolt, Jackson resolved to pursue a different course,
and no longer depend on persons who had so frequently disappointed him. He accordingly despatched messengers to the nearest settlements, with directions to
purchase provisions, at whatever price they could be
procured. This course, to these incumbents on the
nation, afforded an argument much stronger than any
to which he had before resorted. Thus assailed, in a
way they had not before thought of, by being held and
made liable for the amount of the purchases, they exerted themselves in discharge of a duty they had hi-

therto shamefully neglected.   Every expedient had been tried, to urge them to a compliance of the obligations they were under to their government; until the present, none had proved effectual.   In one of his letters, about this time, the general remarks: " I have no doubt, but a combination has been formed, to starve us out, and defeat the objects of the campaign; but M'Gee ought to have recollected that he had disappointed and starved my army once; and now, in return, it shall be amply provided for, at his expense. At this point, he was to have delivered the rations,— and whatever they may cost, at this place, he will be required to pay: any price that will ensure their delivery, I have directed to be given."   The supplying an army by contractors, he had often objected to, as highly exceptionable and dangerous.   His monitor, on this subject, was his own experience.   Disappointment, mutiny, and abandonment by his troops, when in the full career of success, and an unnecessarily protracted campaign, were among the evils already experienced, and which he wished, if possible, to be in future avoided.

79   Under these and other circumstances, which seemed to involve much more serious consequences, the general had but little repose or quietness.   Every thing was working in opposition to his wishes.   The East Tennessee brigade, under the command of Doherty, having been instructed to halt, until adequate supplies should be received at head quarters, had already manifested many symptoms of revolt, and was with much difficulty restrained from returning immediately home. Added to their own discontents, and unwillingness to

remain in service, much pains had been taken by a per-
sonage high in authority, to scatter dissension amongst
them, and to persuade them, that they had been improperly called out, and without sufficient authority ;—
that the draft was illegal, and that they were under no
necessity to serve.   Arguments like these, urged by
a man of standing, were well calculated to answer the
end desired ; what the governing motive was, that gave
rise to a course of conduct so strange, is difficult to be
imagined ; none was ever avowed, and certainly none
can be given, that will account for it satisfactorily. On
the morning that general Doherty was about to proceed to head quarters, he was astonished to find a beating up for volunteers, to abandon his camp, and return
home.   Notwithstanding all his efforts to prevent it,
one hundred and eighty deserted.   His surprise was
still greater, on learning, that a captain from Carter   80
county, had been instructed by major general Cocke,
that in the event of his marching back any number of
the troops, he would take upon himself to discharge
them, on their return to Knoxville. Before this, Cocke 81
had been at the camp of Doherty, and had, by different means, attempted to excite mutiny and disaffection
among the troops. As a reason for being unwilling
to go with them in command, he stated, that they
would be placed in a situation which he disliked to
mention, and one which his feelings would not enable
him to witness : that they were going out to be placed under the command of general Jackson, who would
impose on them the severest trials, and where they
would have to encounter every privation and suffering.
He represented, that at head quarters there was not a

sufficiency of provisions on hand to last five days; nor was there a probability that there would be any change of circumstances for the better;—that should they once be placed in the power of Jackson, he would, with the regular force under his command, compel them to serve as long as he pleased. Expressions like these, to men who had never before been in the field, and coming from one who had already been employed in a respectable command, were well calculated to produce serious impressions. Doherty, who was a brigadier in the first division, was at a loss to know how he should proceed with his own major general, who had obtruded himself into his camp, and was endeavouring to excite revolt; he accordingly despatched an express to head quarters, to give information of what was passing. The messenger arrived, and, in return, received an order to Doherty, commanding him, peremptorily, to seize, and send under guard to Fort Strother, every officer, without regard to his rank, who should be found, in any manner, attempting to incite his army to mutiny. General Cocke, perhaps apprehending what was going on, had retired before this order arrived, and thus escaped the punishment due to so aggravated an offence.

About this time, colonel Dyer was despatched with six hundred men with orders to proceed to the head of the Black Warrior, and ascertain if any force of the Indians was embodied in that quarter, and disperse them, that they might not, through this route, get in the rear of the army, and cut off the supplies. This detachment having proceeded eight days through the ridges along the Cohawba, had fallen in with a trail

the enemy had passed, stretching eastwardly, and had CHAP.
followed it for some distance. Apprehending that the   V.
army might be on the eve of departing from Fort Strother, and being able to gain no certain information of 1814.
the savages, they desisted from the pursuit, and returned to camp.

That there might be no troops in the field, in a situation not to be serviceable, orders were given the
brigadiers, to dismiss from the ranks every invalid, and
all who were not well armed.

General Jackson having, at length, by constant and
unremitted exertions, obtained what supplies were necessary to enable him to proceed, determined to set
out and pursue his course, still further into the ene- March.
my's country. A fear of the consequences to an army, from inaction; a wish that their time might not
be loitered away uselessly; and a consciousness that
a sufficiency of provisions was on the way, and could
be sent to him from the post maintained in his rear,
prompted him to do so. On the 14th, he commenced his march, and crossing the river, arrived, Marches
on the 21st, at the mouth of Cedar creek, which had Strother
been previously fixed on for the establishment of a in quest
fort.* At this place, it became necessary to delay a enemy.
day or two, with a view to detail a sufficient force, for
the protection and safety of this point, and to wait the
coming of the provision boats, which were descending
the Coosa, and which, as yet, had not arrived.

On the 22d of January, the day of the battle of
Emuckfaw, general Coffee, as has been already stated,

* Fort Williams.

CHAP.
V.

1814.

82

83

March.

had been detached to destroy the Indian encampment on the Tallapoosa; having reconnoitred their position, and believing them too strongly posted, to be advantageously assailed by the force he commanded, he had retired, without making the attempt. The position they had chosen was not far from New Youcka, and near the Oakfusky villages. Fortified as it was by nature, and the skill and exertions of the Indians; no other conjecture was entertained, than at this place was intended, a defence of the most determined kind. Learning that the savages were still embodied here, Jackson resolved, so soon as the necessary arrangements could be made to keep open a communication, and preserve in safety his rear, to make a descent on it, and destroy the confederacy; thence, returning to Fort Williams for provisions, to urge forward to the Hickory ground, where he hoped he would be able to put an end to the war.

On the 24th, leaving a sufficient force under brigadier general Johnston, for the protection of the fort, with eight days' provisions he set out for the Tallapoosa, by the way of Emuckfaw. The whole force now with him amounted to less than three thousand effective men; being considerably reduced, by the necessity of leaving behind him strong garrisons at the different forts. At ten o'clock on the morning of the 27th, after a march of fifty-two miles, he reached the village Tohopeka. The enemy, having gained intelligence of his approach, had collected in considerable numbers, with a view to give him battle. The warriors from the adjacent towns, Oakfusky, Hillabee, Eufalee, and New Youcka, amounting to a thousand

or twelve hundred, were ready, and waiting his approach. They could have selected no place, better
calculated for defence; for, independent of the advantages bestowed on it by nature, their own exertions
had greatly contributed to its strength. Surrounded
almost entirely by the river, it was accessible only by
a narrow neck of land, of three hundred and fifty yards
width, which they had taken much pains to secure and
defend, by placing large timbers, and trunks of trees,
horizontally on each other, leaving but a single place
of entrance. From a double row of port holes formed
in it, they were enabled to give complete direction to
their fire, whilst they lay, in perfect security, behind.

General Coffee, at the head of the mounted infantry,
and friendly Indians, had been despatched, early in the
morning, from camp, with orders to gain the southern
bank of the river, encircle the bend, and make some
feint, or manœuvring, by which to divert the enemy
from the point where the attack was intended principally to be waged. He was particularly instructed so
to arrange and dispose the force under his command,
that they might not escape, by passing to the opposite
side in their canoes, with which, it was represented,
the whole shore was lined. Jackson, with the rest of
the army, proceeded to take a post in front of the
breast-work. Having planted his cannon on an eminence, about two hundred yards from the front of the
enemy's line, with a view to break down his defence,
a brisk fire commenced. The musketry and rifles,
which occupied a nearer position, were used, as the
Indians occasionally showed themselves from behind
their works. The artillery was well served, by major

CHAP.
V.
1814.

Bradford, and the fire kept up for some minutes, without making any impression; time, however, was gained, for complete readiness. The signals having now
announced that general Coffee had reached, in safety,
his point of destination, on the opposite side of the
river, had formed his line, and was ready to act, the
order was given to charge. " Never were troops more
eager to be led on, than were both regulars and militia.
They had been waiting with impatience for the order,
and hailed it with acclamations. The spirit that animated them, was a sure augury of the success that was
to follow." Between them, there was no difference ;
both advanced with the intrepidity and firmness of
veteran soldiers. The former, the thirty-ninth regiment, led on by their skilful commander, colonel Williams, and the brave, but ill-fated major Montgomery ;

Battle of
Tohopeka,
or the
Horse-
Shoe.

and the militia, under the command of colonel Bunch,
moved forward, amidst a destructive fire, that continually poured upon them, and were presently at the rampart. Here an obstinate and destructive conflict ensued,
each contending for the port holes, on different sides.
Many of the enemy's balls were welded between the
muskets and bayonets of our soldiers. At this moment, major Montgomery, leaping on the wall, called
to his men to mount, and follow him ; he had scarcely
spoken, when, shot through the head, he fell to the
ground. Our troops had now scaled their ramparts,
when, finding it no longer tenable, the savages retired
back, and concealed themselves amidst the brush and
timber, that lay thickly scattered over the peninsula,
whence they continued resistance, and kept up a gall-
ing and constant fire, until they were again charged,

and forced back. Driven to despair, not knowing
whither to flee, and resolving not to surrender, they saw
no other alternative, than to effect their escape, by
passing in their canoes to the opposite bank of the
river; from this they were, however, prevented, by
perceiving that a part of the army already lined the
other shore. Under these circumstances, the remaining warriors, who yet survived the severity of
the conflict, betaking themselves to flight, leaped
down the banks, and concealed themselves along
the cliffs and steeps, which were covered by the
trees that had been felled from their margin. From
these secreted spots, as an opportunity was afforded,
they would fire, and disappear. General Jackson, perceiving that any further resistance would only involve
them in utter destruction, sent a flag, accompanied by
an interpreter, to propose to them a surrender, and
save the further effusion of blood. Whether the proposal were fairly explained, none but the interpreter
can know; at any rate, instead of being accepted, as
was fully expected would be the case, it was answered
by a fire, which wounded one of the party. Finding
they would not yield, nor abandon the course of desperation, on which they had resolutely fixed their
minds, orders were given to dislodge them. To accomplish this, the artillery was turned against them;
but without producing the effect. Lighted torches
were now thrown down the steeps, which, communicating with the brush and trees, and setting them on
fire, drove them from their hiding places, and brought
them to view. Thus the carnage continued, until
night separated the combatants; when the few mis-

guided savages, who had avoided the havoc and slaughter of the day, were enabled, through the darkness of the night, to make their escape.

Whilst the attack was thus waged, in front of the line, the friendly Indians, in general Coffee's detachment, under the command of colonel Morgan, with captain Russell's company of spies, were effecting much; and no doubt, to the course pursued by them, on the opposite side, was greatly owing the facility with which the breast-work was scaled, and its possession obtained. The village stood on the margin of the river, and on that part of the peninsula most remote from the fortification. At the line were all their warriors collected. Several of the Cherokees, and Russell's spies having swum across, unobserved, and procured some canoes, a considerable number passed over, entered their town, and fired it. No sooner was this discovered, than their attention and opposition was necessarily divided, and drawn to the protection of a point, which they had hitherto believed secure, and where they had not apprehended an attack. Thus assailed from an unexpected quarter,—a force in their rear, and another, still stronger, advancing on their front, afforded the invading army a much easier and less hazardous opportunity of succeeding in the assault, and securing the victory.

This battle gave a death blow to all their hopes; nor did they venture, afterwards, to make a stand. From their fastnesses in the woods, they had tried their strength, agreeably to their accustomed mode of warfare ; in ambuscade, had brought on the attack ; and, in all, failure and disaster had been met. The con-

tinual defeats they had received, were, no doubt, the
reasons of their having so strongly fortified this place,
where they had determined to perish, or be victorious.
That such a resolution had been taken, is conclusive,
from the circumstance of their having permitted their
women and children to remain : these they are always
careful to remove far from danger, and their scenes of
action. The positive assurance of success they now
indulged, had prevented their adhering to this precautionary measure, which, hitherto, they had never overlooked. In this action, the best and bravest of their
warriors were destroyed ; and a .greater loss sustained,
than had been met with in any of their previous con-
tests. Few escaped the carnage. Of the killed, many
were thrown into the river, whilst the battle raged ;—
many, in endeavouring to pass it, were sunk, by the
steady fire of Coffee's brigade ; and five hundred and
fifty-seven were left dead on the ground. Among
the number of the slain, were three of their prophets.
Decorated in a manner wild and fantastic,—the plu-
mage of many birds about their heads and shoulders ;
with savage grimaces, and horrid contortions of the
body, they danced and howled their cantations to the
sun. Their dependents already believed a commu-
nion with heaven sure, which, moved by entreaties, and
offered homage, would aid them in the conflict, and
give a triumph to their arms. Fear had no influence ;
and when they beheld our army approaching, and already scaling their line of defence, even then, far from
being dispirited, hope survived, and victory was still
anticipated. Monohoe, a very considerable one, who
had cheered the broken spirit of the nation, by his

CHAP. pretended divinations, fell, mortally wounded, by a
   V.   cannon shot in the mouth, while earnestly engaged
         in his incantations, and in urging and encouraging his
  1814. troops resolutely to contend.

Four men, who surrendered, and three hundred
women and children, were taken prisoners. That so
few warriors should have sought and obtained safety,
by appealing to the clemency of the victors, to persons
acquainted with the mode of Indian warfare, will not
appear a matter of surprise. It seldom happens that
they extend or solicit quarter : faithless themselves,
they place no reliance on the faith of others ; and, when
overcome in battle, seek no other protection than dex-
terity and haste in retreat afford. Another cause for
85   it may be found in a reason already given, in the attack made by a detachment of general Cocke's division, on the Hillabee clans, who were assailed and put
to the sword, at a moment when, having asked for
peace at discretion, they were expecting it to be given.
This misfortune was occasioned alone by a want of
concert, in the divisions of our army ; but it was past,
and with it was gone, on the part of the savages, all
confidence in our integrity and humanity ; and they
looked and trusted for safety, now, to nothing but their
own bravery. In this contest, they maintained resistance,
fighting and firing from their covert places, long after
the hope, either of success or escape, was, or should
have been at an end, and after the proposal had been
submitted to spare the further useless waste of blood.
A few, who had lain quiet, and concealed under the
cliffs, survived the severity of the conflict, and effected
their retreat, under cover of the night.

Our loss, although considerable, was small, when CHAP.
compared with that of the enemy; the whole estimate, V.
including in it the friendly and Cherokee Indians, being but fifty-five killed, and one hundred and forty-six
1814.
wounded. Of the former was major Montgomery, a
brave and enterprising young officer, of the thirty-ninth
regiment, and lieutenants Moulton and Somerville, who
fell early in the charge.

The object of the present visit being answered, the
general, in pursuance of his first plan, concluded to
return to Fort Williams. Having sunk his dead in
the river,* to prevent their being scalped by the savages, and made the necessary arrangements for carrying off his wounded, he commenced his return march
returns
for the fort, and in a few days reached it in safety.
to Fort
Williams.

---

* Sinking them in the river, in preference to burying them,
was adopted from the consideration, that those of our troops,
who had previously fallen, had been raised, stripped, and
scalped. Many of the Indians at Tohopeka were found in the
clothes of those who had been killed and buried at Emuckfaw.
It is true that this could operate no injury to the dead; yet it
was wished to be prevented for the future. It was a fact well
ascertained, that the Creek nation, generally, were ignorant of
the extent and number of their defeats; and so long as they
could be induced to believe, by those who undertook to account for it in that way, that their missing warriors were still
alive, and had gone on some distant enterprise; or could obtain the scalps of the killed, which they always consider as
certain evidences of victory, the war would still continue. It
was thought, therefore, better to sink than to bury them, as
the enemy would be thereby deprived of those badges of national and individual distinction, the effect of which would
be to shorten the period of the war.

His first object, on his arrival, was to excite, in the breasts of his soldiers, a sense of pride, commensurate with the achievements they had performed, and the valour they had displayed. He was impelled to it from a consciousness that feeling, once subsided, could with difficulty be again aroused; and from a desire to ward off that despondency from his ranks, which had once proved so fatal to his hopes. With a view to these objects, the next day, on parade, before the fort, he published to them this address :

" You have entitled yourselves to the gratitude of your country and your general. The expedition, from which you have just returned, has, by your good conduct, been rendered prosperous, beyond any example in the history of our warfare: it has redeemed the character of your state, and of that description of troops, of which the greater part of you are.

" You have, within a few days, opened your way to the Tallapoosa, and destroyed a confederacy of the enemy, ferocious by nature, and grown insolent from impunity. Relying on their numbers, the security of their situation, and the assurances of their prophets, they derided our approach, and already exulted, in anticipation of the victory they expected to obtain. But they were ignorant of the influence of government on the human powers, nor knew what brave men, and civilized, could effect. By their yells, they hoped to frighten us, and with their wooden fortifications to oppose us. Stupid mortals ! their yells but designated their situation the more certainly; whilst their walls became a snare for their own destruction. So will it

ever be, when presumption and ignorance contend
against bravery and prudence.

" The fiends of the Tallapoosa will no longer mur- der our women and children, or disturb the quiet of our borders.   Their midnight flambeaux will no more illumine their council-house, or shine upon the victim of their infernal orgies.   In their places, a new generation will arise, who will know their duty better. The weapons of warfare will be exchanged for the utensils of husbandry ; and the wilderness, which now withers in sterility, and mourns the desolation which overspreads her, will blossom as the rose, and become the nursery of the arts.   But before this happy day can arrive, other chastisements remain to be inflicted.   It is indeed lamentable, that the path to peace should lead through blood, and over the bodies of the slain : but it is a dispensation of Providence, to inflict partial evils, that good may be produced.

" Our enemies are not sufficiently humbled,—they do not sue for peace.   A collection of them await our approach, and remain to be dispersed.   Buried in ig- norance, and seduced by their prophets, they have the weakness to believe they will still be able to make a stand against us.   They must be undeceived, and made to atone their obstinacy and their crimes, by still further suffering.   The hopes which have so long de- luded them, must be driven from their last refuge. They must be made to know, that their prophets are impostors, and that our strength is mighty, and will prevail.   Then, and not till then, may we expect to make with them a peace that shall be lasting."

CHAP.   Understanding that the enemy was embodied,
   V.   in considerable numbers, at Hoithlewalee, a town
1814.   situated not far from the Hickory ground, he was
         anxious to re-commence his operations, as early as
         possible. The forces under his command, from
         sickness, the loss sustained in the late battle, and some
         discharges that had been given, had been too much
         reduced in strength, to permit him to act as effi-
         ciently as was wished. It was desirable, therefore, to
         effect a junction with the southern army, as soon as
         possible. The North Carolina troops, under the
         command of general Graham, an old and experi-
         enced revolutionary officer; and those of Georgia, un-
      86 der colonel Milton, were announced to be some where
         south of the Tallapoosa, and could be at no great dis-
         tance. To unite with them was an event much desired
      87 by Jackson, as well with a view to push his operations
         more actively, as to be able to procure for his army
         those supplies which he feared his resources might not
         sufficiently afford; for, hitherto, he had received from
         general Pinckney strong assurances, that all complaints
         on this subject would be at an end, so soon as his, and
         the southern division, could unite. No time was to
         be lost, in effecting a purpose so essential. General
         Jackson accordingly determined to leave his sick and
         wounded, and the fort, to the care and command of
         brigadier Johnston, and to set out again for the Talla-
         poosa. On the 7th, with all his disposable force, he
         commenced his march, with the double view of effect-
         ing an union with the army below, and of attacking,
         on his route, the enemy's force, collected at Hoithle-
         walee. His greatest difficulty was in conveying to colo-

nel Milton intelligence of his intended operations. The
friendly Indians, who, from their knowledge of the
country, had been always selected as expresses, were
with difficulty to be prevailed on now, for any such
undertaking. Believing their nation to be embodied,
in larger numbers than any which had been yet encountered, and that, confiding in their strength, they
would be better enabled to go out, searching and spy-
ing through the surrounding country, they at once
concluded, that any enterprise of this kind would be
attended with too great peril and danger, and the difficulty of eluding observation too much increased, for
them to adventure. This circumstance had as yet
prevented the arrangement of such measures as were
best calculated to bring the different divisions to act in
general concert. The necessity, however, of such co-
operation, was too important, at this moment, not to
be effected, if it were possible. Could the enemy, at
the point they now occupied, be brought to fight, and
a decisive advantage obtained over them, dispirited
and broken, they might be induced to submit to any
terms, and the war be ended; but if suffered to escape,
they might again collect, give battle at some fortunate
and unexpected moment, and thereby protract it a considerable time. To prevent this was desirable; and in
no other way could it so certainly be effected, as if, while
the Tennessee troops advanced from the north, the
Carolinians and Georgians should make such a disposition as would prevent an escape, by the enemy's
crossing the river, and passing off to Pensacola and the
Escambia.

Having at length succeeded in procuring confidential messengers, previously to setting out on this expedition, Jackson addressed colonel Milton, and advised
him of his intended movement. To guard against
any accident or failure that might happen, different
expresses were despatched, by different routes. He
informed him that with eight days' provisions, and a
force of about two thousand men, he should, on the
7th, take up the line of march, and proceed directly
for Hoithlewalee; which he expected to reach and attack on the 11th. He urged the necessity of a proper
concert being established in their movements; and either that he should proceed against the same place,
about the same time, or, by making some favourable
diversion in the neighbourhood, contribute to the successful accomplishment of the objects of the expedition.

His point of destination, owing to the floods of rain
which had fallen, and raised the streams to considerable
heights, was not reached until the 13th. This delay,
unavoidable, and not to be prevented, gave the Indians
an opportunity of fleeing from the threatened danger.
On reaching a creek, of the same name, which skirted
the town, it was so swollen as to be impassable. The
savages, gaining intelligence of an approach that was
thus retarded, were enabled to escape, by passing
the river in their canoes, and gaining the opposite
shore. Had colonel Milton fortunately made a different disposition of the troops under his command,
and co-operated with the Tennessee division, by
guarding the southern bank of the river, their escape
would have been prevented, and the whole force, col-

lected here, would either have been destroyed or made
prisoners. Although Jackson, in his letter of the 5th,
had assured him he would reach the enemy on the
11th; and when prevented by high waters and rotten
roads, had again notified him, that he would certainly
arrive and attack him by the morning of the 13th;
and urged him to guard the south bank of the Tallapoosa; still was the request disregarded, and the savages permitted to escape. Learning they were abandoning their position, and seeking safety in flight,
Jackson filed to the right, and overtaking the rear of
the fugitives, succeeded in making twenty-five prisoners. At this time, nothing was heard of colonel Milton; but on the same day, having marched about five
miles from his encampment at Fort Decatur, and approached within four of Hoithlewalee; he, the next
morning, gave notice of an intention to attack the village that day; at this moment the inhabitants and warriors had fled, and the town was occupied and partly
destroyed by a detachment from Jackson's army, that
had succeeded in passing the creek.

The Georgia army being so near at hand, was a
source of some satisfaction, although the escape of the
enemy had rendered their presence of less importance,
than it otherwise would have been. The stock of provisions, with which the march had been commenced
from Fort Williams, was nearly exhausted. Assurances, however, having been so repeatedly given, that
abundant supplies would be had on uniting with the
southern army, and that event being now so near at
hand, all uneasiness upon this subject was at once dispelled. Colonel Milton was immediately applied to,

the situation of the army disclosed, and such aid, as he could extend, solicited. He returned an answer to the general's demand, observing, he had sent some for the friendly Indians, and would, the next day, *lend* some for the remainder of the troops; but felt himself under no obligation to furnish any. Jackson, fully satisfied of its being in his power to relieve him, and that this apparent unwillingness could not, and did not proceed from any scarcity in his camp, assumed a higher ground, and, instead of asking assistance, now demanded it. He stated, that his men were destitute of supplies, and that he had been duly apprized of it; and concluded by ordering him to send five thousand rations immediately, for present relief; and himself and the forces under his command to join him at Hoithlewalee, by ten o'clock the next day. " This order," he remarked, " must be obeyed without hesitation."—It was obeyed. The next day, a junction having been effected, the necessary steps were taken to bring down the provisions deposited at Fort Decatur, and no further inconvenience was afterwards felt for the want of supplies.

Unites with the Georgia army.

Appearances seemed now to warrant the belief, that the war would not be of much longer continuance: the principal chiefs of the Hickory ground tribes were coming in, making professions of friendship, and giving assurances of their being no longer disposed to continue hostilities. The general had been met, on his late march, by a flag from these clans, giving information of their disposition to be at peace. In return they received this answer; that those of the war party who were desirous of putting an end to the contest in

Indians apply for peace.

which they were engaged, and becoming friendly,
must evince their intention of doing so by retiring in
the rear of the army, and settling themselves to the
north of Fort Williams: no other proof than this, of
their pacific dispositions, would be received.   Fourteen chiefs of these tribes had arrived, to furnish
still further evidence of their desire for peace.   They
assured the general that their old king, Fous-hatchée,
was anxious to be permitted to visit him in person,
but was then on his way, with his followers, to settle
above Fort Williams, agreeably to the information he
had received by the flag which had lately returned to
him.

Detachments were out to scour the country on the
south, with orders to break up any collection of the
enemy, that might be heard of in convenient distance.
The main body prepared to advance to the junction of
the two rivers, where, until now, it had been expected
the Indians would make a last and desperate stand.*
Every thing was in readiness to proceed on the march,
when it was announced to the general, that colonel
Milton's brigade could not move.   During the night
before, some of his wagon horses having strayed off,
persons had been sent in pursuit, and were expected

---

* The Hickory ground, or that part of the Creek nation lying in the forks, near where the Coosa and Tallapoosa unite,
was called by the Indians *Holy ground*, from a tradition and
belief among them, that it never had been trod by the foot
of a white man. Acting under the influence of their prophets,
and a religious fanaticism, it was supposed they would make
greater exertions to defend this, than any other portion of their
country.

CHAP. shortly to return with them; when, it was reported, he
   V.   would be ready to go on.   To Jackson, this was a

1814.   reason for delaying the operations of an army, which
as yet he had never learned, nor ever been influenced by.   He had indeed been frequently made to
halt, though from very different causes.   He replied
to the colonel's want of preparation, by telling him,
that in the progress of his own difficulties, he had discovered a very excellent mode of expediting wagons, even
without horses; and if he would detail him twenty
men from his brigade, for every wagon deficient in
horses, he would guarantee their safe arrival at their
place of destination.   Rather than do this, he preferred
to dismount some of his dragoons, and thus avoided
the necessity of halting, until his lost teams should
arrive.

   The army continued its march, without gaining intelligence of any embodied forces of the enemy, and
reached the old Toulossee Fort, situated on the Coosa,
Proceeds   not far from the confluence, at which another was de-
to the   termined to be erected, to be called after the com-
Hickory
ground.   manding general.   Here the rivers approach within an
hundred poles of each other, and, again diverging,
unite six miles below.   At this place, the chiefs of the
different tribes were daily arriving, and offering to submit on any terms.   They all concurred in their statements, that those of the hostile party, who were still
opposed to asking for peace, had fled from the nation, and sought refuge along the coast, and in Pensacola.   General Jackson renewed the assurances he
had previously given; that they could find safety in no
other way, than by repairing to the section of country

already pointed out to them; where they might be
quiet and undisturbed.

To put their friendly professions at once to the test,
he directed them to bring Weatherford to his camp,
tied, that he might be dealt with as he deserved. He
was one of the first chiefs of the nation, and had been
the principal actor in the butchery at Fort Mimms.
Learning from the chiefs, on their return, what had
been required of them by Jackson, he was prevailed
upon, as being perhaps the safer course, to go and
make a voluntary surrender of himself. Having reached the camp, without being known, and obtained admission to the general's quarters, he told him he was
Weatherford, the chief who had commanded at Fort
Mimms, and, desiring peace for himself and his people, had come to ask it. Somewhat surprised, that
one who so richly merited punishment, should so
sternly demand the protection which had been extended to others, he replied to him, that he was astonished
he should venture to appear in his presence; that he
was not ignorant of his having been at Fort Mimms,
nor of his conduct there, for which he well deserved
to die. " I had directed," continued he, " that you
should be brought to me confined; had you appeared
in this way, I should have known how to have treated
you." Weatherford replied, " I am in your power—
do with me as you please. I am a soldier. I have
done the white people all the harm I could ; I have
fought them, and fought them bravely : if I had an
army, I would yet fight, and contend to the last : but
I have none ; my people are all gone. I can now do no
more than weep over the misfortunes of my nation."
Pleased at the firmness of the man, Jackson informed

him, that he did not solicit him to lay down his arms, and become peaceable: " The terms on which your nation can be saved, and peace restored, has already been disclosed: in this way, and none other, can you obtain safety." If, however, he wished still to continue the war, and felt himself prepared to meet the consequences, although he was then completely in his power, no advantage should be taken of that circumstance ; that he was at perfect liberty to retire, and unite himself with the war party, if he pleased ; but if taken, his life should pay the forfeit of his crimes ; if this were not desired, he might remain where he was, and should be protected.

Weatherford answered, that he desired peace, that his nation might, in some measure, be relieved from their sufferings ; that, independent of other misfortunes, growing out of a state of war, their cattle and grain were all wasted and destroyed, and their women and children destitute of provisions. " But," continued he, " I may be well addressed in such language now. There was a time when I had a choice, and could have answered you : I have none now,—even hope has ended.   Once I could animate my warriors to battle ; but I cannot animate the dead. My warriors can no longer hear my voice : their bones are at Talladega, Tallushatchee, Emuckfaw, and Tohopeka. I have not surrendered myself thoughtlessly. Whilst there were chances of success, I never left my post, nor supplicated peace. But my people are gone, and I now ask it for my nation, and for myself. On the miseries and misfortunes brought upon my country, I look back with deepest sorrow, and wish to avert still greater

calamities. If I had been left to contend with the CHAP.
Georgia army, I would have raised my corn on one V.
bank of the river, and fought them on the other; but
your people have destroyed my nation. You are a 1814.
brave man : I rely upon your generosity. You will
exact no terms of a conquered people, but such as
they should accede to : whatever they may be, it would
now be madness and folly to oppose. If they are opposed, you shall find me amongst the sternest enforcers
of obedience. Those who would still hold out, can be
influenced only by a mean spirit of revenge ; and to
this they must not, and shall not sacrifice the last
remnant of their country. You have told us where
we might go, and be safe. This is a good talk, and
my nation ought to listen to it. They shall listen to it."

The earnestness and bold independence of his conduct left no doubt of the sincerity of his professions.
The peace party became reconciled to him, and agreed
to bury all previous animosities. In a few days afterwards, having obtained permission, he set out from
camp, accompanied by a small party, to search through
the forest, for his followers and friends, and persuade
them to give up a contest, in which hope seemed to 90
be at an end, and, by timely submission, to save their
nation from still further disasters.

The present was a favourable moment for preventing further opposition. The enemy, alarmed and
panic struck, were dispersed, and fleeing in different
directions. To keep alive their apprehensions, and
prevent their recovering from the fears with which
they were now agitated, was of the utmost importance.
If time were given them to rally, and form further

CHAP. resolutions, some plan of operation might be concert-
V. ed; and although it might not be productive of any
1814. very serious injury, yet it might have a tendency to
lengthen out the war, and involve those deluded people in still greater woes. Detachments, sufficiently
strong, were accordingly ordered out, to range through
the country, prevent their collecting at any point, and
to scatter and destroy any who might be found concerting offensive operations. Wherever they directed
their course, submission, and an anxious desire for
peace, were manifested by the natives. Those who
were still bent upon a continuance of the war, and
trusted for relief to the aid which their British allies
had promised, and which they had been for some time
expecting, had retired out of the country, towards the
sea; not doubting but the assistance looked for would
shortly arrive, enable them to re-commence hostilities,
with better hopes of success, and regain their country,
which they now considered as lost. Many of the chiefs
and warriors, looking to the defeats they had continually met with, in all their battles; viewing it as impracticable to resist, with any expectation of better fortune,
the numerous forces that were collecting, and threatening them at different points; and anxious to have
spared to them yet a part of their country, determined
to discard all ideas of further resistance, and throw
themselves for safety on the mercy of their conquerors.
To this end, the chief men, from the different tribes,
were daily arriving, asking for peace, and that their
lives might be spared.

General Jackson was not ignorant of the faithlessness
of these people, and how little confidence was to be re-

posed in the professions of an enemy, who, prompted
by fear, would be controlled by its influence, only whilst
those fears were continued. He well knew they had
been too severely chastised, for their friendship or promises to be implicitly relied on, and too much injured
not to feel a disposition to renew the conflict with the
first flattering hope that dawned. Too many difficulties
had been encountered, and too many dangers past, to
bring those savages to a sense of duty, to leave them now,
with no better security than mere professions. Some arrangement was necessary to be made, that should prove
lasting, and ensure certainty. None seemed better
calculated for these ends, than what had been already
announced; that those disposed to throw away the war
club, and renew their friendly relations with the United
States, should retire in the rear of the advance of the
army, and occupy the country about Fort Williams,
and to the east of the Coosa. The effect of such an
arrangement would be this; that the line of posts, already established, would cut them off from any communication with East Florida; and, by being placed
in that part of the nation, inhabited by the friendly Indians, whose fidelity was not doubted, the earliest intelligence would be had of their hostile intentions,
should any be manifested. The proposed conditions
were cheerfully accepted: and the different tribes set
out, to occupy a portion of their country, which alone
promised them protection and safety. Proctor, the
chief of the Owewoha war towns, to whom this promised security from danger had first been made, was
reported to be still at home, and to have abandoned
all intention of moving, in consequence of permission

CHAP. given by the United States' agent to the Creeks, for
V.   him and his warriors to remain at home. On receiving
1814. this information, the general despatched a messenger
       to him, with information, that whether he or the agent
       were to be obeyed, he might decide; but that he would
       treat as enemies all who did not immediately retire to
       the section of country he had pointed out. The chief
       of Owewoha found no difficulty in deciding the ques-
       tion, and prepared to retire where he had been previ-
       ously ordered.

91   Lieutenant colonel Gibson, who had been sent out,
       with a detachment of seven hundred and fifty men,
       returned, and reported, that he had proceeded a con-
       siderable distance down the Alabama river, and had
       destroyed several towns of the war party, but could
       gain no intelligence of a force being any where col-
       lected.

          By the establishment of Fort Jackson, a line of posts
       was now formed, from Tennessee and Georgia to the
       Alabama. The conduct of the Indians clearly mani-
       festing their desire for peace, nothing remained to be
       done, but to organize the different garrisons in such a
       manner, that, should any hostile intention be hereafter
       discovered, it might be crushed, before it should as-
       sume any very threatening aspect. What final steps
       should be taken, and what plans adopted, for perma-
       nent security, were to be deferred for the arrival of
       general Pinckney, who, being in the neighbourhood,
92   would, on the next day, reach Fort Jackson.

General   On the 20th, general Pinckney arrived, and assum-
Pinckney
arrives at ed, in person, the command of the army. The course
head quar-
ters.   pursued by Jackson, towards satisfying the Indians,

that to be peaceable was all that was required of them, meeting his approbation, and understanding that the chiefs and warriors of the nation were retiring, with their families, where they had been directed, he was satisfied hostilities would now cease. Independent of their professions, heretofore given, much of the property plundered at Fort Mimms, and along the frontiers, having been brought in and delivered, no doubt was entertained, but that all further national opposition would be withdrawn. There being no necessity, therefore, for maintaining an army longer in the field, orders were issued, on the 21st, for the troops from Tennessee to be marched home, and discharged; taking care, on the route, to leave a sufficient force, for the garrisoning and protection of the posts already established.

To troops who had been engaged in such hasty and fatiguing marches, who had been so much and so often exposed to hardships and dangers, and who had now, by their zealous exertions in the cause of their country, brought the war to a successful termination, and severely chastised the savages, for their unprovoked outrages upon their defenceless frontiers, it was a pleasure to retire to their homes, from the scenes of wretchedness they had witnessed, and from a contest, where every thing being performed, nothing remained to be done. It was a cheering reflection to them, that, their trials being over, they were retiring to their families and homes, and carrying with them that sweetest and happiest of all consolations, to a war-worn soldier's mind, that, in the trying and difficult situations in which they had been placed, they had acted with honour to themselves, and fidelity to their country.

Whilst these arrangements were making, the friendly Creeks were engaged in pursuing and destroying
their fugitive countrymen, with the most unrelenting
rigour.   To have been at the destruction of Fort
Mimms, was a ground of accusation against a warrior,
which at once placed him without the pale of mercy.
They viewed, or affected to view, this unwarranted and
unprovoked offence, with sentiments of deeper invete-
racy, than did even our own troops. Meeting a small
party, who were on their way to camp, to submit
themselves on the terms that had been previously offered, and understanding they had accompanied Weatherford, in his attack on this fort, they arrested their
progress, and put them to death.   Pursuing a course
of this kind, was well calculated to keep alive the timid
apprehensions of the Indians, and induce them to consider the proffered terms of peace as a stratagem, to
lure them into danger, and effect their destruction :
sensible of this, general Pinckney took immediate
steps to prevent its again recurring.

To see the people of the same nation, marshalled in
opposition to each other, is not a matter of surprise, on
the principles and practice of modern warfare, which
affects to prove it right, to seize on any circumstance,
that may operate prejudicially to an enemy ; but the
patriot, whose bosom swells with a love of country,
will ever view it with abhorrence : and although, from
necessity or policy, he may avail himself of the advantages afforded by such a circumstance, he can never either approve or justify it. Although the war had been
commenced, in opposition to the views and wishes of
the friendly party, yet it was their duty to have united.

Their entering the ranks of an invading army, and
fighting for the extermination of their people, and the
destruction of their nation, was a circumstance which
evidently marked them as traitors to their country,
and justly deserving the severest punishment.

In two hours after receiving general Pinckney's order, the western troops commenced their return march,
and reached Fort Williams, on the evening of the
24th. Immediate measures were adopted, for carrying into effect what had been ordered; to send out detachments, to assail and disperse any of the war party,
that might be found on their route, within striking
distance.

The East Tennessee troops, having a longer period
to serve, were, on that account, selected, to garrison the
different posts. General Doherty was directed to detail
from his brigade seven hundred and twenty-five men,
for the defence of those points, that an open communication might be preserved with Fort Jackson, and to
secure, more effectually, a peace, which, being supposed, for the present, to be founded in the fears and
distresses of the war party, was perhaps not altogether
securely and firmly established.

The general being about to separate from his army,
did not omit to declare to them the high sense he entertained of their conduct, and how well they had deserved of their country. " Within a few days," said
he, " you have annihilated the power of a nation, that,
for twenty years, has been the disturber of your peace.
Your vengeance has been glutted. Wherever these
infuriated allies of our arch enemy assembled for battle, you pursued and dispersed them. The rapidity

of your movements, and the brilliancy of your achievements, have corresponded with the valour by which
you have been animated.   The bravery you have displayed in the field of battle, and the uniform good conduct you have manifested in your encampment, and
on your line of march, will long be cherished in the
memory of your general, and will not be forgotten by
the country you have so materially benefited."

The constant and rapid movements of these troops for
the time they had been in service, had greatly exposed
them ; and although many hardships had been encountered, yet their duty had been performed without murmuring. A retrospect of the last month will show,
that more could scarcely have been done. Fort Williams was reached just four weeks from the time they
had left it, on the expedition to Tohopeka, where they
had met and conquered the enemy ; whence, returning, not with a view to obtain rest, but to recruit the
exhausted state of their provisions, in one week was
this same army on the way to Hoithlewalee, where,
95 supported in their hopes by their prophets, was collected the strength of the nation ; and where, but for
the absence of the Georgia army, they would have
been captured or destroyed, the war ended, and all
apprehension of future resistance quieted. To this
point did they urge forward, over mountains, and
through torrents of continual rain, that rendered the
route almost impassable ; and reached and destroyed,
on the 14th, a town which the inspired men of the nation
had declared was consecrated, and on which no white
man was ever to tread with impunity. On the 17th,
they are found at the confluence of the Coosa and Tal-

lapoosa, treading still their consecrated soil, and driving the panic-struck savages before them; and again,
on the 24th, are at Fort Williams, retiring to their
homes, from the labours they had encountered, and the
conquests they had gained. In such celerity of movement, is to be found the cause, that secured to Jackson and his army, the uniform successes they obtained.
So rapid were his marches, that not unfrequently was
he in the neighbourhood of the enemy, before they
had received any intelligence of his approach; in addition to this, was attached to him the quality, that few
generals ever possessed in a higher degree, of inspiring
firmness in his ranks, and making even cowards brave.
An entire confidence of success, a full assurance of
victory, and a fearlessness and disregard of danger,
were the feelings displayed by himself in all difficult
situations, and those feelings he possessed the happy
faculty of diffusing through his army.

Whether any of the hostile party were still on the
Cohawba, or had fled for safety to the British and Spaniards at Pensacola, was uncertain. To ascertain this
fact,—to disperse them, and destroy their villages, general Johnston was despatched, at the head of five hundred men, with orders to proceed along this river, to
its head branches, effect the object so far as it was
practicable, and re-unite with the main army at Deposit. Jackson reported to general Pinckney, that his
orders had been complied with; that four hundred
troops had been detailed for the protection of Fort
Williams, and that he would leave at the other points,
a force proportioned to their exposed situations. "The
remainder of my troops," he continues, "I shall march

to Tennessee, where I shall discharge them : after which, I shall no longer consider myself accountable for the manner in which the posts may be defended, or the line of communication kept open ;—happy that the time for which I offered my services to my government, and the duties they assigned me to perform, will have terminated together."

The army proceeded on its march, and crossing Tennessee river, reached Camp Blount, near Fayetteville, where they were discharged from further service. Johnston, who had previously fallen in, had destroyed some of the enemy's towns; but had learned nothing of a force being any where embodied along the route he had taken.

On parting from his troops, the general again brought before them the recollection he retained of their faithful and gallant conduct, and the patience with which they had borne the privations and hardships of war. On his return, wherever he passed, the plaudits of the people were liberally bestowed. The ardent zeal he had manifested in the service of his country, the difficulties he had surmounted, and the favourable issue, which, by his exertions, had been given to a contest, that had kept alive the anxieties and fears of the frontier settlers, excited a general gratitude and admiration; all were ready to evince the high sense they entertained, of the success with which every effort had been crowned, and with one accord united in reverence for him, who, by his zealous exertions, and able management, had so greatly contributed to the safety of the country.

CHAPTER VI.

Jackson is appointed a major general, in the service of the
United States.—Is directed to open a negotiation with the
Indians.—Speech of the Big Warrior, a chief of the nation.
—Concludes a treaty with the Creek Indians.—His views
against Pensacola and East Florida.—General Armstrong's
letter.—The Spanish governor is called on for an explanation of his conduct.—His answer.—The adjutant general
is despatched to Tennessee, to raise volunteers.—Jackson
sets out for Mobile.—Orders the Tennessee troops to advance to his assistance.

———

A WAR, from which much greater and more serious injuries had been apprehended, was thus happily
terminated. Although many valuable lives were
lost in the contest, yet were they far less than might
have been expected, in contending with an enemy,
whose wrath knew no bounds, and whose cruelty was
insatiate. To the rapidity with which an army had
been collected, and pushed into the heart of their country, was owing the circumstance that the frontiers were
not stained with the blood of the settlers. Though
humanity may weep over the misfortunes of this
people, and regret that they were sunk in such ir-
retrievable woes, yet there is a consolation left; that if
it be a crime, it is not chargeable on the American
government. Towards them had been exercised every
forbearance. For more than twenty years had the

CHAP. 96
VI.

1814.

CHAP. western people been the victims of their unrelenting
VI. cruelties; and many a parent lives, at this day, whose
1814. recollection treasures a child, that bled beneath their
murderous hands. Cold Water, on the Tennessee,
was long the den of these savages, whence they made
their inroads, and, by their inhuman butcheries, kept
the frontier inhabitants in perpetual alarm. An expedition, acting without the consent of the government,
but with a view to that security their own situation so
much demanded, as early as the year 1787, under general Robertson, made a descent on this settlement,
and destroyed it. This active and resolute measure
ensured them a tranquillity, to which they had hitherto
been strangers. Those who escaped, retired to the
Black Warrior, carrying with them an additional spirit
of revenge, which occasionally displayed itself, in the
murder of our citizens, whenever a favourable opportunity occurred; until the winter of 1813, when their
97 towns were again assailed and destroyed.

The war, in which the United States were engaged
with Great Britain, afforded them, as they believed, a
safe opportunity to satiate again their angry passions.
In addition to former animosities retained, British
emissaries had been among them, engaged to excite
and encourage them to opposition. Arms and ammunition, from Pensacola, having been liberally furnished,
and a belief strongly inspired, that the Americans could
be driven off, and the lands they possessed re-gained by
the Indians, they at once resolved upon the course they
would pursue. The dreadful and cruel assault made
98 on the settlement of Tensaw, was the first intelligence
afforded, of the lengths which they had determined to

go. The security of the frontiers, requiring that efficient measures should be taken to defend them, it was
time for the government to abandon that moderation
and forbearance they had hitherto practised towards
these tribes. The legislature of Tennessee, being in
session at the time, with a promptness highly honourable, called out the forces of the state, without giving
the general government information of the threatened
danger, and waiting the result. To protect an extensive country, by erecting garrisons, and relying on
them for defence, did not appear to Jackson a course
likely to assure its object. He determined, with the
troops he could collect on so sudden an emergency, to
carry the war to their very doors; and, by giving them
employment at home, divert them from their plans,
and force them to adopt measures of defence. Urging
the contractors, therefore, to be diligent in the discharge
of their duties, and to forward supplies, with all possible haste, he took a position at Fort Strother, in the
enemy's country. The battle of Talladega, which
shortly afterwards followed, gave a severe check,
induced them to believe they were contending with a
different kind of people from what they had expected,
and might have convinced them, too, that the promised safety, offered by their prophets, through their
spells and incantations, was mere mockery and non-
sense : yet so deluded were they, and so confidently
believing in the supernatural powers of these men, that
they were ready to attribute a want of success to
circumstances, over which these inspired prophets
could, in future, claim control : but at length, when
it was discovered that the prophets themselves did

CHAP. not escape that fatality which attended their warriors
VI. in battle, they began to think, either that they had
1814. never been commissioned, or that the *Great Spirit*,
for some unknown cause, had become offended, and
99 withdrawn his confidence.

Had Jackson been enabled, at this time, to have
prosecuted the campaign, it might have had a much
earlier conclusion; but although he had, at the first
onset, obtained advantages, from which much benefit
might have arisen, yet, from the want of proper exertions on the part of the contractors, he was halted, and
compelled to retrace his steps back to Fort Strother.
From the delays unavoidably met with here, flowed
those grievances which gave a check to further operations. The winter, against which his troops were
illy provided, was fast approaching; hardships, and
hunger, which was already pressing, with a long and
fatiguing campaign in prospect, presenting a thousand
imaginary difficulties, excited discontents, which presently broke out into open mutiny; and although the
intention of the volunteers, to desert the service, and
retire home, was prevented, by the stern and resolute
conduct of their general, yet they were thereby unfitted for the duties of the field, because entire confidence
was no longer to be reposed. To venture with such
troops, who, whilst the tomahawk and scalping knife
were uplifted, to wreak vengeance on their devoted
frontiers, were coolly construing the effect and meaning
of laws, was too unsafe a reliance, for a commander,
whose first object was to impress on the minds of the
savages, the determination and strength of the government he represented. It was adventuring too largely;

for, should defeat result, the difficulty of drawing
a new army to the field, would be increased, and
that confidence in troops, so essential to complete success, would thereby be lost.   It was believed to be a
safer course, to permit them to depart, and await the
arrival of another force.   These circumstances had a
tendency to encourage the Indians, and protract the
war.   Had the volunteers proceeded with the animation and bravery which characterized them in the battle they had just fought, they would have gradually acquired a confidence, which would have rendered them
an overmatch for Indian valour and cunning ; whilst by
one further successful effort, they might have dispirited
the enemy, and ended the campaign.   But the arrival
of a different description of troops, and the confusion
into which they were thrown at the battle of Enotichopco, had encouraged the savages, and induced
them to think the contest by no means a hazardous
one.   That despondency, which had resulted from
their previous defeats, was from this moment forgotten ; and, again inspirited, they looked to the accomplishment of their object, with hopes of certainty even
greater than before.   Perhaps, however, it is well that
events transpired in the way they did.   Had peace
been restored in consequence of early fears excited, it
might have lasted only until a favourable opportunity
occurred of again breaking it ; but the war having continued, until the hopes, the strength, and spirit of the
nation were exhausted, nothing serious is now to be
apprehended, from any hostile disposition that may
hereafter be manifested.   Other advantages will also
result.   The uniform and uninterrupted successes,

obtained over them, in all our battles, will impress the minds of the savages in our limits, with a higher reverence for the character of our nation, than they have hitherto indulged; give protection to our citizens; and ensure that security to the government, which the mildness it has practised, and the tribute it has constantly given them for their *peace*, has, heretofore, never been able to effect; they will tend to destroy the influence held over them by other nations; and bring them to a conviction, that the United States is the only power, whose hostility they should fear, or whose friendship they should prize.

It was now eight months since general Jackson had left home, to arrest the progress of the Indian war; during most of which time, he had been in a situation of bodily infirmity, that would have directed a prudent man to his bed, instead of the field. During this period, he had never seen his family, or been absent from the army longer than to visit Deposit, and arrange with his contractors some certain plan to guard against a future failure of supplies. His health was still delicate, and rendered retirement essential to its restoration; but his uniformly successful and good conduct, had brought him too conspicuously before the public, for any other sentiment to be indulged, than that he should be placed, with an important command, in the service of the United States.

The resignation of general Hampton, enabled the government, in a short time, to afford him an evidence of the respect it entertained for his services and character. A notice of his appointment as brigadier and brevet major general, was forwarded on the 22d of

May, from the war department. General Harrison having, about this time, for some cause, become disgusted with the conduct of the government towards him, had refused to be longer considered one of her military actors; to supply which vacancy, a commis- sion of major general was immediately forwarded to Jackson.

100

The contest with the Indians being ended; the first and principal object of the government was, to enter into some definitive arrangement, which should deprive of success, any effort that might hereafter be made, by other powers, to enlist these savages in their wars. None was so well calculated to answer this end, as that of restricting their limits, so as to cut off their communication with British and Spanish agents, in 101 East Florida.

The citizens of Tennessee, learning that commissioners were appointed for the accomplishment of this purpose; and believing themselves as much, or more interested than others, in having such a disposition made, as should give complete security to their borders, petitioned the government that one might be selected from their state. The efforts they had made to effect what had been done; and the interests they had involved, were considerations that the president did not scruple to admit. He accordingly associated general Jackson in the mission, and again required his 102 services for the establishment of a peace, on such terms as should promise to be permanent. The circumstance of colonel Hawkins being appointed, was an additional reason, why any solicitude had been felt, or any petition forwarded. He may have been deceived.

and may have founded his opinions upon data presumed to be correct; but his continual declarations, that
the Creek Indians intended a rigid adherence to their
treaties, at the very moment they were planning their
murderous schemes against the frontiers, led the western people to fear, that his agency had lasted too long,
to hope that he would steadily pursue that course,
which the safety and interest of the country required.

On the 10th of July, the general, with a small reti-
nue, reached the Alabama; and on the 10th of August
succeeded in procuring the execution of a treaty, in
which the Indians pledged themselves, no more to list-
en to foreign emissaries,—to hold no communication
with British or Spanish garrisons; guaranteed to the
United States, the right of erecting military posts in
their country, and a free navigation of all their waters.
They stipulated further, that they would suffer no agent
or trader to pass among them, or hold any kind of
commerce or intercourse with their nation, unless specially deriving his authority from the president of the
United States.

United
States
open a ne-
gotiation
with the
Indians.

To settle the boundary, defining the extent of territory to be secured to the Creeks, and that which they
would be required to surrender, was attended with
some difficulty; and was increased by the intrigues of
the Cherokee nation, who sought to obtain from them,
such an acknowledgment of their lines, as would give
them a considerable portion of country, never attached
to their claim. The Creeks had heretofore permitted
this tribe to extend its settlements as low down the
Coosa as the mouth of Wills' creek. It was insisted,
now, in private caucus, that as they were about to sur-

103
104

render all their country, lying on Tennessee river, they CHAP.
should, previously to signing the treaty, acknowledge VI.
the extension of the Cherokee boundary, which would 1814.
secure their claim against that of the United States.
The only reply obtained from the Creeks, was, that
they could not lie, by admitting what did not in reality
exist.

The United States might, without violence to those
feelings benevolence excites, have demanded the whole
country, and either have treated the Indians as vassals,
or admitted them into their national compact, with such
rights of citizenship, as, from their peculiar habits of
life, they were calculated safely to use and enjoy ; but
the humane and generous policy, which had been se-
dulously maintained, in all transactions with the savages, within their limits, induced the government to require, in the cession, only such portion of their country as should bar every avenue to foreign intrigue, and
give additional strength to those sections of the union,
which, from their limited extent of territory, and consequent limited population, were unable to afford sufficient supplies, for the subsistence of an army, or to
give a partial check to the inroads of an invading enemy. The lines defined by the treaty were so arranged, as fully to meet these objects. Sufficient territory was acquired on the south, to give security to the
Mobile settlements, and western borders of Georgia,
which had often felt the stroke of Indian vengeance
and cruelty ; while, at the same time was effected, the
important purpose of separating them from the Seminole tribes, and our unfriendly neighbours in East
Florida. To Madison county, and the frontiers of Ten-

nessee, an assurance of safety was given, by the settlements which would be afforded on the lands stretching along the Tennessee river; whilst the extent of the cession west of the Coosa, would cut off all communication with the Chickasaws and Choctaws, and prevent, in future, the passage of those emissaries from the north-western tribes, who, during the present war, had so industriously fomented the discontents of the Creeks, and excited them to hostility. It is a happy consideration, that whilst these advantages were obtained, no material injury was done those vanquished people. Their country, extensive as it was, presented no inducements to the hunters, which could, as heretofore, be relied on with certainty; and, for all the purposes of agriculture, the part preserved to them was more than sufficient, for fifty times the population it contained. It may appear plausible in theory, but practice will always disprove the idea, that the civilization of Indians can be effected, whilst, scattered through an immense wilderness, they are left to pursue their wandering habits of life. Inured to their own manners, from the earliest period, it certainly would not answer to innovate at once upon their ancient customs; but, were their extensive wilds gradually reduced, so, in proportion, would the benefits resulting from hunting, and wandering through the forest, subside, until at last, necessity would prompt them to industry and agriculture, as the only certain and lasting means of support.

Unwilling to resort to any other mode of living, than that to which they had been always accustomed; and satisfied that their means of subsistence would be lost

in the surrender of their country, they remained obstinately opposed to any arrangement. Before being finally acted upon, the treaty was fully debated in council, and the voice of the nation decided against it.
Jackson had already submitted the views of his government, and now met them in council, to learn their
determination. He was answered by the Big Warrior,
a friendly chief, and one of their first orators, who declared the reluctance they felt, in yielding to the demand, from a conviction of the consequences involved,
and the distresses it must inevitably bring upon them.
The firm and dignified eloquence of this untutored ora-
tor, evinced a nerve and force of expression, that might
not have passed unnoticed, before a more highly polished assembly : the conclusion of his speech is giv-
en, for the satisfaction of such as can mark the bold
display of savage genius, and admire it when discovered. Having unfolded the causes that produced the
war, and admitted that they had been preserved alone
by the army which had hastened to their assistance;
he urged, that although, in justice, it might be required of them, to defray the expenses incurred, by the
transfer of a part of their country, yet the demand was
premature, because the war party was not conquered :
they had only fled away, and might yet return. He
portrayed the habits of the Indians, and how seriously
they would be affected by the required surrender; and
thus concluded :

" The president, our father, advises us to honesty
and fairness, and promises that justice shall be done :
I hope and trust it will be! I made this war, which
has proved so fatal to my country, that the treaty en-

tered into, a long time ago, with father Washington, might not be broken. To his friendly arm I hold fast. I will never break that chain of friendship we made together, and which bound us to stand to the United States. He was a father to the Muscoga people; and not only to them, but to all the people beneath the sun. His talk I now hold in my hand. There sits the agent he sent among us. Never has he broken the treaty. He has lived with us a long time. He has seen our children born, who now have children. By his direction, cloth was wove, and clothes were made, and spread through our country; but the red sticks came, and destroyed all,—we have none now. Hard is our situation, and you ought to consider it. I state what all the nation knows : nothing will I keep secret.

" There is the Little Warrior, whom colonel Hawkins knows. While we were giving satisfaction for the murders that had been committed, he proved a mischief-maker; he went to the British on the lakes; he came back, and brought a package to the frontiers, which increased the murders here. This conduct has already made the war party to suffer greatly : but, although almost destroyed, they will not yet open their eyes, but are still led away by the British at Pensacola. Not so with us : we were rational, and had our senses —we yet are so. In the war of the revolution, our father beyond the waters, encouraged us to join him, and we did so. We had no sense then. The promises he made were never kept. We were young and foolish, and fought with him. The British can no more persuade us to do wrong : they have de-

ceived us once, and can deceive us no more. You
are two great people. If you go to war, we will
have no concern in it; for we are not able to fight.
We wish to be at peace with every nation. If they
offer me arms, I will say to them, You put me in
danger, to war against a people born in our own land.
They shall never force us into danger. You shall never see that our chiefs are boys in council, who will be
forced to do any thing. I talk thus, knowing that father Washington advised us never to interfere in wars.
He told us that those in peace were the happiest people. He told us that if an enemy attacked him, he
had warriors enough, and did not wish his red children
to help him. If the British advise us to any thing, I
will tell you,—not hide it from you. If they say we
must fight, I will tell them, No!"

The war party not being entirely subdued, was but
a pretext to avoid the demand; presuming that if the
council should break up, without any thing being definitely done, they might, in part, or perhaps altogether,
avoid what was now required; but the inflexibility of
the person with whom they were treating, evinced to
them, that however just and well-founded might be
their objections, the policy under which he acted was
too clearly defined, for an abandonment of his demand
to be at all calculated upon. Shelocta, one of their
chiefs, who had united with our troops, at the commencement of the war; who had marched and fought
with them in all their battles; and had attached to
himself strongly the confidence of the commanding
general, now addressed him. He told him of the regard he had ever felt for his white brothers, and with

what zeal he had exerted himself to preserve peace, and keep in friendship with them; when his efforts had failed, he had taken up arms against his own country, and fought against his own people; that he was not opposed to yielding the lands lying on the Alabama, which would answer the purpose of cutting off any intercourse with the Spaniards; but the country west of the Coosa, he wished to be preserved to the nation. To effect this, he appealed to the feelings of Jackson; told him of the dangers they had passed together; and of his faithfulness to him, in the trying scenes through which they had gone.

There were, indeed, none whose voice ought sooner to have been heard than Shelocta's. None had rendered greater services, and none had been more faithful. He had claims, growing out of his fidelity, that few others had: but his wishes were so much at variance with what Jackson considered the interest of his country required, that he was answered without hesitation. " You know," said he, " that the part you desire to retain is that through which the intruders and mischief-makers from the lakes reached you, and urged your nation to those acts of violence, that have involved your people in wretchedness, and your country in ruin. Through it leads the path Tecumseh trod, when he came to visit you : that path must be stopped. Until this be done, your nation cannot expect happiness, nor mine security. I have already told you the reasons for demanding it : they are such as ought not,—cannot be departed from. This evening must determine whether or not you are disposed to become friendly. Your rejecting the treaty will show you to

be the enemies of the United States,—enemies even
to yourselves." He admitted it to be true, that the war was not ended, but that this was an additional reason why the cession should be made ; that then a line would be drawn, by which his soldiers would be able to distinguish and know their friends. " When our armies," continued he, " came here, the hostile party had even stripped you of your country : we re-took it, and now offer it to you ;—theirs we propose to retain. Those who are disposed to give effect to the treaty, will sign it. They will be within our ter-ritory ; will be protected and fed ; and no enemy of theirs or ours shall molest them. Those who are op-posed to it shall have leave to retire to Pensacola. Here is the paper : take it, and show the president who are his friends. Consult, and this evening let me know who will sign it, and who will not. I do not wish, nor will I attempt, to force any of you ;—act as you think proper."

They proceeded to deliberate and re-examine the course they should pursue, which terminated in their assent to the treaty, and the extension of those advan-tages that had been insisted on.*

* It was agreed that the line should begin where the Che-rokee southern boundary crossed the Coosa, to run down that river to Woe-tum-ka, or the Big Falls, and thence eastwardly to Georgia. East and north of this line, containing upwards of one hundred and fifty thousand square miles, remained to the Indians. West and south was secured to the United States. There are not many nations in the world, that would have acted with such justice and lenity towards a vanquished people. The country had been conquered and won, at con-

CHAP.   Every attention had been given, during the nego-
VI.   tiation, to impress on the minds of the savages the

1814.

106   siderable expense, and loss.   Few governments, under such
circumstances, would have done less than to have taken what
best suited their convenience, without attempting to bargain
at all upon the subject; more especially when it occupied a
space of more than two hundred miles, through which the
western people, seeking a market on the ocean, were under
the necessity of passing, on their return home; and where,
for the want of accommodation, numerous exposures and
hardships were encountered.   Scarcely, however, had the
treaty been entered into, when every tribe in the neighbourhood, the Choctaws, Chickasaws, and Cherokees, asserted
their claims, each, to a part of the cession, which frittered it
down to a mere nothing.   The latter set up a title to the
whole extent, lying along the Tennessee river, and succeeded
in having it recognized by the government.   The other two,
gathering confidence from their success, came forward, and
were no less fortunate.   The United States, to remove every
ground of complaint, opened a negotiation with these Indians,
and purchased their interest at the price that was demanded.
When it is considered that these claims were set up by inconsiderable clans, which might, at a word, have been hushed to
silence, it affords the highest eulogy on the justice and mag-
nanimity of our government, that, instead of attempting any
exercise of its power, for the furtherance of its views, their
complaints were heard, and peaceably quieted, by paying them
the equivalent they required.

The liberality of the act is more apparent, when it is taken
into consideration, that the claim of the Creek Indians was
unquestionably the best.   The coming of the other tribes to
this section of country can be traced by Indian traditional
history.   " Some came from the west, beyond the great river
Mississippi; others from the north;" but the same record
knows nothing of the Creeks.   So far back as it extends, they
are known as the most numerous and warlike of the southern

necessity of their remaining in friendship; for, although CHAP.
all apprehensions of their acting in concert, as a na- VI.
tion, had subsided, yet it was important to leave their 1814.
minds favourably impressed, lest the wandering fugitives, scattered in considerable numbers towards the
Escambia and Pensacola, might, by continuing hostile, associate with them more of their countrymen,—
attach themselves to the British, should they appear in
the south, aid them by their numbers, and pilot them
through the country.

This retreat of the savages, in East Florida, was

tribes, and are spoken of as coming out of the ground. Possession, with Indians, is the only evidence of title. Their
country, always defined by natural objects, belongs to the
next occupant, when once they have abandoned it. The tradition of their origin, reaching to a period long anterior to the
time when other tribes settled on their borders, proves them
to have been the first proprietors of the soil: the country was
never abandoned by them: being the most warlike and powerful, it has never been wrested from them by conquest: the
conclusion follows, that they must be still the owners, and
that other tribes, as they allege, have acquired a residence
only through their permission and indulgence. If power, this
improvement on the principles of national law, and legitimate
rule of modern times, had been made the appeal, between a
government strong as the United States, and such inconsiderable Indian hordes, there can be no question, as to the
manner the difference might have been settled : yet the administration, rather than leave themselves open even to suspicion, preferred and obtained the title of these people, at an
expense of at least three hundred and fifty thousand dollars.
Let other nations, if they can, produce an act of theirs, which,
for justice and liberality, can be compared with this.

always looked upon as a place, whence the United States might apprehend serious difficulties to arise. There was no doubt but that the British, through this channel, with the aid of the governor, had protected the Indians, and supplied them with arms and ammunition; nor was it less certain, but that, through their art and address, they had been excited to the outrages which had been heretofore committed. It was an idea entertained by Jackson, at the commencement of the Creek war, that the proper and best mode of procedure would be to push his army through the nation; gain this den, where vegetated so many evils; and, by holding it, effectually cut off their intercourse, and means of encouraging the war: but the unexpected difficulties which we have before noticed, had suppressed the execution of his well-digested plans, and left him to pursue his course as circumstances, and the obstacles met with, would permit. The assistance which, during the war, had been continually afforded these people, from Pensacola, induced him, once more, to turn his attention there; and he now strongly urged on government the propriety of attacking and breaking down this strong hold, whence so many evils had already flowed, and whence greater ones were yet to be expected. His busy mind, actively engaged, while employed in settling all differences at Fort Jackson, was seeking, through every channel that could afford it, information as to the designs of the British against the southern parts of the Union. The idea had been prevalent, and was generally indulged, that, so soon as the severity of approaching winter should put a stop

to active operations on the Canada frontier, with all CHAP.
their disposable force, they would turn their attention VI.
against the southern states, and there attempt to gain
some decisive advantage. New Orleans, with one con- 1814.
sent, was fixed upon as the point that most probably
would be assailed. The circumstance of there being so
many there, who had never been thought to entertain
any well-founded regard for the country in which they
lived, together with a large black population, which it
was feared might be excited to insurrection and massacre, were reasons which strongly led to this conclusion.

General Jackson having understood, that that comfort and aid, which had been already so liberally extended, was still afforded by the Spanish governor to
the hostile Indians, who had fled from the ravages of
the Creek war, cherished the belief that his conduct
was such as deservedly to exclude him from that pro- Views
tection to which, under other circumstances, he would against
be entitled, from the professed neutrality of Spain. At Pensacola
all events, if the improper acts of the Spanish agents
would not authorize the American government openly
to redress herself for the unprovoked injuries she had
received, they were such, he believed, as would justify
any course that had for its object the putting them
down, and arresting their continuance. In this point
of view he had already considered it, when, on his way
to the Alabama, he received certain information, that
about three hundred English troops had landed; were
fortifying at the mouth of the Apalachicola; and were
endeavouring to excite the Indians to war. No time
was lost, in giving the government notice of what

was passing, and the course by him deemed most advisable to be pursued. The advantages to be secured by the possession of Pensacola, he had frequently urged. Whether it was that the government beheld things in a different point of view, or, being at peace with Spain, was willing to encounter partial inconveniences, rather than add her to the number of our enemies, no order to that effect was yet given. In detailing to the secretary of war what had been communicated to him, he remarks : " If the hostile Creeks have taken refuge in Florida, and are there fed, clothed, and protected ; if the British have landed a large force, munitions of war, and are fortifying and stirring up the savages ; will you only say to me, raise a few hundred militia, which can be quickly done, and with such regular force as can be conveniently collected, make a descent upon Pensacola, and reduce it? If so, I promise you, the war in the south shall have a speedy termination, and English influence be for ever destroyed with the savages in this quarter."

Notwithstanding this and other applications to the government, he was still unable to obtain an answer : nothing was returned, that could be construed into a permission of, or command to abstain from, the execution of his project. At length, on the 17th of January, 1815, after the British army had been repulsed at New Orleans, and the descent on East Florida almost forgotten, through the post office department, dated the 18th of July, 1814, he received the following letter from general Armstrong, the then secretary at war :

General Armstrong's letter.

" The case you put is a very strong one : and if all the circumstances stated by you unite, the conclusion is irresistible. It becomes our duty to carry our arms where we find our enemies. It is believed, and I am so directed by the president to say, that there is a dis- position on the part of the Spanish government, not to break with the United States, nor to encourage any conduct on the part of her subordinate agents, having a tendency to such rupture. We must, therefore, in this case, be careful to ascertain facts, and even to distinguish what, on the part of the Spanish authorities, may be the effect of menace and compulsion, or of their choice and policy : the result of this inquiry must govern. If they admit, feed, arm, and co-operate with the British and hostile Indians, we must strike on the broad principle of self-preservation :—under other and different circumstances, we must forbear."

That this state of things did actually exist; that the British were favourably received, and every assistance necessary to a continuance of hostilities extended to the Indians, the government had been already appriz ed, by the frequent communications made to them on the subject. Had this letter reached him in time, it would have at once determined general Jackson on the course to be pursued, and on the execution of his design : how it was so long delayed we know not, nor shall we pretend to conjecture. We would, however, recommend in all cases, where a measure is to be proceeded in, either from necessity, or a well-founded apprehension of its propriety, that the government should adopt it without fear or trembling, or a regard to the consequences involved; nor leave to be determined by the success or failure of the design, whether an officer acting upon his own responsibility, and for the good of his country, shall become the subject of commendation or reproof.

His first attention, on arriving at Fort Jackson, had been directed to a subject, which he believed to be of greater importance than making treaties;—to establish some plan, by which he might be constantly advised, during his stay, of those schemes that were agitating in the south: believing that every passing event might be readily obtained through the Indians, who could go among the British, without in the least exciting suspicion: he had required colonel Hawkins to procure some who were confidential, and might be certainly relied on, to proceed to Deer island, and return as early as they could obtain correct information of the strength, views, and situation of the enemy. In about fifteen days they came back, confirming the statement, that a considerable English force had arrived, and was then in the bay of St. Rose; that muskets and ammunition had been given to the Indians, and runners despatched to the different tribes, to invite them to the coast.

Satisfied that such permissions, by a neutral power, were too grievous to be borne, he addressed a letter to the governor of Pensacola, and assured him he had understood, that every protection and assistance was furnished the enemies of the United States, within his territory; requested him to state whether or not the fact were so, and to surrender to him such of the chiefs of the hostile Indians, as were with him. "I rely," continued he, "on the existing friendship of Spain, and that neutrality which she should observe, as authority for the demand I make." The governor's answer, which shortly afterwards was received, evinc-

ed nothing of that conciliatory temper which was looked for, and left no hope of procuring any other redress,
than that which might be obtained through his fears.
This, however, was a matter which required to be managed with great caution. Spain and the United States
were at peace; to reduce any part of her territory, and
take possession of it, in exclusion of her authority,
might be construed such an aggression, as to induce
her into the war. On the other hand, to suffer her,
with open arms, to receive our enemies, and permit
them to make every preparation within her ports, for
invading and attacking our country, were outrages too
monstrous to be borne, and should, in the opinion of
Jackson, be remedied, let the consequences in prospec-
tive be what they might. Although these things had
been earnestly pressed upon the consideration of the
war department, no answer to his repeated solicitations
on the subject, had been received. On his own responsibility, to advance in the execution of a measure,
which involved so much, when his government was,
and had for some time, been in possession of all the
circumstances, was risking too much. Yet, were it
delayed longer, every day might give Pensacola additional strength, and increase the danger attendant on
its reduction. Undetermined, under considerations
like these, he resolved upon another expedient,—to
despatch a messenger, to lay open to the governor the
ground of his complaint,—to obtain from him a declaration of his intention, as regarded the course he meant
to adopt, and pursue,—and to ascertain whether he designed to make subsisting treaties between the two na-

tions, the basis of his conduct, or to pursue a strange and concealed course, which, under the garb of pretended friendship, cloaked all the realities of war. The propriety of delivering up the hostile Indians, who were with him, to atone for the violation of existing treaties, and the rights of humanity, was again pressed and solicited.

A reply was not concluded on, by the governor, for some time; owing to a very considerable doubt that harassed his mind, whether it would not be more proper to return it without an answer, "in imitation of the conduct of general Flournoy, acting in conformity to the orders of Mr. Madison." But, having considered the matter, quite maturely and deliberately, he at length came to the conclusion, to wave the example set him by the president, and act in obedience to those "high and generous feelings, peculiar to the Spanish character."

108

Letter of
governor
Gonzalez
Manre-
quez.

In answer to the request, that the hostile Indians should be delivered up, he denies that they were with him, "at that time," or that he could, on the ground of hospitality, refuse them assistance, at a moment when their distresses were so great : nor could he surrender them, as he believed, without acting in open violation of the laws of nations,—laws, to which his sovereign had ever strictly adhered, and of which he had already afforded the United States abundant evidence, when he omitted to demand of them "the traitors, insurgents, incendiaries, and assassins of his chiefs, namely, Guiterres, Toledo, and many others, whom the American government protected, and maintained

in committing hostilities, in fomenting the revolution, CHAP.
and in lighting up the flames of discord in the internal VI.
provinces of the kingdom of Mexico."

1814.

To the inquiry, why the English had been suffered
to land in his province arms and ammunition, with a
view of encouraging the Indians to acts of hostility, he
proceeded, with his same " national characteristic," and
asked if the United States were ignorant, that at the
conquest of Florida, there was a treaty between Great
Britain and the Creek Indians, and whether they did
not know, that it still existed between Spain and those
tribes? " But," continued he, " turn your eyes to the
island of Barrataria, and you will there perceive, that
within the very territory of the United States, pirates
are sheltered and protected, with the manifest design
of committing hostilities by sea, upon the merchant
vessels of Spain; and with such scandalous notoriety,
that the cargoes of our vessels, taken by them, have
been sold in Louisiana."

It is difficult to discover, by what system of logic it
was, that governor Manrequez could trace any kind of
analogy, between the United States affording to a few
of the patriots of South America, an asylum from the
chains, oppressions, and persecutions, that were threatened to be imposed on them by Spanish tyranny; and
his permitting within his limits, comfort, aid, and assistance, to be given the savages, that they might be
better enabled to indulge in cruelty towards us. Nor
can it be perceived, how the piracies of Lafite and his
party, at Barrataria, and the successful smuggling
which brought their plunder into port, in open defiance of the law, could operate as a sufficient pretext

c c

for giving protection and indulgence, to an enemy entering his confines, and continuing there, with the avowed intention of waging war against a power, with which Spain professed to be in friendship; and at the very time, too, she claimed to be neutral. Nor can we see the force of the argument, that because England had a treaty with the Creek Indians, which afterwards devolved to Spain, the agents of his Catholic majesty were, in consequence, justified in protecting the savages in their murders, or assisting covertly, as they did, in the war against us : how the conclusions were arrived at, we will leave with the governor to decide, at some moment, when, relieved from those high and honourable feelings, " peculiar to the Spanish character," reason may re-assert her empiry over him, and point the manner he was enabled to work out his strange results.

The governor, however, had taken his ground without suffering his reflections to go to the full extent. He had placed arms in the hands of the savages, " for the purposes of self-defence ;" many of them were flocking down,—more were yet expected. The British had already landed a partial force, and a greater one was shortly looked for. Against this certain and expected strength, added to what his own resources could supply, he believed an American general would not venture to advance. These considerations had led him to assume his lofty tone,—to arraign the conduct of the United States in extinguishing the Indian title on the Alabama,—in disregarding and violating their treaties, and to point out the danger to which the restoration of peace in Europe might shortly expose them. As yet he was ignorant of the energy of the man already near his borders, and who, to march against and break down his fancied security, did not desire to be ordered, but only to be apprized by his country that it might be done. Jackson determined again to address him, and to exhibit fully the grounds of accusation and complaint against him, in a style at least as courtly as his own.

" Were I clothed," he remarks, " with diplomatic powers, for the purpose of discussing the topics em- Letter to the go- braced in the wide range of injuries of which you vernor of complain, and which have long since been adjusted, I Pensaco-la. could easily demonstrate that the United States have been always faithful to their treaties, steadfast in their friendships, nor have ever claimed any thing that was not warranted by justice. They have endured many insults from the governors and other officers of Spain, which, if sanctioned by their sovereign, amounted to acts of war, without any previous declaration on the subject. They have excited the savages to war, and afforded them the means of waging it : the property of our citizens has been captured at sea, and if compensa- tion has not been refused, it has at least been withheld. But as no such powers have been delegated to me, I shall not assume them, but leave them to the represent- atives of our respective governments.

" I have the honour of being entrusted with the command of this district. Charged with its protec- tion, and the safety of its citizens, I feel my ability to discharge the task, and trust your excellency will al- ways find me ready and willing to go forward, in the performance of that duty, whenever circumstances

CHAP.
VI.

1814.

shall render it necessary. I agree with you, perfectly, that candour and polite language should, at all times, characterize the communications between the officers of friendly sovereignties; and I assert, without the fear of contradiction, that my former letters were couched in terms the most respectful and unexceptionable. I only requested, and did not demand, as you have asserted, the ringleaders of the Creek confederacy, who had taken refuge in your town, and who had violated all laws, moral, civil, and divine. This I had a right to do, from the treaty which I sent you, and which I now again enclose, with a request that you will change your translation; believing, as I do, that your former one was wrong, and has deceived you. What kind of an answer you returned, a reference to your letter will explain. The whole of it breathed nothing but hostility, grounded upon assumed facts, and false charges, and entirely evading the inquiries that had been made.

" I can but express my astonishment at your protest against the cession on the Alabama, lying within the acknowledged jurisdiction of the United States, and which has been ratified, in due form, by the principal chiefs and warriors of the nation. But my astonishment subsides, when, on comparing it, I find it upon a par with the rest of your letter and conduct; taken together, they afford a sufficient justification for any consequences that may ensue. My government will protect every inch of her territory, her citizens and their property, from insult and depredation, regardless of the political revolutions of Europe: and although she has been at all times sedulous to preserve a good

understanding with all the world, yet she has sacred CHAP.
rights, that cannot be trampled upon with impunity. VI.
Spain had better look to her own intestine commo-
tions, before she walks forth in that majesty of strength 1814.
and power, which you threaten to draw down upon
the United States.

" Your excellency has been candid enough to admit
your having supplied the Indians with arms. In addition to this, I have learned that a British flag has
been seen flying on one of your forts. All this is done
whilst you are pretending to be neutral. You cannot
be surprised, then, but on the contrary will provide a
fort in your town, for my soldiers and Indians, should
I take it in my head to pay you a visit.

" In future, I beg you to withhold your insulting
charges against my government, for one more inclined
to listen to slander than I am; nor consider me any
more as a diplomatic character, unless so proclaimed
to you from the mouths of my cannon."

Captain Gordon, who had been employed on the
mission to Pensacola, had been enabled, during his
stay, to obtain much more full and satisfactory information than it had pleased the governor to communicate. Appearances completely developed the schemes
that were in agitation, and convinced him that active
operations were intended shortly to be commenced
some where in the lower country. He reported to the
general, that he saw from one hundred and fifty to two
hundred British officers and soldiers, a park of artillery, and about five hundred Indians, under drill of
those officers, armed with new muskets, and dressed
in the English uniform.

Jackson directly brought to the view of the government the information he had received, and again urged
his favourite scheme, the reduction of Pensacola.
" How long," he observed, " will the United States
pocket the reproach and open insults of Spain?   It is
alone by a manly and dignified course, that we can
secure respect from other nations, and peace to our
own.   Temporizing policy is not only a disgrace, but
a curse to any nation.   It is a fact, that a British captain of marines is, and has been for some time, engaged in drilling and organizing the fugitive Creeks,
under the eye of the governor; endeavouring, by his
influence and presents, to draw to his standard as well
the peaceable as the hostile Indians.   If permission
had been given me to march against this place twenty
days ago, I would, ere this, have planted there the
American Eagle; now we must trust alone to our
valour, and the justice of our cause.   But my present
resources are so limited,—a sickly climate, as well
as an enemy to contend with, and without the means
of transportation, to change the position of my army,
that, resting on the bravery of my little phalanx, I can
only hope for success."

Many difficulties were presented ; and although
anxious to carry into execution a purpose which
seemed so strongly warranted by necessity, he was
wholly without the power of moving, even should he
be directed to do so. Acting in a remote corner, which
was detached, and thinly inhabited, the credit of his
government was inadequate to procure those things
necessary and essential to his operations ; while the
poverty of his quarter master's department presented

but a dreary prospect for reliance. But to have all CHAP.
things in a state of readiness for action, when the time
should come to authorize it, he was directing his attention in the way most likely to effect it. The warriors of the different tribes of Indians were ordered to
be marshalled, and taken into the pay of the government. He addressed the governors of Tennessee,
Louisiana, and the Mississippi territory, soliciting them
to be vigilant in the discharge of their duties. Information, he said, had reached him, which rendered
it necessary that all the forces allotted for the defence
of the seventh military district, should be held in a
state of perfect readiness, to march at any notice, and
to any point they might be required. " Dark and
heavy clouds," he continues, "hover around us. The
energy and patriotism of the citizens of your states
must dispel them. Our rights, our liberties, and free
constitutions, are threatened. This noble patrimony of
our fathers must be defended with the best blood of
our country : to do this, you must carry into effect the
requisition of the secretary of war, and call forth your
troops, without delay."

On the day after completing his business at Fort Sets out
Jackson, he had departed for Mobile, to place the for Mobile.
country in a proper state of defence. The third regiment, a part of the forty-fourth and thirty-ninth, were
all the regular forces he could at this time command.
Many reasons concurred, rendering it necessary that a
sufficient force should be brought into the field, as
early as possible. His appeals to the people of Tennessee had been generally crowned with success; and
he had no doubt but that he might yet obtain from

CHAP. them assistance, to enable him to act defensively at
VI. least, should any unexpected emergency arise, until
‿‿‿ the states already applied to, should have their quotas
1814. ready for the field.   On the citizens of Louisiana and
Mississippi he believed he might securely rely, and
that their ardour would readily excite them, to contend with an enemy at their very doors.   Well knowing the delay, incident to bringing militia requisitions expeditiously forth, and fearing that some circumstance might arise, to jeopardize the safety of the
country, before the constituted authorities could act ;
he had already despatched his adjutant general, colonel
Butler, to Tennessee, with orders to raise volunteers,
and have them in readiness tó march to his relief,
whenever it should be required.

Every day's intelligence tended to confirm the belief that a descent would be made,—most probably on
New Orleans.   Anonymous letters were secretly forwarded from Pensacola, which found their way into
the American camp.   Many of the settlers were apprized, by their friends, of the fears they entertained
for their safety, and entreated to retire from the gathering storm, which would soon burst, and entirely involve the lower country in wo and ruin.   Where certainly to expect it, was unknown.   The part bordering
on Mobile might be assailed ; yet, taking into consideration, that no very immediate advantages could be
obtained there, it was an event not much to be apprehended.   The necessity, however, of being prepared
at all points, so far as the means of defence could be
procured, was at once obvious ; for, as the general, in
one of his letters, remarked, " there was no telling
where, or when, the spoiler might come."

There were now too many reasons to expect an
early visit, and too many causes to apprehend danger,
not to wish that an efficient force were at hand.   Colonel Butler was written to, and ordered to hasten forward with the volunteers he could procure, and join
him without delay.   The order reached him at Nashville, on the 9th of September, and he engaged actively in its execution.   He directly applied to general Coffee, to advance with the mounted troops he
could collect.   A general order was issued, bringing
to view the dangers that threatened, and soliciting
those who were disposed to aid in protecting their
country from invasion, to rendezvous at Fayetteville,
by the 28th instant.   The appeal was not ineffectual :
although the scene of their operations was at least
five hundred miles from their homes, the call was
promptly obeyed ; and two thousand able-bodied
men, well supplied with rifles and muskets, appeared,
at the appointed time, to march with the brave general
Coffee, who had so often led his troops to victory and
honour.   Colonel Butler, with his usual activity and
industry, hastened to meet and push on the militia,
under the command of colonel Lowery, which had
been heretofore required for garrisoning the posts in
the Indian country ; whilst captains Baker and Butler,
with the regular troops, lately enlisted, advanced to
Mobile, where they arrived in fourteen days.   By
proper exertions, all things were presently in complete
readiness ; and the troops, in high spirits, set out for
the point to which danger and their country called
them.

CHAP.
VI.

1814.

Orders
the troops
from Ten-
nessee to
advance.

109

CHAPTER VII.

CHAP.
VII.

1814.

WHETHER a force were thus concentrating to act defensively against an invading enemy, or were intended to attack and break down their rallying point in the Spanish territory, whence they had it in their power to make sudden inroads on any part of our coast, as yet all was conjecture. It was a trait in Jackson's character, to lock closely in his bosom all his determinations; it was only to a few, on whom he reposed with unlimited confidence, that any intimation was given of his intentions. The idea could scarcely be entertained, that at this time any hostility was meditated against Pensacola. The frequent applications he had made to the war department, to be indulged in the execution of this purpose, without having obtained any directions or permission to do so, had placed a veto on the project, unless he should venture to assume and risk it on his own responsibility.

It was impossible that he should remain long in CHAP. doubt, as to the course best calculated to assure defence, VII. or as to the ulterior objects of the enemy. Colonel 1814. Nicholls, with a small squadron of his Britannic majesty's ships, arrived, the latter part of August, and took Colonel up his head quarters with governor Manrequez. He Nicholls arrives at was an Irishman, sent in advance by his royal mas- Pensacola ter, to sow dissensions among our people, and draw to his standard the malcontents and traitors of the country. His proclamation, issued to the western and southern inhabitants, full of well-turned periods, false statements, and high sounding promises, it was hoped would lead them to the belief, that their government was forging for them chains; that it had not to redress any injuries of its own, but through the mere dictum of the French emperor, declared war against a power, the freest, the happiest, the most moral and religious on earth. He stated, that he was at the head of a force amply sufficient to reinstate them in those liberties and enjoyments, of which they had been bereaved, by the designs of " a contemptible few." That those disposed to imbrue their hands in the blood of their countrymen might not quietly rest, doubting of the assurances given, he concluded by tendering, as security for all he had said and promised, " the sacred honour of a British officer.* Perhaps he could have 110 vouchsafed nothing, that the American people would not have sooner relied on : it was a pledge in which past experience had told them they could not in safety confide. To them it was a matter of surprise,

* See note A.

that a people from whom they had learned all they had ever known or felt of oppression, should come to make them freer than they were ; or that, groaning themselves under a load of taxes, from which there was scarcely a hope of being ever relieved, they should come, with such apparent compassion, and great benevolence, to take away the burdens of those whom they despised, and on whom, for forty years, they had heaped nothing but contumely and reproach. Where it was this agent of Britain learned, that the citizens of the United States complained of burdens, heavily and unjustly imposed, we know not; satisfied, however, are we, that it was a murmur never breathed by the people at large, They had encountered privations, and borne the " brunt of war ;" yet felt no solicitude that it should cease, until the assailed honour and independence of their country were secured on a basis, firmer than before.

He had waited about two weeks, that his proclamation might take effectual hold, and prepare the inhabitants to open their bosoms to receive him, when this delivering hero, aided by his Indian and Spanish allies, set out, to ascertain the effect it had wrought. His first visit was to Fort Bowyer, situated on the extreme end of a narrow neck of land, about eighteen miles below the head of Mobile bay, and which commands the entrance. With the loss of one of his ships, and an eye, he had the mortification to learn, that he had been addressing an incorrigible race, who could be neither duped, flattered, nor flogged into submission.

111

Septem.

Fort Bowyer had been heretofore abandoned ; and until the arrival of general Jackson in this section of the country, was ill calculated for serious resistance. On perceiving its importance, he immediately directed it to be placed in the best possible state of defence. So effectual was its situation, in a military point of view, as commanding the passes of those rivers which discharge themselves into the bay, that it was with him a matter of surprise it had not been more regarded, and better attended to.

Major Lawrence had the honour to command this spot, the gallant defence of which has given it celebrity, and raised him to an elevated stand in the estimation of his country. That in Pensacola plans of operation were digesting, which had for their object an invasion some where, was a fact to which Lawrence was not a stranger. A disposition to have his little fortress in such a state of readiness, as would place it in his power, should it be their object, to make a brave defence, had prompted him to the most vigorous exertions. His whole strength was but one hundred and thirty men. By this Spartan band was evinced a confidence in each other, and an unshaken resolution, which left their brave commander no room to apprehend dishonour to his flag, even should defeat result.

The 12th of September determined all doubt, as to the object the British had in view. The sentinels brought intelligence, that a considerable force, in Indians, marines, and Spaniards, had landed ; and, the same day, two brigs and sloops hove in sight, and anchored not far distant.

CHAP.   The next day, some disposition was manifested
VII.   by those who had been landed, to bring on the attack;
        but a fire from the fort forced them from their position,
1814.   and compelled them to retire about two miles; whence,
112   attempting to throw up fortifications, they were again
        made to retreat.

            Until the 15th, nothing definitive took place. Early
        on that day, the signals passing from the ships to the
        shore, led Lawrence to believe an assault was intended,
        and would shortly be made. At half after four o'clock
        in the evening, every thing being arranged, the Hermes
        in the van, commanded by sir W. H. Percy, and the
        others close in the rear, anchored within musket shot
        fire of the fort.   From her near position, support-
113   ed by the Caron, and brigs Sophia and Anaconda,
Attack on mounting, in all, ninety guns, she opened her broad-
Fort Bow-
yer.   side.   Colonel Nicholls and captain Woodbine, at the
        head of their detachment, commenced a simultaneous
        attack by land, with a twelve pound howitzer, at
        point blank distance; but, from their sand bank forti-
        fications they were too quickly driven, to be enabled
        to produce the slightest injury; whilst their courage
        was wholly inadequate to carry it by storm.

            The action now raged with considerable violence.
        From the fort and ships was pouring a continual fire.
        The Hermes, having at length received a shot through
        her cable, was driven from her anchorage, and floated
        with the stream.   In this situation, she was thrown
        into a position, where, for twenty minutes, she re-
        ceived a severe raking fire, which did her considerable
        damage.   In her disabled condition, it was no longer

possible to control her, whence, drifting with the cur- CHAP.
rent, she ran upon a sand bank, about seven hundred VII.
yards distant, where, until late at night, she remained 1814.
exposed to the guns from the fort. Her commander,
finding it impracticable to get her off, set her on fire,
and abandoned her. She continued burning, until
eleven o'clock, when she blew up. The Caron, next
in advance to the Hermes, was considerably injured,
and with difficulty got out to sea.

It is worthy of remark, to show the difference
in battle, between the two nations, to mark the conduct of British and American officers, under circumstances precisely similar. Whilst the battle raged, the flag of the van ship was carried away, and
at this moment she had ceased to fire. What had
caused its disappearance, none could tell : no other
opinion was, or could with propriety be indulged, than
that it had been hauled down, with a view to yield the
contest, and surrender. Influenced by this belief, Lawrence, with that generosity characteristic of American
officers, immediately desisted from further firing. The
appearance of a new flag, and a broadside from the ship
next the Hermes, was the first intelligence received,
that such was not the fact; and the contest again raged
with renewed violence. It was but a few minutes,
however, before the flag staff of the fort was also carried away : but so far from pursuing the same generous course that had just been witnessed, the zeal of
the enemy was increased, and the assault more furiously
urged. At this moment, Nicholls and Woodbine, at
the head of their embattled train, perceiving what had
happened, that our " star-spangled banner" had sunk.

CHAP.
VII.
~~~~
1814.

at once presuming all danger had subsided, made a most courageous sally from their strong hold; and, pushing towards their vanquished foes, were already calculating on a rich harvest of blood and plunder: but a well-directed fire checked their progress, dissipated their expectations, and drove them back, with a rapidity, even surpassing the celerity of their advance.

Taking into consideration the inequality of force employed on the opposite sides of this contest, it will appear a matter of surprise, that the attack should have terminated in the way it did ;—that it was not attended with success. This circumstance would be a sufficient evidence of the bravery and correct conduct of its gallant defenders, were there a total absence of all other facts; but their belief, that the best way to avoid disaster was to be in a state of readiness to meet it, and a constant assiduity, which urged them forward, day and night, that they might be in a situation calculated for successful defence, are facts remembered, and entitle them to the highest commendation. From the bay, the attack was waged with a force of six hundred men, and ninety guns, of larger caliber than any opposed to them; whilst upwards of four hundred Indians and other troops were on the shore, in rear of the fort. Lawrence's strength was scarcely a tenth of the enemy's. His fort, hastily prepared, with not more than twenty guns, was ill calculated for stubborn resistance; most of these were of small caliber, whilst many, from being badly mounted, rendered no essential service in the action: yet, with this great inequality, he well maintained the honour of his flag, and compelled the enemy, resting in full confidence of success, to retire, with the loss of his best ship, and two hundred and thirty men killed and wounded; whilst the loss sustained by the Americans did not exceed ten.

Very different were the feelings of the leaders of this expedition, from what they had been on setting out from Pensacola, where every thing had been prepared for giving success to their plans, and where scarcely a doubt had been entertained of the result. Numerous advantages were expected to arise from a victory, not in expectancy, but already looked to as certain;—as an event that could not fail. From it, greater facility would be given to their operations; while Mobile would fall, of course. This being effected, independent of the strong hold already possessed in East Florida, an additional one would be acquired, calculated to prevent all intercourse with New Orleans, from this section of the country, to enable them more easily to procure supplies, and, having obtained their expected reinforcements, to proceed across to the Mississippi, and cut off all communication with the western states. To render the blow effectual was important; that, by impressing at once the inhabitants with an idea of their strength and prowess, the proclamations already disseminated might claim a stronger influence on doubting minds. The force employed, and its disposition, was calculated to attain these wished for events. While the attack should be furiously waged by the ships from the bay, that the yells of three or four hundred savages in the rear should strike the defenders of this fort with such a panic, as to make them, at the first onset, throw down their arms, and clamour for mercy, was a belief so

CHAP.
VII.

1814.

sanguinely indulged, that obstinate resistance had never been thought of. Different was the reality,—instead of triumph, they had met defeat. The only badges of victory they could present the friends, with whom, but a few days before, with flattering promises they had parted, were shattered hulks, that could scarcely keep above the water, and decks covered with dead and wounded.

116 The three vessels that retired were considerably injured, and with difficulty got to sea, leaving Nicholls and Woodbine, with their friends and allies, on the shore, to make good their retreat, as danger and discretion would permit.

On the morning of the 14th, Jackson, fearing, from every thing he had learned, that an attack would be made, had set out, in a boat, from Mobile, to visit Fort Bowyer, examine its situation, and have such arrangements made, as should add to its strength, and obtain that security, which its re-establishment had been designed to effect. He had proceeded down the bay, and arrived within a few miles, when he met an express from Lawrence, bringing intelligence of the enemy's arrival, and requesting that assistance might be immediately sent to his relief. The general hastened back, and reaching Mobile late at night, despatched a brig, with eighty men, under the command of captain Laval. Not being able to reach his point of destination until the next day, and finding every place of entrance blocked up by the besiegers, he ran his brig to the land, determined to wait until night, when, under cover of its darkness, he hoped to succeed in throwing himself into the fort. The battle,

however, having in the mean time commenced, presented new difficulties, and restrained the execution of
his purpose, without encountering greater hazard than
prudence seemed to sanction. The Hermes, on being
driven from her anchorage, had, at the time of her explosion, floated and grounded in a direction that left
her immediately in the rear of the fort, from the position occupied by the brig. This circumstance well
accounted for the mistake with which he was impressed, and led captain Laval to believe his brave countrymen had all perished. Believing they would now
attempt to carry his vessel, he set sail for Mobile, and
reported to the commanding general the destruction
and loss that had happened. Jackson declared it was
impossible; that he had heard the explosion, and was
convinced it was on the water, and not on the shore.
Perhaps his great anxiety, more than any reality, had
constituted this essential difference in sound. If, however, it were as reported, his own situation being
thereby rendered precarious, something was to be
done, to regain a place, for many reasons too important to be yielded. His principal fears were, lest the
strength of the enemy should be greatly increased, before his expected reinforcements should arrive, who
would be thereby enabled to extend his inroads, and
paralyze the zeal of the country. It was no time for
much deliberation on the course most advisable to be
pursued. He determined to retake the fort, at all hazards; and a general order was issued, for the departure of the troops. Every thing was nearly in readiness, when a despatch arrived from Lawrence, bear-

CHAP. ing the pleasing intelligence that all was safe, and that
VII.   the enemy, beaten and vanquished, had retired.

1814.   The conduct displayed by the officers and soldiers
       of this garrison is worthy to be remembered. With
117   troops wholly undisciplined, and against an enemy ten
       times more numerous than themselves, so coolly and
       fearlessly contending, that we cannot wish our country
       better, than that the future defenders of her honour,
       and violated rights, may be as sensibly alive to their
       duty, and act with a like determined bravery.

British   The British had now retired to Pensacola, to dispose
vessels re-
tire to   of their wounded, refit their vessels, and be ready, as
Pensacola.
       soon as circumstances would permit, to make, perhaps,
       another descent, on some less guarded point. So long
       as this, their only place of refuge and retreat on the
       southern coast, was left in their possession, it was im-
       possible to calculate on the consequences that might
       arise. The commanding general was well convinced
       that this was merely a feint, and that the object of
       their wishes and designs, so soon as a sufficient force
       should arrive, would be New Orleans. At this place,
       he believed his presence material, to ascertain and
       guard the most important passes to the city, and con-
       cert some system of general defence. His feelings,
       however, would not permit him to depart, and leave
       the settlements and Mobile open to an attack, from
       forces immediately in the neighbourhood, which might
       reduce them, and thereby gain a position whence they
       might obtain supplies, and be placed nearer the ulti-
       mate point, against which, most probably, their views
       were directed. His regret was indeed great, that, time

after time, without the least success, he had urged and entreated his government, for permission to take possession of a place where so many dangers threatened, and where every assistance and encouragement was afforded the British; and that regret was increased, now, when he saw the very evils engendering and springing into existence, to which he had so often endeavoured to draw their attention, and which were jeopardizing the safety of the whole lower country. To him the defence of this district had been entrusted: it was incumbent on him to render a just account of his stewardship, and zealously to support his well-earned reputation. Unless Pensacola were reduced, it was vain to think of defending the country: it would be involved in ruin,—himself in disgrace. Anxiously concerned for the general good, he saw no channel through which safety could be effected, but by hazarding, on his own responsibility, the reduction of this place.

CHAP. VII.

1814.

Jackson and his government had ever viewed this subject in very different lights: they were not willing to risk a contest with Spain, for the sake of removing what they considered an inconsiderable injury: he thought it of more serious import, and did not believe it could afford even a pretext for rupture between the two nations. If Spain, through her agents, permitted and encouraged a power with whom she was at peace to be thus harassed and annoyed, she deserved to be placed on the list of enemies, and treated accordingly. If, however, Great Britain, taking advantage of the defenceless state of her province, claimed free egress, in exclusion of her authority, she could have no well-

Jackson's determination, and reasons, for proceeding against Pensacola

CHAP. founded cause of complaint against the injured power,
VII. which should hold it until such time as, by bringing a
sufficient force, she might be in a situation to support
1814. her neutrality, and enforce obedience to her laws.
Upon either ground, he believed it might be sufficiently justified. There was one, however, on which
it could be placed, where he well knew nothing could
result, beyond his own injury ; and on this issue he
was willing to trust it. If any complaint should be
made, his government, having never extended to him
an authority, might, with propriety, disavow the act ;
and, by exposing him to censure and punishment, it
would be an atonement for the outrage, and Spain, in
justice, could demand no more. The attack on Mobile point was a confirmation of his previous conjectures, as to the views of the enemy ; and, from that
moment, he determined to advance against and reduce
Pensacola, throw a sufficient force in the Barrancas,
hold them until the principles of right and neutrality
were better respected, and rest the measure on his own
responsibility. Believing this the only course that could
assure ultimate security, he decided with firmness, and
resolved to execute his intentions, so soon as general
Coffee should arrive, with the volunteers, from Tennessee.

It was now rumoured, and generally accredited, that
a very considerable force, under the command of lord
Hill, would shortly sail from England, destined to act
against some part of the United States ; where, none
knew, or could tell ; rumour, and public opinion, fixed upon New Orleans. The importance of this place
was well known to our enemy ; it was the key to the

whole commerce of the western country. Had a de- CHAP.
scent been made on it a few months before, it might VII.
have been taken with all imaginable ease; but the
British had confidently indulged the belief, that they 1814.
could possess it, at any time, without much difficulty. England and France having ended their long-
pending controversy, it was thought that the French
people of Louisiana, sensibly alive to the great be- 118
nefits the English had conferred upon their native
country,—benefits that have prostrated her liberty, and
sunk her, perhaps, in eternal slavery, would, on their
first appearance, hail their deliverers, and at once become their vassals. Independent of this, they saw, in
the black population, the means of exciting insurrection and massacre, and deluging the country in blood.
Whether this kind of warfare, which involves the deepest wretchedness, and equally exposes to ruin, the innocent as the guilty,—the female as the soldier, should
be pursued by a nation professing a high sense of moral feeling; or whether a nation that adopts such a
system, can be entitled to the appellation of honour- 119
able, are questions on which we should not fear even
the decision of an Englishman, could he but divest
himself of that animosity and hatred, which, from infan-
cy, he entertains for the Americans. To this, and many
other acts, equally in violation of the rules that should
govern honourable warfare, may be traced the cause
of those deep-rooted inveteracies, in the breasts of our
citizens, towards those of England, which time, and a
different course of conduct, can alone remove. Why
such hostility has been practised towards us, it is dif-

ficult to determine; unless the crime of the revolution, if it were one, to rise in opposition to the oppression and despotism, under which we then groaned, has disposed them to visit the sins of the father upon the child, with a determination they shall never be forgiven or forgotten. Certain is it, that the United States have received more, and greater insults and injuries, from this power, than from all the other nations of the earth together; the hoary locks of a father, torn off by the merciless Indian,—the innocent, helpless female, bleeding by savage torture,—and the unoffending babe, dragged from the beating bosom of its mother, and butchered in her sight, are cruelties that can be traced to British influence: yet these people and ourselves are descended from the same fathers—speak the same language—are governed by the same laws—and are similar in manners and customs. But to inquire into the causes of national feeling, belongs not to the historian; it is his duty only to detail facts. The war is over; peace is restored; and the two nations, and their citizens, by a mutual respect, and forbearance towards each other, should endeavour to promote that friendship and intercourse, which it is evidently the interest of both to preserve, and which, we hope, will be lasting.

The expected reinforcements were now announced.

Arrival of general Coffee's brigade. General Coffee, with his brigade, had arrived, and halted at the cut off, above Fort St. Stephens. In addition to the force with which he had commenced his march, he was strengthened by the arrival of others, who had followed, and overtaken him at this place; so

that his whole number was now about twenty-eight
hundred. To make the necessary arrangements for an immediate march, general Jackson, on the 26th day of October, repaired to general Coffee's camp.

The difficulty of subsisting cavalry on the route, rendered it necessary that part of this brigade should proceed on foot. Although they had volunteered in the service as mounted men, and had not expected any different disposition to be made of them, yet they cheerfully acquiesced in the order: and one thousand, abandoning their horses to subsist as they could, on the reeds that grew along the river bottoms, prepared to commence the march on foot. Being supplied with rations for the trip, on the 2d day of November the line of march was taken up: and Pensacola was reached on the 6th. The British and Spaniards had obtained intelligence of their approach, and intended attack; and every thing was in readiness to dispute their passage. The forts were garrisoned, and prepared for resistance; batteries were formed in the principal streets; and the British vessels were moored within the bay, and so disposed as to command the main entrance to the town.

The American army, consisting of the greater part of Coffee's brigade, the regulars, and some few Indians, in all about three thousand, had arrived within a mile and a half of this rallying point for our enemies, and formed their encampment. Before any final step was taken, the general concluded to make a further application to the governor, and learn what course he would make it necessary for him to pursue. To take possession, and dislodge the British, was indispensable:

CHAP. to do it under such circumstances, as should impress
VII. the minds of the Spaniards with a conviction, that the
invasion of their territory was a measure adopted
1814. from necessity, and not choice, or a disposition to
November infringe, or violate, their neutral rights, was believed
to be essential. It was rendered the more so, on the
part of Jackson, because a measure of his own, and not
sanctioned or directed by his government. Previously, therefore, to any act of open war, he determined to
try the effect of negotiation, that he might ascertain,
certainly and correctly, how far the governor felt disposed to preserve a good understanding between the
two governments.

Explana- Major Piere, of the forty-fourth regiment, was action of the cordingly despatched, with a flag, to disclose the ob-
conduct of jects intended to be attained by the visit, and to re-
governor quire that the different forts, Barrancas, St. Rose, and
Manre- St. Michael, should be immediately surrendered, to be
quez re- garrisoned and held by the United States, until Spain,
quired. by furnishing a sufficient force, could protect the province, and preserve unimpaired her neutral character.
He was charged by the general with a candid and explicit statement of his views, and instructed to require
of the governor a decisive and positive declaration of
the course he intended to adopt.

This mission experienced no very favourable result.
Major Piere, on approaching St. Michael's, was fired
on, and compelled to return. Whether this were done
by the Spaniards themselves, or by their allies and
friends, who were sojourning with them, was not material. The Spanish flag was displayed on the fort,
and under it the outrage was committed: though it

was a fact well ascertained, that, until the day before,
the British flag had been also associated : this, on the
arrival of Jackson, had been removed, and the colours
of Spain left, which were to afford protection to our
enemies, and a pretext for every injury. This conduct, so unexpected and unprovoked, and withal, so
directly in opposition to the principles and practice of
civilized warfare, might have well determined the general to abstain from further forbearance, and proceed
immediately to the accomplishment of his views : but
a consciousness, that although the reduction of this
place was required by circumstances of the highest necessity, yet, lest it might be blazoned around to his
prejudice, and become a cause of national difficulty,
he was prompted to act with every possible deliberation and caution. A sense of humanity, too, towards
those people, who, he was satisfied, were acting not
from any choice or discretion of their own, but by the
authority of the British, induced a wish for the objects of his visit to be effected, without injury to
them. Determining, therefore, to understand the governor fully, previously to proceeding to extremities,
he again despatched a letter to him, not by any of
his officers, for after such perfidy he was unwilling,
and felt it unsafe, to risk them ; but by a Spanish cor-
poral, who had been taken, on the route, the day before. By him, he required to know why his former
application, instead of being met with a becoming
spirit of conciliation, had been insulted. In answer,
he received from the governor a confirmation of the
opinion previously entertained, that what had been
done was not chargeable to him, but the English ;

that he had no agency in the transaction of which he complained, and assured him of his perfect willingness to receive any overtures he might be pleased to make. This was joyful tidings; and no time was to be lost, in meeting the offer. If negotiation should place in his hands the different fortresses, before information of it was had by the British shipping, lying in the bay, the outward channel would be effectually stopped, and the means of their escape entirely cut off. Major Piere was accordingly sent off, at a late hour of the night, to detail to the governor the reasons which had rendered the present descent proper; and to insist on the conditions already noticed, as alone calculated to assure safety to the United States, and give protection to the province of East Florida. He was particularly instructed to impress on his consideration, that a re-surrender would be made, so soon as Spain, by the arrival of a sufficient force, could protect her territory from the inroads of a power, at war with the United States; and which, through an opening thus afforded, was enabled, and had already done her considerable injury. In his communication to the governor, he remarks, " I come not as the enemy of Spain; not to make war, but to ask for peace; ᵗo demand security for my country, and that respect to which she is entitled, and shall receive. My force is sufficient, and my determination taken, to prevent a future repetition of the injuries she has received. I demand, therefore, the possession of the Barrancas, and other fortifications, with all your munitions of war. If delivered peaceably, the whole shall be receipted for, and become the subject of future arrangement, by our

respective governments; while the property, laws, and
religion of your citizens will be respected. But if
taken by an appeal to arms, let the blood of your subjects be upon your own head. I will not hold myself
responsible for the conduct of my enraged soldiers.
One hour is given you for deliberation, when your determination must be had."

The council was called, the propositions considered, and the conclusion taken, that they could not be
acceded to. As soon as the answer was received,
showing that nothing peaceably could be done, Jackson resolved to push his army forward; and, immediately commencing his march, proceeded to the
accomplishment of his object, determined to effect it,
in despite of danger, and the consequences.

Early on the morning of the 7th, the army was in
motion. To foster the idea, that he would march and
reach the town along the road, on which he was encamped, a detachment of five hundred men was sent
forward, with orders to show themselves in this
direction, and amuse and deceive the enemy; while,
urging rapidly on, with the strength of his army, he
was gaining it at a different and unexpected point.
This stratagem succeeded: the British, looking for
his appearance where the detachment was seen, had
formed their vessels across the bay, and were waiting
his approach, with their guns properly bearing: nor
had they an intimation to the contrary, until our troops
were descried upon the beach, on the east side, where
they were at too great a distance to be annoyed from Our army enters,
the flotilla; and whence, pushing forward, they were and takes posses-
presently in the streets, and covered by the houses. sion of Pensacola

CHAP.   One company, from the third regiment of infantry,
VII.   with two field pieces, formed the advance, led by the
1814. brave captain Laval, who fell, severely wounded, while,
at the head of his command, he was charging a Spanish battery, formed in the street.   The left column,
composed of the regular troops, the third, thirty-ninth,
and forty-fourth regiments, headed by majors Wood-
ruff and Piere, formed the left, next the bay.   The
dismounted volunteers proceeded down the street,
next the regulars : Coffee's brigade next, on their
right : the Mississippi dragoons, commanded by colonel Hinds, and the Choctaw Indians by major Blue,
of the thirty-ninth, advanced on the extreme right of
all.   Captain Laval's party, although deprived of their
leader, moved forward, and, at the point of the bayonet, took possession of the battery in their front.   So
quickly was this effected, that the Spaniards had it in
their power to make but three fires, before they were
forced to abandon it.   From behind the houses and
garden fences, were discharging constant vollies of
musketry, until the regulars arriving, met the Spaniards, and drove them from their positions.   The
governor, panic struck, trembling for the safety of his
city, and remembering the declaration of the general,
that he should not attempt to restrain the irritation of
his soldiers, hastened, bearing a flag in his hand, to
find the commander, and seek to stay the carnage. He
was met by colonels Williamson and Smith, at the
head of the dismounted troops, when, with faltering
speech, he entreated that mercy might be extended,
and promised to consent to whatever might be de
manded.

General Jackson had stopped for a moment, where Laval had fallen, and was at this time in the rear. Receiving information that an offer had been made to comply with all the demands he had made, he hastened to the intendant house, and obtained a confirmation of what he had been previously assured, that the town, arsenals, and munitions of war, should be immediately surrendered.

122

The British vessels in the bay, with the aid of their boats, by which they obtained a more commanding situation, continued to fire upon our troops, as, passing along the principal streets and avenues, they could get them in the range of their guns. Lieutenant M'Call, perceiving some of their boats attempting to take a nearer position, advanced to the beach, with two pieces of heavy cannon, where, open, exposed, and uncovered, he commenced a brisk and well-aimed fire, which drove them back to a more respectful distance.

No time was lost, in procuring what was considered of vital importance,—the surrender of the forts. Although greater benefits would have been derived, had the success of negotiation placed them privately in his hands, without its being known to his enemies, yet even now they were not to be neglected. Their possession was necessary still to his own security,—to check any design that might be in agitation. What was the force opposed to him ; at what moment reinforcements might appear off Pensacola, and thereby give an entire change to things, as they at present existed, were matters of which no certain idea could be formed. To possess the Barrancas, which lay fourteen miles to the west, was a consideration of the first importance; still, until the town and its fortresses were secured, it was improper to withdraw to so great a distance.

Notwithstanding the assurances given, that all differences would be accommodated, and every thing insisted on agreed to, Fort St. Michael was still withheld. Captain Dankins was ordered to take post on Mount St. Bernard, form his batteries, and reduce it. He was in a situation to act, when the commandant, colonel Sotto, ordered his flag taken down, and the fort to be surrendered.

123

It is curious to observe the treachery of the Spaniards, and the unpardonable method they took, to indulge their rancour and spleen. Previously to striking his colours, the commandant had asked permission to fire his guns; to this there could be no objection, and the indulgence was extended; but, faithless and cowardly, he levelled and fired his pieces, charged with grape, at a party of dragoons and Choctaw Indians, who were at a small distance, which killed three horses, and wounded two men. Such unpardonable conduct, independent of other wrongs and injuries, already noticed, might have justified any treatment; the destruction of the garrison would not have been an unmerited chastisement. The general was on his way to Mount St. Bernard, where his artillery was planted, when he received intelligence of what had been done. He determined no longer to confide in persons, whose only object seemed to deceive, but to make the sword the arbiter between them. His cannon were already turned towards the fort, and the resolution taken to batter it down, when it was announced by major Piere that

Conduct and perfidy of the Spaniards.

the capitulation had been agreed on, and a surrender would be made in half an hour. He again forbore to obey that impulse their unwarrantable conduct had so justly excited, and despatched captain Dankins, to insist on an immediate delivery; with directions to carry it by storm, if the demand were not instantly complied with.

Difficulties promised thus peaceably to terminate. The day being far spent, and the general greatly indisposed, no step could be taken to obtain possession of the Barrancas, until the next morning. On the credit of the governor's promises, made first on their entrance into the town, the principal part of the army had been ordered a short distance out. Understanding, at St. Bernard, that what had been required would be done, and that no further delay would be met, the general had set out to the encampment, leaving major Piere behind, with a sufficient force to preserve the town in safety and quietness. He was astonished, early in the morning, to learn that captain Dankins, on reaching St. Michael, the preceding evening, had been threatened to be fired on by colonel Sotto: possession, however, had been yielded, on being made to understand, that if the fort were not delivered instantly, and without further parley, it would be carried forcibly, and the garrison put to the sword. A capitulation was signed: Pensacola, and the different fortresses, were to be retained, until Spain could better maintain her authority; while the rights and privileges of her citizens were to be respected.

Every thing was in readiness, on the following day, to march, and take possession of Barrancas fort. The faithless conduct of yesterday had determined Jackson on the execution of his plans; nor longer to confide in Spaniards' promises. Major Piere was ordered to give the command of the city to colonel Hayne, and report himself at camp, to accompany him on 'the march; but previously to retiring, to require the governor to execute an authority to the commandant of the fort, to deliver it; and, in the event he would not comply, immediately to arrest him, and every public officer, and hold them as prisoners. The order for its delivery had been signed, and the line of march ready to be taken up, to advance and receive it,— peaceably, if the order would effect it—forcibly, if not; when a tremendous explosion, in that direction, fol-

Fort Barrancas is blown up by the British.

124

lowed by two others, in quick succession, excited the apprehension that all was destroyed. To ascertain, certainly, whence the noise had proceeded, major Gales, a volunteer aid, was despatched, with two hundred men, to reconnoitre and obtain intelligence. He presently returned, and confirmed what had been previously apprehended, that the fort was blown up, and the British shipping retired from the bay.

Although the repairing this place might be productive of numerous advantages, as keeping the enemy, during the expected descent on the lower country, from having in their possession a point where they might prepare their expeditions, and where, in despite of every vigilance that could be used, they might obtain ample supplies; yet, inasmuch as the act was unauthorized by his government, Jackson felt himself restrained from incurring any expense, for the re-establishment, of what had been thus treacherously destroyed. Though disappointed in the object he had principally in view, he nevertheless believed that some of the benefits intended and expected would result. This strong hold, which had so long given protection to the southern hostile savages, and where they had been excited to acts of war and cruelty, was assailed, and the Indians taught that even here, safety was not to be found. The valour and good conduct of his troops had impressed on the minds of the Spaniards a respect for the character of his country, which hitherto they had not entertained; and the British, by being dislodged, were prevented from maturing and settling those plans, which were to give efficacy to their future operations against the southern section of the Union : but as the means of maintaining and defending it were destroyed, it was unnecessary to think of garrisoning, and attempting to hold it. It was accordingly concluded to re-deliver all that had been surrendered, and retire to Fort Montgomery. He was the more disposed to do so, believing the British, who had sailed out of the bay, would again make their way to Fort Bowyer, and, with a knowledge of the principal strength of the army being away, seek to aim a blow somewhere on the Mobile. An express was immediately hastened to   125 colonel Sparks, who had been left in command at this place, announcing what had transpired, suggesting apprehensions for his safety, and notifying him, in the event of an attack, to endeavour to parry the danger, until the regular troops should arrive, to support him, who would be urged forward with every industry.

Two days after entering the town, he abandoned it. Previously to retiring, he wrote to governor Manre-

quez ; and, after stating to him the causes which had induced him, justifiably, as he believed, to enter his
territory, he thus concluded: " As the Barrancas, and
the adjacent fortresses have been surrendered to, and
blown up, by the British, contrary to the good faith I
had reposed in your promises, it is out of my power
to protect and guard your neutrality, as otherwise I
should have done. The enemy has retreated ; the
hostile Creeks have fled for safety to the forest; and I
now retire from your town, leaving you to re-occupy
your forts, and protect the rights of your citizens."

Town and
fortresses
are sur-
rendered,
and our
army re-
tires.

Much is due, not only to the calmness and intrepidity of conduct displayed by the troops, in their advance
on the town, against the batteries, that were formed in
the streets, the fort, and the fleet lying in the bay ; but
much more for their orderly, open, and generous conduct towards a people who had wholly outraged every
principle of correct conduct ; and who, even at the
moment when the sword was made the appeal, and the
blow they merited only stayed by humanity, were
still pursuing a course of faithlessness and treachery,
and clearly evincing a disposition to aid and assist our
enemies : yet, under such circumstances, which certainly would have warranted a less lenient course towards them, not a single irregularity was committed, or the rights of individuals at all molested. So
exemplary was the deportment of our officers, and the
conduct of our soldiers, as to extort the Spaniards'
praise, and even to induce the declaration that our Indians behaved with more decency and propriety than
their friends, with whom they had just parted. When
we remember, what is undeniably the fact, that the

British had been always well received by the inhabitants of East Florida, who had rendered them every
assistance and protection in their power; and who,
from their disposition to aid them, had even brought
difficulties upon themselves; ingratitude and injustice
may be well charged upon them, when it is recollected that these friends, who had been so well regarded, on retreating from Pensacola, carried off three or
four hundred slaves, not their own, in despite of the
remonstrances and repeated demands of the owners
to have them restored.

Our loss, in this expedition, was truly inconsiderable. The left column alone met resistance, and had
fifteen or twenty wounded—none killed. It appears,
indeed, strange, that three heavy pieces of artillery,
charged with grape and canister, and three times fired
against a column, advancing through a narrow street,
should not have effected more. Of the number
wounded, was lieutenant Flournoy, a promising young
man, who, having gone out as a volunteer, was, on
account of his merit, promoted to a lieutenancy in the
forty-fourth United States' regiment. By a cannon
shot, he lost his leg. Captain Laval, being too dangerously injured to be moved, was trusted by the general to the clemency of the governor of Pensacola,
who humanely gave him that attention his situation
required.

The Indian warriors, who had taken refuge in
Pensacola, finding themselves abandoned by the British, fled across the country, and sought safety on the
Appalachicola : many were afforded shelter on board
the shipping, from which they were shortly afterwards

CHAP. landed, to prosecute the war after their own manner,
VII. and in their own way. Jackson determined they
1814. should have no rest, or respite from danger, so long
as a warlike attitude was preserved. Recent events
had shown them, that neither the valour of their allies, nor their own exertions, could afford them protection. He believed it an auspicious moment to
pursue them in their retreat; increase still more their
fears and apprehensions; and effectually cut up that
misplaced confidence, which had already well nigh
proved their ruin. Understanding that those who
had been carried off from Pensacola had been landed
on the Appalachicola, and a depot of all necessary
supplies there established, major Blue, of the thir-
Expedi- ty-ninth regiment, was sent off, on the 16th, at the
tion
against head of a thousand mounted men, with orders to fol-
the In- low and attack them, and destroy any of their vil-
dians. lages he might find, on his route. General M'Intosh,
of the Georgia militia, then in the Creek country, was
apprized of the destination, and directed to co-operate,
that the savages might be assailed and dispersed, before they should have it in their power to attempt hostilities against the frontiers. Having effected this object, they were ordered to repair to Mobile, to aid in
its defence.

Shortly after the American army had retired, the
Spaniards commenced rebuilding Forts Barrancas and
St. Rose, which they had lost, through the improper
interference of their friends. Anxious to regain that
confidence they had justly forfeited, the British offered their services, to assist in the re-establishment.
This offer was refused, and an answer returned by

the governor, that when assistance was in fact need- CHAP.
ed, he would make application to his friend, general VII.
Jackson.

1814.

There was nothing now so much desired by the
general, as to be able to depart for New Orleans, where
he apprehended most danger, and where he believed
his presence was most material.   He had already ef- November
fected a partial security for Mobile, and the inhabitants
on its borders; and such as he believed might be preserved, by proper vigilance and activity in those left
in command.   He determined to set out, on the 22d,
for the Mississippi; and, by proper exertions, seek to
place the country in such a situation for defence as the
means within his reach would permit. His health
was still delicate, which almost wholly unfitted him
for the duties he had to encounter : but his constant
expectation of a large force appearing soon on the coast,
impelled him to action. Added to the fatigues incident
to his station, he as yet had no brigadier general in his
district, to relieve him of many of those duties, which
he had neither time, nor bodily strength to meet. General Winchester had been ordered to join him.   He
had not yet arrived, but was daily looked for.   In expectation of his speedy approach, Jackson was making
every necessary arrangement, for investing him with the
command of Mobile, and, for his own departure. Colonel Hayne, the inspector general, had been despatched to the mouth of the Mississippi, to examine if there
were any eligible site, where, by erecting batteries, the
river might be commanded, and an ascent prevented, if through this route sought. General Coffee and
colonel Hinds, with the dragoons from the territory,

CHAP. were ordered to march with their commands, and take
VII. a position as convenient to New Orleans as they could
1814. obtain a sufficiency of forage, to recruit their horses;
having regard to some central point, whence they
might, without loss of time, proceed wherever danger
should be most imminent. Every thing being ar-
General ranged, and general Winchester having reached the
Winches- Alabama, Jackson, on the 22d day of November, left
ter arrives, Mobile, for the city of New Orleans, and reached it
and Jack-
son pro- on the 1st day of December; where his head quar-
ceeds to
New Or- ters, for the present, were established.
leans.

CHAPTER VIII.

Jackson's correspondence with governor Claiborne.—His address to the citizens of Louisiana.—Militia from Tennessee and Kentucky advance; and general plans adopted for defence.—Plan for filling delinquencies in the army.—British shipping arrive on the coast.—Loss of the Sea Horse.—Battle on the lake, and loss of the gun boats.—Jackson reviews the militia.—His address to them.—Expresses sent to generals Coffee and Carroll.—Declaration of martial law, at New Orleans.—The British effect a landing, and Jackson prepares to meet them.

————

GENERAL JACKSON was now on a new theatre, and soon to be brought in collision with an enemy, different from any he had yet encountered : the time had arrived, to call forth all the energies he possessed. His military career, from its commencement, had been obstructed by innumerable difficulties, but far greater were now rising to his view. His body worn down by sickness and exhaustion, with a mind constantly alive to the apprehension, that, with the means given him, it would not be in his power to satisfy his own wishes, and the expectations of his country, were circumstances well calculated to depress him. He was as yet without sufficient strength or preparation, to attempt successful opposition against the numerous and well-trained troops, which were expected shortly at some unprepared point, to enter, and lay

CHAP.
VIII.

1814.

December.

H h

CHAP. waste the lower country. What was to be hoped,
VIII. from the clemency and generous conduct of such a
~~~~~ foe, their march to the city of Washington already an-
1814. nounced; while the imagination painted in lively colours the repetition, here, of scenes of desolation, even
surpassing what had there been witnessed.

126   Louisiana, he well knew, was ill supplied with
arms, and contained a mixed population, of different tongues, who perhaps felt not a sufficient attachment for the soil or government, to be induced to defend them to the last extremity. No troops, arms, or
ammunition, had yet descended from the states of
Kentucky and Tennessee. His only reliance for defence, if assailed, was on the few regulars he had, the
volunteers of general Coffee, and such troops as the
state itself could raise. What might be the final result of things, under prospects gloomy as the present,
should an enemy shortly appear, was no difficult conjecture. His principal fears, at present, were, that
127 Mobile might fall, the left bank of the Mississippi be
gained, all communication with the western states cut
off, and New Orleans be thus unavoidably reduced.
Although continually agitated by such forebodings, he
breathed his fears to none. Closely locking all apprehensions in his own breast, he appeared constantly se-
rene, and as constantly endeavoured to impress a general belief, that the country could and would be successfully defended. The manifestation of such tranquillity, and apparent certainty of success, under circumstances so unpropitious, excited strong hopes, dispelled every thing like fear, and impressed all with
additional confidence.

With the remnant of force he had at command,
and the additional strength to be afforded him from
Kentucky and Tennessee, uncertain in its arrival, undisciplined, and unarmed; to oppose an enemy who
might be already on the coast, and of whose exceeding
valour great and wondrous stories had been already
told; might have sunk into inaction any mind not gift-
ed with uncommon energy, and made it to retire from
a contest, where seemingly insurmountable difficulties
rendered delusive every hope of resistance: yet, firm
and resolute, an increase of difficulties but occasioned
an increase of exertion, and he entered on his forlorn
undertaking, with no other determination than to leave
nothing unessayed,—to ride out the threatening storm
in safety.

While engaged in his operations on the Mobile, and
even while at Fort Jackson, he had kept up a correspondence with the governor of Louisiana, persuading
and urging him to the adoption of such measures, as
might be calculated to give security to the state. From
the information derived through this source, he felt
assured, that little reliance was to be placed on the
great body of the citizens; and that, to gain any decisive advantages from their services, it would be necessary to abandon any thing like temporizing policy, and
pursue a course at once steady and unwavering. Many, indulging the belief that West Florida would
shortly be restored to Spain; and a still greater number, resting in the opinion that the country could not
be successfully defended, had led most well designing
men astray; while Englishmen, Spaniards, and innumerable other foreigners, feeling no attachment to the

government, under which they lived, were, at any time, ready to surrender it to any power that might invade. The requisition made, had been badly filled; many had absolutely refused, even after being drafted, to enter the ranks. At so eventful a crisis as that which was fast approaching, it was painful to discover so great a want of union and regard for their duty, in those very persons on whom he would have to rely, for any sudden emergency. This reluctance to entering the field, there was a propriety in putting down, that the good might not be led astray, from privileges usurped by the designing; and to convince them, that those who shared the care and protection of the government, were under obligations to defend it, whenever required.

Governor Claiborne had been addressed on this subject; and, while the necessity of discouraging such a temper of mind among his citizens was insisted on, he was exhorted to use his exertions, in guarding every pass from the city, that the enemy, hovering in the gulf, might not obtain supplies from the shore. " I regret," said he " to hear of the discontents of your people : they must not exist. Whoever is not for us, is against us. Those who are drafted must be compelled to the ranks, or punished : it is no time to balance : the country must be defended; and he who refuses to aid, when called on, must be treated with severity. To repel the danger with which we are assailed, requires all our energies, and all our exertions. With union on our side, we shall be able to drive our invaders back to the ocean. Summon all your energy, and guard every avenue with confidential patroles, for spies and traitors are swarming around. Numbers will be flocking to your city, to gain information, and corrupt your citizens. Every aid in your power must be given, to prevent any vessels sailing with provisions. By us, the enemy must not be fed. Let none pass; for on this will depend our safety, until we can get a competent force in the field, to oppose attack, or become the assailants. We have more to dread from intestine, than open and avowed enemies: but, vigilance on our side, and all will be safe. Remember, our watch word is victory or death. Our country must and shall be defended. We will enjoy our liberty, or die in the last ditch."

He forwarded, at the same time, an address to the people of Louisiana, and endeavoured to excite them to a defence of their rights and liberties, and to raise in their minds an abhorrence of an enemy, who, by proclamation, and dishonourable stratagem, was seeking to promote disunion, and draw the disaffected to his standard. He pointed out the course the present crisis required them to adopt, and entreated them not to be lured from their fidelity to a country, of all others the freest and happiest, by uniting with a foe, who sought a furtherance of his views, by the most disreputable pretences,—by courting the friendship and aid of even traitors, pirates, and robbers.

" Your government, Louisianians, is engaged in a just and honourable contest, for the security of your individual, and her national rights. The only country on earth, where man enjoys freedom, where its blessings are alike extended to the poor and rich, calls on you to protect her from the grasping usurpation of

Britain :—she will not call in vain. I know that every man, whose bosom beats high, at the proud title of freeman, will promptly obey her voice, and rally round the eagles of his country, resolved to rescue her from impending danger, or nobly die in her defence. Who refuses to defend his rights, when called on by his government, deserves to be a slave,—deserves to be punished, as an enemy to his country—a friend to her foes."

The minds of the people of this state were thus gradually turned to consider of the contest, in which it was certainly expected they would be shortly engaged, that they might be ready and prepared to meet it, when the event should arrive. Preparations for collecting, in sufficient strength to repel an invasion, when it should be attempted, had been carried actively forward. The fiat of the secretary of war had been issued to the governors of the adjoining states: and Jackson had long since anxiously pressed them to hasten the execution of the order, and push their forces to the place of danger, without delay. The ardour felt by the governor of Tennessee, rendered any incentive unnecessary. He was well aware of the importance of activity and exertion, and had used all the authority of his office, to call the requisition forth, and have it in readiness.

Militia are
called out.
The venerable Shelby, of Kentucky, had been no less vigilant, in discharge of the duty required of him. The necessity of despatch, in military matters, and the advantages resulting from it, in his youth, and more advanced age, he had studied and learned in the field of battle. The troops from his state

were immediately organized;—placed under the command of major general Thomas, and proceeded down
the Ohio, to resist the inroads of the enemy.*   It
may be esteemed a circumstance of great good fortune, that Shelby, at a time so perilous as that in which
the United States were placed, during the period of
his services, should have been the chief magistrate of
Kentucky; a state possessing ample resources, and
which might have slumbered in inaction, but for the
energy of him who filled her executive chair. He did
not remain contented with a discharge of those duties,
merely imposed on him by his office; but, feeling the
ardour of his youth revived, excited his citizens by
manly appeals, and inspirited them by his own example. The government had never called upon the
patriotism of this state, that it had not been met with
a becoming zeal by the governor, and as cheerfully
and promptly acquiesced in by his people. The
bravery with which they crowded to the American
standard, at the first onset of danger, where they firmly supported the honour of the nation, enduring cold,
and hunger, and every privation, is remembered, and
will not be forgotten.

William Carroll, who, on the promotion of Jackson
in the army of the United States, had been appointed
a major general, was to command the requisition in-

* Although this requisition was ready to proceed, yet the
state of the quarter master's department was inadequate to
those outfits and supplies necessary to its departure. Thus
situated, individuals of the state came forward, pledged their
funds, and enabled it to set out.

CHAP. tended to be marched from Tennessee. He had issued
VIII. his orders to his division, and, on the 19th of December, the day appointed for their rendezvous, twen-
1814. ty-five hundred of the yeomanry of the state appeared
at Nashville; and, in eight days, embarked on board
their boats, and directed their way to New Orleans,
the place of their destination. To the industry of general Carroll, in hastening those arrangements, which
enabled his division so soon to depart, every respect is
due; for to his fortunate arrival, as will be seen hereafter, is greatly to be attributed the reason that success
did not result to the enemy, in his first assault, or that
Louisiana escaped the impending danger.

The militia, now organized from these two states,
were respectable for their numbers, and commanded by officers, who carried with them entire confidence. In bravery, they were not surpassed by any
troops; yet were they without experience or discipline,
and poorly armed. Many had procured muskets and
bayonets; though the greater part of them had arms
capable of rendering little or no service; and some had
none. To remedy their want of discipline was attended with some difficulty, on account of the slender
means afforded for instruction, while, in boats, they
were descending the river. Carroll's anxiety, however, for the respectable appearance of his troops, and
a still stronger desire entertained, that they might be
in a situation for immediate action, should necessity,
on his arrival, require it, led him to seize even on the
limited opportunities for improvement, that were within his reach. Whenever, from adverse winds, or any
other cause preventing his progress, he was compelled

to stop, his men were immediately brought to receive every information that could, under such circumstances, be communicated; and often, while floating with the stream, the decks of his boats formed a field for their manœuvres. Although in this way, considerable progress was made, and some advantages gained, yet they were but militia-men, and as yet altogether unqualified to meet the veteran troops, with which they were going to contend.

Although general Jackson had obtained his successes, heretofore, with troops of this description, yet he was far from entertaining a belief that they could be relied on, for manœuvring in an open field, against troops who were skilled, and inured to war. None knew better the point of exertion to which militia could be strained; that while successful, and resting with confidence in themselves, none could effect more; but when once dispirited, they became a useless weight. Taught by the recollection of his own difficulties, that forces of this description were ever capricious and refractory, he had heretofore brought to the notice of the secretary of war, a new and different course from what had been before pursued, as being more efficient, less expensive, and better calculated for the purposes of defence. In a letter to him, of the 20th of November, 1814, he observes, " Permit me to suggest a plan, which, on a fair experiment, will do Mode of away or lessen the expenses, under the existing mode supplying delinof calling militia forces into the field. Whenever there quencies happens to be a deficiency in the regular force, in any my. in the arparticular quarter, let the government determine on the necessary number: this should be apportioned among

the different states, agreeably to their respective representations, and called into service for, and during, the
war. The quota wanted will, in my opinion, be soon
raised, from premiums offered by those who are subject to militia duty, rather than be harassed by repeated
drafts. In the mean time, let the present bounty, given
by the government, be also continued. If this be
done, I will ensure that an effective force shall soon
appear in every quarter, amply sufficient for the reduction of Canada, and to drive all our enemies from our
shores."

Such was the course of things, and such the plans
adopted for security and safety, when the general
reached New Orleans. The period was too momentous to afford him a respite from business; and he immediately adopted such measures as could be earliest
effected, and were best calculated for resistance and
defence.

The legislature of Louisiana had been for some
weeks in session; and, through the governor's communication, had been informed of the situation and
strength of the country, and of the necessity of calling
all its resources into action; but, balancing in their
decisions, and uncertain of the best course to be pursued, to assure protection, they as yet had resolved
upon nothing promising certainty and safety, or calculated to infuse tranquillity and confidence in the public
mind. The arrival of Jackson, however, produced a
new aspect in affairs. His activity and zeal in preparation, and his reputation as a brave man and skilful
commander, turned all eyes towards him, and inspired

even the desponding with a confidence they had not before felt.

The volunteer corps of the city were reviewed, and a visit, in person, made to the different forts, to ascertain their situations, and the reliance that might be had on them, to repel the enemy's advance. Through the lakes, their large vessels could not pass : should an approach be attempted, through this route, in their barges, it might be met and opposed by the gun boats, which already guarded this passage; but if, unequal to the contest, they should be captured, it would, at any rate, give timely information of a descent, which might be resisted on the landing, before an opportunity could be had of executing fully their designs. Up the Mississippi, however, was looked upon as the most probable pass, through which might be made an attempt to reach the city ; and here were progressing suitable preparations for defence.

We have already noticed that colonel Hayne had been despatched from Mobile, with directions to view the Mississippi, near its mouth, and report if any advantageous position could be found for the erection of batteries; and whether the re-establishment of the old fort at the Balize could command the river, in a way to prevent its being ascended. That it could not be relied on for this purpose, the opinions of military men had already declared. General Jackson was always disposed to respect the decisions of those, who, from their character and standing, were entitled to confidence: yet in matters of great importance, it formed no part of his creed to attach his faith to the statements of any, where the object being within his reach, it was in his power to satisfy himself. Trusting implicitly in colonel Hayne, as a military man, who, from proper observations, could infer correct conclusions, he had been despatched to examine how far it was practicable to obstruct and secure this channel. His report was confirmatory of the previous information received, that it was incapable, from its situation, of effecting any such object.

General
plans
adopted
for de-
fence.

Fort St. Philips was now resorted to, as the lowest point on the river, where the erection of works could be at all serviceable. The general had returned to New Orleans, on the 9th, from a visit to this place, which he had ordered to be repaired and strengthened. The commanding officer was directed to remove every combustible material without the fort; to have two additional platforms immediately raised; and the embrasures so enlarged, that the ordnance might have the greatest possible sweep upon their circles, and be brought to bear on any object within their range, that might approach either up or down the river. At a small distance below, the Mississippi, changing its course, left a neck of land in the bend, covered with timber, and which obstructed the view. From this point, down to where old Fort Bourbon stood, on the west side, the growth along the bank was ordered to be cut away, that the shot from St. Philips, ranging across this point of land, might reach an approaching vessel, before she should be unmasked from behind it. On the site of Bourbon, was to be thrown up a strong work, defended by five twenty-four pounders, which, with the fort above, would expose an enemy to a cross fire, for half a mile. A mile above St. Philips was to be established a work, which, in conjunction with the others, would command the river for two miles. At Terre au Bœuf, and at the English turn, twelve miles below the city were also to be taken measures for defence; where it was expected by Jackson, with his flying artillery and fire ships, he would be able, certainly, to arrest the enemy's advance. This system of defence, properly established, he believed would give security from any attack in this direction. Fort St. Philips, with the assistant batteries, above and below, would so concentrate their fires, that an enemy could never pass, without suffering greatly, and perhaps being so shattered, that they would fall an easy prey to those still higher up the river. The essential difficulty was to have them commenced, and speedily finished. On returning, he hastened to apprize the governor of his views, and entreated him to aid in their furtherance. It was proposed to submit it to the consideration of the legislature, and to prevail, if possible, with the planters, to furnish their negroes, by whom alone such work could, in so insalubrious a climate, be safely done. " If what is proposed be performed," said he, " I will stand pledged that the invaders of your state shall never, through this route, reach your city." He desired to be informed, early, of the success of the application, and how far the legislature would be disposed to extend their fostering care to the objects suggested; that, in the event of failure, he might have recourse to such resources as were within his reach. " But," added he, " not a moment is to be lost. With energy and expedition, all is safe :—delay, and all is lost."

The plans of operation and defence were projecting on an extensive scale. The only objects of fear were the traitors who infested the city; and to these, after the most incessant exertions, he had well nigh fallen a victim.

The legislature had met his views with becoming zeal; and the necessary measures had been taken, to have the selected points for defence completed in the shortest possible time; which would present, on the Mississippi, barriers, that it was not feared the enemy would be able to pass.

Upon lakes Borgne and Pontchartrain, an equally strong confidence was had, that all would be safe from invasion. Commodore Patterson, who commanded the naval forces, had executed every order with promptness and activity. Agreeably to instructions received from the commanding general, to extend to all the passes on the lakes every protection in his power, he had already sent out the gun boats, under lieutenant Jones. From their vigilance and capability to defend, great advantages were calculated to arise; added to which, the Rigolets, the communication between the two lakes, was defended by Petit Coquille fort, a strong work, under the command of captain Newman, which, when acting in conjunction with the gun boats, it was supposed would be competent to repel any assault that might here be waged. The prospects of defence had been improved, by detachments sent out to fell timber across every small bayou and creek, leading out of the lakes, and through which a passage for boats and barges could be afforded; and to increase the obstruction, by sinking large frames in their beds, and filling

Gun boats
are sent
on lake
Borgne.

them with earth. Guards and videttes were out, to watch every thing that passed, and give the earliest information. In despite of these precautionary mea- sures, treachery opened a way, and pointed the entrance of the enemy to a narrow pass, through which they ef- fected a landing, and reached, previously to being dis- covered, the banks of the Mississippi.

Such were the measures adopted for the protection of Louisiana, against an attack, which, although hither- to resting on conjecture, was supported by too many strong circumstances to admit of doubt. Information of a large force having left England, filled with high hopes and expectations—the attack on Fort Bowyer, and the inflammatory proclamations, already published, with anonymous letters, received from persons in the West Indies and Pensacola, known, and to be relied on, all tended strongly to unfold their views, and to dissipate every thing like doubt.* But the time was at hand when conjecture was giving place to certainty; when the intentions of the enemy were fully develop- ing themselves; and the fact fairly presented, that Louisiana would fall, and her principal city be sacked, unless the brave men, associated to defend her, should stand, firmly resolved to justify the high expectations formed of their valour. Certain information was at British hand, of an English fleet being now off Cat and Ship shipping island, within a short distance of the American lines, arrive on the coast. where their strength and numbers were daily increas- ing.

Lieutenant Jones, in command of the gun boats, on Lake Borgne, was directed to reconnoitre, and ascer-

* See note B.

CHAP.
VIII.
1814.

tain their disposition and force; and, in the event they should attempt, through this route, to effect a disembarkation, to retire to the Rigolets, and there, with his flotilla, make an obstinate resistance, and contend to the last. He remained off Ship island, until the 12th of December; when, understanding the enemy's forces were much increased, he thought it most advisable to change his anchorage, and retire to a position near Malheureux island. This course was rendered more necessary, because affording a safer position, and, in the event of being attacked, a better opportunity of making good his retreat to the Rigolets, where alone he was instructed to attempt opposition. Whoever looks upon a map of the country, will at once discover the importance of the place, if driven into action with a greatly superior force. This, and Chef Menteur, which unite at the entrance to the lake, and form a narrow channel, constitutes the only pass into Pontchartrain. By reaching it, the gun boats would present as formidable an opposition as could be made by all the force that could be brought against them, and put at defiance any effort that could be made, to gain the city through this route.

On the 13th, Jones discovered the enemy moving off in his barges, and directing his way towards Pass Christian. He was not long in doubt, as to the objects probably had in view; for, although at first it was supposed to be "a disembarkation, intended to be landed there, yet, on their passing it, and pursuing their course still further westwardly, he at once concluded an attack on the gun boats was designed." His orders left him no discretion, as to the place he should meet and fight

them. Indeed, his flotilla, although quite inconsider- CHAP.
able in numbers, was of too much consequence to the VIII.
nation, at this juncture, to be inadvertently risked, or
in fact risked at all, unless under circumstances giving 1814.
a decided superiority. In no other way was this to be
obtained, than by reaching the point to which he had
been ordered : this he endeavoured to effect, as soon
as he became satisfied of what was intended by their
present movement. Weighing, therefore, his anchors,
with the design of reaching the position referred to in
his orders, he soon discovered it to be wholly impracticable. A strong wind having blown for some days
to the east, from the lake to the gulf, had so reduced
the depth of water, that the best and deepest channels
were insufficient to float his little squadron. The oars
were resorted to, but without rendering the least assistance : it was immoveable. Recourse was now
had to throwing every thing overboard that could be
spared, to lighten and bring them off ; all, however,
was ineffectual,—nothing could afford relief. At this
moment of extreme peril and danger, the tide coming
suddenly in, relieved from present embarrassment, and
lifting them from the shoal, they bore away from the
attack meditated ; directed their course for the Rigolets ; and came to anchor at one o'clock the next morning, on the west passage of Malheureux isle ; where, at
day, they discovered the pursuit had been abandoned.

At the bay of St. Louis was a small depot of public 129
stores, which had, that morning, been directed, by
lieutenant Jones, to be brought off. Mr. Johnston, on
board the Sea Horse, had proceeded in the execution
of this order. The enemy, on the retreat of Jones.

κ k

CHAP. despatched three of their barges to capture him ; but,
VIII. unable to effect it, they were driven back. An additional force now proceeded against him ; when a smart
1814. action commenced, and the assailants were again com-
130 pelled to retire, with some loss. Johnston, satisfied
that it was out of his power successfully to defend
himself, and considering it hopeless to attempt uniting,
in face of so large a force, with the gun boats off Malheureux, determined to blow up his vessel, burn the
stores, and effect his retreat by land. A prodigious
Loss of explosion, and flames bursting on his view, assured
the Sea Jones of the probable step that had been taken.
Horse.

Early on the morning of the 14th, the enemy's
barges, lying about nine miles to the east, suddenly
weighed their anchors; and, getting under way, proceeded westwardly to the pass, where our gun boats
still lay. The same difficulty they had experienced
yesterday was now encountered. Perceiving the approach of the enemy's flotilla, an attempt was made to
retreat; but in vain. The wind was entirely lulled,
and a perfect calm prevailed ; while a strong current,
setting to the gulf, rendered every effort to retire unavailing. No alternative was at hand; but a single
course was left;—to meet and fight them. At once the
resolution was adopted, to avail themselves of the best
position they could obtain, wait their approach, and
defend themselves, whilst there was a hope of success.
The line was formed, with springs on the cables,
and all were waiting, composedly, the arrival of a foe,
who imagined himself advancing to an easy conquest.
The contest, in so open and unfavourable a situation,
and against so superior a force, promised, indeed, to

be a very unequal one : yet the firmness and bravery
which had always characterized our fearless tars in
battle, were, on this occasion, not to be tarnished. An
unfortunate state of things, which they could not control, had brought them into battle at a moment, and
under circumstances, their discretion did not approve ;
but, being inevitable, every mind was determined on
a desperate stand ; and still, though beaten, to preserve
unsullied their reputation,—their flag from dishonour.

Forty-three boats, mounting as many cannon, with
twelve hundred chosen men, well armed, constituted
the strength of the assailants. Advancing in extended
line, they were presently in reach : and, at half after
eleven o'clock, commencing a fire, the action soon
became general. Owing to a strong current, setting
out to the east, two of the boats, numbers 156 and
163, were unable to keep their anchorage, and floated
about an hundred yards in advance of the line. This
circumstance was unfortunate ; for although it could
by no means be calculated, that victory could be attendant on a conflict, where strength and numbers
were so disproportionate, yet, could the line have been
preserved, the chances for defence would have been
increased,—the opportunity more favourable for inflicting injury, and crippling the foe, while the period of
the contest would have been protracted. Every moment this could have been prolonged would have
proved essentially advantageous ; for soon as the wind
should spring up, which yet continued lulled, the boats
would be rendered more manageable, and an opportunity afforded of retiring from the battle, whenever the
result promised to become fatal.

The enemy, coming up with the two gun boats, in advance of the line, and relying on their numbers and supposed superior skill, determined to board. For this purpose, several of their barges bore down on number 156, commanded by lieutenant Jones, but failed in the attempt; they were repulsed, with an immense destruction, both in their officers and crew, and two of their boats sunk; one of them, with one hundred and eighty men, went down, immediately under the stern of number 156. Again rallying, with a stronger force than before, another desperate assault was made, to board, and carry at the point of the sword, which was again repelled, with considerable loss. The contest was now bravely waged, and spiritedly resisted. Lieutenant Jones, unable to keep on the deck, from a severe wound he had received, retired, leaving the command with George Parker, who no less valiantly defended his flag, until, severely wounded, he was forced to leave his post. No longer able to maintain the conflict, and overpowered by superior numbers, they yielded the victory, after a contest of forty minutes, in which every thing was done that gallantry could do, and nothing unperformed that duty required. The commandant was ably supported by lieutenants Spedder and M'Ever, of numbers 162 and 123, and by sailing masters Ulrick and Deferris, of numbers 163 and 5. The two former were wounded; M'Ever severely, in both arms; in one so badly, as to be compelled to have it amputated. It is unnecessary to take up the time of the reader, in commendation of this Spartan band: their bravery and good conduct will be long remembered and admired,

and excite emotions much stronger than language can
paint. The great disparity of force between the combatants, added to the advantages the enemy derived
from the peculiar construction of their boats, which gave
them an opportunity to take any position that circumstances and safety directed, while the others lay wholly
unmanageable, presents a curious and strange result;
that, while the American loss was but six killed, and
thirty-five wounded, that of their assailants was not
less than three hundred. The British have never afforded us any light upon this subject: but, from every information, and from all the attendant circumstances of the battle, it was even believed to have exceeded this number; of which a large proportion was
officers.*

The British returned to their shipping, at Cat island,
with their prisoners, carrying with them a convincing
argument, to do away the belief with which they had
arrived, that, in this section of country, the inhabitants
were waiting, with open arms, to receive them; and   131
that the forces embodied for its defence would retire,
at the first appearance of danger. It was the same argument which, a few weeks before, had been made to
colonel Nicholls, at Fort Bowyer, and which had produced on his mind such conviction, as to render him

	Boats.	Men.	Guns.
* The British had	43	1200	43
The Americans	5	182	23
	38	1018	20

So that the disparity of force was as eight—seven—and nearly two to one.

unwilling, at that time, that the matter should be further discussed in his presence.

This disaster was announced to general Jackson,
while on a visit to the lakes, whither he had gone to
examine the situation of the different works, there
erected. He heard it with much concern; for on it
important consequences rested. The means of watching the enemy, and ascertaining his projects, were now
cut off, and the necessity imposed, of resorting for
safety, in this direction, to entirely different remedies.

Aided by ours, and the great number of their own
boats, his fears for the safety of Mobile were much
increased. The apprehensions which he had constantly
entertained for this place were of the most lively kind.
Although he had every confidence in the gallant commander at Fort Bowyer, yet he well knew how ineffi-
cient were the exertions of a brave man, when assailed by superior strength and numbers. The security
of this place was to him a matter of the greatest concern. It seems to have been an object that never sufficiently fastened itself on the consideration of our enemy. His own apprehensions of an invasion here, as
affecting much more seriously the interest of the lower
country, was to him a cause of constant uneasiness.
He felt confident, that, while this remained safe, so
might the country adjacent; but if it fell, conquered
by a greatly superior force, the settlements on the
Mobile and Alabama rivers would become tributary,
and New Orleans be involved in the general ruin.
Deeply impressed with the importance of the place, he
had heretofore brought to the view of the secretary of
war the propriety and necessity of adopting such a

course, as should place it entirely out of the reach of
danger. To effect this, he had proposed that a large
frigate, mounting forty-four guns, which, for some
cause, to him unknown, had been left on the stocks,
at Tchifonte, in an unfinished state, should be completed, and applied to this purpose. " Let her," he
remarked, " be placed in the Navy Cove, which will
protect the rear of the fort ; and my life upon it, ten
thousand troops, and all the British fleet, cannot take
the place, nor enter the bay. This will be their point
of attack ; if carried, they will penetrate the Indian nation,—there make a stand, and excite the savages to
war, and the negroes to insurrection and massacre ;—
penetrate, if they can, to the left bank of the Mississippi, and arrest all communication. If they succeed
in this, the lower country falls, of course." Nothing,
however, had ever been done: and the defence now
rested on the means which he himself could reach.
An express was sent to general Winchester, apprizing
him of what had happened ; that all communication
being cut off, he must look to the procuring supplies
for his army, from Tennessee, through the posts established in the Creek country. " The enemy," he
continues, " will attempt, through Pass Huron, to reach
you : watch, nor suffer yourself to be surprised ; haste,
and throw sufficient supplies into Fort Bowyer ; and
guard vigilantly the communication from Fort Jackson, lest it be destroyed. Mobile point must be supported and defended, at every hazard. The enemy
has given us a large coast to guard ; but I trust, with
the smiles of heaven, to be able to meet and defeat

133

him, at every point he may venture his foot upon the land."

Increased vigilance, and enlarged exertions, were now required, to guard the different routes, through which they might seek to make good their progress, and reach the object of their visit. Major Lacoste, commanding the battalion of coloured troops, was ordered, with two pieces of cannon, and a sufficient force, to take post, and defend the Chef Menteur road, that led from the head of lake Borgne to New Orleans. In fact, wherever an inlet or creek, of the smallest size, putting in, justified the belief, that through it an entrance might be effected, suitable arrangements were made, to oppose the passage, and prevent approach. Through the Rigolets was presumed the most probable route the enemy would adventure, that, by gaining lake Pontchartrain, a landing might be made, above or below, or at bayou St. John, opposite the city; and, by a division of their forces, make such a diversion, as, with raw troops, could not be met, under any circumstances of advantage.

This place had been confided to captain Newman, of the artillery. It was an important point, as well for the purposes already named, as being a position whence any movement on the lakes could be discovered. On the 22d, it was reinforced by several heavy pieces of cannon, and an additional supply of men. He was advised by the general, of its consequence, and that it was not to be inconsiderately yielded; but that, in the event he should be compelled to abandon it, every thing being properly secured, he was to make good

his retreat to Chef Menteur, where he would be covered by an additional force: "But," added he "you
are not to retreat, until your judgment is well convinced that it is absolutely necessary to the very salvation of your command."

On the 16th, the militia were reviewed by Jackson.
He had found, on his first arrival at New Orleans,
such a state of despondency manifested by the people,
that to remove it had called forth all his exertions.
His active and incessant endeavours to have defended
every accessible point, and a confidence, constantly
evinced, that his resources were commensurate with
all the purposes of successful resistance, had completely undermined those fears, at first so generally indulged. Lest, from what had lately happened, the same
state of things might be again produced, was the principal cause of appearing before them, to-day, on review; to convince them, by his deportment, that the
safety of the city was not to be despaired of. He directed an address, previously prepared for the purpose, to be read to them. It was drawn in language
breathing the warmth of his own feelings, and well
calculated to communicate and inspire the same glow
to others. He told them that they were contending
for all that could render life desirable; "For your
property and lives;—for that which is dearer than all,
your wives and children;—for liberty, without which,
country, life, and property, are not worth possessing.
Even the embraces of wives and children are a reproach to the wretch, who would deprive them by his
cowardice, of those inestimable blessings. You are
to contend with an enemy who seeks to deprive you

of the least of these,—who avows a war of vengeance and desolation, carried on and marked by cruelties, lusts, and horrors, unknown to civilized nations.

" Natives of the United States! the enemy you are to contend with are the oppressors of your infant political existence—they are the men your fathers fought and conquered, whom you are now to oppose. Descendants of Frenchmen! natives of France! they are English, the hereditary, the eternal enemies of your ancient country, the invaders of that you have adopted, who are your foes. Spaniards! remember the conduct of your allies at St. Sebastian, and recently at Pensacola, and rejoice that you have an opportunity of avenging the brutal injuries inflicted by men who dishonour the human race. Louisianians! your general rejoices to witness the spirit that animates you, not only for your honour, but your safety ; for whatever had been your conduct or wishes, his duty would have led, and yet will lead him to confound the citizen, unmindful of his rights, with the enemy he ceases to oppose. Commanding men who know their rights, and are determined to defend them, he salutes you as brethren in arms; and has now a new motive to exert all his faculties, which shall be strained to the utmost, in your defence. Continue with the energy you have begun, and he promises you not only safety, but victory over an insolent foe, who has insulted you by an affected doubt of your attachment to the constitution of your country. Your enemy is near ; his sails already cover the lakes : but the brave are united ; and if he find us contending among ourselves, it will be for the prize of valour,—and fame, its noblest reward."

Resistance on the lakes being at an end, no doubt
was entertained, but that the moment for action would be, as early as the enemy could make his prepa- rations to proceed.   At what point, at what time, and with a force how greatly superior to his own, were matters wholly resting in uncertainty, and could not be known, until they actually transpired.   All the means for opposition were to be seized on, without delay.   That the hour of attack was not far distant, was confirmed by a circumstance which reflects no considerable honour on the officer in command of the fleet.   The day after the contest on the lakes, Mr. Shields, purser in the navy, was despatched with a flag, to Cat island, accompanied by Dr. Murrell, for the purpose of alleviating the situation of our wounded, and to effect a negotiation, by which they should be liberated on parole.   We are not aware that such an application militated against the usages and customs of war : if not, the flag of truce should have been re- spected ; nor ought its bearer to have been detained as a prisoner.   Admiral Cochrane's fears, that it was a wile, designed to find out his strength and situation, are far from presenting a sufficient excuse for so wanton 134 an outrage on propriety.   If this were apprehended, could not the messengers have been met, at a distance from the fleet, and ordered back, without a nearer ap- proach ?   Had this been done, no information could have been gained, and the object designed to be se- cured by their detention would have been answered, without infringing that amicable intercourse between contending armies, which, when violated or disregard- ed, opens a door to brutal and savage warfare.   Find-

CHAP. ing they did not return, the cause of it was at once
VIII. correctly divined.

135 1814.   Early on the 15th, expresses were sent off, up the
             coast, in quest of general Coffee; to endeavour to pro-
An ex-   cure information of the Kentucky and Tennessee di-
press is
sent in   visions, which it was hoped were not far distant, and
quest of   to urge their speedy approach. In his communication
general
Coffee.   to Coffee, the general observes, " You must not sleep,
             until you arrive within striking distance. Your accus-
             tomed activity is looked for. Innumerable defiles
             present themselves, where your riflemen will be all
             important. An opportunity is at hand, to reap for
             yourself and brigade the approbation of your country."

             In obedience to the order he had received at Mo-
bile, to occupy some central position, where his horses
might be subsisted, and whence he might act as circumstances should require, Coffee had proceeded as
far as Sandy creek, a small distance above Baton
Rouge, where he had halted. His brigade, on its
march, had been greatly exposed, and had encountered
many hardships. The cold season had set in; and,
for twenty days, it had rained incessantly. The waters
were raised to uncommon heights, and every creek
and bayou was to be bridged or swum. Added to
this, their march was through a poor country, but
thinly settled, where little subsistence was to be had,
and that procured with much difficulty. He had been
at this place eight or ten days, when, late on the
night of the 17th, the express, despatched from head
quarters, reached him. He lost no time in executing
the order; and, directing one of his regiments, which,
for the greater convenience of foraging, lay about six

miles off, to unite with him, he was ready in the morning, and marched the instant it arrived. In consequence of innumerable exposures, there were, at this
time, three hundred on his sick list. These being
left, he commenced his march, with twelve hundred
and fifty men. The weather yet continued extremely
cold and rainy, which prevented their proceeding with
the celerity, the exigency of the moment so much required. Coffee, perceiving that the movement of his
whole force, in a body, would perhaps occasion delays,
ruinous to the main object in view, ordered all who
were well mounted, and able to proceed, to advance
with him; while the rest of his brigade, under suitable
officers, were left to follow on, as fast as the weak and
exhausted condition of their horses would permit. His
force, by this arrangement, was reduced to eight hundred men, with whom he moved with the utmost
industry. Having marched eighty miles the last day,
he encamped, on the night of the 19th, within fifteen
miles of New Orleans, making, in two days, a distance
of one hundred and fifty miles. Continuing his advance, early next morning, he halted within four miles
of the city, to examine the state and condition of his
arms; and to learn, in the event the enemy had landed,
the relative position of the two armies.

These brave men, without murmuring, had now
traversed an extent of country, nothing short of eight
hundred miles, and under trials sufficiently severe
to have appalled the most resolute and determined.
They had enrolled themselves, not as volunteers sometimes do, to frolic, and, by peaceable campaigns, to
gain a name in arms; they had done it, knowing that

an enemy, if not already at hand, was certainly expected, with whom they would have to contend, and contend severely. Great reliance was had on them by the
commanding general; and their good conduct, in the
different situations in which they had acted with him,
was a proof how much they deserved it. On inspect-
ing their arms, which consisted principally of rifles,
two hundred were discovered to be greatly injured by
the weather, and unfit for service.

The advance of colonel Hinds, from Woodville,
with the Mississippi dragoons, was no less prompt and
expeditious; an active and brave officer, he was, on
this, as on all other occasions, at his post, ready to act
as was required. Having received his orders, he hastened forward, and effected, in four days, a march of
two hundred and thirty miles.

On the 16th, colonel Hynes, aid-de-camp to general Carroll, reached head quarters, with information
from the general, that he would be down, as early as
possible; but that the situation of the weather, and
high winds, greatly retarded his progress. The steam
boat was immediately put in requisition, and ordered
up the river, to aid him in reaching his destination,
without loss of time. He was advised of the necessity
of hastening rapidly forward; that the lakes were in
possession of the enemy, and their arrival daily looked
for: " But," continued Jackson, " I am resolved,
feeble as my force is, to assail him, on his first landing, and perish, sooner than he shall reach the city."

Independent of a large force, descending with general Carroll, his coming was looked to with additional
pleasure, from the circumstance of his having with him

a boat, laden with arms, which, destined for the defence of the country, he had overtaken on the passage. His falling in with them was fortunate; for, had
their arrival depended on those to whom they had
been incautiously given, they might have come too
late, and after all danger had subsided; as was indeed
the case with others, forwarded from Pittsburg,
which, through the unpardonable conduct of those
who had been entrusted with their management and
transportation, did not reach New Orleans, until after
all difficulties had ended. Great inconvenience was
sustained, during the siege, for want of arms, to place
in the hands of the militia. Great as it was, it would
have been increased, even to an alarming extent, but
for the accidental circumstance of this boat falling
into the hands of the Tennessee division, which impelled it on, and thereby produced incalculable advantage.*

* On the first intimation that the British intended a descent on this section of the United States, general Jackson
had suggested to the secretary of war the scarcity of both
arms and ordnance, and the necessity of having the deficiency remedied, as soon as possible. Mr. Monroe had given the
earliest attention to this subject, and had ordered an ample
supply to be embarked from Pittsburg, sufficiently early
to have reached head quarters, previously to the enemy's
landing. Their transportation down the western waters
had been confided to men, who felt not a sufficient concern
for their speedy arrival, to use the necessary diligence. Whether the government had given any such orders, or it were a
piece of penny-wise economy, suggested by the quarter master, we do not know. The fact, however, is, that a steam
vessel, sailing with much expedition, proposed to carry and
deliver them at New Orleans, in eighteen days, which would

This division, as we have before remarked, had left Nashville on the 19th of last month. Their exertions, without which they could not have arrived in time to have given that assistance and protection which the peril of the moment so much required, entitle them and their commander to every gratitude. But above all, is our gratitude due to that benign Providence, who, having aided in the establishment of our glorious independence, again manifested his goodness and power, in guarding the rights of a country, rendered sacred by the blood of the virtuous, heretofore shed in her defence. It rarely, if ever, happens, that the

have been in time for all the purposes afterwards needed. But he who had the management of this business, because he had it in his power to save a very inconsiderable sum in freight, preferred delivering them to the captain of a large flat bottomed boat, which moved slowly, and which, withal, it was understood, would occasionally stop on the way, to traffic, and trade off the different articles with which she was laden. On all occasions, we would commend the doctrine of economy, when founded on correct principles : but that minister or agent of the government, who, to save a partial expense, hazards the loss of thousands ; or who, through parsimonious views, of any kind whatever, risks the loss of a whole country, evidences such weak and narrow-sighted policy, as can on no ground be justified. This single circumstance, as it afterwards turned out, is sufficient to show the correctness of the position, if argument were necessary to establish it. The general, in a letter to the secretary of war, after the battle of the 8th, remarks, that if he had had a sufficiency of arms, he would have captured or destroyed the whole British army ; and this he might have had, if the agents of the government had executed the duties confided to them, on a scale liberal as the crisis demanded.

Cumberland river admits a passage for boats, so early in the season; but torrents of rain descending swelled the stream, and wafted our troops safely to the Mississippi, where all obstructions were at an end. Their apprehensions lest the blow might be stricken, and the injury done, before they could reach their destined point, had inspired an alacrity and exertion, which brought them to the place of danger and usefulness, in a shorter period of time than even traders had usually employed, when hurrying with their produce to market.

While these preparations were progressing, to concentrate the forces within his reach, the general was turning his attention to ward off any blow that might be aimed, before his expected reinforcements should arrive. Every point, capable of being successfully assailed, was receiving such additional strength and security as could be given. Patroles and videttes were ranged through the country, that the earliest intelligence might be had of any intended movement. The militia of the state was called out *en masse;* and, through the interference of the legislature, an embargo declared, to afford an opportunity of procuring additional recruits for the navy. General Villery, because an inhabitant of the country, and best understanding the several points on the lakes, susceptible of, and requiring defence, was ordered, with the Louisiana militia, to search out, and give protection to the different passes, where a landing might be effected.

To hinder the enemy from obtaining supplies on the shore, a detachment was sent to Pearl river, to prevent any parties from landing, until the stock could

M m

CHAP. be driven from the neighbourhood.   The precaution,
VIII. for some time used, of restricting the departure of
~~~~~~
1814. any vessel with provisions, had greatly disappointed
the expectations of the British, and had even introduced distress into Pensacola.   The governor had solicited the opening a communication, for the relief of
136   the suffering inhabitants of his province. Jackson was
aware that this appeal to his humanity might be a stratagem, having for its object to aid his enemy.   Although the governor, hitherto, had given no flattering
evidence, either of his friendship, his candour, or sincerity, still his statement might be correct; and if so,
the neutrality of his country established a well-founded
claim to the benevolence of the Americans. Balancing
between a desire that these people should not be
seriously injured, and a fear that the application was
intended for a very different purpose, he determined to
err on the side of mercy, and relieve their wants. This
he directed general Winchester, at Mobile, to effect,
if his stock of provisions would permit it.   He was
particularly enjoined that the quantity sent should be
small, and be conveyed by water: " For if," said he,
" the Spaniards are really in distress, and it shall be
taken by the British, it will excite their just indignation towards them, and erase all friendship, while they
will be afforded an additional proof of ours : and the
supply, being inconsiderable, will be of no great benefit to our enemy."

His arrangements were well conceived, and rapidly
progressing; but they were still insufficient; and his
own forebodings assured him, that, to obtain security,
something stronger than had been yet resorted to,

required to be adopted. That there was an enemy in
the midst of his camp, more to be feared than those
who were menacing from abroad, was indeed highly
probable ; while an apprehension indulged, that there
were many foreigners, who, feeling no attachment for
the country, and having nothing to defend, would not
scruple to avail themselves of every opportunity, to
give intelligence of the strength, situation, and arrangement of his camp, excited his fears, and induced
a wish to apply the earliest possible corrective. A
stranger himself, his own conjectures might not have led
to the conclusion ; but information received, before and
soon after his arrival, through different channels, had
awakened a belief, that the country was filled with traitors and spies, who, if not closely guarded, might occasion the worst of consequences. Although he had been
in possession of data, sufficiently strong to confirm
him in the opinion, that the facts were truly as had
been represented, until now, no urgent necessity had
arisen, rendering a resort to rigid measures essential
to the general safety. Abundant evidence of prevailing disaffection had been already obtained, through
governor Claiborne. In a letter to general Jackson,
after his return from Pensacola, he observes, " Enemies to the country may blame your prompt and energetic measures ; but in the person of every patriot,
you will find a supporter. I am well aware of the
lax police of this city, and indeed of the whole state,
with respect to strangers. I think, with you, that our
country is filled with traitors and spies. On this subject, I have written pressingly to the city authorities
and parish judges. Some regulations, I hope, will be

adopted by the first, and greater vigilance be exercised, in future, by the latter."

1814.   Never, perhaps, all the circumstances considered, did any general advance to the defence and protection of a people situated in his own country, where greater room was had to distrust the success of the event, and believe all efforts hopeless. That there should be found, at all times, and in all places, an inconsiderable few, who would not withhold their assent to a change in the form of any government, under which they might live, is not a circumstance to excite surprise. Some might be induced to it, if for no other reason, to alter a condition in life, which, if not improved, could not be worsted ; and in our country particularly, where foreigners are so freely and readily admitted to all our rights and privileges,many of whom being allured not by any attachment, but from motives of cupidity alone, shall we ever have to regret, perhaps, a want of union and energy, at those periods, when they shall be mostly needed. But that disaffection should ever be found in our national councils, is an increased source of regret, and makes it to assume a character of deeper danger. When, therefore, general Jackson was informed by the governor, that the legislature, instead of discharging, with alacrity, diligence, and good faith, the duties which had been confided to them by their constituents, had, under the garb of privilege, endeavoured to mar the execution of measures the most salutary, he might well suppose the country in danger, and suspect a want of fidelity in her citizens. 137 zens. Although we would gladly draw a veil over the conduct of this body, and forgive the error, yet it is

difficult, nor is it necessary to forget that heretofore, at
a moment of expected danger, they exerted themselves
against the establishment of any system of defence.
General Flournoy at that time commanded. Apprehending invasion, he applied to the governor, for what
aid the state could afford. His constitutional resources
were attempted, and an effort made to draw out the
militia : they resisted the requisition ; and that resistance, so far from being discountenanced by the legislature, then in session, was promoted and encouraged,
by their assuming to themselves the right of declaring
the demand illegal, unnecessary, and oppressive.
When popular resentment is once awakened, and opposition to measures, however proper, once begun, the
slightest encouragement impels it on ; but when the
highest authorities become abettors, and, by their
conduct and expressions, give it sanction, the delusion is increased, and soon swells beyond the bounds
where reason can control. Thus supported, the militia stood their ground, and resolutely resisted the call
to defend their country. This example had already
induced the conviction that they were privileged persons, and had reserved to them, on all occasions,
when called for, the right of determining if the call were
regular, where they would prefer to act, and be governed accordingly. When, therefore, the first requisition
made by Jackson, was attempted to be filled, a number
made a tender of their services, as volunteers ; but on
this condition, that they were not to be marched from
the state. The reply made showed they were to act
with a general who knew nothing of temporizing policy, and who would go the entire length that safety

and necessity required. They were assured his object was to defend the country, and that he should do it, at all hazards; that soldiers, who entered the ranks, should forget the habits of social life, and be willing and prepared to go wherever duty and danger called; such he wanted, and none others would he have.

Influenced by these, and other weighty considerations, which were daily disclosed; and from a conviction which he felt was not founded upon light considerations—that the country, without it, could not be saved; he brought to the view of the legislature the propriety and necessity of suspending the writ of *habeas corpus*. They proceeded slowly to the investigation, and were deliberating, with great caution, upon their right and power to adopt such a measure; when the general, sensible that procrastination was dangerous, and might defeat the objects intended to be answered, suspended their councils, by declaring the city and environs of New Orleans under martial law.

Declaration of martial law.

All persons entering the city were required, immediately, to report themselves to the adjutant general; and on failing to do so, to be arrested, and held for examination. None were to depart from it, or be suffered to pass beyond the chain of sentinels, but by permission from the commanding general, or one of the staff: nor was any vessel or craft to be permitted to sail on the river, or the lakes, but by the same authority, or a passport signed by the commander of the naval forces.

The lamps were to be extinguished at nine o'clock at night; after which time, all persons found in the streets, or from their respective homes, without per-

mission, in writing, signed as above, were to be arrest- CHAP.
ed, as spies, and detained for examination. VIII.

At a crisis so important, and from a persuasion that 1814.
the country, in its menaced situation, could not be
saved, by the exercise of any ordinary powers, he believed it best to adopt a course that should be efficient,
even if it partially endangered the rights and privileges
of the citizen. He proclaimed martial law, believing
necessity and policy required it: " Under a solemn
conviction that the country, committed to his care,
could by such a measure alone be saved from utter
ruin; and from a religious belief, that he was performing the most important and sacred duty. By it, he
intended to supersede such civil powers, as, in their
operation, interfered with those he was obliged to exercise. He thought that, at such a moment, constitutional forms should be suspended, for the preservation
of constitutional rights; and that there could be no
question, whether it were better to depart, for a moment, from the enjoyment of our dearest privileges,
or have them wrested from us forever."

This rigid course, however, was by no means well
received. Whether it had for its object good or evil,
whether springing from necessity, or from a spirit of
oppression in its author, with many, was not a material question: it was sufficient for them to consider
it an infraction of the law, to excite their warmest opposition; whilst the *necessitas rei* afforded no substantial argument, to induce a conviction of its propriety. Whether the civil should yield to military
law, or which should have control, with those whose
anxious wishes were for the safety of the state, was not

a matter of deep concern; but to busy politicians, and lukewarm patriots, it opened a field for investigation; and many had arguments at command, to prove it an usurpation of power, an outrage upon government, and a violation of the constitution. Pending the invasion, and while affairs of major importance impended, no occasion was presented of testing its correctness; but so soon as the enemy had retired, and before it was ascertained, whether, at some more fortunate and less guarded point, they might not return, to renew those efforts which had so lately failed, Dominick A. Hall, judge of the United States court for this district, determined to wage a war of authority, and have it decided, if, in any event, the civil power could be deprived of supremacy. Jackson believed his time of too much importance, at so momentous a period, to be wasted in the discussion of civil matters. Giving it, therefore, the attention he believed its officiousness merited, instead of obeying the command, he arrested and ordered him to leave the city. Peace being presently restored, and danger over, the judge renewed the contest; and, causing the general to appear before him, on a process of contempt, for detaining and refusing to obey a writ of habeas corpus, which had been directed to him, amerced him in a fine of a thousand dollars. How far he was actuated by correct motives, in exclusion to those feelings which sometimes estrange the judgment, his own conscience can determine; and how far his proceedings were fair and liberal, will appear hereafter, when, in proper order, we shall be brought to examine this prosecution. For the present, we are confident, that if ever there were a case, that could justify or excuse a departure from the law, its features were not stronger than those which influenced general Jackson, on the present occasion, in suspending the rights of the citizens. If judge Hall were impelled to the course he took, in defence of the violated dignity of the constitution, and to protect the rights of a government, whose judicial powers he represented, whether right or wrong, he deserves not censure; although it might be well replied, that a fairer and more glorious opportunity of showing his devotedness to his country had just passed, when he might truly have aided in defence of her honour, nor left even room for his motives to have been unfairly appreciated.

This strong and efficient measure had not been resorted to, from the mere anticipation of danger; already, sufficient causes existed; and intrigue and stratagem were busily winding their way into our camp: they were either to be put down, or every hope of opposition or successful resistance abandoned. England, never at a loss for varnished statements, to give plausibility to her views, not only held forth the idea that she had come to restore the inhabitants to higher privileges than they enjoyed, but, to render the delusion still more complete, through her emissaries, propagated the belief, that, as the friend of Spain, she had come to restore West Florida to its rightful owner, and the citizens to their lawful sovereign. Composed, as our army at this time was, of heterogeneous materials, Frenchmen, Spaniards, and natives, it required constant efforts, to keep alive excitement, and ward off despondency. Learning the rumours that had been spread among them, and fear-

CHAP.
VIII.
~~~~
1814.

ing they might have an injurious effect, Jackson immediately circulated an address, in which he sought to preserve their ardour and devotion to their country.

" Believe not," he observed, " that the threatened invasion is with a view to restore the country to Spain. It is founded in design, and a supposition that you would be willing to return to your ancient government. Listen not to such incredible tales : your government is at peace with Spain. It is your vital enemy, the common enemy of mankind, the highway robber of the world, that has sent his hirelings among you, to put you from your guard, that you may fall an easier prey. Then look to your liberty, your property, the chastity of your wives and daughters. Take a retrospect of the conduct of the British army, at Hampton, and at other places where it has entered our country : and every bosom, which glows with patriotism and virtue, will be inspired with indignation, and pant for the arrival of the hour, when we shall meet and revenge those outrages against the laws of civilization and humanity."

With the exception of the Kentucky troops, which were yet absent, all the forces expected had arrived. General Carroll had reached Coffee's encampment four miles above the city, on the 21st, and had immediately reported to the commanding general. The officers were busily engaged in drilling, manœuvring, and organizing the troops, and in having every thing ready for action, the moment it should become necessary. No doubt was entertained, but the British would be able to effect a landing at some point ; the principal thing to be guarded against was not to prevent it; for, since the loss of the gun boats, any attempt of this kind could only be regarded as hopeless : but, by preserving a constant vigilance, and thereby having the earliest intelligence of their approach, they might be met at the very threshold, and opposed. Small guard boats were constantly plying on the lakes, to watch, and give information of every movement. Some of these had come in, late on the evening of the 22d, and reported that all was quiet, and that no unfavourable appearance portended in that direction. With such vigilance, constantly exercised, it is truly astonishing that the enemy should have effected an invasion, and succeeded in disembarking so large a force, British without the slightest intimation being had, until they landing, were accidentally discovered emerging from the swamp rive on and woods, about seven miles below the town : why the Mississippi. it so happened, traitors may conjecture, although the truth is yet unknown. The general impression is, that it was through information given by a small party of Spanish fishermen, that so secret a disembarkation was effected. Several of them had settled at the mouth of this bayou, and supported themselves by fish they caught, and vended in the market at New Orleans. Obstructions, as we have already stated, had been ordered to be made on every inlet, and the Louisiana militia been detached for that purpose. This place had not received the attention its importance merited : nor was it until the 22d, that general Villery, charged with the execution of this order, had placed here a small handful of men. Towards day, the enemy, silently proceeding up the bayou, landed, and succeeded in capturing the whole of this party, but two, who, fleeing to the swamp, endeavoured to reach the city; but, owing to the thick undergrowth, and briars, which rendered it almost impervious, they did not arrive, until after the enemy had reached the banks of the Mississippi, and been discovered.

Bayou Bienvenu, through which the landing was made, is an arm of considerable width, stretching towards the Mississippi, from lake Borgne, and about fifteen miles south-east of New Orleans. It had been reported to general Jackson, on the 23d, that, on the day before, several strange sail had been descried, off Terre au Bœuf. To ascertain correctly the truth of the statement, majors Tatum and Latour, topographical engineers, had been sent off, with orders to proceed in that direction, and learn if any thing were attempting there. It was towards noon, of the 23d, when they started. Approaching general Villery's plantation, and perceiving, at a distance, soldiers, and persons fleeing hastily away, they at once supposed the enemy had arrived. What, however, was but surmise, was presently, and on nearer observation, rendered certain; and it was now no longer a doubt, but that the British had landed, in considerable force, and had actually gained, unobserved, the house of general Villery, on the bank of the Mississippi, where they had surprised, and made prisoners, a company of militia, there posted.

Major Tatum, hastening back, announced his discovery. Preparations to act were immediately made by general Jackson. The signal guns were fired, and expresses sent forward, to concentrate the forces; resolving, that night, to meet the invaders, and try his own and their firmness.

CHAPTER IX.

General Jackson concentrates his forces, and marches to fight the enemy.—Alarms of the city.—Mode of attack, and battle of the 23d of December.—British reinforcements arrive during the action.—Arrival of general Carroll's division.—Our army retires from the field.—Effects of this battle.—Jackson establishes a line of defence.—General Morgan is ordered on the right bank of the Mississippi.—Destruction and loss of the Caroline schooner.—Battle of the 28th December.—Conduct of the legislature of Louisiana; their deliberations suspended.—Scarcity of arms, in the American camp.

———

THE hour to test the bravery of his troops had now arrived. The approach of the enemy, flushed with the hope of easy victory, was announced to Jackson, a little after one o'clock in the afternoon. There were too many reasons, assuring him of the necessity of acting speedily, to hesitate a moment, on the course proper to be pursued. Could he assail them, and obtain even a partial advantage, it might be beneficial—it might arrest disaffection—buoy up the despondent—determine the wavering, and bring within his reach resources for to-morrow, which might wholly fail, should fear once take possession of the public mind. It was a moment, too, of all others, most propitious to success. He well knew the greater part of his troops were inured to marching and fatigue, while

CHAP.
IX.

1814.

those opposed to him were just landed from a long voyage, and were as yet without activity, and unfitted for bodily exertion. Moreover, a part only might have arrived from the shipping, while the remainder would be certainly disembarked as early as possible. These circumstances seemed to augment, in his behalf, the chances of victory, if now sought; but if deferred, they might, in a little time, disappear. He resolved, at all events, to march, and that night give them battle. Generals Coffee and Carroll were ordered to proceed immediately from their encampment, and join him, with all haste. Although four miles above, they arrived in the city, in less than two hours after the order had been issued. These forces, with the seventh and forty-fourth regiments, the Louisiana troops, and colonel Hinds' dragoons, constituted the strength of his army, which could be carried into action against an enemy, whose numbers, at this time, could only be conjectured. It was thought advisable to leave Carroll and his division behind; for notwithstanding there was no correct information of the force landed through Villery's canal, yet Jackson feared that this might be only a feint, intended to divert his attention, while, in all probability, a much stronger and more numerous division, having already gained some point, higher on the lake, might, by advancing in his absence, gain his rear, and succeed in their views. Uncertain of their movements, it was essential he should be prepared for the worst, and, by different dispositions of his troops, be ready to resist, in whatever quarter he might be assailed. Carroll, therefore, at the head of his division, and governor Claiborne, with the state militia, were directed to take post on the Gentilly road, leading from Chef Menteur to New Orleans, and to defend it to the last extremity.

Alarm pervaded the city. The marching and countermarching of the troops—the proximity of the enemy—with the approaching contest, and uncertainty of the issue, had excited a general fear. Already might the British be on their way, and at hand, before the necessary arrangements were made to oppose them. To prevent this, colonel Hayne, with two companies of riflemen, and the Mississippi dragoons, was sent forward, to reconnoitre their camp, learn their position and their numbers; and, in the event they should be found advancing, to harass and oppose them at every step, until the main body should arrive.

Every thing being ready, general Jackson commenced his march, to meet and fight the veteran troops of England. An inconsiderable circumstance, at this moment, evinced what unlimited confidence was reposed in his skill and bravery. As his troops were marching through the city, his ears were assailed with the screams and cries of innumerable females, who had collected on the way, and seemed to apprehend the worst of consequences. Feeling for their distresses, and anxious to quiet them, he directed Mr. Livingston to address them in the French language. " Say to them," said he, " not to be alarmed : the enemy shall never reach the city." It operated like an electric shock. To know that he himself was not apprehensive of a fatal result, inspired them with altered feelings ; sorrow was ended, and their grief converted into hope and confidence.

CHAP.
IX.

1814.

Mode of
attack.

The general arrived in view of the enemy, a little before dark. Having previously ascertained, from colonel Hayne, their position, and that their strength was about two thousand men,* he immediately concerted the mode of attack, and hastened to execute it. Commodore Patterson, commanding the naval forces, with captain Henly, on board the Caroline, had been directed to drop down, anchor in front of their line, and open upon them from the guns of the schooner; which being the signal for attack, was to be waged simultaneously on all sides. The fires from their camp disclosed their position, and showed their encampment, formed with their left resting on the river, and extending at right angles into the open field. General Coffee, with his brigade, colonel Hinds' dragoons, and captain Beal's company of riflemen, was ordered to oblique to the left, and, by a circuitous route, avoid their piquets, and endeavour to turn their right wing; having succeeded in this, to form his line, and press the enemy towards the river, where they would be exposed more completely to the fire of the Caroline. The rest of the troops, consisting of the regulars, Plauche's city volunteers, Daquin's coloured troops, the artillery under lieutenant Spoots, supported by a company of marines, commanded by colonel M'Kee, advanced along the bank of the Mississippi, and were commanded by Jackson in person.

* This opinion, as it afterwards appeared, was incorrect. Their number, at the commencement of the action, was three thousand, which was shortly afterwards increased by additional forces.

General Coffee had advanced beyond their piquets, next the swamp, and nearly reached the point to which he was ordered, when a broadside from the Caroline announced the battle begun. Patterson had proceeded slowly, giving time, as he believed, for the execution of those arrangements contemplated on the shore. So sanguine had the British been in the belief that they would be kindly received, and little opposition attempted, that the Caroline floated by the sentinels, and anchored before their camp, without any kind of molestation. On passing the front piquet, she was hailed, in a low tone of voice, but returning no answer, no further question was made. This, added to some other attendant circumstances, confirmed the opinion that they believed her a vessel laden with provisions, which had been sent out from New Orleans, and was intended for them. Having reached what, from their fires, appeared to be the centre of their encampment, her anchors were cast, and her character and business disclosed from her guns. So unexpected an attack produced a momentary confusion; but, recovering, they answered her by a discharge of musketry, and flight of congreve rockets, which passed without injury, while her grape and canister were pouring destructively on them. To take away the certainty of aim afforded by the light of their fires, these were immediately extinguished, and they retired two or three hundred yards into the open field, if not out of the reach of the cannon, at least to a distance, where, by the darkness of the night, they would be protected.

Battle of the 23d December.

140

Coffee had dismounted his men, and turned his horses loose, at a large ditch, next the swamp, in the rear of Lorond's plantation, and gained, as he believed, the centre of the enemy's line, when the signal from the Caroline reached him. He directly wheeled his columns in, and, extending his line parallel with the river, moved towards their camp. He had scarcely advanced more than an hundred yards, when he received a heavy fire, from a line formed in his front : this, to him, was an unexpected circumstance, as he supposed the enemy lying principally at a distance, and that the only opposition he should meet, until he approached towards the levee,* would be from their advanced guards. The circumstance of his coming up with them so soon, was owing to the severe attack of the schooner, which had compelled them to abandon their camp, and form without her reach. The moon shone, but reflected her light too feebly to discover objects at a distance. The only chance, therefore, of producing certain injury, with this kind of force, which consisted chiefly of riflemen, was not to venture at random, but only to discharge their pieces when there should be a certainty of felling the object. This order being given, the line pressed on, and, having gained a position near enough to distinguish, a general fire was given ; it was too severe and destructive to be withstood ; the enemy gave way, and retreated,—rallied,—formed,—were charged, and again retreated. These gallant men, led by their brave commander, urged

---

* Embankments formed along the river, to confine it in its bed.

fearlessly on, and drove them from every position they attempted to maintain. Their general was under no necessity to encourage and allure them to deeds of valour : his own example was sufficient to excite them. Always in the midst, he displayed a coolness and disregard of danger, calling to his troops, that they had often said they could fight—now was the time to prove it.

The enemy, driven back by the resolute firmness and ardour of their assailants, had now reached a grove of orange trees, with a ditch running past it, protected by a fence on the margin. It was a favourable position, promising security, and was occupied with a confidence they could not be forced to yield it. Coffee's dauntless yeomanry, strengthened in their hopes of success, moved on, nor discovered the advantages against them, until a fire from the whole British line shewed their defence. A momentary check was given ; but, gathering fresh ardour, they charged across the ditch, gave a deadly and destructive fire, and forced them to retire. Their retreat continued, until, gaining a similar position, they made another stand, and were again driven from it, with considerable loss.

Thus the battle raged, on the left wing, until the British reached the bank of the river ; here a determined stand was made, and further encroachments resisted : for half an hour, the conflict was extremely violent on both sides. The American troops could not be driven from their purpose, nor the British made to yield their ground ; but at length, having suffered greatly, the latter were under the necessity of taking refuge behind the levee, which afforded a breast-work,

CHAP. and protected them from the fatal fire of our riflemen.
  IX.   Coffee, unacquainted with their position, for the dark-
 1814. ness had greatly increased, already contemplated again
to charge them; but major Moulton, who had discovered their situation, assured him it was too hazardous; that they could be driven no further, and would,
from the point they occupied, resist with the bayonet,
and repel, with considerable loss, any attempt to dislodge them. The place of their retirement was covered, in front, by a strong bank, which had been extended into the field, to keep out the river, in consequence of the first being encroached upon, and undermined in several places: the old one, however, was
still entire, in many parts, and gave them security from
the broadsides of the schooner, which lay off at some
distance. A further apprehension, lest, by moving
still nearer to the river, he might greatly expose himself to the fire of the Caroline, which was yet spiritedly maintaining the conflict, induced Coffee to retire
until he could hear from the commanding general, and
receive his further orders.

During this time, the right wing, under Jackson,
was no less prompt and active. A detachment of artillery, under lieutenant Spotts, supported by sixty
marines, formed the advance, and had moved down
the road, next the levee. On their left was the seventh
regiment of infantry, led by major Piere. The forty-
fourth, commanded by major Baker, was formed on
the extreme left; while Plauche's and Daquin's battalions of city guards, were directed to be posted in the
centre, between the seventh and forty-fourth. The
general had ordered colonel Ross, who, during the

night, acted in the capacity of brigadier general, on
hearing the signal from the Caroline, to move off by
heads of companies, and, having reached the enemy's
line, to deploy, and seek to unite the left wing with
the right of general Coffee's. This order was omitted
to be executed; and the consequence was an early introduction of confusion in the ranks, whereby was prevented the important design of uniting the two divisions.

Instead of marching in column from the first position, the troops were wheeled into an extended line,
and moved off in this order, except the seventh regiment, next the person of the general, which advanced
agreeably to the instructions that had been given.
Having sufficient ground to form on at first, no inconvenience was at the moment sustained: but this
advantage presently failing, the centre was compressed,
and forced in the rear. The river, from where they
were, gradually inclined to the left, and diminished the
space originally possessed: farther in, stood Lorond's
house, surrounded by a grove of clustered orange
trees: this pressing the left, and the river the right
wing to the centre, formed a curve, which threw the
principal part of Plauche's and Daquin's battalions
without the line. This might have been remedied,
but for the briskness of the advance, and the darkness
of the night. A heavy fire from behind a fence, immediately before them, had brought the enemy to view.
Acting in obedience to their orders, not to waste their
ammunition at random, our troops had pressed forward against the opposition in their front, and thereby
threw those battalions in the rear.

A fog rising from the river, which, added to the smoke from the guns, was covering the plain,—gradually diminishing the little light shed by the moon, and greatly increasing the darkness of the night: no clue was left, to tell how or where the enemy were situated.   There was no alternative but to move on, in the direction of their fire, which subjected the assailants to material disadvantages.   The British, driven from their first position, had retired back, and occupied another, behind a deep ditch, that ran out of the Mississippi towards the swamp, on the top of which was a high fence.   Here, strengthened by increased numbers, they again opposed the approach of our troops.   Having waited, until they had come sufficiently near to be discovered, they discharged, from their fastnesses, a fire upon the advancing army.   Instantly our battery was formed, and poured destructively upon them; while the infantry, coming up, aided in the conflict, which was for some time spiritedly maintained.   At this moment, a brisk sally was made upon our advance, when the marines, unequal to the assault, were already giving away.   The adjutant general, and colonels Piatt and Chotard, with a part of the seventh, hastening to their support, drove the enemy, and saved the artillery from capture.   General Jackson, perceiving the advantages they derived from their position, ordered their line to be charged.   It was obeyed with cheerfulness, and executed with promptness. Pressing on, our troops gained the ditch, and, pouring across it a well-aimed fire, compelled them to retreat, and abandon their entrenchment. The plain, on which they were contending, was cut to

pieces, by races from the river, to convey the water. CHAP.
IX.
They were, therefore, very soon enabled to take another situation, equally favourable with the one whence
they had been just driven, where they formed for battle, and, for some time, gallantly maintained themselves; but were at length forced to yield it, and retreat.

The enemy, discovering the firm and obstinate resistance made by the right wing of the American army, and perhaps presuming its principal strength was
posted on the road, formed the intention of attacking
violently the left. Obliquing for this purpose, an attempt was made to turn it. At this moment, Daquin's
and the battalion of city guards were marched up, and,
being formed on the left of the forty-fourth, met and
repulsed them.

The time of the contest prevented many of those
benefits which might have been derived from the artillery. The blaze of the enemy's musketry was the
only light by which they could judge of their positions,
or be capable of taking their own to advantage; yet,
notwithstanding, it greatly annoyed them, whenever it
could be brought to bear. Directed by lieutenant
Spotts, a vigilant and skilful officer, with men to aid
him, who looked to nothing but a zealous discharge
of their duty, it rendered the most essential and important services.

The enemy had been thrice assailed and beaten, and
made to yield their ground for nearly a mile. They
had now retired, and, if found, were to be again sought
for through the dark. The general determined to halt,
and ascertain Coffee's position and success, previously

to waging the battle further, for as yet no communication had passed between them.   He entertained no
doubt, from the brisk firing in that direction, but that
he had been warmly engaged; but this had now nearly subsided; the Caroline, too, had almost ceased her
operations; it being only occasionally, that the noise of
her guns disclosed the little opportunity she possessed
of acting efficiently.

The express despatched to general Jackson, from
the left wing, having reached him, he determined to
prosecute the successes he had gained, no further.
The darkness of the night,—the confusion into which
his own division had been thrown, and a similar one
on the part of Coffee, all pointed to the necessity of
retiring from the field, and abandoning the contest.
The bravery and firmness already displayed by his
troops, had induced the belief, that by pressing on he
might capture the whole British army : at any rate, he
considered it but a game of venture and hazard, which,
if unsuccessful, could not occasion his own defeat. If,
incompetent to its execution, superior numbers or superior discipline should compel him to recede from
the effort, he well knew the enemy would not have te-
merity enough to attempt pursuit. The extreme darkness—their entire ignorance of the situation of the
country, and an apprehension lest their forces might
be greatly outnumbered, afforded him sufficient reasons, on which to ground a belief, that although beat-
en from his purpose, he would yet have it in his power to retire in safety : but on the arrival of the express
from general Coffee, learning the strong position to
which the enemy had retired, and that a part of the left

wing had been detached, and were in all probability
captured, he determined to retire from the contest, nor attempt a further prosecution of his successes. General Coffee was accordingly directed to withdraw, and take a position at Lorond's plantation, where the line had been first formed: and thither the troops on the right were also ordered to be marched.

142

The last charge made by the left wing, had separated, from the main body, colonels Dyer and Gibson, with two hundred men, and captain Beal's company of riflemen. What might be their fate; whether captured, or had effected their retreat, was, at this time, altogether uncertain; be that as it might, Coffee's command was thereby considerably weakened.

Colonel Dyer, who commanded the extreme left, on clearing the grove, after the enemy had retired, was marching in the direction he expected to find general Coffee; he very soon discovered a force in front, and hastened towards it; arriving within a short distance, he was hailed, ordered to stop, and report to whom he belonged: Dyer and Gibson advanced, and stated they were of Coffee's brigade; by this time they had arrived within a short distance of the line, and perceiving the name of their brigade was not understood, their apprehensions were awakened, lest it might be a detachment of the enemy; in this opinion they were immediately confirmed, and wheeling to return, were fired on and pursued. Gibson had scarcely started when he fell; before he could recover, a soldier, quicker than the rest, had reached him, and pinned him to the ground with his bayonet; fortunately the stab had but slightly wounded him.

and he was only held by his clothes: thus pinioned, and others briskly advancing, but a moment was left for deliberation;—making a violent exertion, and springing on his feet, he threw his assailant to the ground, and made good his retreat. Colonel Dyer had retreated about fifty yards, when his horse dropped dead; entangled in the fall, and slightly wounded in the thigh, there was little prospect of relief, for the enemy were briskly advancing: his men being near at hand, he ordered a fire, which, checking their approach, enabled him to escape. Being now at the head of his command,—perceiving an enemy in a direction he had not expected, and uncertain how or where he might find general Coffee, he determined to seek him to the right, and moving on with his little band, forced his way through the enemy's lines, with a loss of sixty-three of his men, who were killed and taken. Captain Beal, with equal bravery, charged through the enemy, carrying off some prisoners, and losing several of his own company.

British re-
inforce-
ment ar-
rives.
This reinforcement of the British had arrived from Bayou Bienvenu, after night. The boats that had landed the first detachment, had proceeded back to the shipping, and having returned, were on their way up the bayou, when they heard the guns of the Caroline; moving hastily on to the assistance of those who had debarked before them, they reached the shore, and knowing nothing of the situation of the two armies, came up in the rear of general Coffee's brigade. Coming in contact with colonel Dyer and captain Beal, they filed off to the left, and reached the British camp.

This part of Coffee's brigade, unable to unite with, or find him, retired where they had first formed, and joined colonel Hinds' dragoons, which had remained on the ground where the troops had first dismounted, to cover their retreat, in the event it became necessary.

Jackson had gone into this battle with a confidence of success; and his arrangements were such as would have ensured it, even to a much greater extent, but for the intervention of circumstances that were not, and could not be foreseen. The Caroline had given her signals, and commenced the battle, a little too early, before Coffee had reached and taken his position, and before every thing was fully in readiness, to attain the objects designed: but it was chiefly owing to the confusion introduced at first into the ranks, which checked the rapidity of his advance,—gave the enemy time for preparation, and prevented his division from uniting with the right wing of general Coffee's brigade.

Colonel Hinds, with one hundred and eighty dragoons, was not brought into action during the night. Interspersed as the plain was, with innumerable ditches, cut in different directions, it was impossible that cavalry could act to any kind of advantage: they were now formed in advance, to watch, until morning, the movements of the enemy.

From the experiment just made, Jackson believed it would be in his power, on renewing the attack, to capture the enemy: he concluded, therefore, to call down general Carroll with his division, and assail him again at the dawn of day. Directing governor Claiborne to remain at his post, with the Louisiana militia, for the defence of the Gentilly road, he despatched an order to Carroll, in the event there had been no appearance of a force during the night, in the direction of Chef Menteur, to hasten and join him with his command; which order was executed by one o'clock in the morning. Previously, however, to his arrival, a

Arrival of general Carroll's division.

different conclusion was taken. From prisoners who had been brought in, and some deserters, it was ascertained, that the strength of the enemy during the battle was four thousand, and, with the reinforcements which had reached them, after its commencement, it was then not less than six :—at any rate, it exceeded his own greatly, even after the Tennessee division should be added. Although very decided advantages had been obtained, yet they had been procured under circumstances that might be wholly lost, in a contest waged in open day, between forces so disproportioned, and by undisciplined troops against veteran soldiers. Jackson well knew it was incumbent upon him, to act a part entirely defensive: should the attempt to gain and destroy the city succeed, numerous difficulties would arise, which might be avoided, so long as he could hold the enemy in check, and halt him in his designs. Prompted by these considerations, —that it was important to pursue a course calculated to assure safety; and believing it attainable in no way so effectually, as in occupying some point, and by the strength he might give it, make up for the inferiority of his numbers; he determined to forbear all further efforts, until he should more certainly discover the views of the enemy, and until the Kentucky troops should reach him, which had not yet arrived. Pursuing this idea, at four o'clock, having ordered colonel Hinds to occupy the ground he was then leaving, and to observe the enemy closely, he fell back, and formed his line behind a deep ditch, that ran at right angles from the river. There were two circumstances, strongly recommending the importance of this place: the swamp, which, from the high lands at Baton Rouge, skirted the river at irregular distances, and was in many places almost impervious, had approached here within four hundred yards of the Mississippi, and hence, from the narrowness of the pass, was more easily to be defended; added to which, there was a deep canal, whence the dirt being thrown on the upper side, already formed a tolerable breast-work. Behind this, his troops were formed, and proper measures adopted for increasing its strength, with a determination never to abandon it; but there to resist to the last, and defend those rights which were sought to be outraged and destroyed.

The soldier who has stood the shock of battle, and knows what slight circumstances often produce decided advantages, will be able, properly, to appreciate the events of this night. Although the dreadful carnage of the 8th of January, hereafter to be told, was in fact the finishing blow, that struck down the towering hopes of those invaders, and put an end to the contest; yet in the battle of the 23d, is to be found, abundant cause, why success resulted to our arms, and safety was given to the country. The British had reached the Mississippi without the fire of a gun, and had encamped upon its banks, as composedly, as if they had been seated on their own soil, and at a dis-

143

tance from all danger. These were circumstances awakening a belief that they expected little opposition, were certain of success, and that the troops with whom they were to contend, would scarcely venture to resist them : resting thus confidently, they would the next day have moved forward, and succeeded in the accomplishment of their designs. Jackson, convinced that an early impression was essential to ultimate success, had resolved to assail them at the moment of their landing, and " attack them in their first position :" we have, therefore, seen him, with a force, inferior by one half, to that of the enemy, at an unexpected moment, break into their camp, and with his undisciplined yeomanry, drive before him the pride of Europe. It was an event that could not fail to destroy all previous theories, and establish a conclusion, our enemy had not before formed, that they were contending against valour inferior to none they had seen ;—before which their own bravery had not stood, nor their skill availed them : it had the effect of satisfying them, that the quantity and kind of troops, it was in his power to wield, must be different from what had been represented ; for, much as they had heard of the courage of the man, they could not suppose, that a general, having a country to defend, and a reputation to preserve, would venture to attack, on their own chosen ground, a greatly superior army, and one, which, by the numerous victories achieved, had already acquired a fame in arms ; they were convinced that his force must greatly surpass what they had expected, and be composed of materials, different from what they had imagined.

The American troops, which were actually engag- CHAP.
ed, did not amount to two thousand men : they con- IX.
sisted of part of

Coffee's brigade and captain Beal's company,   648
The 7th and 44th regiments,   -   -   763
Company of marines and artillery,   -   82
Plauche's and Daquin's battalions,   -   -   488
And the Mississippi dragoons under colonel ⎱
   Hinds, not in the action,   -   ⎰ 186

_____

2167* 144

which for one hour maintained a severe conflict,
with a force of four or five thousand, and retired in
safety from the ground, with the loss of but twenty
four killed, one hundred and fifteen wounded, and
seventy four made prisoners ; while the killed, wounded, and prisoners, of the enemy, were not less than four 145
hundred.

Our officers and soldiers executed every order with
promptness, and nobly sustained their country's character. Lieutenant colonel Lauderdale, of Coffee's
brigade, an officer on whom every reliance was placed,
fell at his post, and at his duty : he had entered the
service, and descended the river, with the volunteers,
under general Jackson, in the winter of 1812—
passed through all the hardships and difficulties of
the Creek war, and had ever manifested a readiness to
act when his country needed his services. Young,

_____

* Colonel Butler, adjutant general of the southern division,
furnished the author with this statement, and vouched for its
correctness.

brave and skilful, he had already afforded evidences of a capacity, which might, in future, have become useful ; his exemplary conduct, both in civil and military life, acquired him a respect, that rendered his fall a subject of general regret. Lieutenant M'Lelland, a valuable young officer, of the 7th, was also among the number of the slain.

Coffee's brigade, during the action, imitating the example of their commander, bravely contended, and ably supported the character they had established. The unequal contest, in which they were engaged, never occurred to them ; nor for a moment checked the rapidity of their advance. Had the British known they were mere riflemen, without bayonets, a firm stand would have arrested their progress, and destruction or capture would have been the inevitable consequence ; but this circumstance being unknown, every charge they made was crowned with success, producing discomfiture, and routing and driving superior numbers before them. Officers, from the highest, to inferior grades, discharged what had been expected of them. Ensign Leach, of the 7th regiment, being wounded through the body, still remained at his post, and in the performance of his duty. Colonel Reuben Kemper, enterprising and self-collected, amidst the confusion introduced on the left wing, found himself at the head of a handful of men, detached from the main body, and in the midst of a party of the enemy ; never did any man better exemplify the truth of the position, that discretion is sometimes the better part of valour : to attempt resistance was idle, and could only eventuate in destruction ; with a mind unclouded by the

peril that surrounded him, he sought and procured his
safety through stratagem. Calling to a group of soldiers who were near, he demanded where their regiment was; lost themselves, they were unable to answer: but taking him for one of their own officers,
they followed, as they were ordered, to his own line,
where they were made prisoners.

The 7th regiment, commanded by major Piere, and
the 44th, under major Baker, aided by major Butler,
gallantly maintained the conflict—forced the enemy
from every secure position he attempted to occupy,
and drove him a mile from the first point of attack.
Confiding in themselves, and their general, who was
constantly with them, exposed to danger and in the
thickest of the fight, inspiring by his ardour, and encouraging by his example, they advanced to the conflict, nor evinced a disposition to leave it, until the
prudence of their commander directed them to retire.

From the violence of the assault already made,
the fears of the British had been greatly excited;
to keep their apprehensions alive was considered important, with a view partially to destroy the over-
weening confidence with which they had arrived, and
compel them to act, for a time, upon the defensive.
To effect this, general Coffee, with his brigade, was
ordered down on the 24th, to unite with colonel Hinds,
and make a show in the rear of Lacoste's plantation.
The enemy, not yet recovered of the panic produced by the first assault, already believed it was in contemplation to urge another attack, and immediately
formed to repel it; but Coffee having succeeded in
recovering some of his horses, which were wander-

ing along the sides of the swamp; and in regaining part of the clothing his troops had lost, returned to the line, leaving to be conjectured the objects of his movement.

The scanty supply of clothes and blankets, that remained to the soldiers, from their long and exposed marches, had been left where they dismounted to meet the enemy. Their numbers were too limited, and the strength of their opponents too well ascertained, for any part of their force to remain and take care of what was left behind: it was so essential to hasten on, reach their destination, and be ready to act, when the signals of the Caroline should announce their co-operation necessary, that no time was afforded them to secure their horses;—they were turned loose, and their recovery trusted entirely to chance. Although many were regained,—many were lost; while most of the men remained with but a single suit to encounter in the open field, and in swamps, covered with water, the hardships of camp, and the severity of winter. It is a circumstance which entitles them to much credit, that under privations so severely oppressive, complaints or murmurs were never heard. This state of things was not of long continuance. The story of their sufferings and misfortunes was no sooner known, than the legislature appropriated a sum of money for their relief, which was greatly increased, by subscriptions, in the city and neighbourhood. Materials being purchased, the ladies, with that Christian charity, and warmth of heart, characteristic of their sex, at once exerted themselves in removing their distresses: all their industry was called into action, and in a little

time, the suffering soldier was relieved. Such generous conduct, in assisting at a moment when so
much needed; while it conferred on those females the
highest honour, could not fail to nerve the arm of the
brave, with new zeal, for the defence of their bene-
factresses. This distinguished mark of their patriotism and benevolence, is still remembered; and often
as these valiant men recount the dangers they have
passed, and with peculiar pride dwell on the mingled honours and hardships of the campaign, they
breathe a sentiment of gratitude to those, who conferred upon them such distinguished marks of their kindness, and, by timely interference, alleviated their misfortunes.

To present a check, and keep up a shew of resistance, detachments of light troops were occasionally
kept in front of the line, assailing and harassing the
enemy's advanced posts, whenever an opportunity was
offered of acting to advantage. Every moment that
could be gained, and every delay that could be extended to the enemy's attempts, to reach the city, was
of the utmost importance. The works were rapidly progressing, and hourly increasing in strength. The militia of the state were every day arriving, and every day
the prospect of successful opposition was brightening.

The enemy still remained at his first encampment.
To be in readiness to repel an assault when attempted,
the most active exertions were made on the 24th and
25th. The canal, covering the front of our line, was
deepened and widened, and a strong mud wall formed
of the earth, that had been originally thrown out. To
prevent any approach until his system of defence

should be in a state of greater forwardness, Jackson ordered the levee to be cut, about an hundred yards below. The river being very high, a broad stream of water passed rapidly through the plain, of the depth of thirty or forty inches, which prevented any approach of troops on foot. Embrasures were formed, and two pieces of artillery, under the command of lieutenant Spotts, early on the morning of the 24th, were placed in a position to rake the road leading up the levee.

He was under constant apprehensions, lest, in spite of his exertions below, the city might, through some other route, be reached and destroyed; and those fears were increased to-day, by a report that a strong force had arrived—had debarked at the head of lake Borgne, and compelled an abandonment of the fort at Chef Menteur. This, however, proved to be unfounded : the enemy had not appeared in that direction, nor had the officer, to whom this fort, so much relied on, had been entrusted, forgotten his duty, or forsaken his post. Acting upon the statement that major Lacoste had retired from the fort, and fallen back on bayou St. John, and incensed that orders, which, from their importance, should have been faithfully executed, had been thus lightly regarded, he hastened to inform him what he had understood, and to forbid his leaving his position. " The battery I have placed under your command, must be defended at all hazards. In you, and the valour of your troops, I repose every confidence ;—let me not be deceived. With us, every thing goes on well : the enemy has not yet advanced. Our troops have covered themselves with glory : it is a noble example, and worthy to be followed by all.

Maintain your post, nor ever think of retreating." To CHAP.
inspire confidence, and ensure safety, colonel Dyer, IX.
and two hundred men, were ordered here, to give 1814.
additional strength, and act as videttes, in advance of
the occupied points.

General Morgan, who, at the English turn, commanded the fort on the east bank of the river, was instructed to proceed as near the enemy's camp as prudence and safety would permit, and, by destroying the
levee, to let in the waters of the Mississippi between
them. The execution of this order, and a similar one,
previously made, below the line of defence, had entirely insulated the enemy, and prevented his march
against either place. On the 26th, however, the commanding general, fearing for the situation of Morgan,
who, from the British occupying the intermediate
ground, was entirely detached from his camp, directed him to abandon his encampment, carry off what
cannon might be wanted, and throw the remainder in
the river, where they could be again recovered, when the
waters receded; to retire to the other side of the river,
and, after leaving an adequate force, for the protection
of Fort Leon, to take a position on the right bank,
nearly opposite to his line, and have it fortified. The
necessity of this movement was imposed by the relative disposition of the two armies. The same cause,
however, that produced this, made it essential that St.
Leon should not be neglected. From every intelligence, obtained through deserters and prisoners, it
was evident that the British fleet would make an effort to ascend the river, and co-operate with the troops
already landed. That this, or a diversion in a differ-

ent quarter, would be attempted, produced exertions to be able to defend at all points.

The forts on the river, well supported with brave men, and heavy pieces of artillery, might, perhaps, deter their shipping from venturing up the Mississippi, and dispose them to seek some safer route, if any could be discovered. Through Pass Barrataria was best calculated for this purpose, where, in all probability, the effort might be made. The difficulty of ascending the Mississippi, from the rapidity of the current, its winding course, and the ample protection already given at St. Philip, Bourbon, and St. Leon, were circumstances to which it was not inferred the British were strangers : nor was it to be expected, that, with a knowledge of them, they would venture here the success of an enterprise on which so much depended. It was a more rational conjecture that they would seek a passage through Barrataria—proceed up on the right bank of the river, and gain a position, where, co-operating with the force on the east side, they might drive our troops from the line they had formed, and, at less hazard, succeed in the accomplishment of their designs. Major Reynolds was accordingly ordered thither, with instructions to place the bayous, emptying through this pass, in the best state of defence—to occupy and strengthen the island —to mount sufficient ordnance, and draw a chain, within cannon-shot, across, the more effectually to guard the route, and protect it from approach. Lafite, who had been heretofore promised a pardon for the outrages he had committed against the laws of the United States, and who had already shown a lively zeal in behalf of his adopted country, was sent with Reynolds. He was selected, because, from the proofs already given, no doubt was entertained of his fidelity, and because his knowledge of the geography, and precise situation of this section of the state, was remarka- bly correct: it was where he had constantly rendez- voused, during the time of cruizing against the mer- chant vessels of Spain, under a commission, obtained at Carthagena, and where he had become perfectly ac- quainted with every inlet to the gulf, through which a passage could be effected.

With these arrangements; treason apart—all anxi- ously alive to the interest of their country, and dispos- ed to protect her; there was little room to appre- hend, or fear disaster. To use the general's own ex- pression, on another occasion; " the surest defence, that seldom failed of success, was a rampart of high- minded and brave men." That there were some of this description with him, on whom he could safely rely, in moments of extreme peril, he well knew; but that there were many, strangers to him and danger; and who had never been called to act in those situa- tions, where death, stalking in hideous round, appals and unnerves even the resolute, was equally certain: whether they would contend with manly firmness— support the cause in which they had embarked, and realize his anxious wishes on the subject, could be only known in the moment of conflict and trial, when, if disappointed in his expectations, the means of re- trieving the evil would be fled, and every thing lost in the result.

As yet the enemy knew nothing of the position of Jackson. What was his situation—what was intended —whether offensive or defensive operations would be pursued, were circumstances on which they possessed no correct knowledge; still, their exertions, to have all things prepared, to urge their designs, whenever the moment for action should arrive, were unremitting. They had been constantly engaged, since their landing, in procuring from their shipping, every thing necessary to ulterior operations. A complete command on the lakes, and possession of a point on the margin, presented an uninterrupted ingress and egress, and afforded the opportunity of conveying what was wanted, in perfect safety to their camp. The height' of the Mississippi, and the discharge of water, through the openings made in the levee, had given an increased depth to the canal, from which they had first debarked—enabled them to advance their boats much further, in the direction of their encampment, and to bring up, with greater convenience, their artillery, bombs and munitions. Thus engaged, during the first three days after their arrival; early on the morning of the 27th, a battery was discovered on the bank of the river, which had been thrown up during the preceding night, and on which were mounted several pieces of heavy ordnance; from it a fire was opened on the Caroline schooner, lying under the opposite shore.

After the battle of the 23d, in which this vessel had so effectually aided, she had passed to the opposite side of the river, where she had since lain. Her ser-

vices were too highly appreciated not to be again desired, in the event the enemy should endeavour to advance.   Her present situation was considered truly an
unsafe one, but it had been essayed in vain, to advance
her higher up the stream.   No favourable breeze had
yet arisen to aid her in stemming the current; and
towing, and other remedies, had been already resorted to, without success.   Her safety might have
been ensured by floating her down under fort St. Leon ;
though it was preferred, as a matter of policy, to
risk her where she was, still, hourly, calculating that a
favourable wind might relieve her, rather than by dropping her with the current, lose those benefits, which,
against an advance of the enemy, she might so completely extend.   Commodore Patterson had left her
on the 26th, by the orders of the commanding general,
when captain Henly made a further, but ineffectual
effort to force her up the current, near to the line, for
the double purpose of its defence and her own safety.

These attempts to get her away, being discovered;
at daylight, on the morning of the 27th, a battery,
mounting five guns, opened upon her, discharging
bombs and red hot shot; it was spiritedly answered,
but without affecting the battery; there being but a
long twelve pounder that could reach.   The second
fire had lodged a hot shot in her main hold, under her
cables, whence it could not be removed, and immediately set fire to the schooner.   The shot, from the battery, were constantly taking effect, firing her in different
parts, and otherwise producing material injury; while
the blaze already kindled under her cables, was rapidly
extending its ravages.   A well grounded apprehension,

R r

of her commander, that she could be no longer de-fended,—the flames bursting out in different parts, and fast increasing, induced a fear, lest the magazine should be soon reached, and every thing destroyed. One of his crew being killed, and six wounded, and there being not the glimmering of hope that she could be preserved, orders were given to abandon her. The crew reached the shore, and in a short time afterwards she blew up.

Schooner
Caroline
blown up.

Although thus unexpectedly deprived of so material a dependence, for successful defence, an opportunity was soon presented, of using her brave crew to advantage. Gathering confidence, from what had been just effected, the enemy left their encampment, and moved in the direction of our line. Their numbers had been increased, and major general Sir Edward Packenham now commanded in person. Early on the 28th, his columns commenced their advance to storm our works. At the distance of half a mile, their heavy artillery opened, and quantities of bombs, balls and congreve rockets, were discharged. It was a scene of terror and alarm, which they had probably calculated would excite a panic in the minds of the raw troops of our army, and make them surrender at discretion, or abandon their strong hold. But our soldiers had afforded abundant proof, that, whether disciplined or not, they well knew how to defend the honour and interests of their country; and sufficient valour not to be alarmed at the reality—still less the semblance of danger. Far from exciting their apprehensions, and driving them from their ground, their firmness still remained unchanged;—still was mani-

Attack of
the 28th
December.

fested a determination not to tarnish a reputation they had hardly earned; and which had become too dear, from the difficulties and dangers they had passed to acquire it, now tamely to be surrendered. These congreve rockets, though a kind of instrument of destruction, to which our troops unskilled in the science of desolating warfare, had been hitherto strangers, excited no other feeling than that which novelty inspires. At the moment, therefore, that the British, in different columns, were moving up, in all the pomp and parade of battle, preceded by these insignia of terror, more than danger, and were expecting to behold their " Yankee foes," tremblingly retire and flee before them, our batteries opened, and halted their advance.

In addition to the two mounted on the works, on the 24th, three other heavy pieces of cannon, obtained from the navy department, had been formed along the line; these opening on the enemy, checked their progress, and disclosed to them the hazard of the project they were on. Lieutenants Crawley and Norris, volunteered, and with the crew of the Caroline rendered important services, and maintained, at the guns they commanded, that firmness and decision, for which, on previous occasions, they had been so highly distinguished. They had been selected by the general, because of their superior knowledge in gunnery; and, on this occasion, gave a further evidence of their skill and judgment, and of a disposition to act, in any situation where they could be serviceable. The line, which, 147 from the labours bestowed on it, was daily strengthening, was not yet in a situation effectually to resist;

this deficiency, however, was well remedied by those who were formed in its rear.

From the river the greatest injury was done. Lieutenant Thompson, who commanded the Louisiana sloop, which lay nearly opposite the line of defence, no sooner discovered the columns approaching, than warping her around, he brought her starboard guns to bear, and forced them to retreat: but from their heavy artillery, the enemy maintained the conflict with great spirit, constantly discharging their bombs and rockets, for seven hours, when, unable to make a breach, or silence the sloop, they abandoned a contest, where few advantages seemed to be presented. The crew of this vessel was composed of new recruits, and discordant materials,—of soldiers, citizens and seamen; who, by the activity of their commander, were so well perfected in their duty, that they already managed their guns with the greatest precision and certainty of effect; and by three o'clock in the evening, with the aid of the land batteries, had completely silenced and drove back the enemy. Emboldened by the effect produced on the Caroline the day before; the furnaces of the enemy were put in operation, and numbers of hot shot thrown from a heavy piece, which was placed behind, and protected by the levee. An attempt was now made to carry it off, when that protection, heretofore had, being taken away, they were fairly exposed to our fire, and suffered greatly. In their endeavours to remove it, "I saw," says commodore Patterson, "distinctly, with the aid of a glass, several balls strike in the midst of the men who

were employed in dragging it away." In this engagement, commenced and waged for seven hours, we received little or no injury. The Louisiana sloop, against
which the most violent exertions were made, had but
a single man wounded, by the fragments of a shell,
which bursted over her deck. Our entire loss did not
exceed nine killed, and eight or ten wounded. The
enemy, being more exposed, acting in the open field,
and in range of our guns, suffered, from information
afterwards procured, considerable injury; at least, one
hundred and twenty were killed and wounded.

Among the killed, on our side, was colonel James
Henderson, of the Tennessee militia. An advanced
party of the British had, during the action, taken post
behind a fence, that ran obliquely to, and not very remote from, our line. Henderson, with a detachment
of two hundred men, was ordered to drive them from
a position, whence they were effecting some injury,
and greatly annoying our troops. Had he advanced
in the manner directed, he would have been less exposed, and enabled more effectually to have secured
the object intended; but, misunderstanding the order,
he proceeded in a different route, and fell a victim to
his error. Instead of marching in the direction of the
wood, and turning the enemy, which would have cut
off their retreat, he proceeded in front, towards the river, leaving them in rear of the fence, and himself and
his detachment open and exposed. His mistake being
perceived from the line, he was called by the adjutant
general, and directed to return; but the noise of the
waters, through which they were wading, prevented
any communication. Having reached a knoll of dry

ground, he formed, and attempted the execution of his order; but soon fell, by a wound in the head. Deprived of their commander, and perceiving their situation hazardous and untenable, the detachment retreated to the line, with the loss of their colonel and five men.

While this advance was made, a column of the enemy was threatening an attack on our extreme left; to frustrate the attempt, Coffee was ordered, with his riflemen, to hasten through the woods, and check their approach. The enemy, although greatly superior to him in numbers, no sooner discovered his movement, than they retired, and abandoned the attack they had previously meditated.

A supposed disaffection in New Orleans, and an enemy in front, were circumstances well calculated to excite unpleasant forebodings. General Jackson believed it necessary and essential to his security, while contending with avowed foes, not to be wholly inattentive to dangers lurking at home; but, by guarding vigilantly, to be able to suppress any treasonable purpose, the moment it should be developed, and before it should have time to mature. Previously, therefore, to departing from the city, on the evening of the 23d, he had ordered major Butler, his aid, to remain with the guards, and be vigilant, that nothing transpired in his absence, calculated to operate injuriously. His fears, that there were many of the inhabitants, who felt no attachment to the government, and would not scruple to surrender, whenever, prompted by their interest, it should become necessary, has been already noticed. In this belief, subsequent circumstances evinced there was no mistake, and showed that to his assiduity and energy is to be ascribed the cause the country was protected and saved. It is a fact, which was disclosed, on making an exchange of prisoners, that, in despite of all the efforts made to prevent it, the enemy were daily and constantly apprized of every thing that transpired in our camp. Every arrangement, and every change of position, was immediately communicated. "Nothing," remarked a British officer, at the close of the invasion, " was kept a secret from us, except your numbers : this, although diligently sought after, could never be procured."

Between the 23d, and the attack on the 28th, to carry our line, major Butler, who still remained at his post in the city, was applied to by Fulwar Skipwith, at that time speaker of the senate, to ascertain the commanding general's views, provided he should be driven from his line of encampment, and compelled to retreat through the city; would he, in that event, destroy it ? It was indeed a curious inquiry, from one who, having spent his life in serving his country, in different capacities, might better have understood the duty of a subordinate officer ; and that even if, from his situation, major Butler had so far acquired the confidence of his general, as to have become acquainted with his views and designs, he was not at liberty to divulge them, without acting criminally. On asking the cause of the inquiry, Mr. Skipwith replied, it was rumoured, and so understood, that if driven from his position, and made to retreat up the coast, general Jackson had it in contemplation to lay the city waste ;

the legislature desired information on this subject, that if such were his intentions, they might, by offering terms to the enemy, avert so great a calamity. That such a sentiment should be entertained by this body, was scarcely credible; yet a few days brought the certainty of it more fully to view, and shewed that they were already devising plans to ensure their safety, even at any sacrifice. While the general was hastening along the line, from ordering Coffee, as we have just observed, against a column of the British on the left, he was hailed by Mr. Duncan, one of his volunteer aids, and informed, that already it was agitated, secretly, by the members of the legislature, to offer terms of capitulation to the enemy, and proffer a surrender. Poised as was the result, the safety or fall of the city resting in uncertainty, although it was plainly to be perceived, that, with a strong army before them, no such resolution could be carried into effect, yet it might be productive of evil, and, in the end, bring about the most fatal consequences. Even the disclosure of such a wish might create parties—excite opposition in the army, and inspire the enemy with renewed confidence. The Tennessee forces, and Mississippi volunteers, it was not feared would be affected by the measure; but it might detach the Louisiana militia, and even extend itself to the ranks of the regular troops. Jackson was greatly incensed, that those whose safety he had so much at heart, should be seeking to mar his best exertions. He was, however, too warmly pressed, at the moment, to give it the attention its importance merited; but, availing himself of the first respite from the violence of the attack waged against

him, he apprized governor Claiborne of what he had
heard,—ordered him closely to watch the conduct
of the legislature, and the moment the project of offering a capitulation to the enemy should be fully disclosed, to arrest the members, and hold them subject
to his further orders. The governor, in his zeal to
execute the command, and from a fear of the consequences involved in such conduct, construed as im-
perative, an order which was merely contingent ; and,
placing an armed force at the door of the capitol, prevented the members from convening, and their schemes
from maturing.   149

We pretend not to ascribe this conduct to disaffection to the government, or treasonable motives. The
impulse that produced it was, no doubt, interest,—
a principle of the human mind which strongly sways,
and often destroys, its best conclusions. The disparity
of the two armies, in numbers, preparation, and discipline, had excited apprehension, and destroyed hope.
If Jackson were driven back, and little else was looked
for, rumour fixed his determination of devoting the
city to destruction : but even if such were not his intention, the wrath and vengeance of the enemy would
probably be in proportion, to the opposition they received. Although these considerations somewhat pal-
liate, they do not justify. The government was represented, in the person of the commanding general, on
whom rested all responsibility, and whose voice, on
the subject of resistance or capitulation, should alone
have been heard. In the field were persons who were
enduring hardships, and straining every nerve, for the
general safety. A few of the members of their own

CHAP.
IX.
1814.

body, too, were there, who did not despond.* Might not patriotism, then, have admonished these men, honoured as they were with the confidence of the people, rather to have pursued a course, having for its object to keep alive excitement, than to have endeavoured to introduce fear and paralyze exertion. Such conduct, if productive of nothing worse, was well calculated to excite alarm. If the militia, who had been hastily drawn to the camp, and who were yet trembling for the safety of their families, had been told, that a few private men, of standing in society, had expressed their opinions, and declared resistance useless, it would, without doubt, have occasioned serious apprehensions ; but, in a much greater degree would they be calculated to arise, when told that the members of the legislature, chosen to preside over the safety and destinies of the state, after due deliberation, had pronounced all attempts at successful opposition, vain and ineffectual.

Here was an additional reason why expedients should be devised, and every precaution adopted, to prevent any communication, by which the slightest intelligence should be had of our situation, already, indeed, sufficiently deplorable. Additional guards were posted along the swamp, on both sides of the Mississippi, to arrest all intercourse ; while on the river, the common highway, watch boats were constantly plying during

* Only four members of the legislature appeared in the field, to defend their country. We regret not knowing the name of one of these persons : those we have learned are, general Garrigue Flojack, major Eziel, and Mr. Bufort, who abandoned their civil duties for the field, where they afforded examples worthy of imitation.

the night, in different directions, so that a log could scarcely pass unperceived. Two flat-bottomed boats, on a dark night, were turned adrift above, to ascertain if vigilance were preserved, and whether there would be any chance of passing in safety to the British lines. The light boats discovered them on their passage, and on the alarm being given, they were opened upon by the Louisiana sloop, and the batteries on the shore, and in a few minutes were sunk. In spite, however, of every precaution, treason still discovered avenues through which to project and execute her nefarious plans, and which constantly afforded information to the enemy, carried to them, no doubt, by adventurous friends, who sought and effected their nightly passage through the deepest parts of the swamp, where it was impossible for sentinels to be kept.*

Much inconvenience was sustained for the want of arms, and much anxiety felt, lest the enemy, through their faithful adherents, might, on this subject also, obtain information; to prevent it, as far as possible, general Jackson endeavoured to conceal the strength and situation of his army, by suffering his reports to be seen by none, but himself and the adjutant general. Many of the troops in the field were supplied with common guns, which were of little service. The Kentucky troops, who were daily expected, were also understood to be badly provided with arms. Uncertain but the city might still contain many articles that would be serviceable, orders were issued to Mr. Girod, mayor of New Orleans, to search every store and house,

* See note C.

and take possession of all the muskets, bayonets, spades, and axes he could find. Understanding too, there were many young men, who, from different pretexts, had not appeared in the field, he was instructed to obtain a register of every man in the city, under the age of fifty, that measures might be concerted for drawin forth those, who had hitherto appeared backward, in engaging in the pending contest.

150   Frequent light skirmishes, by advanced parties, without much effect on either side, were all that took place for several days. Colonel Hinds, at the head of the Mississippi dragoons, on the 30th, was ordered to dislodge a party of the enemy, who, under cover of a ditch that ran across the plain, were annoying our fatigue parties. In his advance, he was unexpectedly thrown between them, and became exposed to the fire of a line, which had hitherto lain concealed and unobserved. His collected conduct, and gallant deportment, gained him and his corps the approbation of the commanding general, and extricated him from the danger he was in. The enemy retired, and he returned to the line, with the loss of five of his men,

CHAPTER X.

Attack of the 1st of January.—General Jackson's line of defence.—Kentucky troops arrive at head quarters.—British
army reinforced; their preparations for attack.—Battle of
the 8th of January, and repulse of the enemy.—American
redoubt carried, and retaken.—Colonel Thornton proceeds against general Morgan's line, and takes possession
of it.—Letter of captain Wilkinson.—British watch word.
—Generous conduct of the American soldiers.—Morgan's
line regained.—General Lambert requests a suspension of
hostilities.—Armistice concluded.—Execution of an American soldier, by the British.

———

THE British were encamped two miles below the CHAP.
American army, on a perfect plain, and in full view.   X.
Although foiled in their attempt to carry our works by
the force of their batteries, on the 28th, they yet re-   1815.
solved upon another attack, and one which they believed would be more successful. Presuming their
failure to have arisen from not having sufficiently
strong batteries, and heavy ordnance, a more enlarged arrangement was resorted to, with a confidence
of silencing opposition, and effecting such breaches in
our entrenchment, as would enable their columns to
pass, without being exposed to any considerable hazard.
The interim between the 28th of December and 1st of
January, was accordingly spent in preparing to execute
their designs. Their boats had been despatched to

the shipping, and an additional supply of heavy cannon landed through Bayou Bienvenu, whence they had first debarked.

During the night of the 31st, they were busily engaged. An impenetrable fog, next morning, which was not dispelled until nine o'clock, by concealing their purpose, aided them in the plans they were projecting, and gave time for the completion of their works. This having disappeared, several heavy batteries, at the distance of six hundred yards, mounting eighteen and twenty-four pound carronades, were presented to view. No sooner was it sufficiently clear to distinguish objects at a distance, than these were opened, and a tremendous burst of artillery commenced, accompanied with congreve rockets, that filled the air in all directions. Our troops, protected by a defence, which, from their constant labours and exertions, they believed to be impregnable, unmoved and undisturbed, maintained their ground, and, by their skilful management, in the end, succeeded in dismounting and silencing the guns of the enemy. The British, through the friendly interference of some disaffected citizens, having been apprized of the situation of the general's quarters,—that he dwelt in a house, at a small distance in the rear of his line, against it directed their first and principal efforts, with a view to destroy the commander. So great was the number of balls thrown, that, in a little while, its porticos were beaten down, and the building made a complete wreck. In this dishonourable design, they were, however, disappointed; for with Jackson it was a constant practice, on the first appearance of danger, not to wait in his quarters, watching events, but instantly to proceed to the line, and be ready to form his arrangements as circumstances might require. Constantly in expectation of a charge, he was never absent from the post of danger; and thither he had this morning repaired, at the first sound of the cannon, to aid in defence, and inspire his troops with firmness. Our guns, along the line, now opened, to repel the assault, and a constant roar of cannon, on both sides, continued until nearly noon; when, by the superior skill of our engineers, the two batteries formed on the right, next the woods, were nearly beaten down, and many of the guns dismounted, broken, and rendered useless. That next the river still continued its fire, until three o'clock; when, perceiving all attempts to force a breach ineffectual, the enemy gave up the contest, and retired. Every act of theirs discovers a strange delusion, and on what wild and fanciful grounds all their expectations were founded. That the American troops were well posted, and strongly defended by pieces of heavy ordnance mounted along their line, was a fact well known; yet a belief was confidently indulged, that the undisciplined collection which constituted the strength of our army, would be able to derive little benefit from such a circumstance; and that artillery could produce but slight advantages in the hands of persons who were strangers to the manner of using it. That many who, from necessity, were called to the direction of the guns, were at first entirely unacquainted with their management, is indeed true; yet the accuracy and precision with which they threw their shot, afforded a convincing argument, either that they possessed the

capacity of becoming, in a short time, well acquainted
with the art of gunnery, or that it was a science, the
acquiring of which was not attended with incalculable
difficulties.

That they would be able to effect an opening, and
march through the strong defence in their front, was
an idea so fondly cherished by our assailants, that an
apprehension of failure had scarcely ever occurred.
So sanguine were they in this belief, that, early in the
morning, their soldiers were arranged along the ditches,
in rear of their batteries, prepared and ready to advance
to the charge, the moment a breach could be made.
Here, protected by their situation from danger, they
remained, waiting the result that should call them to
act. But their efforts not producing the slightest impression, and their rockets not having the effect to drive
our militia away, they abandoned the contest, and retired to their camp, leaving their batteries almost completely destroyed.

Perceiving their attempts must fail, and that such
an effect could not be produced, as would warrant
their advance, another expedient was resorted to, but
with no better success. It occurred to the British
commander, an attack might be made to advantage,
next the woods, and a force was accordingly ordered
to penetrate in this direction, and turn the left of our
line, which was supposed not to extend further than
the edge of the swamp. In this way, it was expected
a diversion could be made, while the reserve columns,
in readiness, and waiting, were to press forward, the
moment it could be effected. Here disappointment
resulted. Coffee's brigade, being already extended

An ad-
vance
made on
general
Coffee's
line.

into the swamp, as far as it was possible for an advancing party to penetrate, brought unexpected dangers
into view, and occasioned an abandonment of the project. That such a design was practicable, and might
be attempted, was the subject of early consideration;
and the necessary precaution had been taken to prevent it. Although cutting the levee had raised the
water in the swamp, and increased the difficulties
of keeping troops there, yet a fear, lest this pass might
be sought by the enemy, and the rear of the line thereby gained, had determined the general to extend his
defence even here. This had been entrusted to general Coffee; and surely a more arduous duty can scarcely be imagined. To form a breast-work, in such
a place, was attended with many difficulties, and
considerable exposure. A slight one, however, had
been thrown up, and the underwood, for thirty or forty
yards, cut down, that the riflemen, stationed for its
defence, might have a complete view of any force,
which, through this route, might attempt a passage.
When it is recollected that this position was to be
maintained night and day, uncertain of the moment of
attack; and that the only opportunity afforded our
troops for rest, was on logs and brush, thrown together, by which they were raised above the surrounding
water; it may be truly said, that seldom has it fallen
to the lot of any to encounter greater hardships: but,
accustomed to privation, and alive to those feelings
which a love of country inspires, they obeyed without
complaining, and cheerfully kept their position, until
all danger had subsided. Sensible of the importance
of the point they defended, and that it was necessary

T t

to be maintained, be the sacrifice what it might, they looked to nothing but a faithful discharge of the trust confided to them.

Our loss, in this affair, was eleven killed, and twenty-three wounded : that of the enemy was never correctly known.   The only certain information is contained in the communication of general Lambert to earl Bathurst, on the 28th instant, where the casualties and losses, from the 1st to the 5th, are stated at seventy-eight.   Many allowances, however, are to be made for this report.   It was written at a time, when, from the numerous disasters encountered, it was not to be presumed the general's mind was in a situation patiently to remember, or minutely to detail them.   From the great precision of our fire, and the injury visibly sustained by their batteries, their loss was, no doubt, considerable.   The enemy's heavy shot having penetrated our entrenchment, in many places, it was discovered not to be as strong as had at first been imagined.   Fatigue parties were again employed, and its strength daily increased.

The British had again retired to their encampment. It was well understood by Jackson, that they were in daily expectation of considerable reinforcements ; though he rested with confidence in the belief, that a few more days would also bring to his assistance the troops from Kentucky.   Each party, therefore, was busily and constantly engaged in preparation, the one to wage a vigorous attack, the other bravely to defend, and resolutely to oppose it.

A reference to the plate will show more fully than any description can, the situation of the American army. It was in the rear of an entrenchment formed CHAP.
X. of earth, and extending in a straight line from the river to the swamp. In its front was a deep ditch, which 1815. had been formerly used as a mill-race. The Mississippi had receded and left this dry, next the river, though American line of defence. in many places the water still remained. Along the line, and at unequal distances, to the centre of general Carroll's command, were mounted guns of different caliber, from six to thirty-two pounds. Near the river, and in advance of the entrenchment, was erected a redoubt, with embrasures, commanding the road, along the levee, and calculated to rake the ditch in front.

We have heretofore stated, that general Morgan was ordered, on the 24th of December, to cross to the west bank of the Mississippi. From an apprehension lest an attempt might be made through Barrataria, and the city reached from the right bank of the river, the general had extended his defence there likewise: in fact, unacquainted with the enemy's views,—not knowing the number of their troops, nor but that they might have sufficient strength to wage an attack in various directions, he had carefully divided out his forces, that he might guard, and be able to protect, at all points. His greatest fears, and hence his strongest defence, next to the one occupied by himself, was on the Chef Menteur road, where governor Claiborne, at the head of the Louisiana militia, was posted. The position on the right was formed on the same plan with the line on the left,—lower down the river, and extending out to the swamp. Here general Morgan commanded.

CHAP.   To be prepared against every possible contingency
X.   that might arise, Jackson had established another line
of defence, about two miles in the rear of the one at
1815.   present occupied, which was intended as a rallying
point, in the event he should be driven from his first
position.   With the aid of his cavalry, to give a momentary check to the advance of the enemy, he expected to be enabled, with inconsiderable injury, to
reach it; where he would again have advantages on his
side—be in a situation to dispute a further passage to
the city, and arrest their progress. To inspirit his own
soldiers, and preserve as great a show as possible of
strength and intended resistance to the enemy, his unarmed troops, which constituted no very inconsiderable number, were here stationed.   All intercourse between the lines, but by confidential officers, was pro-
hibited, and every precaution and vigilance employed,
not only to keep this want of preparation concealed
from the enemy, but even from being known on his
own lines.

Occasional firing, at a distance, which produced
nothing of consequence, was all that marked the interim, from the 1st to the 8th.

Kentucky   On the 4th of this month, the long-expected rein-
troops ar- forcement from Kentucky, amounting to twenty-two
rive at
head quar-hundred and fifty, under the command of major ge-
ters.   neral Thomas, arrived at head quarters; but so ill
provided with arms, as to be incapable of rendering any
considerable service. The alacrity with which the citizens of this state had proceeded to the frontiers, and
aided in the north-western campaigns, added to the
disasters which ill-timed policy or misfortune had pro-

duced, had created such a drain, that arms were not
to be procured. They had advanced, however, to
their point of destination, with an expectation of being
supplied on their arrival. About five hundred had
muskets; the rest were provided with guns, from
which little or no advantage could be expected. The
mayor of New Orleans, at the request of general Jackson, had already examined and drawn from the city
every weapon that could be found; while the arrival
of the Louisiana militia, in an equally unprepared
situation, rendered it impossible for the evil to be effectually remedied. A boat, laden with arms, was
somewhere on the river, intended for the use and defence of the lower country; but where it was, or when
it might arrive, rested alone on hope and conjecture.
Expresses had been despatched up the river, for three
hundred miles, to seek and hasten it on; still there
were no tidings of an approach. That so many brave
men, at a moment of such anxious peril, should be
compelled to stand with folded arms, unable, from
their situation, to render the least service to their country, was an event greatly to be deplored, and did not
fail to excite the feelings and sensibility of the commanding general. His mind, active, and prepared for
any thing but despondency, sought relief in vain;—
there was none. No alternative was presented, but to
place them at his entrenchment in the rear; and, by
the show they might make, add to his appearance and
numbers, without at all increasing his strength.

Information was now received that major general
Lambert had joined the British commander-in-chief,
with a considerable reinforcement. It had been here-

tofore announced in the American camp, that additional forces were expected, and something decisive
might be looked for, so soon as they should arrive.
This circumstance, in connection with others, no less
favouring the idea, led to the conclusion that a few
days more would, in all probability, bring on the
struggle, which would decide the fate of the city. It
was more than ever necessary to keep concealed the
situation of his army; and, above all, to preserve as
secret as possible, its unarmed condition. To restrict
all communication, even with his own lines, was now,
as danger increased, rendered more important. None
were permitted to leave the line, and none from without to pass into his camp, but such as were to be implicitly confided in. The line of sentinels was strengthened in front, that none might pass to the enemy,
should desertion be attempted : still, notwithstanding
this precaution and care, his plans and situation
were disclosed. On the night of the 6th, a soldier
from the line, by some means, succeeded in eluding
the vigilance of our sentinels. Early next morning,
his departure was discovered : it was at once correctly conjectured he had gone over to the enemy,
and would, no doubt, afford them all the information
in his power to communicate. This opinion, as subsequent circumstances disclosed, was well-founded;
and dearly did he atone his crime. He unfolded to
the British the situation of the American line; the
late reinforcements we had received, and the unarmed
condition of many of the troops; and, pointing to the
centre of general Carroll's division, as a place occu-

pied by militia alone, recommended it as the point CHAP.
where an attack might be most safely made. X.

Other intelligence received was confirmatory of the 1815.
belief of an impending attack. From some prisoners, taken on the lake, it was ascertained the enemy British
were busily engaged in deepening Villery's canal, prepara-
with the view of passing their boats and ordnance to attack.
the Mississippi. During the 7th, a constant bustle
was perceived in the British camp.. Along the borders of the canal, their soldiers were continually in
motion, marching and manœuvring, for no other purpose than to conceal those who were busily engaged
at work in the rear. To ascertain the cause of this
uncommon stir, and learn their designs, as far as was
practicable, commodore Patterson had proceeded down
the river, on the opposite side, and, having gained a
favourable position, in front of their encampment, discovered them to be actually engaged in deepening the
passage to the river. It was not difficult to divine
their purpose. No other conjecture could be entertained than that an assault was intended to be made on
the line of defence commanded by general Morgan;
which, if gained, would expose our troops on the left
bank to the fire of the redoubt erected on the right;
and in this way compel them to an abandonment of
their position. To counteract this scheme was important; and measures were immediately taken to prevent the execution of a plan, which, if successful,
would be attended with incalculable dangers. An
increased strength was given to this line. The se- 154
cond regiment of Louisiana militia, and four hundred
Kentucky troops, were directed to be crossed over,

to reinforce and protect it. Owing to some delay and difficulty in arming them, the latter, amounting, instead of four hundred, to but one hundred and eighty, did not arrive until the morning of the 8th. A little before day, they were despatched to aid an advanced party, who, under the command of major Arnaut, had been sent to watch the movements of the enemy, and oppose their landing. The hopes indulged from their opposition were not realized; and the enemy, unmolested, reached the shore.

Morgan's position, besides being strengthened by several brass twelves, was defended by a strong battery, mounting twenty-four pounders, directed by commodore Patterson, which afforded additional strength and security. The line itself was not strong; yet if properly maintained by the troops selected to defend it, was believed fully adequate to the purposes of successful resistance. Late at night, Patterson ascertained that the enemy had succeeded in passing their boats through the canal, and immediately communicated his information to the general. The commodore had already formed the idea of dropping the Louisiana schooner down, to attack and sink them. This thought, though well conceived, was abandoned, from the danger involved, and from an apprehension lest the batteries erected on the river, with which she would come in collision, might, by the aid of hot shot, succeed in blowing her up. It was preferred patiently to await their arrival, believing it would be practicable, with 155 the bravery of more than eight hundred men, and the slender advantages possessed, to maintain our position, and repel the assailants.

On the left bank, where the general in person commanded, every thing was in readiness to meet the assault, when it should be made.   The redoubt on the
levee, was defended by a company of the seventh regiment, under the command of Lieutenant Ross. The
regular troops occupied that part of the entrenchment
next the river.   General Carroll's division was in the
centre, supported by the Kentucky troops, under general John Adair ; while the extreme left, extending for
a considerable distance into the swamp, was protected
by the brigade of general Coffee.   How soon the attack should be waged, was uncertain ; at what moment, rested with the enemy,—with us, to be in readiness for resistance. There were many circumstances,
however, favouring the belief, that the hour of contest
was not far distant, and indeed fast approaching ; the
bustle of to-day,—the efforts to carry their boats into
the river,—the fascines and scaling-ladders that were
preparing, were circumstances pointing to attack, and
indicating the hour to be near at hand. General Jackson, unmoved by appearances, anxiously desired a
contest, which he believed would give a triumph to his
arms, and terminate the hardships of his suffering soldiers.   Unremitting in exertion, and constantly vigilant, his precaution kept pace with the zeal and preparation of the enemy. He seldom slept : he was always
at his post.   His sentinels were doubled, and extended as far as possible, in the direction of the British
camp ; while a considerable portion of the troops were
constantly at the line, with their arms in their hands,
ready to act, when the first alarm should be given.

u u

For eight days had the two armies lain upon the same field, and in view of each other, without any thing decisive being on either side effected. Twice, since their landing, had the British columns essayed to effect by storm the execution of their plans, and twice had failed—been compelled to relinquish the attempt, and retire from the contest. It was not to be expected that things could long remain in this dubious state. Soldiers, the pride of England,—the boasted conquerors of Europe, were there; distinguished generals were their leaders, who earnestly desired to announce to their country, and the world, their signal achievements. The high expectations which had been indulged of the success of this expedition, were to be realized, at every peril, or disgrace would result.

The 8th of January at length arrived. The day dawned; and the signals, intended to produce concert in the enemy's movements, were descried. On the left, near the swamp, a sky-rocket was perceived rising in the air; and presently another ascended from the right, next the river. They announced to each other, that all was prepared and ready, to proceed and carry by storm, a defence which had twice foiled their utmost efforts. Instantly the charge was made, and with such rapidity, that our soldiers, at the out posts, with difficulty fled in.

The British batteries, which had been demolished on the 1st of the month, had been re-established during the preceding night: and heavy pieces of cannon mounted, to aid in their intended operations. These now open-

ed, and showers of bombs and balls were poured upon our line; while the air was lighted with their congreve rockets.   The two divisions, com- CHAP.

manded by Sir Edward Packenham in person, and X.

supported by generals Keane and Gibbs, pressed for- 1815.

ward; the right against the centre of general Carroll's

command,—the left against our redoubt on the levee. 156

A thick fog, that obscured the morning, enabled them

to approach within a short distance of our entrench-

ment, before they were discovered.   They were now

perceived advancing, with firm, quick, and steady

pace, in column, with a front of sixty or seventy deep.

Our troops, who had for some time been in readiness,

and waiting their appearance, gave three cheers, and

instantly the whole line was lighted with the blaze of

their fire.   A burst of artillery and small arms, pour-

ing with destructive aim upon them, mowed down

their front, and arrested their advance.   In our mus-

ketry, there was not a moment's intermission; as one

party discharged their pieces, another succeeded; al-

ternately loading and appearing, no pause could be

perceived,—it was one continued volley.   The co-

lumns already perceived their dangerous and exposed

situation.   Battery No. 7, on the left, was ably served

by lieutenant Spotts, and galled them with an inces-

sant and destructive fire.   Batteries No. 6 and 8 were

no less actively employed, and no less successful, in

felling them to the ground.   Notwithstanding the se-

verity of our fire, which few troops could for a mo-

ment have withstood, some of those brave men press-

ed on, and succeeded in gaining the ditch, in front of

our works, where they remained during the action,

and were afterwards made prisoners.   The horror be-

fore them was too great to be withstood; and already

CHAP.
X.
1815.

were the British troops seen wavering in their determination, and receding from the conflict. At this moment, Sir Edward Packenham, hastening to the front, endeavoured to encourage and inspire them with renewed zeal. His example was of short continuance : he soon fell, mortally wounded, in the arms of his aid-de-camp, not far from our line. Generals Gibbs and Keane also fell, and were borne from the field, dangerously wounded. At this moment, general Lambert, who was advancing at a small distance in the rear, with the reserve, met the columns precipitately retreating, and in great confusion. His efforts to stop them were unavailing,—they continued retreating, until they reached a ditch, at the distance of four hundred yards, where a momentary safety being found, they were rallied, and halted.

The field before them, over which they had advanced, was strewed with the dead and dying. Danger hovered still around ; yet, urged and encouraged by their officers, who feared their own disgrace involved in the failure, they again moved to the charge. They were already near enough to deploy, and were endeavouring to do so ; but the same constant and unremitted resistance, that caused their first retreat, continued yet unabated. Our batteries had never ceased their 157 fire ; their constant discharges of grape and canister, and the fatal aim of our musketry, mowed down the front of the columns, as fast as they could be formed. Satisfied nothing could be done, and that certain destruction awaited all further attempts, they forsook the contest and the field in disorder, leaving it almost entirely covered with the dead and wounded. It was in

vain their officers endeavoured to animate them to fur- CHAP.
ther resistance, and equally vain to attempt coercion. X.
The panic produced from the dreadful repulse they had 1815.
experienced ; the plain, on which they had acted, being
covered with innumerable bodies of their countrymen ;
while, with their most zealous exertions, they had been
unable to obtain the slightest advantage, were circumstances well calculated to make even the most sub-
missive soldier oppose the authority that would have
controled him.

The light companies of fusileers ; the forty-third and
ninety-third regiments, and one hundred men from the
West India regiment, led on by colonel Rennie, were
ordered to proceed, under cover of some chimneys,
standing in the field, until having cleared them, to
oblique to the river, and advance, protected by the
levee, against our redoubt on the right.   This work,
having been but lately commenced, was in an unfinished state.   It was not until the 4th, that general   158
Jackson, much against his own opinion, had yielded
to the suggestions of others, and permitted its projection ; and, considering the plan on which it had been
sketched, had not yet received that strength necessary
to its safe defence.   The detachment, ordered against
this place, formed the left of general Keane's command.
Rennie executed his orders with great bravery ; and,
urging forward, arrived at the ditch. His advance was
greatly annoyed by commodore Patterson's battery on
the left bank, and the cannon mounted on the redoubt ;
but, reaching our works, and passing the ditch, Rennie, sword in hand, leaped on the wall, and, calling to American
his troops, bade them follow ; he had scarcely spoken, carried.

CHAP.
X.

1815.

when he fell, by the fatal aim of our riflemen. Pressed by the impetuosity of superior numbers, who were
mounting the wall, and entering at the embrasures,
our troops had retired to the line, in rear of the redoubt.
A momentary pause ensued, but only to be interrupted, with increased horrors. Captain Beal, with the city
riflemen, cool and self-possessed, perceiving the enemy in his front, opened upon them, and at every discharge brought the object to the ground. To advance,
or maintain the point gained, was equally impracticable for the enemy : to retreat or surrender was the only
alternative; for they already perceived the division on
the right thrown into confusion, and hastily leaving
the field.

General Jackson, being informed of the success of
the enemy on the right, and of their being in possession of the redoubt, pressed forward a reinforcement,
to regain it. Previously to its arrival, they had abandoned the attempt, and were retiring. They were severely galled by such of our guns as could be brought
to bear. The levee afforded them considerable protection ; yet, by commodore Patterson's redoubt, on
the right bank, they suffered greatly. Enfiladed by
this, on their advance, they had been greatly annoyed,
and now, in their retreat, were no less severely assailed. Numbers found a grave in the ditch, before our
line; and of those who gained the redoubt, not one, it
is believed, escaped ;—they were shot down, as fast as
they entered. The route, along which they had advanced and retired, was strewed with bodies. Af-
frighted at the carnage, they moved from the scene,
hastily and in confusion. Our batteries were still

continuing the slaughter, and cutting them down at
every step: safety seemed only to be attainable, when
they should have retired without the range of our shot;
which, to troops galled as severely as they were, was
too remote a relief. Pressed by this consideration,
they fled to the ditch, whither the right division had
retreated; and there remained, until night permitted
them to retire.

Here was a time, the most auspicious that had appeared during the war, to have gained a complete triumph to our arms. What important events, in a nation's history, are often the result of slight occurrences!
and how often are they prevented, by causes no less
inconsiderable! This truth is apparent, in the fate of
this grand expedition, which had been fitted out to
humble our national pride; and which would have
been captured or destroyed, but for the ill-timed policy of the government, or its agents, who, as has been
shown, prevented the arrival of the arms destined for
this place, because an inconsiderable sum was thereby
saved to the nation. A considerable portion of our
troops were inactive and useless, for the want of arms,
to place in their hands. If this had not been the case,
—had they been in a situation to have acted efficiently,
the whole British army must have submitted. But,
situated as Jackson then was, pursuit would have been
rashness; yet, with the additional force which a sufficiency of arms would have placed at his command,
much might have been effected against an enemy
whose ranks were thinned by the unparalleled slaughter
of the day; and who, panic-struck, and fleeing from
the danger before them, were incompetent to resist-

CHAP. ance, and already believed themselves conquered : but
   X.   prudence, under existing circumstances, strongly op-
1815. posed the idea of pursuit, and suggested to the commanding general, that although he had thus signally
achieved even more than he had expected, yet with
the kind of troops it had been effected, inferior in number and discipline, to attempt, even under present advantages, a contest in the open plain, was hazarding
160 too greatly. His reasoning on this subject was certainly correct, and such as feeling and policy sanctioned. If an attack were now urged, and the effort
crowned with success, enough having been already
done, it could reflect but little additional lustre on the
American character : if, however, unsuccessful, the
object of the expedition would be secured to the enemy ; and all that had, for so many days, and under
such weighty privations, been contended for, would,
at the instant, be sacrificed and lost. In addition to
this, his soldiers were most of them owners of the soil,
who had families anxiously concerned for their safety,
and whose happiness depended upon their return : such
men would be a loss to the community, too great to
warrant their being risked for the mere gratification of
pride ; in opposition, too, to those whose trade was war ;
and who, wholly abstracted from every thing like principle, contended in battle, without knowing why, or for
what they fought. The lives of his soldiers, he believed were too valuable to their families, and the
community, to be risked upon a venture not warranted by necessity, nor required by the interest and honour of the country. He preferred, therefore, to adopt
what seemed the safer course ; to continue his position,

which assured protection to the city, and the inhabi- CHAP.
tants, rather than by endeavouring to obtain more, en-　X.
danger the loss of every thing.

1815.

The efforts of the enemy to carry our line of defence
on the left, were seconded by an attack on the right
bank, with eight hundred chosen troops, under the command of colonel Thornton. Owing to the difficulty Colonel
of passing the boats from the canal to the river, and Thornton's ad-
the strong current of the Mississippi, all the troops vance
against
destined for this service were not crossed, nor the op- gen. Mor-
posite shore reached for some hours after the expected gan's line.
moment of attack. By the time he had effected a landing, the day had dawned, and the flashes of the guns
announced the battle begun. Supported by three gunboats, he hastened forward, with his command, in the
direction of Morgan's entrenchment.

Some time during the night of the 7th, two hundred Louisiana militia had been sent off, to watch the
movements of the enemy, and oppose him in his landing : this detachment, under the command of major
Arnaud, had advanced a mile down the river and halted ; either supposing the general incorrect, in apprehending an attack, or that his men, if refreshed, would
be more competent to exertion, he directed them to
lie down and sleep : one man only was ordered to be
upon the watch, lest the enemy should approach them
undiscovered. Just at day, he called upon his sleeping companions, and bade them rise and be ready, for
he had heard a considerable bustle, a little below. No
sooner risen, than confirmed in the truth of what had
been stated, they moved off in the direction they had
come, without even attempting an execution of their

x x

orders. The Kentucky troops, having reached Morgan at five o'clock in the morning, were immediately sent to co-operate with the Louisianians. Major Davis, who commanded, had proceeded about three quarters of a mile, and met those troops hastily retreating up the road; he ascertained from them, that the enemy had made the shore; had debarked, and were moving rapidly up the levee. He informed them for what purpose he had been despatched,—to oppose an approach as long as practicable, and with their assistance, he would endeavour to execute his orders.

The two detachments, now acting together, formed behind a saw-mill-race, skirted with a quantity of plank and scantling, which afforded a tolerable shelter. Davis, with his two hundred Kentuckians, formed on the road next the river, supported by the Louisiana militia on the right. The enemy appearing, their approach was resisted, and a warm and spirited opposition for some time maintained: a momentary check was given. The British again advanced, and again received a heavy fire. At this moment, general Morgan's aid-de-camp, who was present, perceiving the steady advance of the enemy, and fearing for the safety of the troops, ordered a retreat. Confusion was the consequence— order could not be maintained, and the whole fled, in haste, to Morgan's line. Arriving in safety, though much exhausted, they were immediately directed to form, and extend themselves to the swamp; that the right of the entrenchment might not be turned.

Colonel Thornton having reached an orange grove, about seven hundred yards distant, halted; and, examining Morgan's line, found it to " consist of a formi-

dable redoubt on the river," with its weakest and most
vulnerable point towards the swamp. He directly advanced to the attack, in two divisions, against the extreme right and centre of the line; and, having deploy-
ed, charged the entrenchment, defended by about fifteen hundred men. A severe discharge, from the field
pieces mounted along our works, caused the right division to oblique, which, uniting with the left, pressed
forward to the point occupied by the Kentucky troops.
Perceiving themselves thus exposed, and having not
yet recovered from the emotions produced by their first
retreat, they began to give way, and very soon entire- Morgan's
ly abandoned their position. The Louisiana militia line is
carried
gave a few fires, and followed the example. Through by the
the exertions of the officers, a momentary halt was ef- British
fected; but a burst of congreve rockets, falling thickly,
and firing the sugar-cane, and other combustibles
around, again excited their fears, and they moved hastily away; nor could they be rallied, until, at the distance of two miles, having reached a saw-mill-race,
they were formed, and placed in an attitude of defence.

Commodore Patterson, perceiving the right flank
about to be turned, had ceased his destructive fire
against the retreating columns on the other shore, and
turned his guns to enfilade the enemy next the swamp;
but, at the moment when he expected to witness a
firm resistance, and was in a situation to co-operate,
he beheld those, without whose aid all his efforts were
unavailing, suddenly thrown into confusion, and for-
saking their posts. Discovering he could no longer
maintain his ground, he spiked his guns, destroyed his
ammunition, and retired from a post, where he had
rendered the most important services.

CHAP.   In the panic that produced this disorderly flight, at
X.   a moment when manly resistance was expected, are to
1815. be found circumstances of justification, which might
have occasioned similar conduct even in disciplined
troops.   The weakest part of the line, and which was
protected but by a slight ditch, was assailed by the greatest strength of the enemy : this was defended by one
hundred and eighty Kentuckians, who were stretched
out to an extent of three hundred yards, and unsup-
ported by any pieces of artillery.   Thus openly exposed to the attack of a greatly superior force, and
weakened by the extent of ground they covered, it is
not to be wondered at, or deserving reproach, that
they should have considered resistance ineffectual, and
forsaken a post, which they had strong reasons for
believing they could not maintain.   General Morgan
reported to general Jackson the misfortune and defeat
he had met, and attributed it to the flight of those
troops, who had also drawn along with them the rest
of his forces.   It is true, they were the first to flee ;
and equally true, that their example may have had the
effect of producing general alarm ; but in point of situation, those troops materially differed : the one, as
we have shown, were exposed, and enfeebled by the
manner of their arrangement ; the other, considerably
superior in numbers, covered no greater extent of
ground,—were defended by an excellent breast-work,
and several pieces of cannon : with this difference,
the loss of confidence of the former was not without sufficient cause.   Of these facts, commodore
Patterson was not apprized ;—general Morgan was :
both, however, attributed the disaster to the flight of

the Kentucky militia. Upon their information, gene- CHAP.
ral Jackson founded his report to the secretary of war, X.
by which those troops were exposed to censures they 1815.
did not merit. Had all the circumstances, as they
existed, been disclosed, reproach would have been prevented. At the mill-race, no troops could have behaved better : they were well posted, and bravely resisted the advance of the enemy, nor, until an order
to that effect was given, had entertained a thought of
retreating.

The heart-felt joy at the glorious victory achieved
on one side of the river, was clouded by the disaster
witnessed on the other. A position was gained, which
secured to the enemy advantages the most important;
and whence they might annoy our whole line, on the
left bank. But for the precaution of commodore Patterson, in spiking his guns, and destroying the ammunition, it would have been in the power of colonel
Thornton to have completely enfiladed, and rendered
it altogether untenable. Fearful lest the guns might
be unspiked, and brought to operate against him, general Jackson hastened to throw detachments across,
with orders to regain it, at every hazard. To the
troops on the right bank, he forwarded an address,
with a view to excite them to deeds of valour, and inspirit them to exertions that should wipe off the reproach they had drawn upon themselves.* Previously,
however, to their being in readiness to act, he succeeded by stratagem in re-obtaining it, and thus spared
the effusion of blood, which would have been necessary to its accomplishment.

* See note D.

CHAP.   The loss of the British, in the main attack, on the
X.   left bank, has been, at different times, variously
        stated.   The killed, wounded, and prisoners, ascer-
1815.   tained, on the next day after the battle, by colonel
Loss of   Hayne, the inspector general, places it at twenty-six
the Bri- hundred.   General Lambert's report to lord Bathurst
tish.   makes it but two thousand and seventy.   From pri-
        soners, however, and information and circumstances
        derived through other sources, it must have been even
        much greater than is stated by either.   Among them
        was their commander-in-chief, and major-general
        Gibbs, who died of his wounds the next day, besides
        many of their most valuable and distinguished officers;
        while the loss of the Americans, in killed and wound-
        ed, was but thirteen.*

        It appears to have been made a question by the
        British officers, if it would not be more advisable to
        carry general Morgan's line, and refrain from any at-
        tempt on this side the river.   It was believed, that if
        successful in this, they would be able to force general
Captain   Jackson from his entrenchment, and pass, with the
Wilkin-
son's let- main body of the army, in safety to the city.   A letter,
ter.

        * Our effective force, at the line, on the left bank, was
        three thousand seven hundred; that of the enemy at least nine
        thousand.   The force landed in Louisiana has been variously
        reported: the best information places it at about fourteen
        thousand.   A part of this acted with colonel Thornton; the
        climate had rendered many unfit for the duties of the field;
        while a considerable number had been killed and wounded,
        in the different contests since their arrival.   Their strength,
        therefore, may be fairly estimated, on the 8th, at the number
        we have stated; at any rate, not less.

found in the possession of captain Wilkinson, a British officer, who fell in the battle, to a friend at home,
in the war department, speaking on this subject, shows
that a difference of opinion prevailed, and confesses
his own as being decidedly in favour of a vigorous attack on both sides. It bears date late on the night of
the 7th, nor does it appear, although he was a captain
and brigade major, that he, at that time, knew whether
an assault were seriously intended against Jackson's
line, or was designed as a feint, to aid the operations of
colonel Thornton. With the true spirit of a British
officer, however, he indulges a hope of success, with
entire confidence,—entertains no fears for the result,
nor doubts but that the Americans will at once retire
before their superior skill and bravery. A general
order, which must have been received after he had
written, disclosing the manner of attack, on the left,
where he acted, was found with the letter. The fusileers and light troops were there instructed, after reaching our line, to act as a pursuing squadron, and keep
up alarm, while the army on the right would press
closely in the rear. It breathes an assurance of success, and shows with what anxiety they looked to the
approaching morning, as likely to bring with it a successful termination of their labours, and a triumph over
a foe, whose advantages, more than bravery, they supposed, had so long baffled their utmost efforts.

That it was considered, however, an undertaking of
greater magnitude and hazard than they were disposed
to admit, is obvious, from one circumstance. The
officer who leads his troops on a forlorn attempt, not
unfrequently places before them allurements stronger

CHAP.
X.

1815.

British
watch
word.

than either authority or duty.   On the present occa⸗
sion, this resort was not omitted; and inducements
were held out, than which nothing more inviting
could be offered to an infuriated soldiery.*   Let it
be remembered of that gallant but misguided general,
who has been so much deplored by the British nation,
that to the cupidity of his soldiers, he promised the
wealth of the city, as a recompense for their gallantry
and desperation; while, with brutal licentiousness, they
were to revel in lawless indulgence, and triumph, uncontrolled, over female innocence.   Scenes like these,
our nation, dishonoured and insulted, had already witnessed; she had witnessed them at Hampton and Ha-
vre-de-Grace: but it was reserved for her yet to learn
that an officer of high standing, polished, generous,
and brave, should, to induce his soldiers to acts of
daring valour, permit them, as a reward, to insult, injure, and debase, those whom all mankind, even savages, reverence and respect.   The history of Europe,
since civilized warfare began, is challenged to afford
an instance of such gross depravity,—such wanton
outrage on the morals and dignity of society. English
writers may deny the correctness of the charge · it
certainly interests them to do so: but its authen-
ticity is too well established to admit of doubt, while
its criminality is increased, from being the act of a
people, who hold themselves up to surrounding nations, as examples of every thing that is correct and
proper.

161   * " *Booty and beauty,*" was the watch word of Sir Edward
Packenham's army, in the battle of the 8th.

The events of this day afford abundant evidence

of the liberality of the American soldiers, and show a striking difference in the troops of the two nations. While one were allured to acts of bravery and duty, by the promised pillage and plunder of the inhabitants, and the commission of crimes abhorrent in the sight of earth and heaven; the other fought but for his country, and, having repelled her assailants, instantly forgot all enmity, viewed his fallen foe as a brother, and hastened to assist him, even at the hazard of his own life. The gallantry of the British soldiers, and no people could have displayed greater, had brought many of them even to our ramparts, where, shot down by our troops, they were lying badly wounded. When the firing had ceased, and the columns had retired, our troops, with generous benevolence, advanced over their lines, to assist and bring in the wounded, which lay under and near the walls; when, strange to tell, the enemy, from the ditch they occupied, opened a fire upon them, and, though at a considerable distance, succeeded in wounding several. It was enough for our generous soldiers, that they were doing an act which the benevolence of their hearts approved, and, with charitable perseverance, they continued to administer to the wants of these suffering men, and to carry them within their lines, although, in their efforts, they were continually exposed to danger. Let the apologist for crime say, wherefore were acts thus unpardonable committed against men, who were administering to the wants, and relieving the sufferings of the dying countrymen of those, who thus repaid the most laudable humanity, with wanton and useless cruelty.

CHAP.
X.

1815.

A communication, shortly after, from major general Lambert, on whom, in consequence of the fall of generals Packenham, Gibbs, and Keane, the command had devolved, acknowledges to have witnessed the kindness of our troops to his wounded. He solicits of general Jackson permission to send an unarmed party, to bury the dead, lying before his lines, and to bring off such of the wounded as were dangerous. Though, in all probability, it was unknown to general Lambert, what had been the conduct of his troops, on this occasion, and unquestionably not authorized by him, yet Jackson, in answer to his despatch, did not omit to bring it to his view, and to express his utter abhorrence of the act. The request to bury his dead was granted, so far as an approach to our lines could be permitted. Jackson consented that all lying at a greater distance than three hundred yards, should be relieved and the dead buried: those nearer were, by his own men, to be delivered over, to be interred by their countrymen. This precaution was taken, that the enemy might not have an opportunity to inspect, or know any thing of his situation.

General Lambert requests a suspension of hostilities.

General Lambert, desirous of administering to the relief of the wounded, and to be relieved from his apprehensions of attack, proposed, about noon, that hostilities should cease, until the same hour the next day. General Jackson, greatly in hopes of being able to secure an important advantage, by his apparent willingness to accede to the proposal, drew up an armistice, and forwarded it to general Lambert, with directions to be immediately returned, if approved. It contained a stipulation, that hostilities, on the left bank of the

river, should be discontinued from its ratification, but CHAP.
not on the right; and, in the interim, no reinforce- X.
ments were to be sent across, by either party. This 1815.
was a bold stroke at stratagem; and, although it
succeeded, even to the extent desired, was yet attended with considerable hazard.   Reinforcements
had been ordered over, to retake the position lost
by Morgan in the morning; but they had not, at this
time, passed the river, nor could it be expected to
be retaken with the same troops who had yielded it,
when possessing advantages which gave them a decided superiority : this the commanding general well
knew; yet, to spare the sacrifice of his men, which, in
regaining it, he foresaw must be considerable, he was
disposed to venture upon a course, which, he felt assured, could not fail of success. It was impossible his
object could be discovered ; while he confidently believed the British commander would infer from his
proposition, that such additional troops were already
thrown over, as would be fully adequate to the purposes of attack, and greatly to endanger, if not wholly
cut off colonel Thornton's retreat. General Lambert's
construction was such as had been anticipated. Although the armistice contained a request that it should
be immediately signed and returned, it was neglected
to be acted upon, until the next day ; and Thornton
and his command were, in the interim, under cover of
the night, re-crossed, and the ground they occupied left
to be peaceably possessed by the original holders. The
opportunity thus afforded, of regaining a position, on
which, in a great degree, depended the safety of those
on the opposite shore, was accepted with an avidity

its importance merited, and immediate measures taken to increase its strength, and prepare it against any future attack that might be made. This delay of the British commander was evidently designed, that, pending the negotiation, and before it were concluded, an opportunity might be had, either of throwing over reinforcements, or removing colonel Thornton and his troops from a situation believed to be extremely perilous. Early next morning, general Lambert returned his acceptance of what had been proposed, with an apology for having failed to reply sooner: he excused the omission, by pleading a press of business, which had occasioned the communication to be overlooked and neglected. Jackson was at no loss to attribute the delay to the correct motive: the apology, however, was as perfectly satisfactory to him, as any thing that could have been offered; beyond the object intended to be effected, he felt unconcerned, and, having secured this, rested perfectly satisfied. It cannot, however, appear otherwise than extraordinary, that this neglect should have been ascribed by the British general to accident, or a press of business, when it must have been no doubt of greater importance, at that moment, than any thing he could possibly have had before him.

The armistice was this morning concluded, and agreed to continue until two o'clock in the evening. The remaining dead and wounded were now removed from the field, which, for three hundred yards, in front of our line, they had almost literally covered. For the reason already given, our soldiers, within the line of demarkation between the two camps, delivered over to the British, who were not permitted to cross it, the

dead for burial, and the wounded on parole, for which CHAP.
it was stipulated an equal number of American prison- X.
ers should be restored.

1815.

It has seldom happened that officers were more deceived in their expectations, than in the result of this
battle, or where they atoned more severely their error :
their reasoning had never led them to conclude that
militia would maintain their ground, when warmly assailed : no other belief was entertained, than, alarmed
at the appearance, and orderly firm approach of veteran
troops, they would at once forsake the contest, and
in flight seek for safety. At what part of our line they
were stationed, was ascertained by information derived
through a deserter, on the 6th ; and influenced by a
belief of their want of nerve, and deficiency in bravery,
the main assault was urged at this point. They were
indeed militia ; but the enemy could have assailed no
part of our entrenchment, where they would have met
a warmer reception, or where they would have found
greater strength : it was indeed the best defended part
of the line. The Kentucky and Tennessee troops,
under generals Carroll and Adair, were here, who had
already, on former occasions, won a reputation that
was too dear to be sacrificed. These divisions, alter-
nately charging their pieces, and mounting the plat-
form, poured forth a constant stream of fire, that was
impossible to be withstood, repelled the advancing
columns, and drove them from the field, with prodigious slaughter.

There is one fact told, to which general credit seems
to be attached, and which clearly shows what little fear
was entertained of any determined opposition our

CHAP. militia might make. When repulsed from our line,
X. the British officers were fully persuaded that the information given them by the deserter, on the night of
1815. the 6th, was false, and, instead of pointing out the
ground defended by the militia, he had referred them
to the place occupied by our best troops. Enraged at
what they believed an intentional deception, they called their informant before them, to account for the
mischief he had done. It was in vain he urged his
innocence, and, with the most solemn protestations,
declared he had stated the fact truly as it was. They
could not be convinced,—it was impossible that they
had contended against any, but the best disciplined
troops; and, without further ceremony, the poor fellow, suspended in view of the camp, expiated, on a
tree, not his crime, for what he had stated was true, but
their error, in underrating an enemy, who had already
afforded abundant evidences of valour. In all their
future trials with our countrymen, may they be no
162 less deceived.

CHAPTER XI.

THE conflict was ended, and each army occupied
its former position.   In appearance the enemy were
visibly altered : menace was sunk into dejection, and
offensive measures yielded for those which promised
safety.   The attitude so long preserved, was now lain
aside ; and they were perceived throwing up partial
defences, to guard against expected attack.   It had
been already announced, upon good authority, that a
considerable force had succeeded in passing the Balize—made prisoners of a detachment there, and was
proceeding up the Mississippi, to co-operate with the
land forces.   It was intended to aid in the battle of the
8th ; but, failing to arrive, the attack had been made
without it.   Whether the enemy, chagrined and mortified at the failure of an effort, into which the idea of
disappointment had never entered, might not again renew the attack, on the arrival of this force, was a pro

CHAP.
XI.

1815.

CHAP. bable event, and every preparation was making, to be
XI.   again in readiness to repel it.

1815.   Of this formidable advance, no certain intelligence
was received, until the night of the 11th, when a heavy cannonading, supposed to be on Fort St. Philip,
was distinctly heard.   Jackson entertained no fears for
Bombard- the result. The advantages of defence, which his pre-
ment of caution and vigilance had early extended to this pas-
Fort St.
Philip. sage, added to his entire confidence in the skill and
bravery of the officer, to whom it had been entrusted,
led him to believe there was nothing to be apprehended ; and that every thing which duty and bravery could,
would be done. The enemy's squadron, consisting of
two bomb vessels, a brig, sloop, and schooner, were
discovered by the videttes, from Fort Bourbon, on the
morning of the 9th, directing their course up the river;
signals were made,—information communicated, and
every thing in readiness to receive them.   About ten
o'clock, having approached within striking distance,
an assault was commenced on the fort, and an immense
quantity of bombs and balls thrown.   A severe and
well-directed fire, from our water battery, soon compelled them to abandon the attack, and retire about
two miles.   At this distance, they possessed decided
advantages,—having it in their power to reach the fort,
with the shot from their large mortars, while they were
entirely without the range of ours.   The assault continued, without much intermission, from the 9th until
the night of the 17th. They had hitherto lain beyond
the effective range of our shot, and although from their
large mortars the fort had been constantly reached, and
pierced in innumerable places, still, such an effect

had not been produced, as to justify a belief, that they could now, more than at the moment of their arrival, venture to pass. A heavy mortar having been prepared, and turned against them on the 17th, the security they hitherto enjoyed, was taken away : their vessels could now be reached, and considerable effect was discovered to be produced. This circumstance, and an ineffectual bombardment, which, though continued for eight days, had secured no decided advantage, induced them to suspend all further efforts; and on the morning of the 18th, they retired.

Major Overton, who commanded at this place, his officers, and soldiers, distinguished themselves by their activity and vigilance. To arrest the enemy's passage up the river, and from uniting with the forces below the city, was of great importance; and to succeed in preventing it, as much as could be expected. So long therefore as they kept at a distance, nor attempted a final accomplishment of their object, no other concern was felt, than to watch their manœuvres, and adopt such a course as should afford safety to the troops in the garrison; for this purpose, pieces of timber and scantling were used, which formed a cover, and gave protection from their bombs. The store of ammunition was also divided, and buried in different places in the earth, that in the event of accident the whole might not be lost. During the period of the bombardment, which lasted with little intermission for nine days, sleep was almost a stranger in the fort. The night was the time, when most of all it was feared, lest the enemy, aided by the darkness, and assisted by some fortunate breeze, would have it in their power to ascend the river, in despite of every opposition : the constant activity necessary, prevented all opportunities for repose. On a tempestuous night, the wind setting fair to aid them, an attempt was made to pass : to divert the attention of the fort, and favour the chances for ascent, their boats were sent forward to commence an attack. In this, however, they were disappointed, and compelled to abandon the undertaking. At length, after many fruitless efforts, and an immense waste of labour and ammunition, they retired without effecting their purpose, or producing, to us, a greater injury, than the loss of nine of the garrison, who were killed and wounded.

The failure of this squadron to ascend the river, perhaps determined general Lambert, in the course he immediately adopted. His situation before our line was truly unpleasant. Our batteries, after the 8th, were continually throwing balls and bombs into his camp ; and wherever a party of troops appeared in the field, they were greatly annoyed. Thus harassed, —perceiving that all assistance through this channel had failed ; and constantly in apprehension lest an attack should be made upon him, he resolved on availing himself of the first favourable opportunity to depart, and forsake a contest, where every effort had met disappointment, and where an immense number of his troops had found their graves. The more certainly to effect a retreat in safety, detachments had been sent out to remove every obstruction, that could retard their progress through the swamp. To give greater facility to his departure, strong redoubts were erected on the way, and bridges thrown across every creek and bayou, that obstructed the passage. Every thing being thus prepared, on the night of the 18th, he silently decamped, and, proceeding towards the lake, embarked for his shipping, leaving, and recommending to the clemency and hospitality of the American general, eighty of his soldiers, who were too severely wounded to be removed. With such silence and caution was this decampment managed, that the slightest intelligence was not communicated, even to our sentinels, occupying the out posts. Early next morning, the enemy's camp was perceived to be evacuated; but what had become of them, and whither they had gone, could only be conjectured: no information on the subject was possessed. To ascertain the cause of this new and sudden appearance of things, detachments were in readiness to proceed, and reconnoitre their camp, when surgeon Wadsdale, of the staff, arrived at our line, with a letter to general Jackson, from the British commander, announcing his determination to suspend, " for the present, all further operations against New Orleans," and requesting his humanity towards the wounded, whom necessity had compelled him to leave.

Detachments were now sent out, to ascertain the cause of this unexpected state of things; with orders to harass their rear, if a retreat were really intended. But the precaution taken by the enemy, and the ground over which they were retreating, prevented pursuit, in sufficient numbers to secure any valuable result. The system of operations which Jackson had prescribed for himself, he believed was such as policy sanctioned, nor to be abandoned but for advantages evidently certain, and which admitted not of question. To have pursued, on a route protected and defended by canals, redoubts, and entrenchments, would, at least, have been adventuring upon an uncertain issue, where success was extremely problematical.

Thus, at last, in total disappointment, terminated an invasion, from which much had been expected. Twenty-six days ago, flushed with the hope of certain victory, had this army erected its standard on the banks of the Mississippi. At that moment, they would have treated with contempt an assertion, that in ten days they would not enter the city of New Orleans. How changed the portrait, from the expected reality! But a few days since, and they were confident of the hour of triumph, and successful termination of their labours : now, vanquished, beaten, and cut to pieces, at midnight, under cover of its darkness, they are silently abandoning their camp,—breaking to pieces their artillery,—fleeing from an enemy, who, but a little while before, they held in utter contempt, and submitting their wounded to his clemency. A demonstration is given, which a Briton, short of absolute proof, would have been among the last to have admitted, that fourteen thousand troops, who, oftentimes, against the sternest opposition, had signalized themselves in battle, and marched to victory, could, under any circumstances, be beaten, and one-third of them destroyed, by an inferior number of men, who scarcely knew how to form in column, or deploy into lines : but they knew what was of infinitely more service, in nerving with strength the soldier's arm, and dispelling every thing like fear,—that they were contending for their CHAP. rights, against a power which was causelessly seeking XI. their destruction,—for privilege against usurpation,— for liberty, in opposition to oppression:—that they 1815. were fighting for a country they loved, and for enjoyments, which, once lost, could never be regained. Prompted by these considerations, they had entered the field, and under their influence had acted. For their toils and privations, they were amply remunerated: they had met their own and country's expectations,—had saved a city from destruction—its inhabitants from cruelty and dishonour, and were carrying with them that consolation, which the recollection of a faithful discharge of duty never fails to inspire.

There was no certainty that the contest was finally ended. The enemy had indeed retired, and, "for the present," relinquished further operations against the country: but of what continuance their forbearance might be, whether they would not avail themselves of the first flattering opportunity, to renew the struggle, and wipe off the stain of a defeat so wholly unexpected, could not be doubted. The hopes and expectations indulged, in England, of the success of this expedition, had inspired the whole army; and failure had never been anticipated. They had now retired; yet, from their convenient situation, and having command of the surrounding waters, it was in their power, at a short notice, to re-appear, at the same, or some more favourable point,—cause a repetition of the hardships already encountered, and perhaps succeed in the accomplishment of their views. These considerations led general Jackson to conclude, that, al-

CHAP.   though, for the present, there was an abandonment of
XI.   the enterprise, still it behoved him not to relax in his
~~~   system of defence; but be in constant readiness
1815.   to maintain the advantages he had gained; and not to
risk a loss of the country, by a careless indifference, growing out of the belief that danger had subsided. To prevent such a result, suitable arrangements
were made. The enemy being now again at their
shipping, with entire control on the lakes and gulf, it
could not be known at what point they might venture
a second attack. General Jackson determined to
withdraw his troops from the point they had so long
occupied, and place them about the city, whence, to
repel any further attempt that might be made, they
could be advanced wherever it became necessary.
The seventh regiment of infantry remained to protect
the point he was leaving; while, further in advance, on
Villery's canal, where a landing had been first effected,
were posted some of the Kentucky and Louisiana militia. To secure this point more effectually, orders
were given, on the 22d, to throw up a strong fortification, at the junction of Manzant and Bayou Bienvenu; which order was again attempted to be executed,
on the 25th. On both occasions, failure was the result, from the circumstance of the enemy having, on
their retreat, left a strong detachment at this place,
which, from their situation, defied approach by a force
competent to their reduction. Their occupying this
position afforded strong evidence that further hostilities
were not wholly abandoned. To counteract, however, any advantages which might be thence derived,
different points, along the swamp, and in the direction

of Terre au Bœuf, were occupied, and strong works **CHAP.** thrown up, to prevent their again reaching, in this di- **XI.** rection, the banks of the Mississippi.

These arrangements being made, calculated, if not to prevent, at least to give intelligence of an approach, in time to be resisted; on the 20th, general Jackson, with his remaining forces, commenced his march to New Orleans. The general glow excited, at beholding his entrance into the city, at the head of his victorious army, was manifested by all those feelings which patriotism and sympathy inspire. The windows and streets were crowded, to view the man, who, by his vigilance, decision, and energy, had preserved the country from the fate to which it had been devoted. It was a scene well calculated to excite the tenderest emotions. But a few weeks since, and every bosom throbbed for its safety. Fathers, sons, and husbands, urged by the necessity of the times, were toiling in defence of their wives and children. A ferocious soldiery, numerous, and skilled in the art of war, to whom every indulgence had been promised, were straining exertion to effect their object. Every cannon that echoed from the line was perhaps the signal of their approach, and the commencement of indescribable horrors. But those feelings had subsided: the painful scenes, which had lasted so long, were gone. The tender female, relieved from the anguish of danger and suspense, no longer trembled for her safety and her honour: a new order of things had arisen: joy sparkled in every countenance; while scarcely a widow or orphan was seen, to cloud the general transport. The commanding general, under whose banners every thing had been

General Jackson returns to New Orleans.

CHAP. achieved, deliberate, cool, and sparing of the lives
XI. of the brave defenders of their country, had dis-
1815. pelled the storm, which had so long threatened to involve the ruin of thousands ; and was now returning,
safe and unhurt, those who had, with him, maintained
the contest. His approach was hailed with acclamations : it was not the kind of applause, which, resulting from fear, is oftentimes extended by the subject to
some conqueror or tyrant, returning in triumph ; but
that which was extended by citizens to a citizen,
springing from affection, and founded in the honest
sincerity of the heart. All greeted his return, 'and
hailed him as their deliverer.

But amidst the expression of thanks, and honours,
and congratulations heaped upon him, he was not unmindful, that to an energy above his own, and to a
wisdom which controls the destiny of nations, he was
indebted for the glorious triumph of his arms. Relieved from the arduous duties of the field, his first
concern was to draw the minds of all, in thankfulness
and adoration, to that sovereign mercy, without whose
aid, and inspiring counsel, vain are all earthly efforts.
Day of The 23d having been appointed a day of prayer and
thanks-
giving ap- thanksgiving, for the happy deliverance effected by our
pointed. arms, he repaired to the cathedral. The church and altar
were splendidly adorned, and more than could obtain
admission had crowded to witness the ceremony. A
grateful recollection of his exertions to save the country, was cherished by all ; nor did the solemnity of the
occasion, even here, restrain a manifestation of their
regard, or induce them to withhold the honour so no-

bly earned.   Children, robed in white, and represent-   CHAP.
ing the different states, were employed in strewing the   XI.
way with flowers; while, as he passed, the following   1815.
ode saluted his ears.—

> Hail to the chief! who hied at war's alarms,
> To save our threaten'd land from hostile arms;
> Preserv'd, protected by his gallant care,
> Be his the grateful tribute of each fair:
> With joyful triumph swell the choral lay—
> Strew, strew with flow'rs the hero's welcome way.
> Jackson, all hail! our country's pride and boast,
> Whose mind 's a council, and whose arm 's an host;
> Who, firm and valiant, 'midst the storm of war,
> Boasts unstain'd praise—laurels without a tear:
> Welcome, blest chief! accept our grateful lays,
> Unbidden homage, and spontaneous praise;
> Remembrance, long, shall keep alive thy fame,
> And future infants learn to lisp thy name.

When the general reached the church, the reverend administrator of the diocese met him at the door. Addressing him in a strain of pious eloquence, he intreated him to remember, that his splendid achievements, which were echoed from every tongue, were to be ascribed to Him, to whom all praise was due. "Let the votary of blind chance," continued he, "deride our credulous simplicity. Let the cold-hearted atheist look for an explanation of important events, to the mere concatenation of human causes; to us, the whole world is loud in proclaiming a Supreme Ruler, who, as he holds the destiny of man in his hands, holds also the thread of all contingent occurrences: from his lofty throne, he moves every scene below,—infuses his wisdom into the rulers of nations, and executes his un-

3 A

controllable judgments on the sons of men, according to the dictates of his own unerring justice." He concluded his impressive address, by presenting the general with a wreath of laurel, woven for the occasion, and which he desired him to accept as "a prize of victory."

General Jackson, accepting the pledge, presented by the reverend prelate, as a mark of distinguished favour, returned him a reply no less impressive than the address he had received. He was now conducted in, and seated near the altar, when the organ, and church ceremonies commenced, and inspired every mind with a solemn reverence for the occasion.* These being ended, he retired to his quarters, to renew a system of defence, which should ensure entire safety, and ward off any future danger that might arise. The right bank of the Mississippi was now strengthened by additional reinforcements, and a strong position taken on La Fourche, to prevent any passage in that direction. Suitable arrangements for security having been already made below the city, generals Coffee and Carroll were instructed to resume their former encampment, four miles above, where they had been stationed previously to the landing of the enemy. The rest of the troops were arranged at different points, where necessity seemed most to require it, and where they might be convenient for action, on the first appearance of danger.

Previously to general Lambert's departure, articles of agreement had been entered into, by the commanders of the two armies, for an exchange of prisoners; in pursuance of which, sixty-three Americans, taken on

* See note F

the night of the 23d, from the left wing of general Cof- CHAP.
fee's brigade, had been delivered up : the remainder, XI.
principally those who had been taken at the capture of 1815.
our gun boats, were shortly afterwards surrendered by
admiral Cochrane, and an equal number of British prisoners, in our possession, sent off to be delivered at
the Balize.

The enemy had now withdrawn from the shore, all
the troops which had been landed, and occupied their February.
former position at Cat and Ship Island. Mortified
at their unexpected disaster, they were projecting
a plan, by which it was expected a partial advantage would be secured, and the stigma of defeat ob-
literated.

Fort Bowyer had been once assailed, with a consider- 166
able force, by land and water, and failure had resulted.
This post, the key to Mobile, and considered of infinite consequence, had been retained under the command of him, who heretofore had defended it so valiantly. The British commander, turning from those
scenes of disappointment and wretchedness lately witnessed, and anxious to retrieve his fortunes, before
he retired with his shattered and diminished forces,
perceived no place, against which he might proceed, with better founded hopes of success. Its
importance, in a military point of view, has been already shewn : but, dispirited and reduced as the enemy now were, even should they possess it, they would
not have it in their power to derive those advantages,
which were heretofore so greatly apprehended. 167

On the 6th of February, the British shipping appeared off Dauphin Island, fronting the point on which

stood the fort, garrisoned with three hundred and sixty men. Having made the necessary arrangements, on the 8th, an attack was commenced, both from the land and water. The fleet was formed into two divisions; and approached within one and two miles, bearing south and south-west from it. But the principal attack, and that which compelled a surrender, was from the shore, where colonel Nicholls, and Woodbine had carried on their operations, in September. Five thousand troops, aided by pieces of heavy ordnance, and secured from the fire of our guns, by large embankments, urged the assault. Under cover of the two succeeding nights, redoubts were thrown up, and trenches cut through the sand, which enabled them to approach gradually, and without being exposed to the fire of our guns. Twice, on the 8th, were detachments sent out, to effect, by storm, the accomplishment of their purpose; but the fire from the fort compelled an abandonment of their course, and drove them to the necessity of approaching by trenches, protected by strong redoubts. To demolish these from the fort was impracticable, from their strength; and to attempt to prevent their erection, by any sortie, with so weak a force, would have been rash and imprudent. Thus situated, and every thing being ready, to attack and carry the fort, if opposition were still intended, about ten o'clock, on the 11th, the enemy hoisted a flag : major Lawrence raised another. Hostilities ceased, and general Lambert required a surrender. The officers being convoked, with one consent agreed that further resistance would be ineffectual, and could only lead to the unnecessary loss of many valuable

Reduction of Fort Bowyer.

lives. A capitulation was agreed on, and the fort sur- CHAP.
rendered. XI.

General Winchester, who commanded at Mobile, 1815.
having received intelligence of what was passing at the
point, ordered a detachment of a thousand men, under 168
major Blue, to proceed down the bay, and aid in its
defence. This auxiliary force was too late : having
surprised and captured one of the enemy's out piquets,
consisting of seventeen men, and ascertained that a
surrender had already taken place, they returned. Had
this detachment reached its destination, our loss would
have been more severe. The enemy's forces were
too numerous, and their means of attack too effectual,
for any different result to have taken place, even had
major Blue arrived.

It had early been the wish of general Jackson, for
the large frigate, lying at Tchifonte, to be completed,
and placed in defence of Fort Bowyer. We have
before remarked the confidence entertained by him,
that, with the aid of this vessel, no force brought
against the place would be competent to its reduction.
Near it is the only channel a vessel of any size can
pass. This frigate, occupying the passage, would
present as strong a battery as could be brought against
her, and, with the aid of the fort, defy any assault
from the water ; while, from her position, she would
be able to throw her bombs and shot across the narrow
neck of land, in the rear of the point, and arrest the
advance of any number of troops, which, in this way,
should attempt an approach. Yet every necessary
precaution, to defend this important pass, had been al-

together overlooked or disregarded, and more money
spent by the government, in erecting shelters, to protect the frigate from the weather, than would have
been sufficient for her completion.

1815.

169

Legisla-
ture re-
com-
mence
their ses-
sion.

The legislature of Louisiana had re-commenced
their session. The necessity which had induced a suspension of their deliberations, being removed, by the
departure of the enemy, they were no longer restricted
in the exercise of their constitutional privileges. Some
of the members, during the past struggle, had forsaken their official duties, and repaired to the field,
where more important services were to be rendered,
and where they had manifested a zeal and devotion to
their country worthy of imitation. A much greater
part, however, had pursued a very opposite course,
and stood aloof from the impending danger. The
disposition they had shown, on the 28th of December,
to propose a capitulation with the enemy, has been
adverted to : how far it was calculated to estrange the
public sentiment from that conviction, which general
Jackson had, throughout, endeavoured to rivet and impress, " that the country could and would be successfully defended," can be easily imagined. But with
them he had sinned beyond forgiveness. The course
he had adopted,—his arresting their proceedings, and
suspending their deliberations, by placing an armed
force at the door of the capitol, were viewed as in-
fringements upon legislative prerogative,—denounced
as an abuse of power, and the first opportunity seized,
to exhibit their resentment against the man who had
stood forth in opposition to, and defeated their de-

signs. Whether it were better to indulge them in

a heedless course, that led to no other object than individual advancement, or, by interposing a remedy, arrest the foul purpose intended, preserve the nation from dishonour, and avert the dangerous consequences involved, was not a matter requiring much deliberation ; nor was it an act, to justify the legislature in treating with marked disrespect, him who was the efficient cause of all that had been achieved.

No sooner had they resumed the exercise of their duties, than their first concern was to pass in review, the incidents of the last month. To those who had acted vigilantly in the defence of the state, and who, by their toils and exertions, had contributed to its safety, they tendered their thanks. In pursuance of this resolution, the governor addressed the principal officers : but of Jackson, nothing was said. We are not disposed to recriminate on the conduct of this body, though the circumstances present no very favourable appearance. When danger threatened, they were disposed to make terms with the enemy, and obtain their safety by a surrender of the city : from this they were prevented, by a decision of character, that compelled legislative to yield to military authority. Greatly incensed at being thus unexpectedly restrained in the execution of their designs ; no sooner do they resume the duties of their station, than they are lavish in the praise of those who adopted and pursued a course directly contrary to their own ; while, in that commendation and approval, they intentionally neglect the hero to whom their section of country owed its salvation. But to Jackson, this

was an immaterial circumstance : he had a mind incapable of being inflated by applause, or depressed by
unmerited censure.   He knew, full well, that his
countrymen would duly appreciate his conduct, trace
his actions to proper motives, and extend " honour to
whom honour was due."   *Humanum est errare*, was
a maxim from which he claimed no exemption ; but a
conviction resting on his mind, and which alone had
prompted him to the course he had taken, was, that if
he had erred, it was for the general good : if legislative prerogative had been invaded, it was to save the
actors from themselves : if constitutional forms and
provisions had been violated, the country had been
thereby protected from outrage, dishonour, and ruin.
These afforded consolatory reflections, which the neglect or censures of none could disturb, or take away.
Mindful of what he owed to his country, and what
was expected at his hands, he continued a course, calculated to preserve the advantages he had secured, regardless of the cabal and intrigue of party.

Discon-
tents
among the
American
troops.

Appearances in the American camp were about this
time assuming an unfavourable aspect : present danger and alarm being removed, confusion was arising,
and disaffection spreading through the ranks. Pretexts
were sought after, to escape the drudgery of the field.
Many naturalized citizens, who had been brought into
the service, and made to aid in the general defence,
were now seeking an exemption from further control,
and claiming to be subjects of the king of France.
Some were indeed foreigners : but most of them had,
by naturalization, become citizens of the United States.
Notwithstanding this, as French subjects, they were

seeking, and actually procuring, exonerations through
Monsieur Toussard, the consul resident at New Orleans.　No applicant ever went away unsupplied, and
hundreds had obtained his protections, which were
to relieve them from the drudgery of the field, and
the ties due to their adopted country.　Harassed
by such evils, that were every day increasing; and
having strong and satisfactory reasons to believe that
the enemy, then within a few hours sail of the shore,
were constantly advised of his situation, Jackson determined to adopt such measures, as would at once put
down the machinations of the guilty and designing.
Monsieur Toussard, thus manifesting a warmth of
attachment to the English, and a desire to aid them,
for the services they had given in the restoration of
his monarch, was ordered to leave the city,—retire to
the interior of the country, nor venture to return,
until peace were restored.　His countrymen, too,
who were disposed to claim his protection, and abandon the service, were ordered to follow him, and not
to appear again about New Orleans.　The general did
this, with a view to his own security, and from a conviction, that those who thus shamefully sought to avoid
a contest, threatened against a country which they had
adopted, and whose privileges and benefits they had so
long enjoyed, would not scruple, if an occasion offered, to inflict any injury in their power :—he believed
his camp, or its vicinity, by no means a proper place,
where such characters should be permitted to loiter.　170

Our own citizens, too, were giving rise to difficulties, and increasing the danger of the moment.　Mr.
Livingston had arrived on the 10th, from the British

3 B

fleet, whither he had gone to effect a general cartel : through him, admiral Cochrane had announced the arrival of a vessel from Jamaica, with news of a peace having been agreed on by the two countries. This information was immediately caught by the news-mongers, and either from intention, or want of correct intelligence, suddenly appeared in the Louisiana gazette, in an entirely different shape : it stated the arrival of a flag at head quarters, which announced the conclusion of a peace, and requested a suspension of hostilities. The effect of such a declaration would be, to introduce disaffection among the troops, and induce them to believe that their accustomed vigilance was no longer necessary. Sensible of this, general Jackson instructed the editor to alter what he had stated, and exhibit the facts truly as they were. He adopted this course, from an apprehension of serious consequences. One thing he well knew, that the enemy had retired, under circumstances of mortification and humbled feeling, at their complete discomfiture ; nor was it an improbable conjecture, that they would yet seek an accomplishment of their views, through any channel a hope of success could be discerned. Might not this declaration of a peace, and request for the suspension of hostilities, introduced before the public, be a devise to induce a relaxation in his system of operation and defence ; to divert his officers and soldiers from that attention, and activity, so essential to security,—to excite discontents and murmurings, and a desire to be discharged from the further drudgery of a camp? All these dangers he saw lurking beneath it, if false ; and whether true or false, it was foreign to his duty to be

influenced by any thing, not communicated officially
by his government. Fearful of the effects it might
produce, he lost no time in addressing his army:
" how disgraceful," he remarked, " as well as disastrous, would it be, if, by surrendering ourselves cre-
dulously to newspaper publications,—often proceeding
from ignorance, but more frequently from dishonest
design, we should permit an enemy, whom we have
so lately and so gloriously beaten, to regain the advantages he has lost, and triumph over us in turn." A
general order, at the same time, announced that no
publication relating to, or affecting the army, was to
be published in any newspaper, without first obtaining permission. It has been objected, that this prohibition, going to restrict the exercise of a constitutional right, was an outrage on the feelings and liberty
of the country : but if the press be of so sacred and
intactible a character, that it may adopt and pursue a
course, calculated to scatter dissensions, and excite
mutiny in the ranks of an army, when in the very face
of an enemy, without the power of control, it is a circumstance much to be regretted. Reflecting minds
will determine, if an interposition of power were not
necessary, to restrain so dangerous a freedom, and
to avert injury from a country, whose protection the
press, when it seeks to injure, ceases to deserve.

Notwithstanding this prohibition, shortly afterwards,
an anonymous publication appeared in the Louisiana
Courier, calculated to excite mutiny among the troops,
and afford the enemy intelligence of the situation and
disposition of the army. It was now high time, the
general believed, to act with decision, and prove, by

the rigid exercise of authority, that such conduct militated against the police and safety of his camp, and required not to be passed over with impunity. The enemy had heretofore effected a landing, secretly, and without opposition; and although beaten, might again return. If spies were to be nestled in his camp, and permitted to go forth to the world, with the gleanings of their industry, it was folly to believe the enemy would not profit by the information. Martial law still prevailed in New Orleans, and he resolved to put it in execution against those, who manifested such evident disregard of the public good. The editor was immediately sent for to the general's quarters; he stated the author of the piece to be —— Louaillier, a member of the legislature, and was thereupon discharged.

March.   Louaillier was arrested, and detained for trial. This circumstance afforded civilians a fair opportunity of testing, if it were in the power of a commanding general to raise the military above the civil authority, and render it superior by any declaration of his. Application was made to judge Hall, for a writ of habeas corpus, which was immediately issued. The general, to render the example as efficacious as possible, and from information that the judge had been much more officious than his duty required, determined to arrest him also, and thereby at once to settle the question of authority. On a matter involving such important consequences, he believed it best to have it determined in a way calculated to silence opposition, and shew that he was resolved to put down every effort to thwart the measures he had adopted for defence, or which was in-

tended to destroy the police, which he had established CHAP.
for the tranquillity of his camp.   XI.

Instead of surrendering Mr. Louaillier, therefore,   1815.
and acting in obedience to the writ, he seized the person of the judge, and, on the 11th of the month, sent Judge
him from the city, with these instructions, " I have rested.
thought proper to send you beyond the limits of my
encampment, to prevent a repetition of the improper
conduct with which you have been charged. You
will remain without the line of my sentinels, until the
ratification of peace is regularly announced, or until
the British shall have left the southern coast." He
did this, believing he was right, in the declaration of
martial law, and that the good sense of judge Hall
should, at so momentous a period, have taught him a
different course. He did it, because disposed to give
complete effect to his measures,—to silence opposition, and satisfy the refractory and designing, that judicial interference should not mar the execution of his
plans, or afford a screen, behind which treason might
stalk unmolested. He did it, to make the example
effectual, and to obtain, through fear, that security
which could not be had through love of country.

The mind coolly calculating, in the closet, the principles of right and wrong, cannot fairly appreciate the
merits of this question. Proper inferences can be only
drawn, by bearing in recollection all those circumstances which existed at the moment. That a zeal
suited to the occasion, was not felt by all, the events
already adverted to abundantly prove. The course
pursued by the legislature had evidenced a feeling
and conduct, which had forfeited reliance; while the

enemy being, as we have heretofore shown, constantly advised of every thing transacted in the American camp, plainly evinced, that safety and success were to be attained in no other way, than by pursuing a course at once firm and determined.

The militia had already grown tired of the field, and sighed to be discharged from their toils. To impress on their minds a conviction, that, peace being restored, they were unnecessarily detained in service, when it rested on rumour alone; or to attempt, by any course of conduct, to render them more disaffected, carried with it such a degree of criminality and guilt, as could not be permitted, without endangering the safety of the country. This spirit of discontent had become extensively diffused. The different posts, which had been established, could be with difficulty maintained. The Kentucky troops, and two hundred of the Louisiana militia, stationed in defence of Villery's canal, had abandoned their post. Chef Menteur, too, no less important, had been forsaken by one hundred and fifty of the Louisianians, in despite of the remonstrances and exertions of their officers to detain them. Governor Claiborne had been heard to declare, in words of mysterious import, that serious difficulties would be shortly witnessed in New Orleans. For the commanding general, at a time like this, when disaffection was spreading like contagion through his camp, patiently to have stood, and witnessed mutiny fomented and encouraged by persons who, from their standing in society, were calculated to possess a dangerous influence, would have been a crime he never could have sufficiently atoned, had injury resulted. He thought

it time enough to relax in his operations, and ground CHAP.
his arms, when the conclusion of peace should be an-   XI.
nounced, through the proper authorities.   Until then,
believing his duty required it, he resolved to maintain   1815.
his advantages, and check opposition, at every hazard.
To have obeyed the writ would have been idle.   He
had declared the existence of military authority, and
thereby intended to supersede all judicial power.   If
he had obeyed the mandate, it would have been an
acknowledgment of civil supremacy, and a virtual
abandonment of the course he had adopted.   It was
not an improbable event, that the petitioner would be
discharged, on a hearing, because guilty of no offence
cognizable by the civil courts.   He had not levied war
against the country, nor directly aided the enemy ; but
had done that which was paralyzing exertion, scattering dissension, introducing mutiny, and thinning the
ranks of the army.   Either, then, judicial interference
should have been disregarded, or the arrest was wholly
unnecessary.   But whether the course pursued were
right or wrong, the effect was important : good order
was restored, and disorganizers hushed to silence.

On the 13th of the month, two days after the de- 171
parture of judge Hall from the city, an express reach- Peace an-
ed head quarters, with despatches from the war de- nounced.
partment, announcing the conclusion of a peace between Great Britain and the United States, and directing a cessation of hostilities.   A similar communication from his government was received by general
Lambert, shortly afterwards, and, on the 19th, military
operations, by the two armies, entirely ceased.   The
aspect of affairs was now changing : the militia were

discharged from service; bustle was subsiding; and joy and tranquillity every where appearing. A proclamation, by the directions of the president of the United States, was issued, extending pardon and forgiveness for past offences.

Judge Hall, being restored to the exercise of those functions, of which he had been lately bereaved, by military arrest, proceeded, without loss of time, to an examination of what had passed, and to become the arbiter of his own wrongs and injuries. Accordingly, on the 21st, he granted a rule of court for general Jackson to appear, and show cause why an attachment for contempt should not be awarded, on the ground that he had refused to obey a writ issued to him,—detained an original paper belonging to the court, and imprisoned the judge.*

In this case, there was certainly too much room for an improper indulgence of feeling, for the judge, the injured party, to have claimed any kind of interference: it would have been more advisable to have appealed to a jury of his country, and thus brought before a dispassionate tribunal, the question of the illegality of his arrest and detention. But by becoming the prosecutor and arbiter of his own grievances, he placed himself in a situation, where reason could have but little agency, calculated to do injustice, and attach to his decision suspicion and censure. It would have been

* The writ had been detained, and a certified copy given, on account of its having been altered by judge Hall, in a material part. The general's reasons for the detention will be found in his answer, at the end of the volume.

more satisfactory to Jackson, to have met the inquiry
before a less partial tribunal, yet he did not hesitate, although he was well convinced of its being an extra- judicial proceeding, to appear, and submit the grounds which he believed fully acquitted him of all alleged guilt. The trial by jury was secured, generally, in criminal prosecutions, and in all others, except where the law, from conceived necessity, had directed a more summary course. But the authority of courts had al- ready settled, that statutes founded upon a constitutional permission, and which infringed the privilege of jury trial, were never to receive a liberal construction, but to be exercised only in cases, which came strictly within their letter : inasmuch, therefore, as the indignity complained of was not clearly within the provisions of any existing law, it was believed the court possessed no jurisdiction,—that it deserved to be classed with general injuries, and inquired into by a jury. Claiming to himself, this and other exceptions to the jurisdiction, he met the investigation. He was the more disposed to do so, because the busy politicians of the city had condemned his acts, without seeking for the reasons which induced them. An opportunity was now presented, of developing them fully, and bringing to the view of his country, the weighty considerations that had influenced his mind, and to which, in a great measure, were to be ascribed the protection and safety the country had experienced.

On the 24th, his appearance being entered, he stood represented at the bar by John Reid, his aid-de-camp, Prosecution for
and Messrs. Livingston and Duncan. Major Reid contempt
of court.
addressing the court, remarked, that he appeared with

3 c

the general's answer, supported by an affidavit, going
to show, that the rule should be discharged, and no
further proceedings had against him. A curious course
of judicial proceeding was now witnessed. A cause
was to be shown, and yet the judge would determine,
whether it were exceptionable or not, previously to
being heard or seen. The counsel urged in vain, the
propriety of his first hearing, before he decided if the
answer were consonant with propriety. This was over-
ruled. He would first determine what it should be.
If within any of the rules laid down, it should be heard,
—not else.

" If," said he, " the party object to the jurisdiction,
he shall be heard.

" If it be a denial of facts ; or that the facts charged
do not amount to a contempt, he shall be heard.

" If it be an apology to the court ; or show, that by
the constitution and laws of the United States, or in
virtue of his military commission, he had a right to act
as charged, the court will hear him."

Hear ! and you can then decide if it come under
any of these general rules, was replied and argued at
length by his counsel, as being the correct and proper
course.

173   After much time spent in debate, Major Reid was
at length permitted to proceed. He had gotten through
the exceptions reserved as to the jurisdiction, and was
proceeding with the respondent's reasons, showing the
necessity, and consequent propriety, of declaring martial law, when he was again interrupted, because coming within none of the rules laid down. The ears of
the court were closed against every thing, of argument

or reason, and without hearing the defence, the rule CHAP.
was made absolute, and the attachment sued out.   XI.

This process was made returnable on the 31st. The 1815.
general appeared. It was demanded of him to answer
nineteen interrogatories, drawn up with much labour 174
and form, which were to determine as to his guilt or
innocence. He informed the court he would not be
interrogated; that he had, on a former occasion, presented the reasons which had influenced his conduct,
without their producing an effect, or being even heard.
"You would not hear my defence, although you were
advised it contained nothing improper, and ample reasons why no attachment should be awarded. Under
these circumstances, I appear before you, to receive
the sentence of the court, and have nothing further to
add.

"Your honour will not understand me as intending
any disrespect to the court; but as no opportunity has
been afforded me of explaining the reasons and motives by which I was influenced, so is it expected, that
censure will constitute no part of that sentence, which
you imagine it your duty to pronounce."

The judge proceeded to a final discharge of what
he conceived the offended majesty of the laws required,
and fined the general a thousand dollars.

The hall, in which this business was transacted, 175
was crowded with spectators. The indignation manifested by all was great. Having retired from the presence of the court, and passed into his carriage, it was
seized by the people, and carried forcibly to the coffee-
house, amidst the huzzas of an immense concourse,
that surrounded it. Relieved from this display of the

public regard and gratitude, for his exertions in their defence, he retired to his quarters, and, giving his aid a check, sent him to discharge the fine imposed, and thus terminated his contest with the civil authority.

So rivetted was the impression, that the course pursued by the general was correct, and the conduct of judge Hall more the result of spleen than any thing else, that the citizens of New Orleans determined to ward off the effect of his intended injury, by discharging, themselves, the fine imposed. It was only necessary to be thought of, and it was done. So numerous were the persons, entertaining the same feelings on the subject, that in a short time the entire sum was raised, by voluntary contribution. The general, understanding what was in agitation, to spare his own and their feelings, despatched his aid-de-camp to seek the marshal, and thereby avoided the necessity of refusing a favour, intended to be offered, and which he could not have accepted.

Those who are disposed to be informed further upon this subject, and to know if he acted correctly, in declaring martial law, or whether, short of the stern and determined course adopted, he could have effected the important ends he accomplished, and preserved from dishonour, wretchedness, and ruin, the country and its inhabitants, can refer to the able and elegant answer, submitted to the court, and which was refused to be heard. It is replete with reasons, calculated to satisfy the mind that the course he took was required by every principle of propriety and necessity.*

* See note F.

To suspend the writ of habeas corpus, belongs to CHAP. congress, by the constitution. It restricts any inter- XI. ference, but in cases of invasion or insurrection. To 1815. say that it is a privilege which must be continued, until discharged by a law, embracing the circumstances of every case that may arise, is to suppose a something that never can happen. An invasion might be made, a thousand miles from the seat of government, or in the recess of congress, when no authority, competent to act, did exist. The Roman maxim, *inter arma silent leges*, had its origin in the necessities of the republic. In all governments, there are moments of danger and distress, when, no matter how cautiously protected be the rights of the citizens, they must be disregarded, not for the purpose of being destroyed, but more permanently secured. Certainly none but an officer, acting upon an enemy's line, privy to all his intrigues, stratagems, and wiles, can so correctly judge of the emergency, requiring the exercise of such power. He assumes a weighty responsibility; but, with an intelligent world, hazards no more, than to be able to show, that threatening danger, and unavoidable necessity, required him to act. Cases have occurred, wherein the constitution has been violated without reproach. Few generals have respected private property, when the country afforded provisions, and their armies were in want; they have wrested them from the owner. Here, it may be said, compensation and atonement can be offered, but none for the violation of personal liberty : this is a distinction without a difference, because both rights are equally sacred, and the infringement of one, no less a constitutional violation than the other. We

CHAP. would have but little cause to applaud the prudence,
XI.   energy, or good sense of a general, who should suffer
       distress and want in his camp, mutiny in his army,
1815. and ruin to his country, when he possessed the means
of preventing them, but omitted their exercise, because the constitution forbade him to act. Highly as
we may appreciate the man, who, when clothed with
authority, avoids infringing this sacred shield of our
liberty, yet, to hesitate, when surrounded by peril and
danger, would deservedly attach to him the censures
of the patriotic and the good. Whenever individual
rights are trampled on, and personal liberty disregarded and violated, merited reproach will pursue him
whose only justification is, that he possessed the power: but, when founded on necessity,—demanded by
the exigency of the moment, and obviously resorted
to, for the protection and safety of the country, it will
be excused, approved, nay even commended : nor
will the act be punished, unless some victim to it
should chance to sit in judgment.

176   The war being now ended, it was indispensable to
hasten the necessary arrangements, to relieve from the
toils of the field, those brave men, who had so long
been struggling in their country's defence. The necessary measures to effect this were adopted. The
Militia   Tennessee, Kentucky, and Mississippi troops had
are dis- taken their departure. General Gaines being invested
charged. with the command, in a few days, general Jackson left
New Orleans for Nashville. The good wishes and
friendship of the people followed him : there were some
who rejoiced ; they were those, however, who, in moments of peril, had stood aloof from danger, or sought

to increase it. They had no unpleasant sensations, at

being relieved from the presence of one who, they believed, was well acquainted with the abandoned course they had pursued : but the great body of the citizens, mindful of his vigilance, and the weighty privations he had encountered for their safety and protection, fondly cherished a recollection of what he had done. Previously to breaking up his camp, he addressed his army, and declared the high sense he entertained of those valiant men, who, with him, had toiled in the field, and who, by perseverance and fidelity, had obtained safety for their country, and honour for themselves.*

On his return, the respect of all was manifested in his behalf :—all evinced a partiality for the man whose signal achievements had raised his country to a high and dignified standing, and whose unremitting exertions had closed the war with a lustre that enlightened even the blots of its commencement. He carried with him a consciousness of having discharged his duty ; and although, from necessity, he had been compelled to the exercise of rigid severity, which he would gladly have avoided, yet now, when feeling was lulled, and danger past, he beheld nothing to excite regret, or convince him he was wrong. If, however, he could before have doubted, this general manifestation of public regard was sufficient to quiet his apprehensions. The citizens of the United States were yet too virtuous, merely because of his victories, to bestow such unqualified approbation, could they have believed that

* See note G.

when vested with power, he had wantonly trampled on the rights of individuals, and outraged the sacred principles of the constitution. Yet was this approval of his conduct not only evinced by citizens of the country where he passed, but by congress and the legislatures of the different states,—all bore testimony to the propriety of his measures, by the commendations they bestowed.

177

General Jackson returns to Nashville.

A tedious journey of eight hundred miles brought him to Nashville, where he was gratified with a further evidence of a people's regard. An immense concourse was collected, to greet his return, and welcome his arrival. They had long known him as among the number of their best and most respectable citizens; but curiosity had a new incentive: until now, they had not beheld him as one, who, to protect his country, knew no difficulty too great to be encountered,—who, by his firmness and unconquerable perseverance, amidst surrounding dangers, had shielded her from foreign and intestine foes. An elegant address, drawn up and delivered by Mr. Grundy, welcomed his return. Relieved from this further display of public confidence, the more grateful, because from those who were his acquaintances, neighbours, and friends, he retired home, to enjoy that repose, to which, for eighteen months, he had been a stranger.

His person and character.

In the person of general Jackson, is perceived nothing of the robust or elegant. He is six feet and an inch high, remarkably straight and spare, and weighs not more than a hundred and forty-five pounds. His conformation appears to disqualify him for hardship; yet, accustomed to it from early life, few are capable

of enduring fatigue to the same extent, or with less injury. His dark blue eyes, with brows arched and projecting, possess a marked expression; but when, from
any cause, excited, they sparkle with peculiar lustre and
penetration. In his manners he is pleasing,—in his
address commanding; while his countenance, marked
with firmness and decision, beams with a strength and
intelligence that strikes at first sight. In his deportment, there is nothing repulsive. Easy, affable, and familiar, he is open and accessible to all. Influenced by
the belief, that merit should constitute the only difference in men, his attention is equally bestowed on honest poverty, as on titled consequence. No man,
however inconsiderable his standing, ever approached
him on business, that he did not patiently listen to his
story, and afford him all the information in his power.
His moral character is without reproach, and by those
who know him most intimately, he is most esteemed.
Benevolence, in him, is a prominent virtue, that never
passed distress, without seeking to assist and relieve.
He is, however, not without some of those foibles,   178
which heaven always mingles in the composition of
man. Vice and virtue are often found in the same
bosom, which, like light and shade in a picture, reflect
each other in brighter contrast. Deriving from his
birth a temper irritable and hasty, it has had the effect
to create enemies, and involve him in disputes, which
have sometimes brought him to the field of individual contest. On this subject, he has been heard
to remark, that, throughout life, he had made it a settled rule, never to insult, or wantonly assail, the feelings of any. Controlled by this golden rule, and in-

fluenced by reason, we should doubtless seldom err ; but it is a misfortune incident to nature, that the mind, when irritated, not unfrequently adduces improper conclusions from premises, and ascribes intention to conduct and language, in themselves innocent. Wise is he, peculiarly blest, and greatly to be envied, who, in every situation, before he acts, can deliberately think. It was this quality, which, on his entering the army, induced many to fear he would prove too rash for a safe commander,—that occasions would arise, when he would suffer his judgment to be estranged, through the improper exercise of feeling. Events have proved the fallacy of the conjecture, and shown, that there were none who reasoned more dispassionately on the fitness and propriety of measures,—none more cautious, where caution was necessary, or more adventurous, when daring efforts were required. Few generals had ever to seek for order, amidst a higher state of confusion, or obtained success through more pressing difficulties. The effects he produced, under circumstances gloomy and inauspicious, now through his eloquence and persuasion, and again by his firmness, portrays a character for decision, and a mind intimate and familiar with human nature. That the hireling soldier, prodigal of his life, because his sovereign orders, and the mere echo of his superiors, should entertain a respect for his commander, is too commonly the case, to excite surprise : of such materials, general Jackson's army was not composed ; they were freemen,—citizens ; yet, with the exception of those who abandoned him, in his first advance against the Indians, there was scarcely one who served with

him, officer or soldier, that was not warmly and parti- CHAP.
cularly attached to him.

General Jackson possesses ambition, but it rests on
virtue; an ambition, which, regulated by a high sense
of honour, leads him to desire " that applause which
follows good actions,—not that which is run after."
No man is more disposed to hear and respect the
opinions of others, and none where much is at stake,
and at conflict with his own, less under their influence.
He has never been known to call a council of
war, whose decisions, when made, were to shield
him from responsibility or censure. His council of
war, if doubting himself, was a few officers, in whom
he fully confided, whose advice was regarded, if their
reasons were conclusive ; but these not being satisfactory, he at once adopted and pursued the course suggested by his own mind.

Much as we may delight to range through the field
of battle, in quest of acts, to fix a hero's character,
yet inconsiderable circumstances often mark it much
more strongly : it is then that the mind, retiring from
every thing like motive, gives a loose to impulse, and
acts from feeling alone. The general, who meets and
repels his country's foes, is not unfrequently impelled
by ambition, and a recollection that a nation's gratitude
will succeed his efforts : but when, amidst the general
carnage, he is seen acting as a Christian, and sympa-
thizing in others' woes, his character is marked by
virtue, and more truly ennobled. At the battle of
Tohopeka, an infant was found, pressed to the bosom
of its lifeless mother. This circumstance being made
known to general Jackson, he became interested for

the child, directed it to be brought to him, and sought to prevail on some of the Indian women to take care of and rear it. They signified their unwillingness to do so, and that, inasmuch as all its relations had fallen in the battle, they would prefer it should be killed. The general, after this disclosure, determined he would not entrust it with them, but become himself the protector and guardian of the child. Bestowing on the infant the name of Lincoier, he adopted it into his family, and has ever since manifested the liveliest zeal towards it, prompted by benevolence, and because its fate bore a strong resemblance to his own, who, in early life, and from the ravages of war, was left in the world, forlorn and wretched, without friends, or near relations.

Of the two great parties, which have distracted our country, general Jackson is attached to the republican. In his first political career, he rallied on the side of the people. During Mr. Adams' administration, when the party was few and inconsiderable, he appeared on the side of the rights of man, espousing and advocating the principles of tolerance and free will; until, disgusted with the mode of administering the government, he retired from the legislative councils of the nation. He is not, however, one of those blind infatuated partizans, who holds the opinions of others in derision, and determines on the good or bad qualities of a man, accordingly as he belongs to this or the other sect; but, influenced by the belief, that there are many base and designing, and amiable and virtuous men on both sides, acts on the liberal principle, that

" Worth makes the man, and want of it the fellow."

Could such sentiments be generally diffused, of what importance would they not be to our country! We are aware of the opinion indulged by many wise politicians, that parties ensure a nation's safety, by acting as spies on, and correctors of, each other's conduct. Such an idea may answer, in a country where individuals' rights are merged in the exaltation of a few, and where the contest is for the loaves and fishes, and not in relation to difference in opinion: but in ours, whose government is derived from the people, so long as they continue virtuous and intelligent, and will duly appreciate their rights, no such auxiliary can be essential, either to her happiness or tranquillity. Already we have witnessed it the cause of innumerable evils; but for the hopes and expectations of a designing power, which, through our dissensions and domestic broils, believed she would be able seriously to affect us, we might have remained at peace, and preserved the lives of many of our valuable citizens. That there should be a difference of opinion among us, is certainly nothing strange: it is only in governments absolutely despotic, that the oppressed and trembling subjects imbibe the sentiments of the sovereign and his ministers, and appear to think with them, because they dare not assert their own opinions. Our constitution, on this subject, bars every check, and leaves our conduct, words, and actions free; yet, were our prudence consulted and regarded, it would long since have told us, that party rancour was carried much too far, both for our own and the honour of our country. We are far, however, from supposing that it is a circumstance, whence foreign powers can ever derive an advantage, by which

CHAP. materially to endanger our rights.   Although we may
  XI. differ, as to the best mode of administering the govern-
1815. ment, a circumstance which happens to all in propor-
       tion as liberty is enjoyed ; and although, as has been
       the case, party spirit may be carried beyond what rea-
       son or prudence may sanction, yet against the invaders
       of our rights, our union is strong, and all parties are
       the same.   Should the period ever arrive, when our
       nation shall be vitally assailed, it will be perceived
       that all advantages calculated to arise from our jarrings,
       are delusive ; that there will be but one party, all ral-
       lied in defence of a country, believed by them to be
       the freest and happiest, resolved to swim, or sink to-
       gether.

  179   The proclamations disseminated by Great Britain
       to the people of the United States, were mockery,—
       an insult to our understandings, and a reflection on
       her own : but the divisions she saw, prevailing among
       us, were no doubt the inducement. If ever there were
       a time, when she could have even partially effected the
       disorganization so industriously endeavoured to be
       fomented, and reached us through our differences, it
       was before she had, by an unusual, and hitherto un-
       practised system of warfare, destroyed all confidence,
       and excited our just indignation against her ; and be-
       fore, too, she had so effectually aided to subvert the
       liberty of France, and plunge her in a state of absolute
       vassalage, when, throughout, the professed and openly
       avowed object was to rescue from oppression, and
       make her " free indeed."   When such an example,
       with all its wretched and fatal consequences, is held

up to view, well may nations spurn every external in-   CHAP.
terference, however plausibly it may be offered.   XI.

The principles of our government are at variance   1815.
with war—those of her citizens no less so. If, amidst
the general confusion of the world, we have been forced into a struggle, it was for the preservation of our
rights, and to resist aggressions which had become too
numerous and grievous to be longer borne. With nations, as with individuals, a submission to insult but authorizes a repetition; and forbearance under injuries is
construed into imbecility to redress them. We boast not
of any thing acquired by our contest.   Conquest and
power were not the inducements to its commencement :
what was sought has been attained. We have secured
from other nations a respect, which our peaceful habits
had forfeited. We have brought more closely into view
our own strength, and our own resources; and shown
our enemies, that, however we may be solicitous for
peace, and opposed to war, there is a point, where even
patience becomes exhausted. But, above all, our contest has had the effect of drawing closer the cords of
our union,—quieting party opposition, and allaying discontent. In future, therefore, when we shall be told we
have gained nothing by the war, laying aside all other
considerations, we will point to our union, which it has
more strongly and indissolubly cemented, as of greater
importance than any thing that has happened, since the
all-glorious hour our Independence was declared.   180

THE END.

NOTES.

Note A—page 211.

Proclamation of colonel Nicholls to the southern and western inhabitants.

NATIVES of Louisiana! on you the first call is made, to assist in liberating from a faithless, imbecile government, your paternal soil : Spaniards, Frenchmen, Italians, and British, whether settled, or residing for a time in Louisiana, on you, also, I call, to aid me in this just cause : the American usurpation in this country must be abolished, and the lawful owners of the soil put in possession. I am at the head of a large body of Indians, well armed, disciplined, and commanded by British officers—a good train of artillery, with every requisite, seconded by the powerful aid of a numerous British and Spanish squadron of ships and vessels of war. Be not alarmed, inhabitants of the country, at our approach ; the same good faith and disinterestedness, which has distinguished the conduct of Britons in Europe, accompanies them here ; you will have no fear of litigious taxes imposed on you, for the purpose of carrying on an unnatural and unjust war ; your property, your laws, the peace and tranquillity of your country, will be guaranteed to you by men, who will suffer no infringement of theirs ; rest assured, that these brave red men only burn with an ardent desire of satisfaction, for the wrongs they have suffered from the Americans ; to join you, in liberating these southern provinces from their yoke, and drive them into those limits, formerly prescribed by my sovereign. The Indians have pledged themselves, in the most solemn manner, not to injure, in the slightest degree, the persons or properties of any but enemies. A flag over any door, whether Spanish, French, or British, will be a certain protection ; nor dare any Indian put his foot on the threshold thereof, under penalty of death from his own countrymen; not even an enemy will an Indian put to death, except resisting in arms; and as for injuring helpless women and children, the red men, by their good conduct, and treatment to them, will (if it be possible,) make the Americans blush for their more inhuman conduct, lately on the Escambia, and within a neutral territory.

Inhabitants of Kentucky, you have too long borne with grievous impositions—the whole brunt of the war has fallen on your brave sons; be imposed on no longer, but either range yourselves under the standard of your forefathers, or observe a strict neutrality. If you comply with either of these offers, whatever provisions you send down, will be paid for in dollars, and the safety of the persons bringing it, as well as the free navigation of the Mississippi, guaranteed to you.

Men of Kentucky, let me call to your view, (and I trust to your abhorrence) the conduct of those factions, which hurried you into this civil, unjust, and unnatural war, at a time when Great Britain was straining every nerve, in defence of her own, and the liberties of the world—when the bravest of her sons were fighting and bleeding in so sacred a cause—when she was spending millions of her treasure, in endeavouring to pull down one of the most formidable and dangerous tyrants, that ever disgraced the form of man—when groaning Europe was almost in her last gasp—when Britons alone showed an undaunted front—basely did those assassins endeavour to stab her from the rear; she has turned on them, renovated from the bloody, but successful struggle—Europe is happy and free, and she now hastens, justly, to avenge the unprovoked insult. Show them that you are not collectively unjust: leave that *contemptible few* to shift for themselves: let those slaves of the tyrant send an embassy to Elba, and implore his aid; but let every honest, upright American spurn them with united contempt. After the experience of twenty-one years, can you longer support those brawlers for liberty, who call it freedom, when themselves are free? Be no longer their dupes—accept of my offers—every thing I have promised in this paper, I guarantee to you, on the *sacred honour* of a *British officer.*

Given under my hand, at my *head quarters,*

Pensacola, this 29th day of August, 1814.

EDWARD NICHOLLS.

Note B—page 255.

Letter to commodore Daniel T. Patterson.

Pensacola, 4th December, 1814.

SIR,—I feel it a duty to apprize you of a very large force of the enemy off this port, and it is generally understood New Orleans is the object of attack. It amounts, at present, to about eighty vessels, and more than double that number are momentarily looked for, to form a junction; when an immediate commencement of their operations will take place. I am not able to learn, how, when, or where the attack will be made; but I understand that they have vessels of all descriptions, and a large body of troops. Admiral Cochrane commands; and his ship, the Tonnant, lies, at this moment, just outside the bar. They certainly appear to have swept the West Indies of troops, and probably no means will be left untried to obtain their object.—The admiral arrived only yesterday noon.   I am yours, &c.

N * * *

Note C—page 323.

Letter from Charles K. Blanchard to general Jackson.

New Orleans, March 20, 1814.

SIR,—I have the honour, agreeably to your request, to state to your excellency, in writing, the substance of a conversation that occurred between quarter master Peddie, of the British army, and myself, on the 11th instant, on board his Britannic Majesty's ship Herald. Quarter-master Peddie observed, that the commanding officers of the British forces were daily in the receipt of every information from the city of New Orleans, which they might require, in aid of their operations, for the completion of the objects of the expedition;—that they were perfectly acquainted with the situation of every part of our forces, the manner in which the same was situated, the number of our fortifications, their strength, position, &c. As to the battery on the left bank of the Mississippi, he described its situation, its distance from the main post, and promptly offered me a plan of the works. He furthermore stated, that the above information was received from seven or eight persons, in the city of New Orleans, from whom he could, at any hour, procure every information necessary to promote his majesty's interest.

Note D—page 349.

Address of major general Jackson, on the 8th of January, to the troops on the right bank of the river.

While, by the blessing of heaven, one of the most brilliant victories was obtained by the troops under my immediate command, no words can express the mortification I felt, at witnessing the scene exhibited on the opposite bank. I will spare your feelings and my own, nor enter into detail on the subject. To all who reflect, it must be a source of eternal regret, that a few moments' exertion of that courage you certainly possess, was alone wanting, to have rendered your success more complete than that of your fellow-citizens in this camp. To what cause was the abandonment of your lines owing? To fear? No! You are the countrymen, the friends, the brothers of those who have secured to themselves, by their courage, the gratitude of their country; who have been prodigal of their blood in its defence, and who are strangers to any other fear than disgrace—to disaffection to our glorious cause. No, my countrymen, your general does justice to the pure sentiments by which you are inspired. How then could brave men, firm in the cause in which they were enrolled, neglect their first duty, and abandon the post committed to their care? The want of discipline, the want of order, a total disregard to obedience, and a spirit of insubordination, not less destructive than cowardice itself, are the causes which led to this disaster, and they must be eradicated, or I must cease to command. I desire to be distinctly understood, that every breach of orders, all want of discipline, every inattention of duty, will be seriously and promptly punished; that the attentive officers, and good soldiers, may not be mentioned in the disgrace and danger, which the negligence of a few may produce. Soldiers! you want only the will, in order to emulate the glory of your fellow-citizens on this bank of the river—you have the same motives for action; the same interest, the same country to protect; and you have an additional interest, from past events, to wipe off reproach, and show that you will not be inferior, in the day of trial, to any of your countrymen.

But remember! without obedience, without order, without discipline, all your efforts are vain. The brave man, inattentive to his duty, is worth little more to his country than the coward who deserts her in the hour of danger. Private opinions, as to the competency of officers, must not be indulged, and still less expressed ; it is impossible that the measures of those who command should satisfy all who are bound to obey ; and one of the most dangerous faults in a soldier, is a disposition to criticise and blame the orders and characters of his superiors. Soldiers ! I know that many of you have done your duty ; and I trust, in future, I shall have no reason to make any exception. Officers ! I have the fullest confidence, that you will enforce obedience to your commands ; but, above all, that by subordination in your different grades, you will set an example to your men ; and that, hereafter, the army of the right will yield to none, in the essential qualities which characterize good soldiers ;—that they will earn their share of those honours and rewards, which their country will prepare for its deliverers.

ANDREW JACKSON,
Major General commanding.

———

Note E—page 370.

Address delivered to major general Andrew Jackson, by the reverend W. Dubourg, administrator apostolic of the diocese of Louisiana.

GENERAL,—While the state of Louisiana, in the joyful transports of her gratitude, hails you as her deliverer, and the assertor of her menaced liberties—while grateful America, so lately wrapped up in anxious suspense, on the fate of this important city, is re-echoing from shore to shore your splendid achievements, and preparing to inscribe your name on her immortal rolls, among those of her Washingtons—while history, poetry, and the monumental arts, will vie in consigning to the admiration of the latest posterity, a triumph perhaps unparalleled in their records—while thus raised, by universal acclamation, to the very pinnacle of fame, how easy had it been for you, general, to forget the Prime Mover of your wonderful successes, and to assume to yourself a praise, which must essentially return to that exalted source, whence every merit is derived. But, better acquainted with the

nature of true glory, and justly placing the summit of your ambition, in approving yourself the worthy instrument of Heaven's
merciful designs, the first impulse of your religious heart was to
acknowledge *the signal interposition of Providence*—your first
step, a solemn display of *your humble sense of His favours.*

Still agitated at the remembrance of those dreadful agonies,
from which we have been so miraculously rescued, it is our pride
to acknowledge, that the Almighty has truly had the principal
hand in our deliverance, and to follow you, general, in attributing
to his infinite goodness, the homage of our unfeigned gratitude.
Let the infatuated votary of a blind chance deride our credulous
simplicity; let the cold-hearted Atheist look for the explanation
of important events, to the mere concatenation of human causes :
to us, the whole universe is loud in proclaiming a Supreme Ruler,
who, as he holds the hearts of man in his hands, holds also the
thread of all contingent occurrences. " Whatever be His intermediate agents," says an illustrious prelate, " still on the secret
orders of His all-ruling providence, depend the rise and prosperity, as well as the decline and downfal of empires. From His
lofty throne, he moves every scene below, now curbing, now let-
ting loose, the passions of men ; now infusing His own wisdom
into the leaders of nations ; now confounding their boasted prudence, and spreading upon their councils a spirit of intoxication ;
and thus executing His uncontrollable judgments on the sons of
men, according to the dictates of His own unerring justice."

To *Him*, therefore, our most fervent thanks are due, for our
late unexpected rescue. It is *Him* we intend to praise, when
considering you, general, as the *man of his right hand*, whom he
has taken pains to fit out for the important commission of our defence. We extol that fecundity of genius, by which, under the
most discouraging distress, you created unforeseen resources,
raised, as it were, from the ground, hosts of intrepid warriors,
and provided every vulnerable point with ample means of defence.
To *Him* we trace that instinctive superiority of your mind, which
at once rallied around you universal confidence ; impressed one
irresistible movement to all the jarring elements of which this
political machine is composed ; aroused their slumbering spirits,
and diffused through every rank, the noble ardour which glowed
in your own bosom. To *Him*, in fine, we address our acknowledgments for that consummate prudence, which defeated all the

combinations of a sagacious enemy, entangled him in the very snares which he had spread for us, and succeeded in effecting his utter destruction, without exposing the lives of our citizens. Immortal thanks be to His Supreme Majesty, for sending us such an instrument of His bountiful designs! A gift of that value is the best token of the continuance of His protection—the most solid encouragement, to sue for new favours. The first which it emboldens us humbly to supplicate, as nearest our throbbing hearts, is that you may long enjoy the honour of your grateful country; of which you will permit us to present you a pledge, in this wreath of laurel, the prize of victory, the symbol of immortality. The next is a speedy and honourable termination of the bloody contest, in which we are engaged. No one has so efficaciously laboured as you, general, for the acceleration of that blissful period: may we soon reap that sweetest fruit of your splendid and uninterrupted victories.

*   *   *   *

General Jackson's reply.

REVEREND SIR,—I receive, with gratitude and pleasure, the symbolical crown, which piety has prepared. I receive it, in the name of the brave men who have so effectually seconded my exertions;—they well deserve the laurels which their country will bestow.

For myself, to have been instrumental in the deliverance of such a country, is the greatest blessing that heaven could confer. That it has been effected with so little loss—that so few tears should cloud the smiles of our triumph, and not a cypress leaf be interwoven in the wreath which you present, is a source of the most exquisite pleasure.

I thank you, reverend sir, most sincerely, for the prayers, which you offer up for my happiness. May those your patriotism dictates, for our beloved country, be first heard: and may mine, for your individual prosperity, as well as that of the congregation committed to your care, be favourably received—the prosperity, wealth, and happiness of this city, will then be commensurate with the courage and other qualities of its inhabitants.

Note F—page 388.

Answer submitted by major general Jackson, on a rule to show cause why an attachment for contempt should not issue against him.

This respondent has received a paper, purporting to be the copy of a rule of the district court of the United States for Louisiana, in a suit entitled " The United States *vs.* A. Jackson ; commanding him to show cause why an attachment should not issue against him, for divers alleged contempts of the said court." Before he makes any answer whatever to the said charges, he deems it necessary to protest, and he does hereby protest against, and reserve to himself all manner of benefit of exception to, the illegal, unconstitutional, and informal nature of the proceedings instituted against him : it appearing, by the said proceeding—

I. That witnesses have been summoned by process of subpœna, in a suit or prosecution of the United States against him, when in fact, there is no such suit or prosecution legally pending in said court.

II. That the said rule was obtained at the instance of the attorney of the United States, for the district of Louisiana, who had no right officially to ask for or obtain it ; the duties of the attorney being, by law, restricted to the prosecution of " all delinquents for *crimes* and *offences,* cognizable under the authority of the United States, and all civil actions in which they shall be concerned." As this proceeding is not pretended to be a civil action, to bring it within the purview of the duties of the attorney, it must be a prosecution for a crime or offence, cognizable under the authority of the United States. But the facts stated in the rule do not constitute any " crime or offence, cognizable under this authority." The courts of the United States have no common law jurisdiction of crimes or offences ; if, therefore, the facts stated in the rule are not made such by statute, they are not cognizable by the courts : but the statutes have been searched, and no such provision can be found ; therefore, the facts charged are not offences which are either cognizable by this court, or liable to be prosecuted by the attorney for the United States.

III. That if this be a prosecution for a *crime* or *offence* under the authority of the United States, the mode of proceeding is both unconstitutional and illegal : the 7th and 8th amendment to the constitution contain many provisions, directly contrary•to the mode of proceeding by attachment, for contempt; particularly the 7th amendment, that no person shall be deprived of life, liberty, or property, without due process of law ; and of the 8th, that, in all criminal prosecutions, the accused shall enjoy the right of a speedy trial, by an impartial jury ; and in the 32d section of the law *for punishing certain crimes against the United States*, is contained a conclusive implication, if not an express provision, that no offence can be prosecuted, except by *information* or *indictment ;* neither of which have been filed, in this instance. The respondent, therefore, concludes those heads of exceptions, by the dilemma, that, if the proceeding be a prosecution for a *crime* or *offence*, cognizable by the authority of the United States, it is both unconstitutional and illegal in its present form ; and if it be not such a prosecution, then has the attorney of the United States no right to institute it ; his ministry by law extending only to them.

IV. That this court has no right to issue an attachment for any contempt whatever ; or to punish the same, in any other cases than those prescribed by the 17th section of the judiciary act, which confines such authority to the punishment, by fine and imprisonment, for contempt in any *cause or hearing before the same*—whereas, by the rule, nor the affidavits, does it appear, that the alleged contempts were offered in any *cause* or *hearing* before the said District Court ; on the contrary, all the acts complained of as contempts, are stated to have been done in relation to an ex-parte application made to the judge of the said court, at his chambers, at a time when his court was in vacation, and not in a *cause or hearing before the court.*

V. That no attachment ought to issue, for neglecting or refusing a return to an habeas corpus, issued and returnable out of court : the statutes on that subject, both in England and in the United States, wherever they have been re-enacted, contain express penalties for this offence ; doubtless for the reason that such *neglect* or *refusal*, in relation to an act done, not in a *cause* or *hearing* pending in court, but in an ex-parte proceeding at a judge's chambers, could not be punished, by attachment, as a contempt.

VI. That no act in relation to the writ of habeas corpus, or the allowance of the same, in the case mentioned in the said rule, can be considered as a contempt; because the judge of this honourable court, by the 14th section of the judiciary act of the United States, is expressly inhibited from issuing any writ of habeas corpus, except in cases of prisoners " in custody, under, or by colour of the authority of the United States, or committed for trial before some court of the same; or who are necessary to be brought into court to testify; neither of which circumstances appear, either in the writ, the allowance of the same, or the affidavit on which it was founded. This court, then, having no jurisdiction of the case, according to a decision of the Supreme Court of the United States, this respondent had a right to consider the service as a trespass.

VII. That, by the said writ, no place was designated, at which the same should be returned.

VIII. That the writ was served on the respondent, long after the return thereof, by reason whereof he could not have complied with the tenour, had he been so disposed.

IX. The said writ of habeas corpus issued in an irregular manner, and the respondent was in no wise compelled by law to obey it; inasmuch as the name of the judge, allowing the same, was not *signed* on the writ with his proper hand writing: nor were the words, " according to the form of the statute," marked thereon—both which are positively required, by the statutes regulating the issuing of such process; and without which they need not be obeyed. Should it be objected, that the English statutes are not binding here, it is answered that the United States are without a a statutory provision on the subject; and that the introduction of the writ of habeas corpus generally, must introduce it, as it stood at the time of making the constitution.

X. That if the allowance on the back of the affidavit, contrary to the express words of the statute, be deemed sufficient, yet the respondent was not bound to pay any attention to the writ of habeas corpus, because the same was not issued in conformity with the allowance given on the fifth day of March; this was for a writ returnable on the next day, and afterwards altered, so as to bear date on the sixth of the same month, returnable on the succeeding morning, which would have been the 7th; whereas the writ actually issued, bore date the 6th, and was returnable the same day—

thus varying materially from the allowance. This circumstance is an excellent illustration of the wisdom of the statutory provision, which requires that the writ itself be signed by the judge.

Under all which protestations and exceptions;—without submitting to the jurisdiction of the said court, or acknowledging the regularity of the proceedings, but expressly denying the same— This respondent, in order to give a fair and true exposition of his conduct, on every occasion in which it may be drawn into question—

Saith—

That previously to, and soon after, his arrival in this section of the seventh military district, he received several letters and communications, putting him on his guard against a portion of the inhabitants of the state, the legislature, and foreign emissaries in the city. The population of the country was represented as divided, by political parties and national prejudices; a great portion of them attached to foreign powers, and disaffected to the government of their own country, and some, as totally unworthy of confidence. The militia was described as resisting the authority of their commander-in-chief, and encouraged in their disobedience, by the legislature of the state. That legislature characterised as politically rotten, and the whole state in such a situation as to make it necessary to look for defence, principally from the regular troops, and the militia from other states. Among those representations, the most important, from the official station of the writer, were those of the governor. On the 8th of August, 1814, he says—

"On a late occasion, I had the mortification to acknowledge my inability to meet a requisition from general Flournoy; the corps of this city having, for the most part, resisted my orders, being encouraged in their disobedience by the legislature of the state, then in session; one branch of which, the senate, having declared the *requisition* illegal and oppressive, and the house of representatives having rejected a proposition to approve the measure. How far I shall be supported in my late orders, remains yet to be proved. I have reason to calculate upon the patriotism of the interior and western counties. I know also that there are many faithful citizens in New Orleans; but there are others, in whose attachment to the United States *I ought not to confide.* Upon the whole, sir, I cannot disguise the fact, that if Louisiana should be attacked, we must principally depend for security upon the prompt movements of the regular force under your command, and the militia of the western states and territories. At this moment, we are in a very unprepared and defenceless condition : several important points of defence remain unoccupied, and in case of a sudden attack, this capital would, I fear, fall an easy sacrifice."

On the 12th of the same month, the respondent was told—

" On the native Americans, and a vast majority of the Creoles of the country, I place much confidence, nor do I doubt the fidelity of many Europeans, who have long resided in the country ; but there are others, much devoted to the interest of Spain, and whose partiality to the English, is not less observable, than their dislike to the American government."

In a letter of the 24th, the same ideas are repeated—

" Be assured, sir, that no exertions shall be wanting, on my part ; but I cannot disguise from you, that I have a very difficult people to manage : to this moment, no opposition to the requisition has manifested itself, but I am not seconded with that *ardent zeal*, which, in my opinion, the crisis demands. We look with great anxiety to your movements, and place our greatest reliance for safety, on the energy and patriotism of the western states. In Louisiana, there are many faithful citizens ; these last persuade themselves, that Spain will soon re-possess herself of Louisiana, and they seem to believe, that a combined Spanish and English force will soon appear on our coast. If Louisiana is invaded, I shall put myself at the head of such of my militia as will follow me to the field, and, *on receiving, shall obey your orders.* I need not assure you of my entire confidence in you, as a commander, and of the pleasure I shall experience, in supporting all your measures for the common defence ; but, sir, a cause of indescribable chagrin to me is, that I am not at the head of a willing, and united people : native Americans, native Louisianians, Frenchmen, and Spaniards, with some Englishmen, compose the mass of the population—among them, there exists much jealousy, and as great differences in political sentiments, as in their language and habits. But, nevertheless, sir, if we are supported by a respectable body of regular troops, or of western militia, I trust I shall be able to bring to your aid, a valiant and faithful corps of Louisiana militia : but if we are left to rely *principally on our own resources,*

I fear existing jealousies will lead to distrust, so general, that we shall be able to make but a feeble resistance."

On the 8th of September, the spirit of disaffection is said to be greater than was supposed—the country is said to be filled with *spies* and *traitors:* " Inclosed you have copies of my late general orders. They may, and I trust will be obeyed ; but to this moment, my fellow-citizens have not manifested all that union and zeal, the crisis demands, and their own safety requires. There is in this city a much *greater spirit of disaffection* than I had anticipated ; and among the faithful Louisianians, there is a *despondency* which palsies all my preparations ; they see no strong regular force, around which they could rally with confidence, and they seem to think themselves not within the reach of seasonable assistance, from the western states. I am assured, sir, you will make the most judicious disposition of the forces under your command ; but excuse me for suggesting, that the presence of the seventh regiment, at or near New Orleans, will have the most salutary effect. The garrison here at present is alarmingly weak, and is a cause of much regret : from the great mixture of persons, and characters, in this city, we have as much to apprehend from within, as from without. In arresting the intercourse between New Orleans and Pensacola, you have done right. Pensacola is, in fact, an enemy's post, and had our commercial intercourse with it continued, the supplies furnished to the enemy, would have so much exhausted our own stock of provisions, as to have occasioned the most serious inconvenience to ourselves. I was on the point of taking on myself, the prohibition of the trade with Pensacola : I had prepared a proclamation to that effect, and would have issued it the very day I heard of your interposition. Enemies to the country may blame you for your prompt and energetic measures ; but, in the person of every patriot, you will find a supporter. I am very confident of the very lax police of this city, and indeed throughout the state, with respect to the visits of strangers. I think, with you, that our country is filled with spies and traitors : I have written pressingly on the subject, to the city authorities and parish judges.—I hope some efficient regulations will speedily be adopted by the first, and more vigilance exerted for the future, by the latter."

On the 19th of September, speaking of the drafts of militia, he says—

" The only difficulty I have hitherto experienced in meeting
the requisition, has been in this city, and exclusively from some
European Frenchmen, who, after giving their adhesion to Louis
XVIII., have, through the medium of the French consul, claimed
exemption from the drafts, as French subjects. The question of
exemption, however, is now under discussion, before a special
court of inquiry, and I am not without hopes, that these ungrate-
ful men, may yet be brought to a discharge of their duties."

On the necessity of securing the country against the machinations of foreigners, he, on the 4th of November, informed the respondent—

" You have been informed of the contents of an intercepted letter, written by colonel Coliel, a Spanish officer, to captain Morales, of Pensacola.—This letter was submitted for the opinion
of the attorney general of the state, as to the measures to be pursued against the writer. The attorney general was of opinion,
that the courts could take no cognizance of the same; but that
the governor might order the writer to leave the state, and in
case of refusal, to send him off by force. I accordingly, sir, ordered colonel Coliel to take his departure, in forty-eight hours,
for Pensacola, and gave him the necessary passports. I hope
this measure may meet your approbation. It is a just retaliation
for the conduct lately observed by the governor of Pensacola,
and may induce the Spaniards residing among us, to be less
communicative, upon those subjects which relate to our military
movements."

With the impressions this correspondence was calculated to
produce, the respondent arrived in this city, where, in different
conversations, the same ideas were enforced, and he was advised,
not only by the governor of the state, but very many influential
persons, to proclaim martial law, as the only means of producing
union, overcoming disaffection, detecting treason, and calling
forth the energies of the country. This measure was discussed
and recommended to the respondent, as he well recollects, in the
presence of the judge of this honourable court, who not only made
no objection, but seemed, by his gestures and silence, to approve
of its being adopted. These opinions, respectable in themselves,
derived greater weight from that which the governor expressed,
of the legislature, then in session. He represented their fidelity

as very doubtful; ascribed design to their prolonged session; and appeared extremely desirous that they should adjourn.

The respondent had also been informed, that in the house of representatives, the idea, that a very considerable part of the state belonged to the Spanish government, and ought not to be represented, had been openly advocated, and favourably heard. The co-operation of the Spaniards with the English, was, at that time, a prevalent idea.—This information, therefore, appeared highly important. He determined to examine, with the utmost care, all the facts that had been communicated to him; and not to act upon the advice he had received, until the clearest demonstration should have determined its propriety. He was then almost an entire stranger, in the place he was sent to defend, and unacquainted with the language of a majority of its inhabitants. While these circumstances were unfavourable to his obtaining information, on the one hand, they precluded, on the other, a suspicion that his measures were dictated by personal friendship, private animosity, or party views. Uninfluenced by such motives, he began his observations. He sought for information, and, to obtain it, communicated with men of every description. He believed that even then he discovered those high qualities, which have since distinguished those brave defenders of their country:— that the variety of language, the difference of habit, and even the national prejudices, which seemed to divide the inhabitants, might be made, if properly directed, the source of the most honourable emulation. Delicate attentions were necessary to foster this disposition; and the highest energy, to restrain the effects, that such an assemblage was calculated to produce; he determined to avail himself of both, and with this view, called to his aid, the impulse of national feeling, the higher motives of patriotic sentiment, and the noble enthusiasm of valour. They operated in a manner which history will record; all who could be influenced by those feelings, rallied, without delay, round the standard of their country. Their efforts, however, would have been unavailing, if the disaffected had been permitted to counteract them by their treason, the timid to paralyze them by their example, and both to stand aloof in the hour of danger, and enjoy the fruit of victory, without participating in the danger of defeat.

A disciplined, and powerful army was on our coast, commanded by officers of tried valour, and consummate skill; their fleet had already destroyed the feeble defence, on which, alone, we could rely, to prevent their landing on our shores. Their point of attack was uncertain—a hundred inlets were to be guarded, by a force not sufficient in number for one; we had no lines of defence; treason lurked among us, and only waited the moment of expected defeat, to show itself openly. Our men were few, and of those few, not all were armed; our prospect of aid and supply was distant and uncertain; our utter ruin, if we failed, at hand, and inevitable: every thing depended on the prompt and energetic use of the means we possessed—on calling the whole force of the community into action; it was a contest for the very existence of the state, and every nerve was to be strained in its defence. The physical force of every individual, his moral faculties, his property, and the energy of his example, were to be called into action, and instant action. No delay,—no hesitation,—no inquiry about rights, or *all* was lost; and every thing dear to man, his property, life, the honour of his family, his country, its constitution and laws, were swept away by the avowed principles, the open practice of the enemy with whom we had to contend. Fortifications were to be erected, supplies procured, arms sought for, requisitions made, the emissaries of the enemy watched, lurking treason overawed, insubordination punished, and the contagion of cowardly example to be stopped.

In this crisis, and under a firm persuasion that none of those objects could be effected by the exercise of the ordinary powers confided to him—under a solemn conviction that the country committed to his care could be saved by that measure only from utter ruin—under a religious belief, that he was performing the most important and sacred duty, the respondent proclaimed martial law. He intended, by that measure, to supersede such civil powers, as in their operation interfered with those he was obliged to exercise. He thought, in such a moment, constitutional forms must be suspended, for the permanent preservation of constitutional rights, and that there could be no question, whether it were best to depart, for a moment, from the enjoyment of our dearest privileges, or have them *wrested* from us forever. He knew, that if the civil magistrate were permitted to exercise his usual functions, none of the measures necessary to avert the awful fate that threatened us, could be expected. Personal liberty cannot exist at a time when every man is required to become a soldier. Private property cannot be secured, when its use is indispensable to the public safety. Unlimited liberty of speech is incompatible with the discipline of a camp; and that of the press more dangerous still, when made the vehicle of conveying intelligence to the enemy, or exciting mutiny among the troops. To have suffered the uncontrolled enjoyment of any of those rights, during the time of the late invasion, would have been to abandon the defence of the country: the civil magistrate is the guardian of those rights; and the proclamation of martial law was therefore intended to supersede the exercise of his authority, so far as it interfered with the necessary restriction of those rights; *but no further*.

The respondent states these principles explicitly, because they are the basis of his defence, and because a mistaken notion has been circulated, that the declaration of martial law only subjected the militia in service to its operation. This would, indeed, have been a very useless ceremony, as such persons were already subject to it, without the addition of any other act. Besides, if the proclamation of martial law were a measure of necessity,—a measure, without the exercise of which the country must unquestionably have been conquered, then does it form a complete justification for the act. If it do not, in what manner will the proceeding by attachment for contempt be justified? It is undoubtedly and strictly a criminal prosecution; and the constitution declares, that in all criminal prosecutions, the accused shall have the benefit of a trial by jury; yet a prosecution is even now going on in this court, where no such benefit is allowed. Why? From the alleged necessity of the case, because courts could not, it is said, subsist without a power to punish promptly by their own act, and without the intervention of a jury. Necessity then may, in some cases, justify a departure from the constitution: and if, in the doubtful case of avoiding confusion in a court, shall it be denied in the serious one of preserving a country from conquest and ruin? The respondent begs leave to explain, that in using this argument, he does not mean to admit the existence of necessity in the case of attachment; but to show that the principle of a justification from necessity is admitted, even in that weaker case.

3 G

If the legislature of the United States have given to courts the power to punish contempts, it is no answer to this defence, for two reasons—first, because the words of the law do not necessarily exclude the intervention of a jury ; and secondly, if they do, the law itself is contrary to the words of the constitution, and can only be supported on the plea of necessity ; to which head it is referred by the English writers on the subject.

The only responsibility which has been incurred in the present case, is that which arises from necessity. This, the respondent agrees, must not be doubtful ; it must be apparent, from the circumstances of the case, or it forms no justification. He submits all his acts, therefore, to be tested by this rule.

To the forcible reasons which he has detailed, as impelling him to this measure, he ought to add, that he has since, by the confession of the enemy himself, received a confirmation of the opinions, which he had then good reason to believe ; that there were men among us so depraved, as to give daily and exact information of our movements, and our forces ; that the number of those persons was considerable, and their activity unceasing. The names of those wretches will probably be discovered ; and the respondent persuades himself, that this tribunal will employ itself, with greater satisfaction, in inflicting the punishment due to their crimes, than it now does in investigating the measures that were taken to counteract them.

If example can justify, or the practice of others serve as a proof of necessity, the respondent has ample materials for his defence ; not from analogous construction, but from the conduct of all the different departments of the state government, in the very case now under discussion.

The legislature of the state, having no constitutional power to regulate or restrain commerce, on the —— day of December last, passed an act, laying an embargo—the executive sanctioned it, and, from a conviction of its necessity, it was acquiesced in. The same legislature shut up the courts of justice, for four months, to all civil suitors—the same executive sanctioned that law, and the judiciary not only acquiesced, but solemnly approved it.

The governor, as appears by one of the letters quoted, undertook to inflict the punishment of exile upon an inhabitant, without any form of law, merely because he thought that an individual's presence might be dangerous to the public safety.

The judge of this very court, duly impressed with the emergency of the moment, and the necessity of employing every means of defence, consented to the discharge of men, committed and indicted for capital crimes, without bail, and without recognizance; and, probably under an impression that the exercise of his functions would be useless, absented himself from the place where his court was to he holden, and postponed its session, during a regular term.

Thus the conduct of the legislative, executive, and judiciary branches of the government of this state, have borne the fullest testimony of the existence of the necessity, on which the respondent relies.

The unqualified approbation of the legislature of the United States, and such of the individual states as were in session, ought also to be admitted, as no slight means of defence; inasmuch as all these respectable bodies were fully apprized of his proclamation of martial law, and some of them seem to refer to it, by thanking him for the energy of his measures.

The respondent, therefore, believes he has established the necessity of proclaiming martial law. He has shown the effects of that declaration; and it only remains to prove, in answer to the rule, that the power assumed from necessity, was not abused in its exercise, nor improperly protracted in its duration.

All the acts mentioned in the rule, took place after the enemy had retired from the position they had at first assumed—after they had met with a signal defeat, and after an unofficial account had been received of the signature of a treaty of peace. Each of these circumstances might be, to one who did not see the whole ground, a sufficient reason for supposing that further acts of energy and vigour were unnecessary. On the mind of the respondent, they had a different effect. The enemy had retired from their position, it is true; but they were still on the coast, and within a few hours' sail of the city. They had been defeated, and with loss; but that loss was to be repaired by expected reinforcements. Their numbers still much more than quadrupled all the regular forces which the respondent could command; and the term of service of his most efficient militia force was about to expire. Defeat, to a powerful and active enemy, was more likely to operate as an incentive to renewed and increased exertion, than to inspire them with despondency, or to paralyze their efforts. A treaty, it is true, had been probably signed; yet it might not be ratified. Its contents had not transpired, and no reasonable conjecture could be formed, that it would be acceptable. The influence which the account of its signature had on the army, was deleterious in the extreme, and showed a necessity for increased energy, instead of a relaxation of discipline. Men, who had shown themselves zealous, in the preceding part of the campaign, now became lukewarm in the service. Those whom no danger could appal, and no labour discourage, complained of the hardships of the camp. When the enemy were no longer immediately before them, they thought themselves oppressed, by being detained in service. Wicked and weak men, who, from their situation in life, ought to have furnished a better example, secretly encouraged this spirit of insubordination. They affected to pity the hardships of those who were kept in the field; they fomented discontent, by insinuating that the merits of those to whom they addressed themselves, had not been sufficiently noticed or applauded; and to so high a degree had the disorder at length risen, that at one period, only fifteen men and one officer, out of a whole regiment, stationed to guard the very avenue through which the enemy had penetrated into the country, were found at their post. At another point, equally important, a whole corps, on which the greatest reliance had been placed, operated upon by the acts of a foreign agent, suddenly deserted their post.

If, trusting to an uncertain peace, the respondent had revoked his proclamation, or ceased to act under it, the fatal security by which we were lulled, might have destroyed all discipline, have dissolved all his force, and left him without any means of defending the country against an enemy, instructed, by the traitors within our own bosom, of the time and place, at which he might safely make his attack. In such an event, his life might have been offered up; yet it would have been but a feeble expiation, for the disgrace and misery, into which, by his criminal negligence, he had permitted the country to be plunged.

He thought peace a probable, but by no means a certain event. If it had really taken place, a few days must bring the official advice of it; and he believed it better to submit, during those few days, to the salutary restraints imposed, than to put every thing dear to ourselves and country at risk upon an uncertain contingency. Admit the chances to have been a hundred or a thousand to one in favour of the ratification, and against any renewed attempts of the enemy ; what should we say or think of the prudence of the man, who would stake his life, his fortune, his country, and his honour, even with such odds in his favour, against a few days' anticipated enjoyment of the blessings of peace ? The respondent could not bring himself to play so deep a hazard ; uninfluenced by the clamours of the ignorant and the designing, he continued the exercise of that law, which necessity had compelled him to proclaim ; and he still thinks himself justified, by the situation of affairs, for the course which he adopted and pursued. Has he exercised this power wantonly or improperly ? If so, he is liable ; not, as he believes, to this honourable court for contempt, but to his government for an abuse of power, and to those individuals whom he has injured, in damages proportioned to that injury.

About the period last described, the consul of France, who appears, by governor Claiborne's letter, to have embarrassed the first drafts, by his claims in favour of pretended subjects of his king, renewed his interference ; his certificates were given to men in the ranks of the army ; to some who had never applied, and to others who wished to use them as the means of obtaining an inglorious exemption from danger and fatigue. The immunity derived from these certificates not only thinned the ranks, by the withdrawal of those to whom they were given, but produced the desertion of others, who thought themselves equally entitled to the privilege ; and to this cause must be traced the abandonment of the important post of Chef Menteur, and the temporary refusal of a relief ordered to occupy it.

Under these circumstances, to remove the force of an example which had already occasioned such dangerous consequences, and to punish those who were so unwilling to defend what they were so ready to enjoy, the respondent issued a general order, directing those French subjects, who had availed themselves of the consul's certificates, to remove out of the lines of defence, and far enough to avoid any temptation of intercourse with our enemy, whom they were so scrupulous of opposing. This measure was resorted to, as the mildest mode of proceeding against a dangerous and increasing evil ; and the respondent had the less scruple of his power, in this instance, as it was not quite so strong as that which governor Claiborne had exercised, before the invasion, by the advice of his attorney-general, in the case of colonel Coliel.

It created, however, some sensation ;—discontents were again fomented, from the source that had first produced them. Aliens and strangers became the most violent advocates of constitutional rights, and native Americans were taught the value of their privileges, by those who formally disavowed any title to their enjoyment. The order was particularly opposed, in an anonymous publication. In this, .the author deliberately and wickedly misrepresented the order, as subjecting to removal all Frenchmen whatever, even those who had gloriously fought in defence of the country; and, after many dangerous and unwarrantable declarations, he closes, by calling upon all Frenchmen to flock to the standard of their consul—thus advising and producing an act of mutiny and insubordination, and publishing the evidence of our weakness and discord to the enemy, who were still in our vicinity, anxious, no doubt, before the cessation of hostilities, to wipe away the late stain upon their arms. To have silently looked on such an offence, without making any attempt to punish it, would have been a formal surrender of all discipline, all order, all personal dignity and public safety. This could not be done; and the respondent immediately ordered the arrest of the offender. A writ of habeas corpus was directed to issue for his enlargement. The very case which had been foreseen, the very contingency on which martial law was intended to operate, had now occurred. The civil magistrate seemed to think it his duty to enforce the enjoyment of civil rights, although the consequences which have been described, would probably have resulted. An unbending sense of what he seemed to think his station required, induced him to order the liberation of the prisoner. This, under the respondent's sense of duty, produced a conflict which it was his wish to avoid.

No other course remained, than to enforce the principles which he had laid down as his guide, and to suspend the exercise of this judicial power, wherever it interfered with the necessary means of defence. The only way effectually to do this, was to place the judge in a situation, in which his interference could not counteract the measures of defence, or give countenance to the mutinous disposition that had shown itself in so alarming a degree. Merely to have disregarded the writ, would but have increased the evil, and to have obeyed it, was wholly repugnant to the respondent's ideas of the public safety, and to his own sense of duty. The judge was therefore confined, and removed beyond the lines of defence.

As to the paper mentioned in the rule, which the respondent is charged with taking and detaining, he answers, that when the writ was produced by the clerk of this honourable court, the date of its issuance appeared to have been altered from the 5th to the 6th. He was questioned respecting the apparent alteration, and acknowledged it had been done by judge Hall, and not in the presence of the party who made the affidavit. This material alteration, in a paper that concerned him, gave the respondent, as he thought, a right to detain it, for further investigation, which he accordingly did; but gave a certified copy, and an acknowledgment that the original was in his possession.

The respondent avows, that he considered this alteration in the date of the affidavit, as it was then explained to him by the clerk, to be such evidence of a personal, not judicial, interference, and activity, in behalf of a man charged with the most serious offence, as justified the idea then formed, that the judge approved his conduct, and supported his attempts to excite disaffection among the troops.

This was the conduct of the respondent, and these the motives which prompted it. They have been fairly and openly exposed to this tribunal, and to the world, and would not have been accompanied by any exception or waver of jurisdiction, if it had been deemed expedient to give him that species of trial, to which he thinks himself entitled, by the constitution of his country. The powers which the exigency of the times forced him to assume, have been exercised exclusively for the public good; and, by the blessing of God, they have been attended with unparalleled success. They have saved the country; and whatever may be the opinion of that country, or the decrees of its courts, in relation to the means he has used, he can never regret that he employed them.

ANDREW JACKSON,

Major general commanding 7th military district.

Note G—page 391.

*Address to the troops at New Orleans, after the annunciation of
peace.*

The major general is at length enabled to perform the pleasing
task of restoring to Tennessee, Kentucky, Louisiana, and the
territory of the Mississippi, the brave troops who have acted
such a distinguished part, in the war which has just terminated.
In restoring these brave men to their homes, much exertion is
expected of, and great responsibility imposed on, the commanding
officers of the different corps. It is required of major generals
Carroll and Thomas, and brigadier general Coffee, to march their
commands, without unnecessary delay, to their respective states.
The troops from the Mississippi territory and state of Louisiana,
both militia and volunteers, will be immediately mustered out of
service, paid, and discharged.

The major general has the satisfaction of announcing the approbation of the president of the United States to the conduct of
the troops under his command, expressed, in flattering terms,
through the honourable the secretary at war.

In parting with those brave men, whose destinies have been so
long united with his own, and in whose labours and glories it is
his happiness and his boast to have participated, the commanding
general can neither suppress his feelings, nor give utterance to
them as he ought. In what terms can he bestow suitable praise
on merit so extraordinary, so unparalleled? Let him, in one
burst of joy, gratitude, and exultation, exclaim—" These are the
saviours of their country—these the patriot soldiers, who tri-
umphed over the invincibles of Wellington, and conquered the
conquerors of Europe!" With what patience did you submit to
privations—with what fortitude did you endure fatigue—what
valour did you display in the day of battle! You have secured to
America a proud name among the nations of the earth—a glory
which will never perish.

Possessing those dispositions, which equally adorn the citizen
and the soldier, the expectations of your country will be met in
peace, as her wishes have been gratified in war. Go, then, my
brave companions, to your homes; to those tender connexions,
and blissful scenes, which render life so dear—full of honour,
and crowned with laurels which will never fade. When participating, in the bosoms of your families, the enjoyment of peaceful life, with what happiness will you not look back to the toils

you have borne—to the dangers you have encountered? How will all your past exposures be converted into sources of inexpressible delight? Who, that never experienced your sufferings, will be able to appreciate your joys? The man who slumbered ingloriously at home, during your painful marches, your nights of watchfulness, and your days of toil, will envy you the happiness which these recollections will afford—still more will he envy the gratitude of that country, which you have so eminently contributed to save.

Continue, fellow soldiers, on your passage to your several destinations, to preserve that subordination, that dignified and manly deportment, which have so ennobled your character.

While the commanding general is thus giving indulgence to his feelings, towards those brave companions, who accompanied him through difficulties and danger, he cannot permit the names of Blount, and Shelby, and Holmes, to pass unnoticed. With what generous ardour and patriotism have these distinguished governors contributed all their exertions, to provide the means of victory! The recollection of their exertions, and of the success which has resulted, will be to them a reward more grateful, than any which the pomp of title, or the splendour of wealth, can bestow.

What happiness it is to the commanding general, that, while danger was before him, he was, on no occasion, compelled to use, towards his companions in arms, either severity or rebuke. If, after the enemy had retired, improper passions began their empire in a few unworthy bosoms, and rendered a resort to energetic measures necessary for their suppression, he has not confounded the innocent with the guilty—the seduced with the seducers. Towards you, fellow-soldiers, the most cheering recollections exist, blended, alas! with regret, that disease and war should have ravished from us so many worthy companions. But the memory of the cause in which they perished, and of the virtues which animated them while living, must occupy the place where sorrow would claim to dwell.

Farewell, fellow-soldiers. The expression of your general's thanks is feeble; but the gratitude of a country of freemen is yours—yours the applause of an admiring world.

ANDREW JACKSON,
Major General commanding.

3 H

EDITIONS OF THE JOHN REID
AND JOHN HENRY EATON
LIFE OF ANDREW JACKSON

1. Reid, John and Eaton, John Henry, *The Life of Andrew Jackson, Major General, In the Service of the United States, Comprising, A History of The War In the South, From the Commencement of the Creek Campaign, to the Termination of Hostilities Before, New Orleans.* (Philadelphia, M. Carey and Son, 1817). This is the rare first edition which is by far the best history of all.

2. Eaton, John Henry, *The Life of Andrew Jackson, Major General In the Service of the United States, Comprising, A History of the War In the South, From the Commencement of the Creek Campaign, to the Termination of Hostilities Before, New Orleans.* (Philadelphia, S. F. Bradford, 1824). This printing looks very much like the first edition but has been modified to a considerable degree.

3. ————, *The Life of Andrew Jackson, Major General in the Service of the United States, Comprising a History of the War In the South, From the Commencement of the Creek Campaign to the Termination of Hostilities before New Orleans.* (Cincinnati, Hatch and Nichols, 1827). This printing is an unchanged reprint of the 1824 edition, and might be a pirated edition.

4. ————, *The Life of Major General Andrew Jackson: Comprising A History of the War In the South; From the Commencement of the Creek Campaign to the Termination of Hostilities Before New Orleans.* Addenda: Containing *A Brief History of the Seminole War, And Cession and Govern-*

ment of Florida. (Philadelphia: McCarty and Davis, 1828). This printing was reprinted in smaller print on cheap paper and a considerable amount of material was removed in an apparent effort to shorten the work. This cut is compensated for by the addition of a chapter on the Seminole War.

5. ———, *Memoirs of Andrew Jackson, Late Major-General and Commander In Chief of the Southern Division of the Army of the United States.* Compiled by a citizen of Massachusetts. (Boston, Charles Ewer, 1828). This printing was unsigned by Eaton and has been reorganized. This work was probably an effort by Eaton to make the voting public think another author was writing a favorable account of Jackson and was very likely not a pirated edition.

6. ———, *Some Account of General Jackson, Drawn Up From the Hon. Mr. Eaton's Very Circumstantial Narrative, And Other Well-Established Information Respecting Him.* By a gentleman of the Baltimore Bar. (Baltimore, H. Vicary, Matchett, 1828). This work printed in boldface type on cheap paper is a summary of the regular editions.

7. ———, *Memoirs of Andrew Jackson, Late Major General and Commander In Chief of the Southern Division of the Army of the United States.* by a citizen of Massachusetts. (Philadelphia, 1833). This is a reprint of the Charles Ewer 1828 edition.

8. ———, *Memoirs of Andrew Jackson, Late Major General and Commander In Chief of the Southern Division of the Army of the United States.* by a citizen of Massachusetts. (Philadelphia, 1834). This is a reprint of the Charles Ewer 1828 edition.

9. ———, *Memoirs of Andrew Jackson, Late Major General and Commander In Chief of the Southern Division of the Army of the United States.* by a citizen of Massachusetts. (Philadelphia, 1839). This is a reprint of the Charles Ewer 1828 edition.

10. ———, *Life of Andrew Jackson Embracing Anecdotes Illustrative of His Character. The Young American's Library.* (Philadelphia, Lindsay and Blakeston, 1845). This is

an abbreviated edition written for young people and was
based on the original Life of Andrew Jackson. It has some
additional material including a brief account of Jackson's
life as President.

11. ———, *Memoir of General Andrew Jackson, Containing A Full Account of His Indian Campaign and Defense of New Orleans . . . together with His Veto of the Bank bill; Proclamation to the nullifiers; Farewell Address to which is added the Eulogy of Honorable George Bancroft* (Auburn, N. Y., J. C. Darby and Company, 1845) . This work is a modification of the 1828 Charles Ewer edition with some material added. It is not at all certain whether or not Eaton wrote the additions to this work.

12. ———, *Memoirs of Andrew Jackson, Late Major General and Commander In Chief of the Southern Division of the Army of the United States.* Compiled by a citizen of Massachuetts. (Philadelphia, 1847) . This is a reprint of the 1828 Charles Ewer edition.

13. ———, *Memoirs of Andrew Jackson, Late Major-General and Commander In Chief of the Southern Division of the Army of the United States.* Compiled by a citizen of Massachusetts. (Philadelphia, Lippincott, Grambo, 1850). This is another reprint of the 1828 Charles Ewer edition.

14. ———, *Memoirs of Andrew Jackson, Late Major-General and Commander In Chief of the Southern Division of the Army of the United States.* Compiled by a citizen of Massachusetts. (Philadelphia, Lippincott, Grambo, 1852) . This is another reprint of the 1828 Charles Ewer edition.

15. ———, *Memoirs of Andrew Jackson, Late Major-General and Commander-in-Chief of the Southern Division of the U. S.* Compiled by a citizen of Massachusetts. (Philadelphia, Lippincott, Grambo and Co., 1853). This is a reprint of the 1828 Charles Ewer edition.

16. ———, *Memoirs of Andrew Jackson, Late Major-General and Commander In Chief of the Southern Division of the United States.* Compiled by a citizen of Massachusetts.

(Philadelphai, Lippincott, 1855). This is a reprint of the 1828 Charles Ewer edition.

17. ———, *The Complete Memoirs of Andrew Jackson Seventh President of the United States Containing a Full Account of His Military Life and Achievements, With His Career as President.* (New York, John W. Lovell, Company [date ?]). This book is identical to the Charles Ewer 1828 edition and even seems to have used the same plates, down to page 334. Pages 334 to 362 added a brief account of the remainder of Jackson's life. There is no author listed but it is unlikely that the additional material was written by Eaton.

18. ———, *The Complete Memoirs of Andrew Jackson, Seventh President of the United States. Containing a Full Account of His Military Life and Achievements, With His Career As President.* (Philadelphia, Claxton, Remsen, and Haffelfinger, 1878). The text and plates of this book are identical to the Charles Ewer 1828 edition down to page 334. There is some additional material added to the end of this book but it it unlikely that this part was written by Eaton.

19. ———, *The Complete Memoirs of Andrew Jackson, Seventh President of the United States. Containing A Full Account of His Military Life and Achievements, With His Career As President.* (New York, Hurst and Company, 1885). This edition used the same plates as the 1828 Charles Ewer edition through page 334. A new chapter, containing a brief account of Jackson as President, was added following page 334. It is unlikely that the new material was written by John H. Eaton.

20. ———, *Leben des Generals-Majors Andreas Jackson, Enthaltend eine Geschichte des Kriegs im Suden, Vom Anfange des Feldzugs Gegen die Creeks, bis zur Beendigung der Feindseligkeiten von Neu-Orleans. Zusatze: Enthaltend eine Kurze Geschiehte des Krieges Gegen die Seminolen und Uebergabe und Regierung von Florida. Von Johann Heinrich Eaton . . . Uebers, Von G. F. Jager, Reading, Pennsylvania 1831.* This is a German translation of either Eaton's 1824 or 1828 edition.

21. ———, *Leben und Feldzuge des Generals Andreas Jackson, Geschichte seines Krieges Gegen die Creeks, Seines Feldzuges im Suden und Seiner Demuthigung der Seminolen. Von Johann Heinrich Eaton* . . . (Philadelphia, Kiderlen und Stollmeyer, 1837). This is another German translation of the Eaton 1824 or 1828 edition.

EDITOR'S NOTES

1. The first sentence has been eliminated from later editions.

2. The author made few changes in the 1824 edition but cut almost all of the remaining Preface, from this point, in the 1828 version.

3. This paragraph saved in 1828 edition.

4. This paragraph retained in 1828 edition. The Preface in the 1824 edition is not greatly different from the 1817 printing, but in 1828 Eaton removed all reference to Reid.

CHAPTER I

5. Jackson's date of birth was removed from later editions.

6. A sentence was added in 1828 suggesting that his mother had stimulated Jackson's love of liberty. This of course shows Eaton's interest in adding a good political credit such as Jackson's love of liberty.

7. Since Reid undoubtedly obtained this information concerning Jackson's early life from the General himself, it is probably as accurate as any available.

8. A paragraph was added in the 1824 edition which apparently was an attempt by Eaton to give a more understandable account of Jackson's capture. This does not seem to change the meaning of the work. See 1824 edition, p. 12. See Appendix A.

9. In the 1824 and later editions a long paragraph was added here eulogizing Jackson. See 1824 edition, pp. 16–17. See Appendix B.

10. A substantial addition was made here which praised Jackson's work in the U. S. Senate and in a note at the bottom of the page listed Jackson among those who voted for the repeal of the alien law and the stamp act. Eaton obviously added this for political reasons. See 1824 edition, p. 18. See Appendix C.

11. This was reworded in the 1824 edition to make Jackson seem unselfish and more of a common man. The change is as follows: "Unambitious to those distinctions and honors which young men are usually proud to possess; finding too that his circumstances and condition in life, were not such as to permit his time and attention to be devoted to public matters, he determined to yield them into others' hands, and to devote himself to agricultural pursuits; and accordingly settled himself on an excellent farm, ten miles from Nashville, on the Cumberland river; where for several years he enjoyed all the comforts of domestic and social intercourse." See pp. 19–20 of 1824 edition.

12. James Wilkinson's rank was changed to Brigadier General in 1824 edition. See p. 22.

13. In the 1824 edition Eaton removed all names from this condemnation. He probably thought that these men and their friends might support Jackson for President if they were not condemned. See p. 24 of 1824 edition.

14. In the 1824 edition, Eaton added the following to the end of this paragraph: ". . . and that he would arrest and confine the first officer who dared to enter his encampment with any such object in view." See p. 25 of 1824 edition.

15. Eaton placed the blame directly on Wilkinson in the 1824 edition as follows, "The next morning, however, when everything was about to be packed up, acting doubtless from orders, and intending to produce embarrassment, the Quartermaster entered . . ." See 1824 edition, p. 26.

CHAPTER II

16. Mention of General Cocke was removed from 1828 edition. See 1828 edition, p. 18.

17. During his campaigns against the Creek Indians, Jackson never seemed to have realized that there were any hostile Indians living east of the Chattahoochee River. He never conducted any military operations in that area and seems to have thought the Indians found on the lower Chattahoochee, Flint, and Apalachicola Rivers, were Seminoles. These were actually the lower Creeks and many of them were still hostile in 1815 at the end of the War of 1812. The only campaign against these Creeks and their Seminole friends was led by the Creek agent, Benjamin Hawkins, who

led a force of loyal Indians against those hostiles in late 1814. See Frank L. Owsley, Jr., "British and Indian Activities in Spanish West Florida During the War of 1812," *Florida Historical Quarterly,* (October, 1967), XLVI, 111–123; Charles Cameron to Earl Bathurst, October 28, 1813, Colonial Office 23/60, Public Record Office, London, England.

18. In the 1828 edition Eaton eliminated "Anglo" from "Anglo-Americans." He apparently realized that all Americans were not "Anglo-Americans" and did not wish to offend potential voters. See p. 19 of 1828 edition.

19. Tecumseh visited the Creeks in 1811, not 1812, but some of Tecumseh's Prophets remained with the Creeks until their final defeat. See Thomas P. Abernethy, *The South in the New Nation 1789–1819* (Baton Rouge, 1961), 367; Hawkins to the Secretary of War, January 7, 1812, Letters to the Secretary of War, RG 107, National Archives, Washington, D.C.

20. In 1824 Eaton changed this from Alabamians to Alabama Indians. He doubtless did not wish to offend the white voters of Alabama. See p. 30 of 1824 edition.

21. Although local British officials may have aided and advised Tecumseh, the British Government, in London, knew nothing of his activities with the Southern Indians until the end of 1813, and had definitely not sent him to arouse the Creeks. See Earl Bathurst to Charles Cameron, January 21, 1814, Colonial Office 24/17, Public Record Office, London, England.

22. For some reason Eaton removed "on Duck River" from the 1824 and later editions. He seems to have removed a number of local place names in later editions and one explanation may be that he believed that since his work now had a national audience, most people would not know the location of these places. See p. 31 in 1824 edition.

23. For well over a year after the visit of Tecumseh the Creek Indians engaged in a civil war. During this conflict many Indians who followed the Peace Party were killed by the hostiles. See George Stiggins manuscript 43, mss. I–V, Lyman Draper Collection, Wisconsin State Historical Society, Madison, Wisconsin, pp. 47–52.

24. This note was eliminated from 1828 edition.

25. Eaton added a comment in 1824 edition that this group of Indians was commanded by Weatherford.

26. It is to Reid's credit as an accurate historian that he correctly claimed that the Spanish furnished the Creeks with only ammunition. Many contemporary accounts wrongly claim that the Spanish supplied the Indians with arms as well. See Elizabeth Howard West, ed., "A Prelude to the Creek War of 1813–1814," *The Florida Historical Quarterly* (1940), XVIII, 249–266.

27. Once again Reid's work shows unusual accuracy, since most accounts greatly overestimate the number of persons killed in this battle. This place usually is spelled Mims rather than Mimms. See J. P. Kennedy to F. L. Claiborne, September 26, 1813, Thomas H. Palmer, ed., *The Historical Register of the United States* (Washington, 1812–1816), IV, Part 2, 332; Claiborne to the editors of the *Republican, Mississippi Republican,* March 25, 1814.

28. In 1824 all explanation of why Jackson had a fractured arm is removed. There is no mention of his fight with the Benton brothers. See p. 34, 1824 edition.

29. This paragraph was rewritten in 1824 and made less bloody. See pp. 35–36 in 1824 edition.

30. In the 1828 edition, Eaton mentioned Jackson's health but removed the reference to his arm. Presumably this is further effort to ignore the Benton fight. See 1828 edition, p. 25.

31. This entire paragraph was removed from the 1828 edition down to "with pressing importunity, he had addressed himself to the contractors. . ." It is apparent that Eaton wanted to smooth over the fight between Jackson and General Cocke as much as possible. Cocke was a political figure of some importance in East Tennessee and doubtless Eaton wanted East Tennessee votes. See p. 27 of 1828 edition.

32. This section starting with "to General Flournoy. . ." and ending with "the assistance of the Governor of Tennessee, was also earnestly sought," was removed from the 1828 edition. Apparently the reason for this removal was because of the mention of Cocke and the East Tennessee division. See 1828 edition, p. 28.

33. Turkey Town was a Cherokee settlement.

34. All reference to a junction with General White, part of Cocke's command, was removed from the 1828 edition. See p. 30 in 1828 edition.

35. All of this material starting with "the Army had advanced but a short distance. . ." and ending with ". . . should his other

resources fail." in the middle of page 47, has been removed from the 1828 edition. See 1828 edition, p. 31.

36. General John Floyd, commanding the troops which were advancing into the Creek Nation from Georgia, had the same problem of obtaining rations for his men. Apparently Georgia was no more able to feed its troops than Tennessee. See John Floyd to Mary Floyd, October 7, 1813, copies of letters written during the War of 1812–14 by General John Floyd to his daughter Mary H. Floyd, presented to General John Floyd Chapter, National Society of the United States Daughters of 1812—by Laura E. Blackshear, copy in the Georgia Department of Archives, Atlanta, Georgia.

37. This paragraph starting "on the 20th October, Colonel Dyer. . ." was left out of the 1828 edition. See p. 31, 1828 edition. It appears especially in the 1828 edition that Eaton did not wish to mention the exploits of anyone but Jackson.

38. Cocke's name was left out of the 1824 and later editions. See 1824 edition, pp. 32 and 33.

39. In the 1824 edition, and later, a line was added at the end, "In fact many of the women united with their warriors, and contended in the battle with fearless bravery." Clearly Eaton was trying to show that Jackson's army had no choice but to kill women. See 1824 edition, p. 35.

CHAPTER III

40. This paragraph relating to General White was left out of the 1828 edition although White's name remained in the next paragraph. See 1828 edition, p. 34.

41. All reference to Turkey Town was omitted from the 1828 edition. See 1828 edition, p. 34.

42. This reference to General Cocke was retained in the 1828 edition.

43. This refusal of Colonel Bradley to move up was omitted from the 1828 edition. See 1828 edition, p. 37.

44. Had this break in Jackson's lines not developed, it is probable that the entire force of Indians would have been killed or captured. Such a loss on the part of the hostiles might very well have led them to ask for peace at this time.

45. "From acting in obedience to his order" was omitted from

the 1828 edition. Probably this change would make the new print-ing less damaging to White. See 1828 edition, p. 38.

46. The statement that: "Perhaps jealousy in no inconsiderable degree, was the moving spring to his conduct" was deleted from the 1828 edition. See p. 39. Although criticism of Cocke was not entirely removed from the 1828 edition it was reduced as much as possible.

47. The section dealing with tripes was omitted from 1828 edi-tion. Perhaps it was considered indelicate. See 1828 edition, p. 40.

48. A long paragraph was added in 1824 describing Jackson's dividing the acorns he was eating with one of his men, an incident no doubt supposed to show that Jackson was generous and also shared the hardships of his men. See 1824 edition, pp. 66–67. See Appendix D.

49. Many accounts of this period indicate that the army was actually facing starvation. However, while they were certainly on reduced rations and probably hungry, they never resorted to eating their horses. This would indicate that they were not actually starving.

50. Starting with ". . . these were still further embittered . . ." and ending with "freely distributed as were their words of advice and condolence," all this section was omitted from the 1828 edi-tion. Eaton probably felt that describing this discontent added nothing to the stature of Jackson.

51. This entire section concerning General Cocke was omitted from the 1828 edition, starting with "shortly after the battle of Talladega. . ." and ending with ". . . the speedy accomplishment of the objects of the expedition" on p. 73.

52. This was slightly changed in the 1824 and later editions and M'Gee's name was omitted. See 1824 edition, p. 82.

53. The men were originally enlisted for one year starting December 10, 1812. However, they were released on April 20, 1813, but recalled on October 11, 1813. The men insisted that their term would expire December 10, 1813, but Jackson believed that they had enlisted for a full year of service and that the time they were at home between April 20 and September 4, 1813, did not count on their year of enlistment. He insisted that his men had about five and one-half months more to serve in order to complete their enlistment. See John Spencer Bassett, *The Life of Andrew Jackson* (New York, 1931), pp. 80–87, 101–108.

54. A paragraph of praise for Jackson was added here in the 1824 and later editions. See pp. 91 and 92 of 1824 edition. See Appendix E.

55. This entire paragraph on the arrival of General Cocke was omitted from the 1828 edition. See p. 58 in 1828 edition.

56. The entire remainder of this page starting with "they, however, further. . ." was omitted from 1828 edition. Apparently Eaton considered this section critical of Jackson's men and was bad for politics. See 1828 edition, p. 60.

57. A paragraph was added here in the 1824 and later editions, praising Jackson and blaming most of the difficulties on the contractors. See 1824 edition, p. 103. See Appendix F.

58. Allcorn's name was omitted from the 1824 edition and the whole reference to the actions of the Colonel was deleted from the 1828 edition. See p. 105 in 1824 edition and p. 63 in 1828 edition. Chapter III in the 1828 edition ends with "abandoned the campaign."

CHAPTER IV

59. Mention of General Roberts and the arrest of the officers was omitted from 1828 edition. See 1828 edition, p. 64.

60. A paragraph was added here in 1824 and later editions, in which Eaton commented on the poor qualities of militia troops. See 1824 edition, p. 107.

61. This section starting with "this opinion must, I suppose, agreeably . . ." and ending with "I shall not be at liberty to use," on next page, was deleted from 1828 edition. See 1828 edition, p. 68.

62. This entire section starting with "General Roberts, who. . ." and ending at the bottom of p. 109 with "sentenced, by a court martial, to be cashiered," has been omitted from the 1828 edition. See 1828 edition, p. 69.

63. Roberts' name was dropped from 1824 edition. See p. 118.

64. Major Bradley's name was removed from 1824 edition. See p. 118. Eaton appears to have deleted names from this edition either because he did not wish to anger the persons or because they might detract from Jackson.

65. Major General Cocke was referred to in 1824 and later edi-

tions as "your General." See 1824 edition, p. 121. Again this was probably done for political reasons.

66. Colonel Lilliard was referred to in 1824 and later editions as "the commanding officer." See 1824 edition, p. 125.

67. This entire paragraph starting "As nothing. . ." was omitted from the 1828 edition. See 1828 edition, p. 74.

68. The section starting with "General Cocke had been directed. . ." and ending with ". . . had been ordered to raise," on p. 118, has been deleted from the 1828 edition. See p. 74, 1828 edition.

69. Most of this paragraph has been omitted in the 1828 edition. Apparently Eaton did not wish to remind the reader that Jackson had great difficulty in raising an army. See 1828 edition, p. 76.

70. All of this material dealing with the mutiny of troops starting with "that officer, whose feelings. . ." has been removed from the 1828 edition. This deletion includes all of pp. 122 and 123, ending at the bottom of p. 123 with ". . . the charges were withdrawn." See 1828 edition, p. 76. It seems likely that this section could be left out without affecting the overall account of the war and certainly it did not enhance Jackson's reputation. Therefore the 1828 "campaign biography" skips the whole issue.

71. The 1828 edition mentions only "two hundred friendly Indians" and omits their tribal designations of Cherokees and Creeks. See 1828 edition, p. 76. It is possible that with Jackson's support of Indian removal, Eaton did not wish to stimulate any sympathy for these tribes.

72. In the 1824 and later editions "a thousand men" is changed to "900 new recruits." This was probably a change to a more accurate figure. See 1824 edition, p. 132.

73. "Through the body" and "through the head" are omitted from the 1828 edition. See p. 79. Eaton seems to have continued a policy of cleaning up the gore in his third edition.

74. Reid's account of this battle was based to a considerable degree on his own observations as a participant. The account not only reflects a knowledge of the reports appearing in the Jackson papers but adds considerable detail not found anywhere else. For this reason Reid's version of this battle was probably the most accurate and complete account available anywhere.

75. The 1828 edition deleted the title "Execution of a Soldier" and did not mention General Cocke. The reference to Cocke was replaced by "mutiny with the East Tennessee Brigade." See 1828 edition, p. 87. The execution of Private John Woods was probably one of the most unpopular acts Jackson ever committed and one which many persons at the time considered unnecessary. Eaton undoubtedly played down this execution as much as possible for political reasons.

76. Several lines were deleted from the 1828 edition starting with "his parting interview" and ending on p. 140 with ". . . commencement of the campaign." There was no apparent reason for this change, unless Eaton wished to reserve all praise for Jackson. See 1828 edition, p. 87.

77. This sentence, critical of Cocke, starting "This officer. . ." was eliminated from 1828 edition. See p. 88.

78. This section was rewritten in the 1828 edition to indicate that this was the second time Woods had been convicted of mutiny. According to Eaton's 1828 edition, Woods had been pardoned the first time, and the reader is allowed to believe that this was done by Jackson. Eaton contends that Woods simply could not be allowed a second pardon, since it would weaken the whole army. See 1828 edition, p. 89. See Appendix W.

79. A section was added to 1824 and later editions indicating the great difficulties Jackson was having in keeping up his army and conducting a campaign. Eaton apparently thought that this showed Jackson's ability to deal with adversity. See pp. 153–154, 1824 edition and p. 90 in 1828 edition.

80. Captain Carter's name was removed from 1824 edition. See p. 154.

81. The 1828 edition omitted a long section starting with "Before this, Cocke. . ." and ending on p. 147 with ". . . all who were not armed." Eaton once again was clearly trying to ignore the conflict between Jackson and Cocke. See p. 91 in 1828 edition.

82. In 1824 and later editions Eaton clarified the location of these places by saying that they were near Horseshoe Bend.

83. Although it is not clear in this text, Fort Williams was built as an advanced supply base for this campaign against the Creeks

encamped on the Tallapoosa. See Bassett, *The Life of Andrew Jackson,* p. 115.

84. In the 1824 edition this passage was reworded for clarity. There does not seem to be much change in overall meaning. See 1824 edition, pp. 161–162.

85. This passage starting with "Another cause. . ." and ending with "but their own bravery," was omitted from the 1828 edition. See p. 97 in 1828 edition. Eaton once more left out a reference to General Cocke and his division.

86. Most of Milton's force, if not all of it, was made up of regulars. Most of his men were part of the Third Regiment. See Thomas Pinckney to H. V. Milton, March 6 and March 8, 1814, and Milton to Pinckney, March 10, 1814, enclosures in Pinckney to the Secretary of War, March 17, 1814, Letters to the Secretary of War, RG 107, National Archives, Washington, D.C.

87. A good many minor changes appear in the 1828 edition at this point. However, they seem to have been made in an effort to clarify rather than change the meaning of the passage. See 1828 edition, p. 99.

88. Colonel Homer V. Milton, a regular army colonel, did not feel compelled to take orders from a militia officer. Pinckney had ordered Milton to collect supplies for Jackson's army, but the Colonel, an active commander, wished to take some independent action against the Indians before joining Jackson. Pinckney eventually solved this dispute by taking personal command of the combined forces. See Jackson to Pinckney, April 14, 1814, enclosure in Pinckney to the Secretary of War, April 18, 1814, Letters to the Secretary of War; Thomas Pinckney, General Orders, April 21, 1814, Jackson Papers, Library of Congress, Washington, D.C.

89. William Weatherford was one of the best war leaders of the hostile faction and may have been considered temporary war chief, but he was certainly not one of the principal chiefs of the nation. See H. S. Halbert and T. H. Ball, *The Creek War of 1813 and 1814* (University, Alabama, 1969), p. 149.

90. Apparently Weatherford lived up to his word and helped enforce the peace. According to later reports from the hostile Indians in Florida, several of the American raiding parties which searched West Florida for hostiles were led or guided by Weatherford. These Indians reported that Weatherford was absolutely merciless in dealing with those who continued to be hostile. See

(unsigned) to Lt. Samuel Jackson, July 19, 1814, ms 2328, Cochrane Papers, National Library of Scotland, Edinburgh, Scotland.

91. This entire paragraph concerning Colonel Gibson was
omitted from the 1828 edition. See p. 108 in the 1828 edition. This
follows Eaton's plan of concentrating on Jackson.

92. It was only after Pinckney arrived that the disagreements
between Colonel Milton and Jackson were settled.

93. Weatherford himself may have led some of these parties.
(See above note.) Although Eaton did not realize it, a large number of the persons killed at Fort Mims were friendly Indians and
mixed bloods. It is therefore not at all surprising that the friendly
Indians wanted revenge against those hostiles who had attacked
Fort Mims. See Halbert and Ball, *The Creek War of 1813 and
1814,* p. 147.

94. This is a rather harsh judgment since many of the friendly
Indians were put to death by the hostile faction at Fort Mims and
other places. Clearly there was no love between the factions once
the war started. Nevertheless, this view toward the friendly Indians
may explain why Jackson was so harsh toward them in the peace
settlement. If this statement accurately reflected Jackson's views,
it was probable that Jackson was comparing the friendly Indians
with the loyalists of the American Revolution whom he doubtless
still hated.

95. The 1828 edition omitted "and where, but for the absence
of the Georgia Army, they would have been captured or destroyed,
the war ended, and all apprehension of future resistance quieted."
See p. 111 in 1828 edition. Eaton apparently thought it undesirable
politically to be critical of Georgia.

CHAPTER VI

96. The first three pages of this chapter were omitted from the
1828 edition. This omission starts with "A war, from which much
greater. . ." on page 177 and ending on page 180 with ". . . had
become offended, and withdrawn his confidence." Apparently
Eaton felt that the condemnation of the British found in this
section was not good politics in 1828. See 1828 edition, p. 112.

97. So far as the Creek Indians were concerned, this was a gross
exaggeration. Except for the period just prior to the war, the
Creeks had been very peaceful for a number of years. The expedi-

tion in 1787 might have caused the Creeks near the Tennessee border to remain at peace, but they had also been at peace along their other borders, and on their western frontier, with the Mississippi Territory, they had developed a close friendly relationship with the white settlers.

98. An examination of British and Spanish records indicated that Eaton and other contemporary writers were incorrect in their belief that English agents aroused the Creeks to war. The evidence showed that while some British merchants and local officials in Canada and the Bahamas may have encouraged Indian hostilities against the United States, the Government in London made no effort to arouse the Creeks. The London Government officially encouraged the Creeks to keep the peace until after they entered a war with the United States. The London Government did not discover the Creek hostilities until January, 1814, and British aid did not arrive until May, 1814. Tecumseh's role, at least in the South, was unknown to the authorities in London. The Spanish, however, following the seizure of Mobile in April, 1813, did all they could to persuade the Creeks to attack the United States. Unfortunately for the Indians, the Spanish at Pensacola were so poorly supplied that they could furnish no arms to the Creeks and provided only small amounts of ammunition. See F. L. Owsley, Jr., "British and Indian Activities in Spanish West Florida During the War of 1812," *The Florida Historical Quarterly* (October, 1967), XLVI, 111–123.

99. A paragraph was added here in the 1824 edition, concerning the death of the Prophet Monohoe. This paragraph was left out of the 1828 edition. See 1824 edition, p. 192; also Appendix G.

100. There was a considerable addition here in the 1824 edition which seems to be explanatory. See 1824 edition, pp. 195–196. See Appendix H.

101. This paragraph has substantial changes which in effect leave out the Tennessee political pressure and indicate that the harsh treaty came from Jackson's orders from the War Department. See 1824 edition, pp. 196–197. See Appendix I.

102. The 1828 edition omitted any reference to a conflict with Hawkins. Jackson replaced General Pinckney as a commissioner to make peace with the Creeks. He ignored Pinckney's instructions, which had been to demand only a small land cession from the Creeks, and acting on his own authority demanded that the Creeks

give up a substantial part of their land. Although this was done without authority from Washington, the cession was eventually accepted. See M. B. Pound, *Benjamin Hawkins Indian Agent* (Athens, Georgia, 1951), pp. 234–235; Pinckney to Benjamin Hawkins, April 23, 1814, John S. Bassett, *Correspondence of Andrew Jackson*, 6 vols. (Washington, 1926–1933), II, 1–2 note; Secretary of War to Pinckney, March 17, 1814, Letters sent, Military Affairs, VII, RG 107, National Archives, Washington, D.C.

103. Eaton added a paragraph here in an attempt to justify Jackson's harsh actions in making the Creek settlement. He also included his copy of his instructions from Secretary of War Armstrong. See 1824 edition, pp. 198–199. See Appendix J.

In the 1828 edition Eaton also added a note concerning Henry Clay's attack on the treaty of Fort Jackson. This comment attempted to show Jackson's arch political enemy in a very unfavorable light. See 1828 edition, pp. 116–117.

104. The paragraph starting with "to settle the boundary, defining the extent of territory. . ." and ending on p. 185 with "in reality exists," was omitted from the 1828 edition. See 1828 edition, pp. 116–117.

Eaton apparently did not wish to get into a discussion of Cherokee-Creek problems in 1828.

105. Starting with "there are not many nations. . ." the remainder of this note through page 192 was omitted from the 1828 edition. See 1828 edition, pp. 121–122. Although this note was a strong defense of the harsh treaty of Fort Jackson, Eaton probably thought that by 1828 it was better to ignore the controversy caused by this treaty.

106. A paragraph was added here in 1824 and later editions concerning some land which the Creeks wished to give Hawkins and Jackson. Eaton claimed that Jackson wanted to refuse the land offered him, but would have allowed Hawkins to accept his grant. Eaton undoubtedly tried to use this to show Jackson's unselfishness. See 1824 edition, pp. 207–209. See Appendix K.

107. There was a paragraph added to the 1824 edition, at this point, explaining Jackson's attitude toward the British at Pensacola. In this he claimed that he would have marched at once against the British at Pensacola had he not wished to avoid a breach of Spanish neutrality. He did not wish to cause embarrassment for Washington. He considered that if he had marched at

this time he could have trapped and destroyed the whole British force.

108. The correct spelling of the Spanish Governor's full name is Don Mattio Gonzales Manrique.

109. Eaton once again followed his practice of omitting names from the 1828 edition, mentioning only Coffee and leaving out Colonel Butler, Colonel Lowery, Captains Baker and Butler. See 1828 edition, p. 134.

CHAPTER VII

110. Starting with "perhaps he could have. . . ," the rest of this paragraph was omitted from the 1828 edition. See 1828 edition, p. 138. Eaton apparently deleted this material to make the work less anti-British.

111. The author has chosen to ignore the dissatisfaction of New England with the war.

112. The paragraph starting "the next day. . ." and ending with ". . . made to retreat" was omitted from the 1828 edition, for no apparent reason. See 1828 edition, p. 137.

113. Only the *Hermes* and the *Sophie* got into firing position because of adverse wind and ebb tide. See W. H. Percy to Alexander Cochrane, September 16, 1814, Admiralty 1/505, Public Record Office, London, England.

114. According to English records the British marines and Indians in this engagement numbered between 200 and 250 men. See Edward Nicolls to Alexander Cochrane, November 17, 1814, mss. 2328, Cochrane Papers.

115. English records claim that their losses in this engagement were 24 killed and 44 wounded. See Nicolls to Cochrane, November 17, 1814, mss. 2328, Cochrane Papers.

116. British reports do not indicate that the remaining ships were badly damaged; only one of them had been in action. Also the men were not left ashore by a retreating fleet. Their gun, wounded, and heavy equipment were taken on board ship and they marched back to Pensacola in good order. See Robert Henry to Nicolls, September 20, 1814, and Nicolls to Cochrane, November 17, 1814, mss. 2328, Cochrane Papers.

117. This paragraph starting with "the conduct displayed. . ."

and ending with ". . . determined bravery" was omitted from the 1828 edition. Eaton appears to have tried to remove all passages from this work which praised anyone except Jackson. See 1828 edition, p. 141.

118. Eaton deleted "benefits that have prostrated her liberty and sunk her, perhaps, in eternal slavery. . ." from the 1828 edition. This again is doubtless an effort to make the work less anti-British. See 1828 edition, p. 143.

119. Again trying to make the work less anti-British Eaton, in the 1824 edition, changed ". . . can be entitled to the appellation of honourable. . ." to ". . . merits countenance from the civilized world." See 1824 edition, p. 212.

120. In his continued effort, especially in 1828, to be friendlier to the British, Eaton eliminated ". . . if it were one, to rise in opposition to the oppression and despotism, under which we then groaned. . ." See 1828 edition, p. 143.

121. A substantial section praising Jackson's success is added in the 1824 and later editions to the paragraph ending ". . . to General Coffee's camp." See 1824 edition, p. 243. See Appendix L.

122. Eaton removed from the 1828 version this paragraph starting with "the British vessels. . ." and ending with ". . . respectful distance." There is no apparent reason for this except that it praises the action of Lieutenant McCall rather than Jackson. See 1828 edition, p. 149.

123. Captain Dankins' name is omitted from the 1824 edition. See p. 252 of 1824 version.

124. Again removing names, Major Gales was changed to "one of his aids" in the 1828 printing. See p. 151 of this edition.

125. Jackson's decision to withdraw from Pensacola was probably influenced by his receipt of positive intelligence that a British expedition was on its way to attack New Orleans. See Cochrane to John W. Croker, December 7, 1814, Admiralty 1/508, Public Record Office; Juan Ventura Morales to Alexandro Ramirez, November 3, 1817, *Boletin del Archivo Nacional,* XIII (Habana, 1914), January-February, 1914, pp. 15–16.

CHAPTER VIII

126. In 1828 Eaton omitted this section starting with "Louisiana, he well. . ." and ending with ". . . the last extremity." See

1828 edition, page 157. Eaton probably considered this to be offensive to the voters of Louisiana.

127. Jackson has been criticized for his commitment to Mobile, but the original British plan was to attack Mobile first and move overland against New Orleans. This is the plan correctly described here. Later British plans were to seize Mobile and attack New Orleans through the Mississippi Sound, by boat. The final British plan to bypass Mobile and attack New Orleans directly probably did not come until a month or two before the attack, and may not have been decided until after the British failure to capture Fort Bowyer. See Owsley, "British and Indian Activities in Spanish West Florida During the War of 1812," pp. 116–122; Cochrane to Croker, June 20, 1814, Admiralty 1/506, Public Record Office; Cochrane to [Lord Melville], November 22, 1814, War of 1812 Manuscripts, Lilly Library, Indiana University, Bloomington, Indiana; Cochrane to Croker, December 7, 1814, Admiralty 1/508, Public Record Office.

128. In the 1828 edition Eaton deleted the paragraph starting "The Plans of Operation. . ." and ending with ". . . fallen a victim." He doubtless thought that this might seem insulting to the voters of New Orleans. See 1828 edition, p. 163.

129. Eaton deleted this entire paragraph starting with "At the bay of St. Louis. . ." and ending with ". . . had been taken." on page 258. Apparently this was omitted as a means of shortening the work and eliminated material not directly relating to Jackson. See p. 166 in 1828 edition.

130. Eaton rewrote this page in the 1824 edition. He added some details including the name of the British commander [Captain Lockyer]. This information had probably become available to Eaton after the 1817 edition was published. This new information does not change the basic meaning of the work. See pp. 279–280 in 1824 edition, and p. 67 in the 1828 edition.

131. Eaton omitted, from the 1828 edition, the section starting ". . . and that the forces" and ending on p. 262 with "discussed in his presence." Eaton left the note concerning the number of boats engaged in the battle in the 1828 edition but deleted the comment "so that the disparity of force was eight-seven-and nearly two to one." See p. 168 in 1828 edition. This material deleted was probably left out in an effort to shorten the work.

132. This loss of the gunboats was a real disaster to Jackson. Not only had he lost his scouts but had the gunboat fleet been at its authorized strength of twenty-five boats, the British would have been unable to land through the Mississippi Sound at all. See C. S. Forester, *The Age of Fighting Sail: The Story of the Naval War of 1812* (New York, 1956), pp. 267–269; William Jones to Daniel Patterson, October 18, 1813, and March 7, 1814; Letters sent by the Secretary of the Navy to Officers, RG 45, National Archives, Washington, D.C.

133. Jackson was apparently referring here to an attack on Mobile with an overland assault on the river. This was the original British plan. The General was probably correct in his estimate of the situation regarding the frigate. This vessel was usually referred to in the records as a block ship and was of about six foot draft. The records suggest that this vessel would carry around 30 heavy guns, about as many as a small frigate, but the fact that it could operate freely in the shallow water of the Mississippi Sound, the lakes and Mobile Bay would have greatly complicated a British assault on any of these points. If added to the authorized strength of 25 gunboats which the Navy was supposed to have for the defense of the approaches to New Orleans, it is probable that the British would have found an attack on Mobile very difficult and a landing at New Orleans impossible. This conclusion is supported by British records which complain bitterly that the Admiralty had not supplied enough shallow draught vessels to transport and supply properly the forces to be landed at New Orleans, much less engage a shallow water American naval force. The British considered themselves very lucky to be able to capture Jones' five gunboats and admitted that this battle caused a strain on their already limited supply of small boats and barges. Any larger American naval squadron would have forced the abandonment of the New Orleans attack. The British fleet off the Gulf Coast was enormous, but none of the large ships could enter any of the sounds and bays near New Orleans and were therefore worthless as an assault force on that city. See *Ibid.*, and Patterson to Jones, January 25, 1814 and February 14, 1814, Letters Received by the Secretary of the Navy from Commanders 1804–1886, RG 45, National Archives.

134. It is reported by some students of the battle that Mr. Shields and Dr. Murrell were not considered to be prisoners of

the British. It is also suggested that these two men misled the British by permitting themselves to be overheard discussing the size of Jackson's army. In so doing they helped to convince the enemy falsely that the Americans had an enormous army at New Orleans. See Jane Lucas de Grummond, *The Baratarians and the Battle of New Orleans* (Baton Rouge, 1968), pp. 67–68.

135. Eaton added a paragraph here in 1824 edition. This paragraph explains how Mr. Shields and Dr. Murrell tried with some success to convince the British that 20,000 men were in New Orleans. This was added information which no doubt became available to Eaton after the 1817 edition was published. See pp. 288 and 289 in the 1824 edition, and previous note. See Appendix M.

136. The 1828 edition deleted the comment "Jackson was aware that this appeal to his humanity might be a stratagem, having for its object to aid his enemy." Eaton doubtless thought that Jackson would sound more generous if this comment were removed. See 1828 edition, p. 177.

137. About one-third of a page of new material was added here in the 1824 edition. This material was a section praising the citizenry, and while it had little significance, it was likely intended to appeal to the voters. See p. 298 of 1824 edition.

138. During his tenure as commander of the seventh military district, which included New Orleans, General Thomas Flournoy somehow managed to antagonize nearly everyone in his district both civilian and military. Considering his personality it is not surprising that he received little or no cooperation from the Louisiana legislature or anyone else. Jackson, who made a much better impression on the people of Louisiana, received abundant aid from them. See Thomas Flournoy to the Secretary of War, January 31, 1813, and March 14, 1814, Letters to the Secretary of War; the *New Orleans Gazette,* January 14, 1814.

CHAPTER IX

139. Jackson has been criticized for not using General Carroll's troops in his attack since this additional strength might have enabled him to win a complete victory over the British. However, the decision to place Carroll in a position to watch the Gentilly road was based on excellent intelligence. The original British

plan had been to attack New Orleans from the rear through Lake Ponchartrain. This British plan was abandoned only when Admiral Cochrane discovered that his orders to collect light draft boats at Jamaica had not been followed. Lacking the necessary boats the British did not attempt the landing. However, Jackson had fairly complete information concerning their original plan, and therefore had no choice but to guard against it. See Alexander Cochrane to John W. Croker, December 7, 1814, and December 16, 1814, mss. 2349, Cochrane Papers.

140. The fire from the *Caroline* caused few if any casualties, but did disrupt and demoralize the British to the extent that their defense was badly disorganized. See Harry L. Coles, *The War of 1812* (Chicago, 1965), pp. 218–220.

141. Once the battle started, the British extinguished their camp fires. After this the ship's officers could locate the enemy only by the musket flashes, but when the land action eased off targets became scarce. See Coles, *The War of 1812,* pp. 217–220; Wilburt S. Brown, *The Amphibious Campaign for West Florida and Louisiana 1814–1815* (University, Alabama, 1969), pp. 101–105.

142. Eaton omitted from the 1828 edition the paragraph starting with "The last charge. . ." and ending with ". . . considerably weakened." This seems to have been done to shorten the work. See p. 194 of the 1828 edition.

143. In the 1824 edition Eaton added a paragraph here which was a good example of the praise of Jackson. See pp. 325 and 326 in the 1824 edition. See Appendix N.

144. In the 1828 edition Eaton removed Hinds' unit from this list and placed it in a footnote. This changed the total number he listed as taking part in this action from 2167 to 1981. See 1828 edition, p. 199.

145. British losses in this engagement were 46 killed, 167 wounded and 64 captured. See Brown, *The Amphibious Campaign for West Florida and Louisiana 1814–1815,* p. 104.

146. These "proofs" probably referred to the accounts of British offers to him along with intelligence of British operations which he had supplied to the Americans. For a good account of the actions of the Baratarians see Jane Lucas de Grummond, *The Baratarians and the Battle of New Orleans.*

147. In the 1828 edition Eaton condensed into one short para-

graph this section starting with "The line, which, from the labours. . ." to ". . . with the loss of their colonel and five men," on p. 318. See 1828 edition, p. 208. Apparently Eaton made this drastic cut to shorten the book and possibly because the information did not directly concern Jackson.

148. From the first, the British greatly overestimated the number of men on the American side. See Harry Coles, *The War of 1812*, p. 221.

149. In the 1824 and later editions Eaton added two paragraphs here to explain Jackson's order concerning the disruption of the Louisiana Legislature. He states in part that Claiborne overreacted and that it had not been Jackson's intent to close the Legislature. There were undoubtedly many Louisianians who still resented this action and no doubt Eaton wished to make Jackson's order seem less offensive. See 1824 edition, pp. 346–348. See Appendix O.

150. This last paragraph starting with "Frequent light skirmishes. . ." was omitted from the 1828 edition. Presumably this shortened the 1828 edition and the omitted material added little to the glory of Jackson.

CHAPTER X

151. In the 1824 edition Eaton added a few lines here describing Jackson's treatment of one of the men who complained that his cotton bales were being used as part of the rampart. See 1824 edition, p. 357.

152. Some accounts indicate that the British had opened fire on the American lines without bothering to determine the range. Because of this failure a large part of the bombardment was fired over the American lines, landing several hundred yards to the rear in an open field, where it did no damage. See Coles, *The War of 1812*, p. 224.

153. Some of the Kentucky troops were supplied with rifles but the number is undetermined. In spite of statements that it was the American rifleman who defeated the British, evidence indicates that only a small part of Jackson's army was armed with rifles. See Lambert to Bathurst, January 29, 1814, War Office 1/141, Public Record Office, London, England.

154. Jackson was clearly concerned about this threat, but since

these guns, well supplied with shot, had not been able to drive out the British, it seems unlikely that they could have driven out the Americans. This would have been even less probable considering the great difficulty faced by the British in bringing up ammunition and supplies. It does seem strange that Jackson did not make any efforts to strengthen his line against a raking fire.

155. Eaton, apparently acting on later information, increased the American strength on the west bank of the Mississippi from 800 to 1500 men in the 1824 edition. See 1824 edition, p. 364.

156. Sir Edward's name is usually spelled Pakenham not Packenham.

157. Some accounts of this battle give proper credit to the role of the artillery in defeating the British. Others credit the accuracy of the rifle. However, Eaton, who must have had Jackson's personal approval of this work, praises the artillery and musketry. The term musketry undoubtedly includes rifle fire but except for mentioning Captain Beal's rifles and the death of Colonel Rennie by rifle fire, Eaton makes little mention of this weapon. Previously the author indicates that General Coffee's men were largely armed with rifles but little is said on this subject concerning other units. All but a few of General Carroll's men were armed with muskets, as were most of the armed Kentucky troops. Accounts indicate that there were some rifle companies on the main line but because of its more rapid fire and bayonet, Jackson placed men armed with the musket along most of his front. Coffee's riflemen were placed in the woods on the far end of the line which was not expected to receive the main attack. Jackson appears to have placed his remaining rifle companies as pickets and in strategic spots along the line to act as sharpshooters. He evidently expected the heavy fire which would repel the main British assault to come from muskets. Since the main assault did come on Carroll's sector his expectations were entirely fulfilled. The British attack was actually broken by the fire of muskets and artillery, not rifles.

158. Eaton omitted this section starting with "It was not. . ." and ending with ". . . its safe defence. . ." from the 1828 edition. See 1828 edition, p. 225. Eaton probably believed that it did not favor Jackson to admit that he had been so weak as to yield to the incorrect suggestions of others.

159. Here again Eaton stresses artillery.

160. Eaton added a paragraph in the 1824 and later editions in which he stated that Jackson refused to let Colonel Hinds counterattack because it would cost too many American lives and might endanger the American army by weakening it. This was probably a correct estimate of Jackson's reason for not ordering a counter attack, but in adding this Eaton praises Jackson for being a calm and wise commander. See 1824 edition, pp. 371–372. See Appendix P.

161. In 1833, Jackson apparently tried to confirm the use of this phrase. Charles G. Vaughn claimed to have statements from all the surviving British staff officers who denied that they or Pakenham had ever used "Booty and beauty" as a password. Vaughn admits that some of the troops might have used it. General William Carroll also denied that he had ever heard the British use this term. See Charles G. Vaughn to Jackson, July 14, 1833, first series and William Carroll to Jackson, August 4, 1833, second series, Jackson Papers, Library of Congress.

162. In the 1824 edition, Eaton added about ten lines to glorify the fighting ability of the Americans, especially the yeomanry or common men. See p. 387 of 1824 edition.

CHAPTER XI

163. The remainder of this paragraph, starting with "A heavy mortar. . ." has been omitted from the 1828 edition. See 1828 edition, p. 239. Eaton probably omitted this detail to shorten the work.

164. The section starting with ". . . for this purpose pieces. . ." and ending with ". . . might not be lost," was also removed from the 1828 edition. See 1828 edition, p. 239. Once again Eaton seems to have been trying to shorten the 1828 edition.

165. Although Jackon's army was short of small arms, he apparently never experienced a shortage of cannon powder or balls. This excellent stock was apparently supplied by the Navy which had a large store at New Orleans. Additional powder was probably furnished by the Baratarians. For some indication of the size of the naval supply, see Paul Hamilton to William Helms, July 8, 1814, Miscellaneous Letters Sent by the Secretary of the Navy, RG 45, National Archives, Washington, D.C.

166. This entire paragraph starting with "Fort Bowyer" and

ending with "greatly apprehended," was omitted from the 1828 edition. See 1828 edition, p. 246. Apparently this cut was simply another of Eaton's efforts to trim the length of the 1828 edition.

167. English reinforcements had more than restored their army's losses at New Orleans. The state of British morale remained poor. See Brown, *The Amphibious Campaign for West Florida and Louisiana 1814–1815,* p. 159, 166.

168. In the 1828 edition the entire section starting with "General Winchester. . ." and ending on page 374 with ". . . sufficient for her completion," was omitted from the 1828 edition. This was replaced with a long, almost three-page discussion of the execution of six men for mutiny and desertion. Jackson had been widely attacked for permitting this execution and apparently Eaton believed that Jackson's side of the case needed to be told. In any event, Eaton produced a long defense of the General's action. See 1828 edition, pp. 247–249. See Appendix X.

169. This decision was made by Secretary of the Navy Jones who considered the cost of the ship being built at New Orleans was far too great. He apparently believed that the naval station at New Orleans was wasting money and even hinted at the possibility of corruption at the base. In anger at these expenses, he ordered all work on this vessel stopped. See William Jones to Daniel Patterson, October 18, 1813, and March 7, 1814, Letters Sent by the Secretary of the Navy to Officers, RG 45, National Archives.

170. Eaton added a paragraph here to the 1824 edition. Probably based on new information, this explains that Jackson used the previous years' voter lists as a means of throwing out many of the certificates of French citizenship, signed by Monsieur Toussard, the French Consul. See 1824 edition, pp. 407–408. See Appendix Q.

171. This paragraph was greatly reworded and expanded in the 1828 edition. See 1828 edition, p. 257. Eaton did not change the meaning here but was apparently trying to clarify the actions.

172. The section starting with "But the authority. . ." and ending with ". . . strictly within their letter. . ." is omitted from the 1828 edition. Eaton probably considered this attack on the courts to be unpopular in 1828. See 1828 edition, p. 258.

173. This paragraph starting with "After. . ." is omitted in

the 1828 edition down to ". . . rules laid down." See 1828 edition, p. 259. Eaton probably left this out because it seems to be an attack on the courts, and as in footnote above would be unpopular at that time.

174. There is a large addition in the 1824 edition to this paragraph starting with "This process. . ." and ending with ". . . further to add." Eaton, in the expanded version, tells how Jackson defended himself and puts him in a favorable light in his speech to the crowd. See 1824 edition, pp. 417–418. See Appendix R.

175. In 1824 Eaton greatly enlarged the section starting "The hall, in which . . ." and ending with ". . . have accepted." on page 388. In the 1824 edition, this expansion runs to almost four pages. See 1824 edition, pp. 419–423. Eaton added this material, which glorifies Jackson, to show that the crowd favored him. See Appendix S.

176. Eaton added three pages here defending Jackson's actions in declaring martial law in New Orleans and his arrest of Judge Hall. This is an excellent example of Eaton's uncritical support of Jackson which was added to the 1824 campaign biography. See 1824 edition, pp. 425–428. See Appendix T.

177. In the 1824 edition, Eaton added a paragraph here showing Jackson's honors. See 1824 edition, p. 430.

178. This section starting with "He is, however, not with . . ." and ending with ". . . particularly attached to him," on p. 395 has been rewritten and expanded to almost four pages in the 1824 edition. In this increased glorification of Jackson, Eaton explains away each of his bad traits and makes them normal and human, if not even virtues. See pp. 432–436 in the 1824 edition. See appendix U.

179. Eaton added a paragraph here. This is a comment on the country and makes little change in the work. See the 1824 edition, p. 440. See appendix V.

180. Eaton added a quotation here, but it does nothing to change the meaning of the work. See 1824 edition, p. 442.

EDITOR'S BIBLIOGRAPHY AND APPENDICES

BOOKS DEALING WITH ANDREW JACKSON AND
THE WAR OF 1812

Abernethy, Thomas P. *The South in the New Nation, 1789–1819.*
Baton Rouge: Louisiana State University Press, 1961.

Adams, Henry. *History of the United States of America during the
Second Administration of James Madison.* Vol. II. New York:
Charles Scribner's Sons, 1904.

Armstrong, John. *Notices of the War of 1812.* 2 vols. New York:
Wiley & Putnam, 1840.

Arthur, Stanley Clisby. *The Story of the Battle of New Orleans.*
New Orleans: Louisiana Historical Society, 1915.

———. *Jean Laffite, Gentleman Rover.* New Orleans: Harmon-
son, 1952.

Bassett, John S. *The Life of Andrew Jackson.* 2 vols. Garden City:
Doubleday, Page & Co., 1911.

Beirne, Francis F. *The War of 1812.* New York: E. P. Dutton and
Co., Inc., 1949.

Bernardo, C. Joseph, and E. H. Bacon. *American Military Policy.*
Harrisburg, Pa.: Military Service Publishing Co., 1955.

Brackenridge, H. M. *History of the Late War.* Philadelphia: James
Kay, Jr., 1839.

Brannan, John. *Official Letters of the Military and Naval Officers
of the Untied States, During the War with Great Britain in the
Years 1812, 13, 14, and 15.* Washington, D. C.: Way and
Gideon, 1823.

Brant, Irving. *James Madison, Commander-in-Chief.* Indianapolis:
Bobbs-Merrill, 1961.

Brooks, Charles. *The Seige of New Orleans.* Seattle: University of
Washington Press, 1961.

Brown, John P. *Old Frontiers; The Story of the Cherokee Indians From the Earliest Times to the Date of Their Removal West, 1838*. Kingsport: Southern Publishers Inc., 1938.

Brown, Wilburt S. *The Amphibious Campaign for West Florida and Louisiana, 1814–1815*. University, Alabama: University of Alabama Press, 1969.

Buchanan, John. *The History of the Royal Scots Fusilliers: 1678–1918*. London: Thomas Nelson & Sons, 1925.

Buell, Augustus C. *A History of Andrew Jackson*. 2 vols. New York: Charles Scribner's Sons, 1904.

Burt, A. L. *The United States, Great Britain, and British North America from the Revolution to the Establishment of Peace after the War of 1812*. New Haven, Conn.: Yale University Press, 1940.

Butler, Lewis. *Annals of the King's Royal Rifle Corps*. 4 vols. London: John Murray, 1923.

Caughey, John W. *McGillivray of the Creeks*. Norman: University of Oklahoma Press, 1959.

Chapelle, Howard I. *The History of the American Sailing Navy*. New York: Norton, 1949.

Chidsey, D. B. *The Battle of New Orleans*. New York: Crown, 1961.

Claiborne, John Francis Hamtramck. *Life and Times of Gen. Sam Dale, The Mississippi Partisan*. New York: Harper and Brothers, 1860.

————. *Mississippi as a Province, Territory and State with Biographical Notices of Eminent Citizens*. Jackson, Miss.: Power and Barksdale, 1880.

Claiborne, Nathaniel Herbert. *Notes on the War in the South; With Biographical Sketches of the Lives of Montgomery, Jackson, Sevier, the Late Gov. Claiborne, and Others*. Richmond: William Ramsay, 1819.

Cobbett, William. *Life of Andrew Jackson*. New York: Harper and Brothers, 1834.

Codrington, Sir Edward. *Memoirs of Admiral Sir Edward Codrington*. 2 vols. Ed. by his daughter, Lady Jane B. Bouchier, London: Longmans, Green and Co., 1873.

Coles, Harry L. *The War of 1812*. Chicago: University of Chicago Press, 1965.

Cooke, John Henry. *A Narrative of Events in the South of France and of the Attack on New Orleans*. London: T. & W. Boone, 1835.

Cooper, John Spencer. *Rough Notes of Seven Campaigns*. 2nd ed. Carlisle: G. & T. Coward, 1914. (Originally published 1869.)

Cotterill, Robert S. *The Southern Indians; The Story of the Civilized Tribes Before Removal*. Norman: University of Oklahoma Press, 1954.

Cox, Isaac Joslin. *The West Florida Controversy, 1789–1813 A Study in American Diplomacy*. Gloucester, Mass.: Peter Smith, 1967.

Cullum, G. W. ed. *Campaigns of the War of 1812–15*. New York: Miller, 1879.

Dawson, H. B. *Battles of the United States by Sea and Land*. 2 vols. New York: 1958.

deGrummond, Jane L. *The Baratarians and the Battle of New Orleans*. Baton Rouge: Louisiana State University Press, 1961.

Drake, Benjamin. *Life of Tecumseh, and His Brother the Prophet: with a Historical Sketch of the Shawnoe [sic] Indians*. Cincinnati: E. Morga and Company, 1841.

Eggleston, George Cary. *Red Eagle and the Wars with the Creek Indians of Alabama*. New York: Dodd, Mead Company, 1878.

Forester, C. S. *The Age of Fighting Sail*. Garden City, N. Y.: Doubleday, 1956.

Fortescue, J. W. *A History of the British Army*. 13 vols. London: Macmillan Co., 1899–1930.

Fortier, Alcée. *A History of Louisiana*. 4 vols. New York: Goupil & Co. of Paris, 1903.

Gatschet, Albert Samuel. *A Migration Legend of the Creek Indians, With a Linguistic, Historic, and Ethnolographic Introduction*. 2 vols. Philadelphia: D. G. Brinton, 1884–88.

Gayarré, Charles. *History of Louisiana*. 4 vols. New York: William D. Widdon Publishers, 1866.

Gleig, George R. *The Campaigns of the British Army at Washington and New Orleans*. London: John Murray, 1847.

Goodwin, Philo A. *Biography of Andrew Jackson, President of the United States*. New York: R. H. Towner, 1833.

Halbert, H. S. and Ball, T. H. *The Creek War of 1813 and 1814*. University, Ala.: University of Alabama Press, 1969.

Horsman, Reginald. *The Causes of the War of 1812*. Philadelphia: University of Pennsylvania Press, 1962.

———. *The War of 1812*. New York: Alfred A. Knopf, 1969.

Jacobs, James R. *Tarnished Warrior: Major General James Wilkinson*. New York: Macmillan, 1938.

James, Marquis. *Andrew Jackson the Border Captain*. Indianapolis: Bobbs Merrill Company, 1933.

James, William. *A Full and Correct Account of the Military Occurrences of the Late War between Great Britain and the United States of America*. 2 vols. London: Privately printed, 1818.

Johns, Richard and P. H. Nicolas. *The Naval and Military Heroes of Great Britain or Calendar of Victory*. London: Henry G. Bohn, 1860.

Johnson, Gerald W. *Andrew Jackson, An Epic in Homespun*. New York: Milton Balch and Co., 1927.

King, G. *Creole Families of New Orleans*. New York: Macmillan, 1921.

Knox, Dudley W. *A History of the United States Navy*. New York: G. P. Putnam and Sons, 1936.

Latour, A. Lacarriere. *Historical Memoir of the War in West Florida and Louisiana*. Translated from the French by H. P. Nugent. Philadelphia: John Conrad & Co., 1816.

Leckie, Robert. *The Wars of America*. New York: Harper and Row, 1968.

Lossing, Benson John. *The Pictorial Field-Book of the War of 1812, or, Illustrations, by Pen and Pencil, of the History, Biography, Scenery, Relics, and Traditions of the Last War for American Independence*. New York: Harper and Brothers, 1868.

McAfee, Robert B. *History of the Late War In the Western Country*. Bowling Green, Ohio: 1919. Reprint from 1816 version Historical Publications Company.

Mahan, A. T. *Sea Power in Its Relations to the War of 1812*. 2 vols. Boston: Little, Brown & Co., 1905.

Martin, François-Xavier. *The History of Louisiana*. New Orleans: James A. Gresham, 1882.

Nolte, Vincent. *The Memoirs of Vincent Nolte: Reminiscences in the Period of Anthony Adverse*. Translated from the German. New York: G. Howard Watt, 1934. (Originally published in the U.S., 1854.)

Parton, James. *Life of Andrew Jackson*. 3 vols. Boston: Houghton, Mifflin and Co., 1887-88.

Pickett, Albert James. *History of Alabama, and Incidentally of Georgia and Mississippi, from the Earliest Period.* 2 vols. Charleston: Walker and James, 1851.

Pound, Merritt B. *Benjamin Hawkins, Indian Agent.* Athens: University of Georgia Press, 1951.

Pratt, Julius W. *Expansionists of 1812.* Gloucester, Mass.: Peter Smith, 1957.

Ramsay, David. *History of the United States, From Their First Settlement as English Colonies, in 1607 to the Year 1808, or the Thirty-third of their Sovereignty and Independence.* 3 vols. Philadelphia: M. Carey and Son, 1818.

Rankin, Hugh ed. *The Battle of New Orleans: A British View.* New Orleans: The Hauser Press, 1961.

Remini, Robert V. *Andrew Jackson.* New York: Harper and Row, 1969.

Roosevelt, Theodore. *The Naval War of 1812.* 4th ed. New York: G. P. Putnam's Sons, 1889.

Silver, James W. *Edmund Pendleton Gaines Frontier General.* Baton Rouge: Louisiana State University Press, 1949.

Sinclair, H. *The Port of New Orleans.* Garden City, N. Y.: Doubleday, 1942.

Smith, Zachary F. *The Battle of New Orleans.* (Filson Club Publications, No. 19.) Louisville, Ky.: John P. Morton & Co., 1904.

Snelling, William Joseph. *A Brief and Impartial History of the Life and Actions of Andrew Jackson.* Boston: Stimpson and Clapp, 1831.

Starkey, Marion L. *The Cherokee Nation.* New York: A. A. Knopf, 1946.

Stoddard, William Osborn. *Andrew Jackson and Martin Van Buren.* New York: F. A. Stokes, 1887.

Surtees, William. *Twenty-five Years in the Rifle Brigade.* Edinburgh: Wm. Blackwood, 1833.

Tatum, Howell. "Major Howell Tatum's Journal," ed. John Spencer Bassett, *Smith College Studies in History,* VII (1921–22), Nos. 1, 2, 3.

Walker, Alexander. *Jackson and New Orleans.* New York: J. C. Derby, 1856.

Watson, Thomas E. *Life and Times of Andrew Jackson.* Thompson, Georgia: Jeffersonian Publishing Co., 1912.

Whitaker, Arthur P. *The Spanish American Frontier; 1783–1795.* New York: Houghton Mifflin Co., 1927.

Wilkinson, James. *Memoirs of My Own Times.* 3 vols. Philadelphia: Abraham Small, 1816.

Woodward, Grace S. *The Cherokees.* Norman: University of Oklahoma Press, 1963.

Wright, J. Leitch, Jr. *William Augustus Bowles Director General of the Creek Nation.* Athens: University of Georgia Press, 1967.

ARTICLES AND PERIODICALS DEALING WITH
ANDREW JACKSON AND THE WAR OF 1812

Adams, Reed McC. B. "New Orleans and the War of 1812," *Louisiana Historical Quarterly,* 16 (April, July, October, 1933):221–234, 478–503, 681–703, and 17 (January, April, July, 1934): 169–182, 349–363, 502–523.

Ainsworth, Walden L. "An Amphibious Operation that Failed," *United States Naval Institute Proceedings,* 71 (February, 1945): 193–202.

Barbour, Violet. "Privateers and Pirates of the West Indies," *American Historical Review,* 17 (April, 1911):543–565.

Brooks, Philip C. "Spain's Farewell to Louisiana, 1803–1821," *Mississippi Valley Historical Review,* 27 (July, 1940):29–42.

Boyd, Mark F. "Events at Prospect Bluff on the Apalachicola River, 1808–1818," *The Florida Historical Quarterly,* 14 (October, 1937):55–96.

Cable, George W. "The Creoles in the American Revolution," *Century Magazine,* 25 (February, 1883):538–550.

———. "The End of Foreign Dominion in Louisiana," *Century Magazine,* 25 (March, 1883):643–654.

———. "Plotters and Pirates of Louisiana," *Century Magazine,* 25 (April, 1883):852–866.

———. "Who Are the Creoles?" *Century Magazine,* 25 (January, 1883):384–398.

Calkins, Carlos G. "The Repression of Piracy in the West Indies, 1814–1825," *United States Naval Institue Proceedings,* 37 (December, 1911):1187–98.

Carpenter, Edwin H., Jr. "Latour's Report on Spanish American Relations in the Southwest," *Louisiana Historical Quarterly,* 30 (July, 1947) :715–717.

"A Contemporary Account of the Battle of New Orleans by a Soldier in the Ranks," *Louisiana Historical Quarterly*, 9 (January, 1926):11–15.

Cusacks, Gaspar. "Lafitte, the Louisiana Pirate and Patriot," *Louisiana Historical Quarterly*, 2 (October, 1919):418–438.

Dart, Henry P., ed. "Andrew Jackson and Judge D. A. Hall," *Louisiana Historical Quarterly*, 5 (October, 1922):509–570.

———. "Jackson and the Louisiana Legislature, 1814–15," *Louisiana Historical Quarterly*, 9 (April, 1926):221–280.

Dickson, Colonel Sir Alexander. "Artillery Services in North America in 1814 and 1815," *Journal of the Society for Army Historical Research*, 8 (April, July and October, 1929):79–112, 147–178, 213–226.

Doster, James F. "Letters Relating to the Tragedy of Fort Mims: August-September, 1813," *The Alabama Review*, 14 (October, 1961):269–285.

Espy, William, ed. "General Court Martial Held at the Royal Barracks, Dublin, for the Trial of Brevet Lieutenant Colonel Hon. Thomas Mullins, Captain of the 44th Regiment of Foot, July 11 to August 1, 1815," *Louisiana Historical Quarterly*, 9 (January, 1926):33–110.

Faye, Stanley. "Privateers of Guadeloupe and Their Establishment in Barataria," *Louisiana Historical Quarterly*, 23 (April, 1940): 428–444.

———. "Privateersmen of the Gulf and Their Prizes," *Louisiana Historical Quarterly*, 22 (October, 1929):1012–94.

Fisher, Ruth A. "The Surrender of Pensacola as Told by the British," *American Historical Review*, 54 (January, 1949): 326–329.

Forrester, Cecil S. "Victory at New Orleans," *American Heritage*, 8 (August, 1957):4–9, 106–108.

Galpin, William F. "American Grain Trade to the Spanish Peninsula," *American Historical Review*, 28 (October, 1922):24–44.

Gayarré, Charles E. "Historical Sketch of Pierre and Jean Lafitte," *Magazine of American History*, 10 (October and November, 1883):284–298, 389–396.

Goodrich, Caspar F. "Our Navy and the West Indian Pirates," *United States Naval Institute Proceedings*, 42 (January, 1916): 1459–1475.

Hardin, J. Fair. "The First Great River Captain," *Louisiana Historical Quarterly*, 10 (January, 1927):27–28.

Henry, Robert S. "Tennesseans and Territory," *Tennessee Historical Quarterly,* 12 (September, 1953):195–203.

Holland, James W. "Andrew Jackson and the Creek War: Victory at the Horseshoe," *The Alabama Review,* 21 (October, 1968):243–275.

King, Grace, trans. and ed. "Marigny's Reflections on the New Orleans Campaign," *Louisiana Historical Quarterly,* 6 (January, 1923):61–85.

Liljegren, Ernest R. "Jacobinism in Spanish Louisiana, 1792–1797," *Louisiana Historical Quarterly,* 22 (January, 1939):47–97.

Lister, Walter B. "Portrait of a Pirate," *American Mercury,* 7 (February, 1926):214–219.

McAlister, L. N. "Pensacola During the Second Spanish Period," *The Florida Historical Quarterly,* 32 (January-April, 1959): 281–327.

McClellan, Edwin. "The Navy at New Orleans," *United States Naval Institute Proceedings,* 50 (December, 1924):2041–2060.

Maclay, Edgar S. "Battle of New Orleans Half Won at Sea," *Magazine of History,* 16 (January, 1913):29–34.

Mahon, John K. "British Strategy and Southern Indians: War of 1812," *The Florida Historical Quarterly,* 44 (April, 1966):285–302.

Mills, Dudley, Colonel, Royal Engineers. "The Duke of Wellington and the Peace Negotiations at Ghent," *Canadian Historical Review,* 2 (March, 1921):19–32.

Mississippi Republican, Washington, Mississippi, 1812–1815.

Morgan, David B. "General Morgan's Defense of Conduct of Louisiana Militia" (a letter written at Madisonville, April 15, 1817), *Louisiana Historical Quarterly,* 9 (January, 1926):16–29.

Niles' Weekly Register, Baltimore, 1812–1815.

Owsley, Frank L., Jr. "British and Indian Activities in Spanish West Florida During the War of 1812," *The Florida Historical Quarterly,* 46 (October, 1967):111–123.

————. "Jackson's Capture of Pensacola," *The Alabama Review,* 19 (July, 1966):175–185.

————. "The Fort Mims Massacre," *The Alabama Review,* 24 (July, 1971):192–204.

Parsons, Edward A. "Jean Lafitte in the War of 1812, a Narrative Based on the Original Documents," *Proceedings of the American Antiquarian Society,* 50 (October, 1940):205–24.

Ritchie, Carson I. A. "The Louisiana Campaign," *Louisiana Historical Quarterly*, 44 (January to April, 1961):13–103.

Stephen, Walter W. "Andrew Jackson's Forgotten Army," *The Alabama Review*, 12 (April, 1959):126–131.

"Subaltern in America," *Blackwood's Edinburgh Magazine*, 21 (January to June, 1827):243–58, 417–33, 531–42, 719–26, and 22 (July to December, 1827):74–82, 316–28.

Tousard, Louis de. "Letters re Battle of New Orleans," *Magazine of History*, 25 (July, 1917):40–42.

Trussel, John B. B., Jr. "Thunder by the River," *Field Artillery Journal*, 39 (July-August, 1949):173–75.

Wellesley, Arthur, Duke of Wellington. "Letter of Duke of Wellington (May 22, 1815) on the Battle of New Orleans," *Louisiana Historical Quarterly*, 9 (January, 1926):5–10.

West, Elizabeth H. "A Prelude to the Creek War of 1813–1814," *The Florida Historical Quarterly*, 18 (April, 1940):247–266.

Wright, J. Leitch, Jr. "A Note on the First Seminole War as Seen by the Indians, Negroes, and Their British Advisers," *The Journal of Southern History*, 34 (November, 1968):565–575.

———. "British Designs on the Old Southwest: Foreign Intrigue on the Florida Frontier, 1783–1803," *The Florida Historical Quarterly*, 14 (April, 1966):265–284.

Published Documents

Adams, John Quincy. *The Duplicate Letters, the Fisheries, and the Mississippi. Documents Relating to Transactions at the Negotiation of Ghent*. Washington: Davis and Force, 1822.

Bassett, John S., ed. *Correspondence of Andrew Jackson*. 6 vols. Washington: Carnegie Institution, 1926–1933.

Carter, Clarence E., ed. *The Territory of Mississippi 1809–1817*. vol. 6, 1938. *The Territorial Papers of the United States*. Washington: Government Printing Office, 1934–.

Lowrie, Walter, *et al.*, ed. *The American State Papers, Documents, Legislative, and Executive of the Congress of the United States*. 39 vols. Washington: Government Printing Office, 1832–61.

Richardson, James D., ed. *A Compilation of the Messages and Papers of the Presidents 1789–1897*. 10 vols. Washington: Government Printing Office, 1896–1899.

Rowland, Dunbar, ed. *Official Letter Books of W. C. C. Claiborne, 1801–1816*. 6 vols. Jackson, Mississippi: State Department of Archives and History, 1917.

Official Manuscript Sources

Archivo General de Indias, Seville, Spain.
1. Papeles Procedentes de Cuba, Legajo 1794–1795, 1856.

British Public Record Office, London, England.
1. Admiralty Office 1, vols. 505–509.
2. Admiralty Office 50, vols. 87, 122.
3. Colonial Office 23, vols. 58–61.
4. Colonial Office 24, vol. 17.
5. Foreign Office 5, vols. 139–140.
6. Foreign Office 72, vols. 180, 219.
7. War Office 1, vols. 141–144.
8. War Office 6, vol. 2.
9. Admiralty I, vols. 505, 509, 4360.
10. Admiralty 50, vol. 87, vol. 122.

Georgia Department of Archives and History, Atlanta, Georgia.
1. Governor's Letterbook, Nov. 28, 1809–May 18, 1814.
2. Executive Minutes, Oct. 4, 1812–Apr. 20, 1814, Governor David Bridie Mitchell, and Peter Early.
3. Georgia Military Affairs, vol. 3.

Mississippi Department of Archives and History, Jackson, Mississippi.
1. Executive Journal of David Holmes, Governor of the Mississippi Territory, 1810–1814.

National Archives, Washington, D. C.
Record Group 45
1. Letters sent by the Secretary of the Navy to Officers.
2. Miscellaneous Letters Sent by the Secretary of the Navy.
3. Letters Received by the Secretary of the Navy from Commanders, 1804–1886.
4. Letters Received by the Secretary of the Navy from Captains.
Record Group 107
1. Letters Sent, Military Affairs, vols. 7–8.
2. Letters to the Secretary of War.

3. Letters Sent by the Secretary of War, Indian Affairs, 1800–1824.
4. Letters Sent to the President by the Secretary of War, 1800–1863, vol. 1.

UNOFFICIAL MANUSCRIPT COLLECTIONS

Alabama Department of Archives and History, Montgomery, Alabama.
1. Manuscript Section
   A. The John Coffee Papers.
   B. The Henry S. Halbert Papers.
   C. The A. B. Meek Manuscript, "History of Alabama."
   D. The Albert J. Pickett Papers.
2. Military Section, Books 205 and 207. Typed copies of letters relating to the Creek War.
Florida Historical Society, University of South Florida, Tampa, Florida.
1. The Cruzat Papers.
2. The Greenslade Papers.
Georgia Department of Archives, Atlanta, Georgia.
1. The collected letters of Benjamin Hawkins (typed copies from originals located here and in other archives).
2. Copies of letters written during the War of 1812–14 by General John Floyd to his daughter Mary Hazzard Floyd, presented to the General Floyd Chapter, National Society of the Daughters of 1812 by Laura E. Blackshear (a copy in this archives).
3. Creek Letters (a collection of typed copies).
4. The John Floyd Papers.
5. The Benjamin Hawkins Papers.
Indiana University, Lilly Library, Bloomington, Indiana.
1. War of 1812 manuscripts collection.
Library of Congress, Washington, D. C.
1. The Andrew Jackson Papers.
2. The Benjamin Hawkins Papers.
Mississippi Department of Archives and History, Jackson, Mississippi.
1. The J. F. H. Claiborne Collection, "Letters relating to the

Indian Wars, 1812–1816," Letterbook "F."
Mobile Public Library, Mobile, Alabama.
  1. The John Forbes Papers.
National Library of Scotland, Edinburgh, Scotland.
  1. The Papers of Admiral Alexander Forrester Inglis Cochrane
    (portion dealing with Indians is designated MS 2328).
National Maritime Museum, Greenwich, England.
  1. The Codrington Collection, designated Cod/7.
State Historical Society of Wisconsin, Madison, Wisconsin.
  1. The Lyman Draper Manuscript Collection.
    A. The Georgia, Alabama, and South Carolina Papers, series
      V, vol. 1.
    B. The Tecumseh Papers, series YY, vols. 1–13.
Tennessee Historical Society, Nashville, Tennessee.
  1. The John Coffee Papers.
  2. The Emil Hurja Collection.
  3. The Andrew Jackson Papers.
  4. Miscellaneous files (contain many letters on the Creek War).
  5. The John Reid Manuscript, "Life of Andrew Jackson,"
Tennessee State Library, Nashville, Tennessee.
  1. The Joseph Carson Papers.
  2. The Andrew Jackson Papers.
Tulane University, Howard-Tilton Memorial Library, New Orleans, Louisiana.
  1. Andrew Hynes Collection.
  2. Louisiana Historical Association Collection.
  3. David Rees Collection.
University of Georgia, The University of Georgia Libraries, Athens, Georgia.
  1. The Telamon Cuyler Collection.
University of Oklahoma, University of Oklahoma Libraries, Norman, Oklahoma.
  1. The Eloise D. Smock Collection.

APPENDIX A

The following paragraph was substituted in the 1824 edition for the sentence "They had approached the house by a route through the woods, and thereby eluded the vigilance of a sentinel who had been posted on the road.

Those young men, with a view to security, had placed their horses in the wood, on the margin of a small creek, and posted, on the road which led by the house, a sentinel, that they might have information of any approach, and in time to be able to elude it. But the tories, who were well acquainted with the country and the passes through the forest, had, unfortunately, passed the creek at the very point where the horses and baggage of our young soldiers were deposited, and taken possession of them. Having done this, they approached cautiously, the house, and were almost at the door before they were discovered. To escape was impossible, and both were made prisoners. *(page 12, 1824 edition)*

APPENDIX B

The following was added to the 1824 edition after "he determined to remain." on line 24.

To one of refined feelings, the prospect before him was, certainly, not of an encouraging cast. As in all newly settled countries must be the case, society was loosely formed, and united by but few of those ties which have a tendency to enforce the performance of moral duty, and the right execution of justice. The young men of the place, adventurers from different sections of the country, had become indebted to the merchants; there was but one laywer in the country, and they had so contrived, as to retain him in their business; the consequence was, that the merchants were entirely deprived of the means of enforcing against those gentlemen the execution of their contracts. In this state of things Jackson made his appearance at Nashville, and while the creditor class looked to it with great satisfaction, the debtors were sorely displeased. Applications were immediately made to him for his professional services, and on the morning after his arrival he issued seventy writs. To those prodigal gentlemen, it was an alarming circumstance; their former security was impaired; but that it might not wholly depart, they determined to force him, in some way or other, to leave the country; and to effect this, broils and quarrels with him were to be resorted to. This, however, was soon abandoned, satisfied, by the first controversy in which they had involved him, that his decision and firmness was such as to leave no hope of effecting any thing through this channel. Disregarding the opposition raised to him, he continued, with care and industry, to press forward in his professional course, and his attention soon brought him forward, and introduced him to a profitable practice. *(page 16-17, 1824 edition)*

APPENDIX C

The following was added to the 1824 edition after "to raise him to still higher honours, he was chosen . . ." on line 19.

a senator of the United States congress, and took his seat on the 22d day of November, 1797. About the middle of April, business of an important and private nature, imposed on him the necessity of asking leave of absence, and returning home. Leave was granted, and before the next session he resigned his seat. He was but a little more than thirty years of age, and hence, scarcely eligible, by the constitution, at the time he was elected. The sedition law, about which so much concern and feeling has been manifested through the country, was introduced into the senate, by Mr. Lloyd, of Maryland, in June, and passed that body on the 4th of July following; hence the name of Jackson, owing to the leave of absence which had been granted him in April, does not appear on the journals. On the alien law, however, and the effort to repeal the stamp act, he was present, resting in the minority, and on the side of the Republican principles of the country. *(page 18, 1824 edition)*

APPENDIX D

The following long section was added to the 1824 edition

after the paragraph ending in "for the hospital department."

On this campaign, a soldier one morning, with a woebegone countenance, approached the general, stating that he was nearly starved, that he had nothing to eat, and could not imagine what he should do. He was the more encouraged to complain, from perceiving that the general, who had seated himself at the root of a tree, waiting the coming up of the rear of the army, was busily engaged in eating something. The poor fellow was impressed with the belief, from what he saw, that want only attached to the soldiers, and that the officers, particularly the general, were liberally and well supplied. He accordingly approached him with great confidence of being relieved; Jackson told him, that it had always been a rule with him never to turn away a hungry man when it was in his power to relieve him. I will most cheerfully, said he, divide with you what I have, and putting his hand to his pocket, drew forth a few acorns, from which he had been feasting, adding it was the best and only fare he had. The soldier seemed much surprised, and forthwith circulated amongst his comrades, that their general was actually subsisting upon acorns, and that they ought, hence, no more complain. From this circumstance was derived the story heretofore published to the world, that Jackson, about the period of his greatest suffering, and with a view to inspirit them, had invited his officers to dine with him, and presented for their repast, water and a tray of acorns. *(page 66–67, 1824 edition)*

APPENDIX E

The following long section was added to the 1824 edition after the paragraph ending in "pregnant with important consequences."

Calculating philosophers may maintain the opinion, that conduct like that pursued on this occasion, deserves no other name than rashness: it certainly was determined, and proved in the end decisive. At such a moment, hesitation must have been succeeded by a defeat of purpose, and an entire abandonment by his troops. To have been forsaken in such a manner, and under such circumstances, no expectation could have been entertained of drawing to the service, in any short time, additional troops. The consequence must have been, that the enemy, not subdued, but only exasperated, might, unmolested, have assailed our unprotected frontiers, and drenched them in the blood of our defenseless citizens. These anticipations were alarming, and only to be prevented by some effort, bold and daring, as the one attempted. It was hazardous, yet it succeeded. *(page 91–92, 1824 edition)*

APPENDIX F

The following section was added to the 1824 edition after the paragraph ending "I know nothing by which I can hope to hold them."

Few men had ever imposed on them the necessity of contending with greater difficulties. The volunteers, proud of the name, and conceiving themselves superior to the militia, had just fought their first battle; and if suffering had not destroyed their early excitement, the same fervour with which they sat out might have still continued; but the negligence, or interested views of contractors, had introduced such discontents, as that to repress them, boldness and energy were required. But to effect this, as events proved, was impracticable, inasmuch as the termination of one difficulty seemed but the commencement of another. It is not wonderous then, that the patience of the general should have been exhausted; or in the address presented he should have indulged those feelings which the occasion and the circumstances were so well calculated to inspire. *(page 103, 1824 edition)*

APPENDIX G

A section was added to the 1824 edition following the para-

graph ending "had become offended, and withdrawn his confidence."

The death of Monohoe, at the battle of Tohopeka, is
strongly illustrative of the infatuations under which these
deluded and ignorant people laboured. They did not at all
doubt, but, as their prophets had told them, that having
been spoiled of their hunting grounds, they were again to
re-occupy them through the aid of a new people, who from
beyond the great waters were coming to assist in their recovery. A confidence in what those soothsayers disclosed,
would also, they believed, produce the effect of protecting
and guarding them from wounds and injury when engaged
in battle. All those idle and marvellous stories were confided
in; but when, at this battle, one of their principal prophets
fell, and by a cannon shot received in the mouth, they
adopted the opinion, that the character of the wound was a
judgment on his false pretensions, and forthwith were departed from those visions of faith which previously they had
entertained. *(page 192, 1824 edition)*

APPENDIX H

The 1824 edition has a section added to the paragraph
ending with ". . . immediately forwarded to Jackson." This
is reproduced as follows:

which reached him the day after the notification of his first
appointment, and before he had been enabled to return an
answer whether or not it would be accepted. The important
services which he had rendered, added to the rank which,
under authority of his state, he had held, might well induce
a doubt whether the appointment first conferred was at all
complimentary, or one which, in justice to his own character, he could have accepted. Whatever of objection
there might or could have arisen, on this subject was
removed by the subsequent appointment of major-general,
made on the resignation of Harrison, and which was accepted. *(page 195–196, 1824 edition)*

APPENDIX I

There were several major changes in the 1824 edition in the paragraph following ". . . British and Spanish agents, in East Florida." These are as follows:

No treaty of friendship or of boundary had yet been entered into by the government with the Indians; they remained a conquered people, within the limits, and subject to the regulations and restrictions which had been prescribed in March, by general Jackson, when he retired from their country. He was now, by the government, called upon to act in a new and different character, and to negotiate the terms upon which an amicable understanding should be restored between the United States and these conquered Indians. But for the government to proceed on the principles of equal and reciprocal treaty stipulations, was in reference to the expensive war imposed on them, and the unprovoked manner in which it had been begun, not to be expected. Those Indians had broken without cause the treaty they had made, outraged humanity, and murdered our unoffending citizens. Under such circumstances, by the peace now to be concluded, to negotiate with, and as heretofore recognize them as an independent and sovereign people, comported not with propriety, nor was demanded by any of the ties of moral duty. General Jackson, therefore, was directed to treat with them as a conquered people, and to prescribe, not negotiate, the terms and conditions of a peace. Colonel Hawkins, who for a considerable time past, had been the agent to this nation, was also associated in the mission. With the western people the appointment was not acceptable, and much solicitude was felt from an apprehension of his influence and weight of character amongst the Indians; and a fear that his partialities and sympathies might incline him too much to their interest. Colonel Hawkins may have been deceived, and may have founded his opinions upon data presumed to be correct; but when it occurred to them that previously to the commencement of hostilities, his repeated declarations had been, that the Indians would maintain a rigid adherence to their treaties, and remain at peace, they were far from being satisfied that he should be connected in the negotiation contemplated to be entered into. *(page 196–197, 1824 edition)*

APPENDIX J

A section was added to the 1824 edition after the paragraph ending with ". . . the president of the United States." The addition is as follows:

The stipulations and exactions of this treaty were in conformity with instructions issued from the department of war, and differs in expression from what has been usually contained in instruments of a similar kind. It breathes the language of demand, not of contract and agreement; and hence has general Jackson been censured for the manner after which the negotiation was concluded. The course however, which was pursued, is readily justified by the terms and expressions of the order under which he acted, and which prevented the exercise of discretion. General Armstrong, who at that time was in the cabinet, and spoke the sentiments of the president, in a letter addressed to Jackson on the 24th of March, uses the following remarks. "It has occurred to me, that the proposed treaty with the Creeks, should take a form altogether military, and be in the nature of a *capitulation;* in which case, the whole authority of making and concluding the terms, will be in you exclusively as commanding general. Accompanying which were instructions formally drawn up, and which were to constitute the basis on which the negotiation was to rest. *(page 198–199, 1824 edition)*

APPENDIX K

A section was added to the 1824 edition after the paragraph ending in ". . . the extension of those advantages that had been insisted on.

In the progress of this business another difficulty arose: the council insisted that there should be inserted in the treaty a reservation of certain tracts of land; one for colonel Hawkins, in consideration of his fidelity to them as an agent; and another to Jackson, because of the gratitude felt towards him for his exertions in their favour against the hostile Creeks. To this the general objected. It was personal as it regarded himself, and he was unwilling to appear in any point of view, where suspicion could attach, that he had availed himself of his official situation to obtain personal benefits; fully aware, that however the facts might be, selfish considerations would be imputed as an inducement to what was done. He refused, therefore, to have it inserted; and for the further reason, that the instructions under which he was acting, required it to be a capitulation, not a treaty. The next morning, however, when they met in council to sign the instrument, the chiefs delivered to the general a paper, expressing a wish, and disclosing their reasons, that a reservation to himself,—colonel Hawkins, and Mayfield, who being made a prisoner in his youth, had always resided in the nation, might be assented to: and requested it to be forwarded on and made known to the government. Jackson consented to do so, and to recommend its adoption; but that the reservation they had thought proper to request, if assented to, he would accept of on no other terms than that their father the president should dispose of it, and apply the proceeds to those of the nation on whom distress and poverty had been brought by the war. Mr. Madison subsequently brought this matter to the consideration of the Senate of the United States, and in recommending its adoption, highly complimented the delicacy with which the proposition had been met by general Jackson: it was, however, never acted on and assented to by the Senate. *(page 207–209, 1824 edition)*

APPENDIX L

A substantial section was added, in the 1824 edition, to the end of the paragraph ending in ". . . repaired to General Coffee's camp."

A dependence on himself to further the objects of the government and the cause of the country, had been his constant lot from the commencement of his military career; and a similar resort or failure to the enterprise, was now to be assayed. Money was wanted—the quarter-masters were destitute of funds, and the government credit was insufficient to procure the necessary means to change the position of an army: thus situated, with his own limited funds, and loans effected on his credit and responsibility, he succeeded in carrying his plans into effect, and in hastening his army to the place of its destination. *(page 243, 1824 edition)*

APPENDIX M

A substantial addition was included in the 1824 edition following the paragraph ending in ". . . the cause of it was at once correctly divined."

The British admiral was very solicitous, and resorted to various means to obtain from these gentlemen information of the strength and condition and disposition of our army; but so cautious a reserve was maintained, that from them nothing could be elicited. Shields was perceived to be quite deaf and calculating on some advantage to be derived from this circumstance, he and the Doctor were placed at night in the green room, where any conversation which occurred between them could readily be heard. Suspecting, perhaps, something of the kind, after having retired, and every thing was seemingly still, they began to speak of their situation— the circumstances of their being detained, and of the prudent caution with which they had guarded themselves against communicating any information to the British admiral. But, continued Shields, how greatly these gentlemen will be disappointed in their expectations, for Jackson with the twenty thousand troops he now has, and the reinforcements from

Kentucky, which must speedily reach him, will be able to destroy any force that can be landed from these ships. Every word was heard, and treasured, and not supposing there was any design, or that he presumed himself overheard, they were beguiled by it, and at once concluded our force to be as great as it was represented; and hence no doubt arose—the reason of that prudent care and caution with which the enemy afterwards proceeded; for, as was remarked by a British officer, the actual strength of general Jackson's army, though repeatedly sought after, could never be procured; it was a desideratum not to be obtained. *(page 288–289, 1824 edition)*

APPENDIX N

A substantial section was added to the 1824 edition following the paragraph ending in ". . . to be outraged and destroyed."

Promptitude in decision, and activity in execution, constituted the leading traits of Jackson's character. No sooner had he resolved on the course which he thought necessary to be pursued, than with every possible despatch he hastened to its completion. Before him was an army proud of its name, and distinguished for its deeds of valour. Opposed to which was his own unbending spirit, and an inferior, undisciplined and unarmed force. He conceived, therefore, that his was a defensive policy; that by prudence and caution he would be able to preserve, what offensive operation might have a tendency to endanger. Hence, with activity and industry, based on a hope of ultimate success, he commenced his plan of defence, determining to fortify himself effectually, as the peril and pressure of the moment would permit. When to expect attack he could not tell; preparation and readiness to meet it, was for him to determine on, all else was for the enemy. Promptly, therefore, he proceeded with his system of defence; and with such thoughtfulness and anxiety—that until the night of the 27th, when his line was completed, he never slept, or for a moment closed his eyes. Resting his hope of safety here, he was every where, through the night, present, encouraging his troops, and hastening a completion of the work. The concern and excitement produced by the mighty object before him, were such as overcame the demand of nature, and for five days and fours nights, he was without sleep and constantly employed. His line of defence being completed on the night of the 27th, he, for the first time since the arrival of the enemy, retired to rest and repose. *(page 325–326, 1824 edition)*

APPENDIX O

There is a substantial section added to the 1824 edition following the paragraph ending with ". . . their schemes from maturing."

The purport of this order was essentially misconceived by the governor; or, perhaps, with a view to avoid subsequent inconveniences and complaints, was designedly mistaken. Jackson's object was not to restrain the legislature in the discharge of their official duties; for although he thought, that such a moment, when the sound of the cannon was constantly pealing in their ears, was inauspicious to wholesome legislation, and that it would have better comported with the state of the times for them to abandon their civil duties and appear in the field, yet was it a matter indelicate to be proposed; and it was hence preferred, that they should adopt whatever course might be suggested by their own notions of propriety. This sentiment would have been still adhered to; but when through the communication of Mr. Duncan, they were represented as entertaining opinions and schemes adverse to the general interest and safety of the country, the necessity of a new and different course of conduct was at once obvious. But he did not order governor Claiborne to interfere with, or prevent them from proceeding with their duties; on the contrary, he was instructed, so soon as any thing hostile to the general cause should be ascertained, to place a guard at the door, and keep the members to their post and to their duty. My object in this, remarked the general, was, that then they would be able to proceed with their business without producing the slightest injury: whatever schemes they might entertain would have remained with themselves, without the power of circulating them to the prejudice of any other interest than their own. I had intended to have had them well treated and kindly dealt by; and thus abstracted from every thing passing without doors, a better opportunity would have been afforded them to enact good and wholesome laws; but governor Claiborne mistook my order, and instead of shutting them in doors, contrary to my wishes and expectation, turned them out.

Before this he had been called on by a special committee of the legislature to know what his course would be should necessity compel him from his position? If, replied the general, I thought the hair of my head could divine what I should do, forthwith I would cut it off: go back with this answer; say to your honourable body, that if disaster does overtake me, and the fate of war drives me from my line to the city, they may expect to have a very warm session. And what did you design to do, I enquired, provided you had been forced to retreat. I should, he replied, have retreated to the city, fired it, and fought the enemy amidst the surrounding flames. There were with me men of wealth, owners of considerable property, who, in such an event, would have been amongst the foremost to have applied the torch to their own buildings; and what they had left undone, I should have completed. Nothing for the comfortable maintenance of the enemy would have been left in the rear. I would have destroyed New Orleans—occupied a position above on the river—cut off all supplies, and in this way compelled them to depart from the country. *(page 346–348, 1824 edition)*

APPENDIX P

A section was added to the 1824 edition following ". . . contest in the open plain, was hazarding too greatly."

Colonel Hinds was very solicitous, and in person applied to the commanding general for leave to pursue, at the head of his dragoons, the fleeing and broken columns of the enemy: Jackson, however, would not permit it. "My reason for refusing," he remarked, "was, that it might become necessary to sustain him, and thus a contest in the open field be brought on: the lives of my men were of value to their country, and much too dear to their families to be hazarded where necessity did not require it; but above all, from the numerous dead and wounded stretched out on the field before me, I felt a confidence that the safety of the city was most probably attained, and hence, that nothing calculated to reserve the good fortune we had met should be attempted." *(page 371–372, 1824 edition)*

APPENDIX Q

A section was added to the 1824 edition following paragraph ending in ". . . where such characters should be permitted to loiter."

Particular care and caution had been early taken that embarrassments on the score of citizenship might not arise. Danger threatening, it was no difficult matter to perceive, that on the ground of being subjects of a foreign power, and owing no allegiance to the United States, many would assert a neutrality and exemption from the fatigues and dangers of the field. If entitled to this character, then was it fair they should receive whatever of immunity could attach to their claim; yet if in prosperous times they had asserted their right to be citizens,—participated in our privileges, and drawn to themselves all the benefits appertaining to that relation, then was there every justice in demanding of them the military services which were exacted of others: but as the language spoken was not vernacular, any inquiry on this subject, calculated to result in certainty, was attended with difficulty. Fortunately, however, a warmly contested election, the pre-

ceding summer, had taken place at New Orleans, and a register of the votes on the occasion had been preserved. To this
document then, the general resorted, and with this unan-
swerable argument, that those who had voted, and thereby
participated in the highest privileges of the country, should
not now be permitted to deny, or throw off, a citizenship thus
established. By this mean, he rendered in a great degree,
inoperative, the French consul's certificates and compelled
to the field, spite of their consular protection, every man
whose name could be traced on the election roster. *(page
407–408, 1824 edition)*

APPENDIX R

The paragraph starting with "This process was made returnable on the 31st" was greatly enlarged in the 1824 edition.

This process was made returnable the 31st: and on that
day the general appeared. Public feeling was excited, and the
crowd, on the tiptoe of expectation, were anxiously waiting
to know what punishment the judge would think due to acts
which all agreed had mainly contributed to the success of
our cause. Jackson, previously apprized of the popular fervor
towards him, and solicitous that nothing on his part should
be done calculated to give it impulse, practised more than
usual caution: and now when it had become necessary to appear in public, to ward himself from crimes imputed, he
threw off his military costume, and assuming the garb of a
citizen, the better to disguise himself, entered alone the hall,
where the court was sitting. Undiscovered amidst the concourse which was present, he had nearly reached the bar,
when, being perceived, the room instantly rung with the
shouts of a thousand voices. Raising himself on a bench and
moving his hand, to procure silence, a pause ensued. He
then addressed himself to the crowd; told them of the duty
due to the public authorities; for that any impropriety of

theirs would be imputed to him, and urged, if they had any regard for him, that they would, on the present occasion, forbear those feelings and expressions of opinion. Silence being restored, the judge rose from his seat, and remarking, that it was impossible, nor safe, to transact business as such a moment, and under such threatening circumstances, directed the marshal to adjourn the court. The general immediately interfered, and requested that it might not be done. "There is no danger here; there shall be none—the same arm that protected from outrage this city, against the invaders of the country, will shield and protect this court, or perish in the effort." This declaration had the effect to tranquilize the feelings and apprehensions of the judge; and the business of the court was proceeded with. It was now demanded of him to answer nineteen interrogatories, drawn up with much labour, and in studied form, which were to determine as to his guilt or innocence. He informed the court he should not be interrogated; that, on a former occasion, he had presented the reasons which had influenced his conduct, without their producing an effect, or being even listened to. "You would not hear my defence, although you were advised it contained nothing improper, and ample reasons why no attachment should be awarded. Under these circumstances, I appear before you, to receive the sentence of the court, having nothing further in my defence to offer. *(page 417–419, 1824 edition)*

APPENDIX S

The paragraph starting with "The hall, in which business was transacted, . . ." was greatly expanded in the 1824 edition as follows:

The hall in which this business was transacted was greatly crowded, and excitement every where prevailed. No sooner was the judgment of the court pronounced, than again were sent forth shouts of the people. He was now seized and forcibly hurried from the hall to the streets, amidst reiterated cries of huzza for Jackson, from the immense concourse that surrounded him. They presently met a carriage in which a lady was riding, when, politely taking her from it, the general was made, spite of entreaty, to occupy her place: the horses being removed, the carriage was drawn on, and halted at the coffee-house, into which he was carried, and thither the crowd followed, huzzaing for Jackson, and menacing violently the judge. Having prevailed on them to hear him, he addressed them with great feeling and earnestness; implored them to run into no excesses; that if they had the least gratitude for his services, or regard for him personally, they could evince it in no way so satisfactorily, as by assenting, as he most freely did, to the decision which had just been pronounced against him. "That the civil was the paramount and supreme authority of the land. He had never pretended to any thing else, nor advocated a different doctrine. He had departed from its rules, because that they were too feeble for the state of the times. By a resort to martial law, he had succeeded in defending and protecting a country, which, without it, must have been lost; yet under its provisions he had oppressed no one, nor extended them to any other purpose than defence and safety; objects which its declaration was intended alone to effect." "I feel," continued he, "sensible for those marks of personal regard which you have evinced towards me; and with pleasure remember those high efforts of valour and patriotism which so essentially contributed to the defence of the country. If recent events have shown you what fearless valour can effect, it is a no less important truth to learn, that submission to the civil authority is the first duty of a citizen. In the ardous necessity imposed on me, of defending this important and interesting city, imperious circumstances compelled me, either to jeopardize those important interests which were confided to me, or to take upon myself the responsibility of those measures which have been termed *high handed,* but which, I thought, absolutely essential for defence. Thus situated, I did not hesitate—I could not. I risked all consequences; and you have seen me meet the penalty of my aggression, and bow with submission to the sentence of the law. Had the penalty imposed reached the utmost extent of my ability to meet it, I should not have murmured or complained; nor now, when it is ended, would I forbear a similar course were the same necessity and circumstances again to recur. If the offence with which I am now charged had not been committed, the laws by which I have been punished would not now exist: Sincerely do I rejoice in their maintenance and safety, although the first vindication of their violated supremacy has been evinced in the punishment of myself. The order and decorum manifested by you, amidst various circumstances of strong excitement, merits my warmest acknowledgments. I pray you, permit that moderation to continue. If you have any regard for me, you will not do otherwise than yield respect to the justice of the country, and to the character of its ministers; that feeling and disposition will, I trust, always characterize you; and evince on your part, as firm a disposition to maintain inviolate and unimpaired the laws of the country, as you have recently shown to defend yourself against invasion and threatened outrage." Mr. Davasac, who had acted in the capacity of volunteer aid, being requested by the general, rose, and in the French language, repeated the substance of the remarks previously delivered by Jackson. He urged zealously the maintenance of peace and good order, and thus produced tranquillity to excited feeling.

Being at length relieved from this warm display of gratitude and regard manifested towards him for the exertions he had made in their defence, Jackson retired to his quarters, and giving a check to his aid-de-camp, sent him to discharge the fine imposed, and to terminate his contest with the civil authority. He was greatly consoled at learning, through various respectable channels, that all was tranquil, and that against the judge nothing of indignity of unkindness was longer meditated.

So riveted was the impression, that the course pursued by the commanding general was correct, and the conduct of judge Hall more the result of spleen than any thing else, that the citizens of New Orleans determined to ward off the effect of his intended injury, by discharging, themselves, the fine imposed. It was only necessary to be thought of, and it was done. So numerous were the persons, entertaining the same feelings on the subject, that in a short time the entire sum was raised by voluntary contribution. The general understanding what was in agitation, to spare his own and their feelings, had despatched his aid-de-camp to seek the marshal, and thereby avoided the necessity of refusing a favour, intended to be offered, and which he could not have accepted. Without, however, any knowledge of his wishes, or consulting at all his feelings on the subject, they proceeded in the arrangement, and, by subscription, the entire amount was in a short time raised, and desposited to his use in bank, and notice thereof given. But it was not accepted; though refused in a manner the most delicate. In reply, he declared the obligations felt for this renewed evidence of regard; and, although he could not accept of it, yet as it was the result of the most generous feeling, he solicited that the amount might be applied to the assistance and relief of those whose relatives, during the siege, had fallen in battle. The proposition made was acceded to, and the amount subscribed, and which had been designed expressly for his relief, was disposed of for the benefit of the widow and the fatherless. *(page 419–423, 1824 edition)*

APPENDIX T

A substantial section was added to the 1824 edition following the paragraph ending in ". . . to it should chance to sit in judgment."

Much as has been said of this declaration of martial law, and greatly as it has been complained of, yet is it difficult to conceive what other course for safety could, with equal effect, have been resorted to. None will pretend, that it was not an infraction of constitutional right; though none can seriously entertain a belief, under all the circumstances, that imperious necessity did not demand the introduction of some similar, if not presisely such a measure. Although so much has been said and written of this imputed aggression on the rights of the citizen; and although it has so often been denounced as a high handed act of tyranny, yet when the measure itself, and all its incidents, are fully examined, nothing of oppression or injustice can be traced. Jackson alone was the sufferer: he suffered by the fine imposed on him, and by torrents of abuse, which ever since have been lavishly poured upon him. A member of the legislature, who had not merely attempted, but in fact succeeded in exciting mutiny and insubordination in the army, when in the very face of an enemy, and the arrest of the judge, who, by a too officious interference, seemed to stand forth a participant in the offence, constitutes the whole of what took place under the declaration of martial law. Judge Hall was not imprisoned: it was simply an arrest. During the siege, he had absented himself from the city, and gone to Baton Rouge. He had afforded neither by example or advice, any assistance to our cause, while the enemy was present; but had retired on the first appearance of danger, nor returned until it had disappeared. Whether they would reappear, and where, could not be told; and hence, whatever necessity may have induced the declaration, that same necessity imperiously demanded its continuance. On his arrest, he was merely sent to a distance, and placed at liberty under an order containing no other restriction, than that he should not approach the city nearer than twelve miles.

Louaillier was detained under guard and brought before a court-martial, of which general Gaines was president, charged under the second section of the rules and articles of war, as one "owing allegiance to the United States of America, and found lurking as a spy about the encampment:" for the reason, however, that the inflammatory and mutinous publication which had occasioned his arrest, could not be shown to have been conveyed to the enemy, he was acquitted—the *quo animo* being from this circumstance in the proof not sufficiently apparent. That none might be uninformed of the law, the following official notice had been circulated through the public journals.

Head Quarters, 7th Military District

SECT. 2. And be it further enacted, that in time of war, all persons *not citizens* of, or *owing* allegiance to the United States of America, who shall be found lurking as spies in or about the fortifications or encampments of the armies of the United States, or any of them, shall suffer death, according to the law and usage of nations, by sentence of a general court-martial.

The city of New Orleans and its environs being under martial law, and the several encampments and fortifications within its limits, it is necessary to give publicity to the above section, for the information of all concerned.

By command.

ROBERT BUTLER, *Adjutant-General*

Conversing with general Jackson, once, concerning the declaration of martial law, he expressed himself after the following manner. "I very well knew the extent of my powers, and that it was far short of that which necessity and my situation required. I determined, therefore, to venture boldly forth, and pursue a course correspondent to the difficulties that pressed upon me. I had an anxious solicitude to wipe off the stigma cast upon my country by the destruction of the capital. If New Orleans were taken, I well knew that new difficulties would arise, and every effort be made to retain it; and that if regained, blood and treasure would be the sacrifice. My determination, therefore, was formed, not to halt at trifles, but to lose the city only at the boldest sacrifice; and to omit nothing that could assure success. I was well aware that calculating politicians, ignorant of the difficulties that surrounded me, would condemn my course; but this was not material. What became of me, was of no consequence. If disaster did come, I expected not to survive it; but if a successful defence could be made, I felt assured that my country, in the objects attained, would lose sight of, and forget the means that had been employed." *(page 425–428, 1824 edition)*

APPENDIX U

Although some of the material was published in the 1817 edition, the 1824 printing greatly expanded the work in the section following "Benevolence, in him, is a prominent virtue, that never passed distress, without seeking to assist and relieve."

It is imputed to him, that he derives from his birth a temper irritable and hasty, which has had the effect to create enemies, and involve him in disputes. In a world like this, exemption from every fault is not to be expected; to a higher destiny is perfection reserved! For purposes wiser than men can conjecture, has it been ordained, that vice and virtue shall exist together in the human breast, tending like the happy blending of light and shade in a picture, to reflect each other in brighter contrast. Some of those foibles and imperfections therefore, which heaven usually mingles in the composition of man, are to be looked for; and must be found with every one. In Jackson, however, those defects of character exist to an extent limited as with most men; and the world is in error in presuming him under a too high control of feeling and passion. A fixed devotion to those principles which honour sanctions, peculiarly attaches to him, and renders him scrupulously attentive to his promises and engagements of every description. Preserving system in his monied transactions, his fiscal arrangements are made to correspond with his resources, and hence his every engagement in relation to such subjects, is met with marked punctuality, not for the reason that he is a man of extraordinary wealth, but rather, because he has method, and with a view to his resources, regulates properly his *balance of trade.*

No man has been more misconceived in character. Many on becoming acquainted with him have been heard to admit the previous opinions which they had entertained, and how great had been their mistake. Rough in appearance—positive and overbearing in his manner, are what all upon a first introduction expect to find; and yet none are possessed of milder manners, or of more conciliating address. The public situations in which he has been placed, and the circumstances which surrounded him, are doubtless the cause that those opinions have become so prevalent; but they are opinions which an acquaintance with him tends speedily to remove. The difficulties and embarrassments under which he laboured at New Orleans, were such as might well have perplexed, and thrown the mind aside from every thing of mildness. Arms and ammunition were wanted; the country was in an unprepared and defenceless situation: whatever could be done was to be decided on promptly, and executed speedily. Mutiny, through designing men was introduced, and disaffection stalked about. Night or day there was no respite from duties of the most important and responsible kind; and yet, under all these circumstances, embarrassing as they were, the evidence of temper and impropriety charged by his enemies, to use their own language, is, that he turned the legislature out of doors, and arrested and detained one of its members, with the judge who interposed for his relief.

If it be true, that his principles and sentiments on some subjects, be at variance with those practiced upon, and deemed correct by others, it is the effect of education, and of early impressions upon his mind, by which a particular bent has been given to it. Speaking one day of his mother, he observed, "one of the last injunctions given me by her, was never to institute a suit for assault and battery, or for defamation; never to wound the feelings of others, nor suffer my own to be outraged; these were her words of admonition to me; I remember them well, and have never failed to respect them; my settled course through life has been, to bear them in mind, and never to insult or wantonly to assail the feelings of any one; and yet many conceive me to be a most ferocious animal, insensible to moral duty, and regardless of the laws both of God and man."

Controlled by a rule so golden, as always to respect the feelings of others, mankind would doubtless seldom err; and seldom would disputes and differences in society arise. It is a misfortune, however, incident to the very nature of man; occasionally to be under the influence of excitement; and then error of conclusion may be the consequence. Wise is the man, peculiarly blest, and greatly to be envied, who in every situation, before he acts, can deliberately think, and correctly decide. It was this received impression respecting general Jackson, which, on his entering the army, induced many to fear he would prove too rash for a safe commander; that occasions might arise, when he would suffer his judgment to be estranged, through an improper exercise of feeling. Events early proved the fallacy of the conjecture, and showed that there were none who reasoned more dispassionately on the fitness and propriety of measures,—none more cautious were caution was necessary, or more adventurous, when daring efforts were required. Few generals had ever to seek for order, amidst a higher state of confusion, or obtained success through more pressing difficulties. The effects he produced, under circumstances gloomy and inauspicious—now through his eloquence and persuasion, and again by his firmness, portrays a character for decision, and a mind intimate and familiar with human nature. That the hireling soldier,— the mere echo of his superiors, prodigal of life, because his sovereign orders it, should entertain respect for his commander, is too commonly the case to exite surprise: of such materials, general Jackson's army was not composed; they were freemen,—citizens; yet, with the exception of those who abandoned him in his first advance against the Indians, there was scarcely one that served with him, officer, or soldie,r that was not particularly and warmly attached to him; ready to serve him under any circumstances. The best evidence of private worth, and private character, it to be derived from those who know us most intimately,—from our acquaintances and neighbours, who see and know us, stripped of that concealment which hangs on character when surveyed at a distance. Tested by this rule, general Jackson stands well, for by those who know him most intimately he is most esteemed.

Light and trifling pleasantries often mark character as distinctly as things of consequence. General Jackson one day during the siege of New Orleans, was approached by an officer of the militia, who stated his desire to leave the service, and return home; for that he was made *game of,* and called by the company Pewter Foot. He manifested great concern, and an anxious desire to be relieved from his unpleasant situation. The general, with much apparent sympathy for him, replied, that he had ascertained there was a practice in the camp of giving nick-names; and had understood too, that very many had dared to call him *Old Hickory:* now, said he, if you prefer mine, I am willing to exchange; if not, remain contented, and perform your duty faithfully, and soon as we can get clear of those troublesome British, our wrongs shall be enquired into by a court-martial, and the authors punished; for then, and not till then, shall we have an end of those insults. The effect was happy, and induced the complaining officer to retire, perfectly satisfied to learn, that his grievance would be united with the general's, and both ere long be effectually redressed. *(page 432–436, 1824 edition)*

APPENDIX V

The section following "Although we may differ, as to the best mode of administering the government, a circumstance which . . ." was greatly expanded in the 1824 edition.

Although we may, and do differ, as to the best mode of administering the government, a circumstance which happens to all countries in proportion as liberty is enjoyed; and although, as has been the case, party spirit may be carried beyond the bounds where reason or prudence should give sanction, yet against the invaders of our rights, our union will prove strong, and all parties be the same. Should the period ever arrive, when our nation shall be vitally assailed, it will be perceived that all advantages calculated to arise from our jarrings are delusive; that then there will be but one party, all rallied in defence of a country believed by them to be the freest and happiest in the world, resolved to swim or sink together. It is very true, that the history of the late war presents some melancholy facts, at variance with this opinion; but such has been the odium and just indignation of the country towards its actors, that any future recurrence of such acts should not be anticipated. Involved in war, every citizen of the country is bound in some form or other, to yield assistance, and steadily to maintain it; and that man, or combination of men, who in such a time of peril, shall stand opposed to the constituted authorities, if any other manner than the constitution authorizes, should be considered, if not the enemy, at least, not the friend of the country. *(page 440, 1824 edition)*

APPENDIX W

Compare the following paragraph with the last paragraph on page 142.

The execution of a private (John Woods,) sentenced by a court martial, on a charge of mutiny, produced at this time some excitement, and a salutary effect. On a similar charge he had before been found guilty, and pardoned. That mutinous spirit, so prejudicial to an army, and which frequently had broken into the camp, was necessary to be checked. This second offence, in the same individual, afforded a fit occasion for example; and to evince, that although militia when at their fire sides at home, might boast exemption from control, yet in the field those high notions were to be abandoned and subordination preserved. Painful as it was to the feelings of General Jackson, he viewed it as a sacrifice essential to the preservation of good order, and left the sentence of the court to be inflicted without interposing his pardoning power. *(page 89, 1828 edition)*

APPENDIX X

In the 1828 edition Eaton made substantial changes in the section starting with "General Winchester, who commanded at Mobile, having . . ." and ending with "The Legislature of Louisiana had re-commenced . . ." That section as it appears in 1828 is as follows:

Previous to this attack, an alarming and threatening disturbance appeared amongst the troops at Fort Jackson, and which, on the 22d January, resulted in six of them being found guilty and sentenced to execution at Mobile, on a charge of mutiny and desertion. On the 24th of May, 1814, Governor Blount, acting under instructions from the Secretary of War, required one thousand men for a tour of *six months,* to be drawn from the division of General Jackson, who at that time was a militia general in the service of the state; not the United States. Acting upon the order, the requisition was made, and on the 20th of the suceeding month (June) the required quota was rendevouzed, and marched to garrison the different forts in the Creek Country, bordering on Mobile. Between the 18th and 20th of September, before half the period for which they were mustered had expired, and for which by the government they subsequently were paid, a portion of this regiment becoming weary of the service, an alarming mutiny arose, which resulted in the desertion of two hundred. They claimed to be entitled to a discharge, for the reason, that the term was but for three months. Preparatory to a departure, and to strengthen themselves in their mutinous design, a paper was circulated to obtain the signatures of those who should be willing to act in concert, and depart together. To obtain supplies for the return march, the bake house in which was deposited the contractor's stores, was broken open and demolished. The cattle procured with great difficulty and expense for the subsistence of the troops, were taken, and killed. Sufficient supplies for their return being thus obtained, and the authority of officers in command place at open defiance, on the morning of the 20th of September, in a tumultuous manner, about two hundred abandoned their post and their duty, and set out for home. Early as news of this act of insubordination reached headquarters, a proclamation was issued commanding an arrest of the mutineers: some were taken and forcibly brought back; others voluntarily returned. For their trial a court martial was organized; and which, with one exception, was composed exclusively of officers from their own regiment, and who of course could not be presumed to entertain any feelings of unkindness or prejudice.

The court, consisting of five regular and two supernumerary members, proceeded to an examination and trial of these offenders, and sentenced six of them to be shot: the rest were condemned to a humilitating, though less severe punishment; part of their pay was to be stopped—their lost time to be made up by further service; their heads to be shaved; and at the expiration of their term to be drummed out of camp. Because of age and inexperience, some were recommended to the clemency of the General, and accordingly were pardoned. The residue of these offenders never received any other punishment than having their term of service enlarged, correspondent to the loss occasioned by the desertion. Pay during the period of the desertion was afterwards withheld by the government, who thereby recognized, and adopted the proceedings of the court. In behalf of those condemned to death, nothing of request or negotiation being presented from the court, they were left to their fate, without an exercise on the part of the General, of his respiting or pardoning power. The session of this court was at Mobile, nearly two hundred miles from New Orleans, where General Jackson, from the 1st of December, had been actively and busily engaged. Of the merits of the cases, and the extent of the imputed guilt, he could know nothing, unless as presented by the court, where rested both the fact and the law. To the recommendation of the court the General assented at once, and gave pardon and forgiveness to those thus presented to his consideration and clemency.

The course pursued towards these offenders was imperiously demanded by justice. The British army, to be sure, had on the 19th abandoned the siege of New Orleans, but they were yet a strong and powerful foe, and entirely in command of the water. When and where an effort might be made to strike a further blow could not be known; all the information possessed upon this subject, was a communication from General Lambert to the commanding general of the American army, made at leaving his position before New Orleans, that he had determined "to suspend for the present all further operations." For General Jackson to be on the alert—to guard every assailable point, and to protect from disaffection and mutiny the army, was required by every consideration of necessity to himself, and interest to the country. At such a moment of uncertainty and peril, to permit the army to be wasted and destroyed through riot and desertion, must have resulted in consequences most disastrous. Who pardoneth the guilty, murdereth the innocent, is a remark no less trite than true. If feeling apart from judgment had been exercised, these men might have lived to atone their error, or else again to set prejudicial and injurious examples. In doubtful cases, or where example may be dispensed with, mercy may plead successfully, but her voice ought never to be heard where the demands of justice are clearly ascertained, and the safety of a whole country warns against it. The enemy had retired, though they were yet powerful; and although "for the present all further operations were suspended," it was in their power to renew assault at any time. Official intelligence of peace, through an express from the government, was not communicated to General Jackson until the 13th of February, two days after the capture of Fort Bowyer; nor until the 19th, when similar information was received by General

Lambert, did hostilities between the two armies terminate. At such time, and under such circumstances, justice, not mercy, should have claimed control. Had those offenders been pardoned, with no propriety afterwards could an effort have been made to arrest mutiny and insubordination, no matter to what untoward length both might have proceeded. Mercy so mistaken, at a period so threatening, might have carried with it consequences highly pernicious, and furnished an example, the force and effect of which might not afterwards have been provided against. *(page 247–249, 1828 edition)*

APPENDIX Y

MEMOIR OF JOHN REID

"My dear General, Dear General, Dr. Gen., Dear, Sir, Sir," ran the salutations in the many letters Andrew Jackson received from his service men. One letter more formally put by John Reid began, "Bgr. Genl A. Jackson," and for lack of time due to the exigencies of war ended merely "John Reid" with no complimentary close or title. In one of Jackson's hurried letters, the first few lines were single spaced, but it ended in a double spaced careless scrawl and with no complimentary close and was signed "Andrew Jackson, Maj. Gen." [1] Some of Jackson's letters ended "Yr friend" or "Adieu." [2] Reid and Jackson referred to each other as The Major and The General. Thus matters ran for Major John Reid, aide and military secretary to General Jackson through the Indian wars and at the battle of New Orleans and until his death.[3] How was their relationship established and how did it grow?

Jackson's father, Andrew Jackson, a poor and humble pioneer, and his mother, Elizabeth Hutchinson, daughter of a man who wove Irish linen,[4] left Carrickfergus, in County Antrim, Ireland, in the spring of 1765 on an emigrant ship bound for . . . the Carolina coast.[5] Jackson was born in 1767 in the Waxaws in South Carolina.[6] Reid's ancestry consisting of three brothers—Thomas, John, and Andrew— were migrants from the adjoining county, County Down, Ireland. His parents were Captain Nathan Reid and Sophia Thorpe Reid of New London in Bedford County, Virginia, and he, their eldest child, was born in 1784.

After acquiring from the teachers in the neighborhood, the elementary parts of education, he was put to school at New London Academy, where the vivacity of his mind, his attention to study, and the manly openness of his character soon gained him the notice and respect of all. In all the literary exercises of the school, he was invariably distinguished.[8] After completing his academic studies at Lexington in Rockbridge County, he studied law,[9] and in 1806 was granted a law certificate in Bedford County.[10] At length he decided to practice his profession in another state and moved to Tennessee, then a sparsely settled wilderness, and located in Rutherford County. Two years later, in 1809, he married and moved to Franklin, in Williamson County, and entered upon the practice of law. His acquaintance with Elizabeth Branch Maury, who became his wife, probably began when her father, Major Abram Maury, attended sessions of the Legislature in Murphreesboro, then the capital of the state as well as the seat of Rutherford County.[11]

The war began and steps were taken to prepare for General Jackson's expedition to Natchez, Mississippi. Upon the recommendation of Colonel Thomas H. Benton, who lived in Franklin and who was serving on General Jackson's staff, young Reid was appointed aide and military secretary, and his appointment signed by General Jackson was in the handwriting of Colonel Benton.[12]

The massacre at Fort Mims occurred August 30, 1814, but it was not known in Nashville until September 18, and that information, of course, started a frenzied activity to raise an army and send to the Creek Nation. Under date of October 4, 1814, Major John Reid wrote to his father, "The whole state is under arms. Nothing is now seen but the movement of troops, nor heard but the beating of drums . . . Five thousand troops are marching from the State under General Jackson. They will unite somewhere in the Creek Nation with three thousand from Georgia. I have been at the General's headquarters in Nashville until a few days ago, when I came to complete my preparations to join him on the march. I start tomorrow. I go with him in the capacity of an aide."

The major's letters from this date on through the battle of New Orleans afford valuable light upon the conduct of the war.[13] These were written with an easy freedom and unpretending grace . . . , always affording evidence of a superior understanding, of a gentle and refined nature, and an unaffected modesty; while underlying them are to be perceived qualities of the manliest type, a high sense of honor, indisputable courage, and an unselfish patriotism.[14]

Jackson's proclamations have aroused the admiration of readers for their stirring and direct appeal, but not all of them were written by him. Major Reid, his secretary, imbibed his spirit so faithfully that he could write in the true Jacksonian manner.[15]

It was with pleasure that he witnessed the wrinkles in Jackson's face, so deeply furrowed by exposure and affliction, at length curl into an expression of complacency and self-enjoyment when the Battle of Horseshoe Bend was won.[16] Young John Reid then entered the race for Congress only to return to his General on August 24, 1814, when he received a letter from him in New Orleans dated "eleven o'clock at night." He hastened to be reunited with him and when he arrived was worn completely down by exposure and privations. Yet, he happily noted the ardour with which all orders of men were animated when the General appeared before them.[17]

Major John Reid suffered a sudden and untimely death though not at the edge of the sword but rather in the privacy of the home of his parents. The disease that took him away was termed by some as pneumonia,[18] and by others as a mysterious fever.[19] In the genealogy notes of his family it was set down as typhoid pneumonia. He died on January 18, 1816, at the age of thirty-one.[20] General Jackson wrote a letter of condolence to Major Reid's father,[21] and Mrs. Jackson also sent a very kind letter to his mother.[22] In Case No. 3 of the North Room (Museum) of The Hermitage, Home of General Andrew Jackson, the uniform and hat of Major Reid are preserved.[23] Negative No. 734 is available at the Hermitage for precious small oval-shaped photographs to be made of him, erect and with piercing eyes, "the handsomest man in the army." [24]

Andrew Jackson had turned Reid loose among his papers to write his biography,[25] only four chapters of which had been completed at Reid's death. Later General Jackson turned the papers over to Major John Eaton, who completed the book.[26] It was published by M. Carey and Son, Philadelphia, for the benefit of the children of John Reid, with Lydia R. Bailey, printer, 1817.[27]

November 1973   HELEN REID ROBERTS

NOTES

1. *Passim,* The Papers of Andrew Jackson, 1st Series, Vol. 15–16, 1813–1814, Reel 8, The Tennessee State Library and Archives.
2. John Spencer Bassett, editor, *Correspondence of Andrew Jackson,* III, 447.
3. S. G. Heiskell, *Andrew Jackson and Early Tennessee History,* 401.
4. Augustus C. Buell, *History of Andrew Jackson,* 30.
5. *Ibid.,* 16.
6. Marquis James, *Andrew Jackson the Border Captain,* 12.
7. Daisy I. Read, *New London Today and Yesterday,* 77–78.
8. *National Intelligencer,* Washington, D. C., May 30, 1816.
9. Read, *New London Today and Yesterday,* 81.
10. Manuscript Unit of Archives and Records Section of The Tennessee State Library and Archives, Reel 113.
11. Princess Lazarovich-Hrebelianovich genealogy (unpublished), 25.
12. Heiskell, *Andrew Jackson and Early Tennessee History,* 401.

13. *Ibid.*, 403–404.
14. *The Commercial Gazette,* January 13, 1883.
15. Bassett, *Correspondence of Andrew Jackson,* I, xxv.
16. Heiskell, *Andrew Jackson and Early Tennessee History,* 407.
17. *Ibid,* 408, 411.
18. Read, *New London Today and Yesterday,* 80.
19. James, *Andrew Jackson the Border Captain,* 297.
20. Princess Lazarovich-Hrebelianovich genealogy (unpublished), 7.
21. Heiskell, *Andrew Jackson and Early Tennessee History,* 417.
22. *Ibid.,* 418.
23. Mary C. Doris, compiler, *The Hermitage Home of General Andrew Jackson,* 35.
24. James, *Andrew Jackson the Border Captain,* 172.
25. *Ibid.,* 289.
26. Read, *New London Today and Yesterday,* 80.
27. John Reid & John Henry Eaton, *The Life of Andrew Jackson,* Title Page.

APPENDIX Z
DEATH NOTICE—MAJOR JOHN REID

OBITUARY

On the 18th instant, departed this life, at his father's seat, in Bedford, Va. Major JOHN REID, of the United States' Army, the well known aide of Gen. Jackson, in his transactions against the Creeks and the British. The evening preceeding that on which he died, he was in the finest health and spirits. About midnight he complained of chilliness; medical assistance was called in before breakfast, and additional aid was sent for during the day, but all to no purpose, the disease every hour visibly increased; in the evening the warm bath was about to be applied, but suspended on account of his exhausted condition, he was turned over on his side for temporary relief, and appeared to sink into a gentle sleep; but he awoke no more; the etherial spirit had forsaken its mansion, and the hero who had, for his country's sake, fearlessly braved the cannon and the sabre on the 8th of January, 1815, fell a victim to a fever of twenty-one hours' continuance, on the 18th of January, 1816. Would that he could have lived long enough to complete the history which he had announced to the world, and in the composition of which he was busily engaged.

His loss is the more to be deplored by his family, as it is the second it has experienced this year: for the day after the Major arrived from Washington, whither he had accompanied his beloved General, he saw his sister Maria, a blooming girl of 18, expire. Imagine, then, reader, if thou canst, the poignant anguish his aged father, his disconsolate mother, his bereaved consort, and his other relations, must feel at his death!

Social and agreeable in private life, gallant in the field, in integrity he had but few equals and no superior.

Nat. Int.

[Reported in the *Richmond Enquirer,* February 3, 1816.]

EDITOR'S INDEX TO THE
LIFE OF ANDREW JACKSON

EDITOR'S INDEX TO THE
APPARATUS CRITICA

EDITOR'S INDEX TO THE
APPARATUS CRITICA